WILEY
OFFICE
HANDBOOK

SECOND EDITION

THE
WILEY
OFFICE
HANDBOOK
SECOND EDITION

Reference Guide
Word Finder
WP Guides

RITA KUTIE
VIRGINIA HUFFMAN

John Wiley & Sons

New York · Chichester · Brisbane · Toronto · Singapore

Library of Congress Cataloging in Publication Data

Kutie, Rita, 1930-
    The Wiley office handbook.
(Wiley Series in Office Information Systems)

    Includes indexes.
    1. Commercial correspondence—Handbooks, manuals,
etc.   2. English language—Business English—Handbooks,
manuals, etc.   3. Word processing—Handbooks, manuals,
etc.   I. Huffman, Virginia, 1928-   II. Title.
HF5726.K868   1980   652   83-16707
ISBN 0-471-87055-2

Printed in United States of America

10 9 8 7 6 5 4

PREFACE

Information processing is done by means of electronic technology in many offices today. Nonetheless, the most essential skill for secretarial and clerical positions is the ability to use the English language well: to punctuate, spell, proofread, and edit. This book has been written to provide information to those who wish to perfect their use of English and follow conventional formats in the preparation of business documents.

Sections 1, 2, and 3 contain concise reference materials to help solve language problems. Typewritten examples are provided to illustrate the rules outlined in the text. Section 4 is an alphabetical list of frequently confused and misued words. Both meaning and parts of speech are specified to assist the user in selecting the appropriate word.

Section 8 offers suggestions for improving proofreading and editing skills. For help with formats refer to Sections 5 and 6 and to the illustrations found in those sections.

Section 7 includes guides for the operator of word processing keyboards; it also includes information about the various kinds of word processing equipment and a glossary of word processing terms. The appendix contains a variety of material occasionally needed by the machine transcriptionist, word processor, or correspondence secretary.

Rita Kutie
Virginia R. Huffman

CONTENTS

Contents **xi**

THE

WILEY
OFFICE
HANDBOOK

SECOND EDITION

SECTION 1
Language Use
Guides

Language Use includes five divisions: PUNCTUATION, NUMBERS, CAPITALIZATION, GRAMMAR, and SPELLING.

In PUNCTUATION, major marks of punctuation are presented in alphabetic order. Rules for the use of each punctuation mark together with typewritten examples of the application of these rules are given.

In NUMBERS, general rules for determining whether to spell out a number or whether to type it in figures are presented. Special rules that are applied to typing particular categories of figures such as weights, measures, time, and distance are then presented.

In CAPITALIZATION, rules and examples illustrating the use of these rules are covered.

The GRAMMAR division deals with the most troublesome rules and constructions. The list of entries is alphabetic. Those typed in all caps are subject entries explaining a grammatical rule. Those entries typed in lower case are frequently misused words. Explanations and examples of both correct and incorrect usage are often given.

In SPELLING, rules are presented that can help the machine transcriber, word processor, or correspondence secretary. Rules for hyphenating prefixes and suffixes and a list of common prefixes and suffixes together with their meanings are given.

Throughout the Language Use section and on other occasions throughout *The Wiley Office Handbook* you will notice WP/IP NOTES. The WP/IP NOTES, shaded entries, provide guidelines and suggestions for users of WP/IP equipment.

Punctuation

Apostrophe

1. As a Symbol

The apostrophe may be used as a symbol for feet in bills or tables; it may be used to indicate the omission of figures; it may be used in contractions to indicate the omission of letters.

```
Isn't the most common size 2' x 4'?

I took the class in June of '83.
```

2. In Plurals

For the sake of clarity, the plural of a small letter is formed by adding 's. The plural of a capital letter does not require an apostrophe with the exceptions of A, I, and U.

```
a's  b's  x's  Ds  Fs  A's  I's  U's
```

NOTE: Plural numbers do not require an apostrophe, for example, 1970s, 1s, 2s, and so on.

3. To Show Possession

Add the apostrophe and s to a singular noun to show possession.

```
Jan's report card was her best this
year.
```

Add only the apostrophe after plural nouns ending in s to show possession.

NOTE: The apostrophe is usually omitted in company and organization names that are possessive.

```
The doctors' offices are all in the
medical building.

He plans to attend Teachers College.
```

Add an apostrophe and s to a plural noun that does not end in s to show possession.

```
The sale will include men's suits,
women's hats, and children's
overalls.
```

To indicate joint or common possession of two or more persons, use the possessive with the last noun in the series. Separate possession of two or more persons is shown by adding the possessive to each of the nouns.

```
We went to Marilyn and Frank's house
after the movie.
```

```
Marilyn's and Frank's ideas about
good books are very different.
```

Add an apostrophe and s to a proper name of one syllable that ends in s to show possession. Add only an apostrophe to a proper name of more than one syllable that ends in s to show possession.

```
Charles's bill came to $74; Robert
Sanders' was only $71.
```

As a rule, nouns referring to inanimate things should not be in the possessive. Use an *of* phrase instead.

```
Not: that car's          But: the paint of
     paint                    that car

     the house's              the windows
     windows                  of that
                              house
```

4. In Contractions

Use an apostrophe to indicate the omission of letters in contractions.

```
isn't              is not
doesn't            does not
it's               it is
let's              let us
```

NOTE: A period is not used after a contraction.

Asterisk

1. In Footnotes

Use an asterisk to refer the reader to a footnote at the bottom of the page.

```
The number of small business
failures is increasing.*

*U.S. Department of Commerce Statistics
```

2. To Indicate Omissions

Use an asterisk to indicate omissions of words that are considered unsuitable for printing or to indicate omission of an entire paragraph.

```
In their negotiations, both
management and labor were calling
each other **** liars and thieves,
mostly for the sake of getting
attention.
```

Brackets

1. Within Quotes

Use brackets within quotes when you wish to add a comment or correction.

```
Sarah said, "I'll be there promptly
[you know her 'promptly'] at 8:30."
```

2. Within Parentheses

Use brackets to enclose parenthetical expressions that fall within parenthetical expressions.

```
(This [October 27] will be the first
meeting of the group.)
```

NOTE: If the bracket is not available on your machine, it can be made as follows:

/‾‾ ‾‾/

WP/IP NOTE:

Most word processors have a bracket key. If yours does not, type the bracket as follows: type a diagonal, code backspace, underscore, index up one line, underscore. The closing bracket is prepared by reversing this procedure.

Colon

1. After Introductory Expressions

Use a colon after such expressions as *these*, *as follows*, and *the following*, which introduce a series or list of items.

> The slippers are available in the
> following sizes: small, medium, and
> large.

Use a colon after a statement that introduces a long direct quotation or a formal rule or principle.

> You should know this important rule:
> Always place commas and periods
> inside the quotation marks.

> Another thing to remember is: "Haste
> makes waste."

Use a colon after a statement that introduces an explanation or an example.

> He has his mind set on only one
> profession: law.

2. After Salutations

In a business letter, use a colon after the salutation unless you are using open punctuation.

```
Gentlemen:          Dear Ms. Taylor:
```

3. Between Hours and Minutes

Use a colon to separate hours and minutes when time is expressed in figures.

NOTE: Omit the :00 when time is expressed as an even clock hour.

```
If the bus is scheduled to leave at
3 p.m., we should be at the station
by 2:30.
```

NOTE: When typed, the colon is followed by two spaces unless used with expressions of time or ratio, for example, 2:30; 2:1.

Comma

1. In Compound Sentences

When the independent clauses in a compound sentence are joined by a conjunction, use a comma before the conjunction unless the clauses are very short. Each clause, in order to be independent, must contain a subject and a predicate.

```
She liked the movie but John did
not. (short)
```

```
The twins look very much alike, and
I couldn't tell them apart for
several months. (long)
```

2. After Introductory Words, Phrases, or Clauses

Use a comma after such words as *consequently, finally, therefore,* used to introduce a sentence.

```
Yes, we want to attend the banquet.
```

Use a comma after an introductory phrase if it is long or if it includes a gerund, infinitive, or participle.

```
By purchasing now, you will save 10
percent. (includes gerund)

At the second light, turn left. (long
prepositional phrase)

In order to reach the top, you must
work hard. (includes infinitive)
```

Use a comma following an adverbial clause at the beginning of a sentence.

```
When you receive your order, please
check the contents thoroughly.
```

Unless omitting the comma would cause misreading, do not use a comma after a short introductory prepositional phrase.

```
By April 15 we should have the
final test results.
```

3. In a Series

Use a comma between each item in a series of words or phrases. When the last of a series of three or more items is preceded by *and*, *or*, or *nor*, use a comma before the conjunction as well as between the other items.

```
Sue, Louise, and Harry will attend
the meeting.
```

Do not use a comma before the & sign in a company name.

```
The building was designed by Jones,
Jones & Jones.
```

Use a comma before and after the abbreviation *etc.* when it closes a series.

```
The sale of dresses, coats, suits,
etc., will begin on Wednesday.
```

4. With Appositives and Names in Direct Address

Use commas to set off a noun or a noun phrase that does not restrict the meaning of a preceding noun or pronoun.

> One of the secretaries, a graduate
> of our college, could type 90 words
> a minute.

Do not use commas to set off essential words or closely related appositives.

> Their brother Jim is expected
> home for Thanksgiving.

Use commas to set off the name of a person who is being addressed directly.

> Thank you, Leonard, for your help.

5. With Restrictive and Nonrestrictive Words, Phrases, or Clauses

Use commas to set off a word, phrase, or clause that is nonrestrictive (nonessential) to the sentence.

> Our company, incidentally, bought a
> new dictating system. (word)

> The secretaries, who are new to
> word processing, are eager to have
> equipment installed. (clause)

> It seemed, for a change, that all
> the work in the center was
> completed. (phrase)

Do not use commas if the word, phrase, or clause is restrictive (essential) to the sentence.

> They accidentally noticed the error
> in playout. (word)

> The secretaries who are in word
> processing will use the dictating
> system. (clause)

```
We can look for a change in that
situation very soon. (phrase)
```

6. With Direct Quotations

Use commas to set off a direct quotation (exact words spoken or written by someone else).

```
"Will you meet the plane," she
asked, "or shall I take a cab
home?"
```

7. With Dates and in Addresses

Use commas before and after the year when the year follows the day or month; separate the day of the week from the rest of a date with a comma.

```
He was born on Friday, September 28,
```

EXCEPTION: If a month-year date is used as an adjective, omit the comma before and after the year, for example, the June 1983 issue of the magazine.

Use a comma between the city and the state, but do not use a comma between the state and the ZIP Code.

```
Please send a copy to Mr. John
Lewis, 345 State Street,
Painesville, Ohio 44077.
```

```
He lived in Rockford, Illinois,
most of his life.
```

8. Between Parallel Adjectives

Use a comma to separate two or more parallel adjectives in a series; however, use the hyphen to connect compound adjectives when they precede a noun that they modify.

```
The well-groomed lady wore a long,
flowing gown.
```

9. Between Consecutive Numbers

Use a comma to separate unrelated groups of figures that come together.

> In 1983, 372 accidents were insured under Policy 82–643221.

NOTE: Use a comma to separate thousands, hundred thousands, millions, and so on, in numbers of four or more digits.

Do not use commas in numbers that represent years, page numbers, telephone numbers, ZIP Codes, serial numbers, and so on.

10. In Titles and Degrees

In titles and degrees it is acceptable to use or not to use a comma preceding the title or degree following a person's name. However, consistency must be maintained throughout the document. Within a sentence, if a comma is used before the degree, one must also be used following the degree.

> The letter was addressed to William Daugherty Jr. but was delivered to William Daugherty Sr.
>
> George Sykes, Ph.D., made the presentation.
>
> or
>
> George Sykes Ph.D. made the presentation.

NOTE: Do not use a comma before or after Roman or Arabic numerals used in personal titles.

> The book belongs to Ellwood James III.

11. In Company Names

Use a comma preceding an abbreviation such as Inc. in a company name. However, if the comma is not written into the legal name, no comma is used. Within a sentence, a comma must also follow the abbreviation when one precedes it.

> The company is Zucco & Sons Inc.

> Bentley Brothers, Ltd., has been contracted for the renovation.

12. When Words Are Omitted

Use a comma when a word or words are omitted from a sentence.

> Betsy wants to do some weaving;
> Dale, some pottery.

> Carol is in Columbus; Gary, in Madison.

Dash

1. Before Summarizing Words

Use a dash before a word that follows and summarizes a series at the beginning of a sentence.

> Dresses, coats, suits--these are but a few of the items available at the outlet store.

2. For Greater Emphasis

A dash may be used in place of other marks to achieve greater emphasis.

> Harry O'Brien--he's an excellent lawyer--could advise you. (instead of parentheses)

> The movie--in case you're interested-- is excellent. (instead of commas)

> There is only one place she calls home--New York. (instead of a colon)

```
I like that class--it has been a big
help to me in my job. (instead of a
semicolon)
```

NOTE: When typing a dash, use two hyphens and do not leave a space before, between, or after them.

Never use a comma, semicolon, colon, or period before an opening dash. When necessary, use a question mark or exclamation point before a closing dash.

Be very selective in using dashes as substitutes for other punctuation marks. The forcefulness of the dash is greatly diminished when it is overused.

WP/IP NOTE:

On some WP/IP equipment it is necessary to use two "coded" or "required" hyphens to form the dash or they may be dropped during playback.

Diagonal

1. In Fractions

To type fractions that are not on the typewriter, use the diagonal.

```
His hat is size 6 7/8.
```

NOTE: The mixed number is written with a space after the whole number. If a "made" fraction is used, do not use the machine fractions within the same material.

2. In Certain Expressions and Abbreviations

Use the diagonal in expressions such as his/her, s/he, and/or, MT/ST, c/o.

Ellipsis

Ellipsis marks (three spaced periods with one space before and after each period) are used to show the omission of words from a quotation. When the words are omitted at the end of a sentence, use three spaced periods followed by the necessary terminal punctuation for the sentence as a whole.

```
Mary said, "It is a language of ...
great beauty; it is interesting but
difficult ...."
```

Exclamation Point

Use an exclamation point after a word, phrase, or sentence to show strong feeling.

```
Oh no!  How could I lose my keys?

I hate to work on Saturdays!
```

WP/IP NOTE:

If your keyboard does not have the exclamation point, make one by using the apostrophe, coded backspace, and period. The exclamation point is always followed by two spaces.

Hyphen

1. In Numerals

Use a hyphen in compound numerals from twenty-one to ninety-nine.

```
Twenty-seven people attended the
meeting.
```

Use a hyphen with fractions that are written in words and used as adjectives.

```
We hope to pass the resolution by at
least a four-fifths majority.
```

Do not hyphenate other fractions written as words.

```
He took one half; she took the other.
```

2. With Prefixes

```
self-important          co-worker
```

3. To Replace *To* or *Through*

Use a hyphen to take the place of *to* or *through* in certain statistical writing and in tables and charts.

```
Read pp. 12-29 during the week of
September 19-23.
```

NOTE: The hyphen is typed with no spaces before or after.

4. In Compound Adjectives

Use the hyphen to join the words of a compound adjective preceding a noun that it modifies.

```
First-class mail is sorted before
9:30 a.m.

23-year-old man But: he is 23 years old

high school graduate But: high school-
level material

39-story building

entry-level salaries
```

5. Suspended Hyphen

Retain the hyphen in a series of hyphenated words having the same ending. Space once after each suspending hyphen unless a comma is required at that point.

```
There have been great changes over
the last four- or five-year period.
```

6. In Word Division

Use a hyphen to indicate division of a word at the end of a line.

```
The magnetic media type-
writer has had an enormous
impact on the office.
```

WP/IP NOTE:

Many WP/IP keyboards have special rules for hyphens. If the hyphen is required in a word, such as X-ray, that hyphen may need to be "coded." If a hyphen is only temporary, it is not coded and is dropped during playback unless it appears at the end of a line.

With the wraparound feature available on most equipment, a hyphen is treated the same as any character. Therefore, if a unit containing a hyphen enters the end-of-line zone, the entire unit moves to the next line. An example is a telephone number. If it is desirable to carrier return at a required hyphen, it may be necessary to type a hard carrier return after the hyphen.

Parentheses

1. With References

Use parentheses to set off references to illustrations, charts, diagrams, pages or chapters of books, and similar items.

```
The section on transcription (see
pages 120-129) will be very helpful
to you.
```

2. With Enumerated Items

Enclose numbers or letters in parentheses when they precede enumerated items that are not displayed on separate lines.

```
The test will cover the following:
(1) commas, (2) semicolons, and (3)
colons.
```

3. In Place of Commas and Dashes

Use parentheses in place of commas or dashes to set off and de-emphasize expressions that are not necessary to the meaning or completeness of a sentence.

```
She returned to Denver (her
hometown) for her vacation.
```

4. With Money Amounts

When money amounts are written in words, write the amount in figures enclosed in parentheses.

```
Five hundred seventy-eight dollars
($578)
```

5. With Other Punctuation

If the item in parentheses falls within a sentence, make sure that any punctuation needed at that point falls outside the closing parenthesis.

```
If you will let me know soon (this
week), I will get you the tickets
you need.
```

If the item in parentheses falls within a sentence, do not capitalize the first word of the item in parentheses.

```
I want you to meet Mrs. Bruce (she's
our new typing teacher) when you
come to Cleveland.
```

If the item in parentheses falls within a sentence, do not use a question mark or an exclamation point within parenthetical material if the sentence ends with an identical punctuation mark.

```
In the next school term (are you
planning to enroll?) we hope to
offer word processing courses.
```

```
Shall we invite a guest speaker
(will our attendance warrant it) to
the next meeting?
```

If the item in parentheses is to be incorporated at the end of a sentence, the punctuation needed to end the sentence goes outside the closing parenthesis.

> The meeting was held on January 27 (Tuesday).

6. As Separate Sentences

If the item in parentheses is to be treated as a separate sentence, the preceding sentence should close with its own punctuation mark; the item in parentheses should begin with a capital; ending punctuation should be placed before the closing parenthesis; no other punctuation mark should follow the closing parenthesis.

> She spoke for an hour on word processing. (She offered many new ideas.) After the talk, there was a question-and-answer period.

Period

1. After Sentences

Use a period to mark the end of a complete declarative sentence.

> I bought a sweater and three pair of slacks.

2. After Condensed Statements

Use a period after a condensed statement, which is usually a word or phrase used as an answer to a question or as a transitional expression.

> When do I need the information? Tomorrow.

> Now, the requirements. The first one is punctuality.

3. With Abbreviations

Use periods with abbreviations of personal and professional titles, academic degrees, seniority terms, and a.m. and p.m.

```
Mr.  Dr.  Ph.D.  Jr.  Ms.  B.S.  a.m.
p.m.
```

4. With Numbers

Use a period as a decimal point in amounts of money, percentages, and other amounts consisting of whole numbers plus decimal fractions or simply decimal fractions. Omit .00 after even amounts of dollars.

```
$1,245.98    $10    6.2 percent
```

5. With Numbers in Outlines and Lists

Use a period after each number and letter in an outline or list except those numbers and letters that are enclosed in parentheses or followed by a parenthesis. (See: Outline Formats, p. 347).

NOTE: The period at the end of a sentence or condensed sentence is followed by two typewritten spaces. The period at the end of an abbreviation is followed by only one typewritten space.

WP/IP NOTE:

Normally, the number or letter preceding each item in a list or outline is followed by two spaces. However, WP/IP equipment is frequently set up with a tab grid with stops every five spaces. Please note the following suggestions to create an acceptable format under these circumstances.

Outlines

1. Set your left margin five spaces farther to the left than you want the margin.

2. Tab once; type I; tab; type the statement.

3. When typing II, tab once; type a code backspace; type the II.

(See: Reports and Technical Typing Guides, WP/IP Note, p. 345.)

Lists

In order to leave room for the "tens" digit in a list, do the following:

1. Space one time. Type "1." Tab. Type the statement. Carrier return. Follow this procedure through "9."

2. Number "10" is typed at the margin.

6. With Headings

Use a period followed by two spaces after a heading when text follows on the same line. A period is not used if the heading stands on a line alone.

```
Boston Terrier.  This breed is an
excellent pet for children as it is
especially good natured.

Dogs

Known as man's best friend, this
animal is the most common of
children's pets.
```

Question Mark

1. After Sentences

Use a question mark after a sentence that asks a direct question.

```
What time may we expect you?
```

2. In a Series of Questions

Use a question mark after each question in a series of brief questions relating to the same subject and verb.

```
Do they serve shrimp? lobster?
smelts?
```

3. After Condensed Questions

Use a question mark after a condensed question, which is usually a word or a phrase that follows a statement.

```
She didn't attend the workshop. Why?
```

4. To Indicate Uncertainty

The question mark is enclosed in parentheses within a sentence to indicate uncertainty about a stated fact.

```
The library has five (?) copies of
the best-seller.
```

NOTE: The question mark is followed by two spaces at the end of a sentence or condensed sentence. However, within a sentence it is followed by only one space.

Quotation Marks

1. With Direct Quotations

Use quotation marks to enclose direct quotations. However, long quotations that are set off from the body of the material by being single spaced and indented need not be enclosed with quotation marks.

```
"The campaign will not be over until
November 4," Jerry said.

"Bill just left. He will be back
soon," Ethel said.
```

NOTE: For treatment of long quotations, see pp. 367-368.

2. Within Quotation Marks

Use the single quotation mark to indicate a quotation within a quotation.

```
She said, "We must be, as the poet
said, 'One for all and all for
one.'"
```

NOTE: When quoted material falls within single quotation marks, use double quotation marks.

> Lois said, "When Mr. Baker asked,
> 'Did you mark it "Return
> Requested"?' I answered. 'Yes.' "

3. With Titles

Use quotation marks to enclose titles of articles, short poems, lectures, reports, and chapters of books.

> Have you read the chapter titled
> "Making Corrections"?

4. With Terms and Expressions

Use quotation marks to enclose words that are unusual in a technical or trade sense; words introduced by expressions such as *marked, labeled,* and *signed*; slang or poor grammar used on purpose; words used humorously or ironically; formal definitions of words; and translations of foreign words.

> The package was marked "Handle With
> Care."

> The job at the needlework shop was
> "sewed up" before I got there.

5. With Well-Known Sayings and Proverbs

Do not use quotation marks to enclose well-known sayings and proverbs.

> She still believes there's a pot of
> gold at the end of the rainbow.

6. With Other Punctuation Marks

Periods and commas always go inside the closing quotation mark. Periods and commas also always go inside the single closing quotation mark.

> "I think," Don said, "that my
> favorite poem is 'Trees.'"

Semicolons and colons always go outside the closing quotation mark. Semicolons and colons also always go outside the single closing quotation mark.

```
He said, "I will call you tomorrow";
however, he still hasn't called.
```

A question mark or an exclamation point goes inside the closing quotation mark when it applies only to the quoted material; it goes outside the closing quotation mark when it applies to the entire sentence.

```
She asked, "How did you enjoy
Vermont?"
```

```
Why did Janet keep saying, "We'll
never make it"?
```

If the quoted material and the entire sentence each require the same punctuation mark, use only one mark—the one that comes first.

```
Have you seen the ad that starts,
"Why sacrifice quality?" (quoted
question at the end of a question)
```

The closing parenthesis goes inside the closing quotation mark when the parenthetical element is part of the quotation; it goes outside the closing quotation mark when the quotation is part of the parenthetical element.

```
The teacher was "old (thirty)"
according to my five-year-old
daughter.
```

7. Quotations Standing Alone

When a quoted sentence stands alone, put the ending punctuation mark inside the closing quotation mark.

```
"May I see you tomorrow?"
```

8. Quotations at the Beginnings of Sentences

When a quoted statement is at the beginning of a sentence and is followed by an expression such as *she stated*, use a comma before the closing quotation mark and omit the period.

> "I'd like another cup of coffee," he
> said.

When a quoted question or exclamation occurs at the beginning of a sentence, do not insert a comma but keep the necessary mark of punctuation.

> "May I have another cup of coffee?"
> she asked.

Omit punctuation at the closing quotation mark when a quoted word or phrase occurs at the beginning of a sentence unless it is necessary for the construction of the sentence.

> A "stellar performance" was the
> description given by several of the
> critics.

> "A Sweet Treat," last year's slogan
> for the Maple Sugar Festival, will
> be used again this year.

Semicolon

1. In Compound Sentences

Use a semicolon to separate independent clauses in a compound sentence when no conjunction is used to join the clauses.

> Barbara is shopping now; I expect
> her to return at noon.

When independent clauses are joined by a conjunctive adverb (*accordingly, however,* or a similar word), use a semicolon before the adverb and a comma after it.

> You may still sign up for the class;
> however, you will be asked to pay a
> late fee.

When independent clauses are joined by a coordinate conjunction (*and, but, or, nor*) and one or both of them contain internal commas, use a semicolon before the conjunction, if necessary, to prevent misreading. Otherwise, use a comma before the conjunction.

```
I like pears, apples, and grapes;
but Rita prefers peaches,
strawberries, and blueberries.
```

2. In a Series

When one or more of the items in a series is punctuated with commas, use semicolons between the items to prevent misreading. If misreading is unlikely, commas are strong enough.

```
We visited Sebring, Ohio; Smethport,
Pennsylvania; and Olean, New York.
```

```
If possible, Carol and Dick will be
here for the picnic, but they won't
stay all weekend.
```

NOTE: The semicolon is typed followed by only one space.

Underscores

1. With Titles

Underscore titles of books, magazines, newspapers, pamphlets, long poems, movies, plays, and other literary and artistic works.

```
He sent me the latest issue of
Newsweek.
```

2. With Words

Underscore words referred to as words, words accompanied by definitions, and foreign expressions accompanied by English translations. Once an expression of foreign origin has become established as part of the English language, underscoring is no longer necessary.

Do not confuse the word
<u>personal</u> with <u>personnel</u>.

What will be the rate per annum?

3. For Emphasis or Importance

To give special emphasis or importance to words, the under-score is used. However, use this punctuation sparingly as an overuse diminishes its effectiveness.

Please answer that letter <u>at once</u>.

NOTE: Do not underscore ending punctuation.

WP/IP NOTE:

With most word processing equipment it is possible to un-derscore individual words by use of the word underscore feature, or to underscore continuously by use of the begin and end underscore features. Use a coded automatic un-derscore if available or use code backspaces and manual underscoring. On older equipment (such as the Mag II), if several lines of type are to be underscored solid, it is some-times desirable to insert a stop code at the end of that pas-sage and to do the underscoring manually. Also, with equipment that demands underscores be kept with words, it is acceptable to underscore the words and not the spaces.

4. Statistical Symbols

In technical writing it is proper to underscore symbols that represent a statistic.

The <u>F</u>-ratio is .0475.

The two groups of <u>n</u>'s were not equal.

Numbers

General Rules

1. Numbers 1 Through 10

As a general rule, numbers 10 and under are spelled out; figures are generally used for numbers over 10. However, use figures for numbers referred to as numbers or accompanied by symbols or abbreviations. Figures are also used with weights, temperatures, and measurements.

> There were three special buses going to the game.
>
> At least 250 people will be there.
>
> Section No. 1   7 pcs.   @39c
> 3 percent   4 feet

NOTE: In very formal reports or correspondence, write all numbers in words if they can be expressed in one or two words. Consider a hyphenated number as one word.

2. Numbers Beginning Sentences

At the beginning of a sentence, a number should be spelled out. If the number is large, rewrite the sentence if possible so that the number is not at the beginning of the sentence.

> Twenty-five members attended the rally.
>
> The rally was attended by 25 members.

3. Two Numbers Together

Use a comma to separate unrelated groups of numbers that come together. However, when two numbers occur together and one is part of a compound modifier, write one number in words and the other one in figures. Usually, the shorter number is spelled out.

During 1983, 723 applications were received.

There are three 27-story apartment buildings on Lake Road.

There were 14 three-room apartments in the building.

4. Fractions

Write a fraction in words when it stands alone.

It must be approved by a two-thirds majority.

5. Mixed Numbers

Mixed numbers (whole numbers plus fractions) are written in figures.

5 1/2   25 1/4

NOTE: Fractions that are not on the keyboard are typed with the diagonal. Space between a whole number and a made fraction. Be consistent—don't combine made fractions with machine fractions.

He said it was worth 2 1/3 times that much.

Special Rules

1. Dates

When the day follows the month, do not include the ordinal ending *st*, *nd*, *rd*, or *th*. When the day precedes the month or stands alone, use the ordinal ending or write it in words.

We plan to get together before June 15.

The 19th of June is the date Joan mentioned to me.

Will we see you at the picnic on the eighth?

2. Times of Day

Use figures with a.m. and p.m. Omit :00 for time on the hour except in tabulated material for uniformity.

> The package should arrive before
> 10 a.m.

3. Addresses

Always use figures for numbers in addresses except numbered street names *One* through *Ten* and the house number not be used in an address. Use an ordinal only if needed for clarity.

> Their office is at One Erieview Plaza.
>
> 224 East 48 Street, Apt. 702 But:
> 224 48th Street
> Atlanta, GA 30309
>
> We will move to 2 Lakeshore Boulevard.
>
> The corporate offices are on Seventh Avenue.

4. Money

Figures and the word *cents* are used for amounts under a dollar and figures with the *$* sign for an amount of a dollar or more. Omit .00 with even dollar amounts except in tabulations for the sake of uniformity. However, when an amount under a dollar is related to other amounts of a dollar or more, follow this example:

> Cheese was $1.89 a pound, ham was
> $1.98 a half pound, and bread was
> $.59 a loaf.
>
> The newspaper was 35 cents.

5. Ages

Unless age is used as a significant statistic, spell it out when given in years only. When any combination of years, months, and days is used, express it in figures.

On her birthday she will be
seventeen.

Henry Brown, 47, is the new board
member of our company.

Mary's baby is 3 months 5 days old
today.

6. Percentages

Use figures with the word *percent* when expressing percentages. The % symbol is used only in technical material and must be repeated with each percentage.

Almost 75 percent of those polled
indicated agreement with the new
law.

7. Discount Terms

Periods of time related to discount terms are expressed in figures.

If you pay within 10 days, you will
receive the discount.

8. Measurements

Figures are used for weights, dimensions, and other measurements that have a technical significance.

The elevation of the top platform
is 150 feet 2 inches.

9. Size, Serial, and Similar Numbers

Use figures for size, serial, and similar numbers. Capitalize *serial, model, No.,* and so on when used.

We returned the Model 24
machine. We prefer Style No. 20.

10. Indefinite Numbers and Very Large Numbers

Spell out indefinite numbers. However, use figures to express approximate amounts of money. Money in round amounts of a million or more may be expressed partially in words.

```
The election cost about $1,000, and
fewer than a hundred people voted
on the $10 million project.
```

11. Phone Numbers

No space is required after an area code, which is enclosed in brackets. A space is used between a telephone number and an extension number. *Extension* is always abbreviated and capitalized. A capital X may be used in place of Ext.

```
(412)953-7137
953-7000 (Ext. 7022)
           or
953-7000 (X7022)
```

Capitalization

Beginning Words

1. Of Sentences

Capitalize the first word of a sentence or a condensed statement.

> The white beach stretched on for miles.
>
> Now, to take care of the next problem.

2. Of Direct Quotations

Capitalize the first word of a direct quotation that is a complete sentence.

> Cheryl asked, "Did you like New England?"

3. Of Displayed Items

Capitalize the first word of each item displayed in a list or an outline.

> The committee was made up of the following:
>   Business representatives
>   Teachers
>   Consultants

4. Of Complimentary Closings

Capitalize the first word of a complimentary closing.

> Sincerely, Cordially yours, Very truly yours,

33

5. Of Sentences That Follow Colons

Capitalize the first word of a sentence that follows a colon.

> He gave me these directions: Turn left at the stop sign, and follow that road for two miles.

6. Of Questions Within Sentences

Capitalize the first word of a question within a sentence.

> The biggest problem seems to be, When will the construction be completed?

> EXCEPTION: This house is pretty, isn't it?

Names and Titles of Persons

1. Of Names, Nicknames, and Words Used as Names

Capitalize names and words used as names.

> I thought Kristy would be at Vickie's party.

> Akron is called the Rubber City.

> The one they called Masked Man rode off on his white horse.

2. Before Names

Capitalize a title that precedes the name of a person unless the name is in apposition to the title.

> The article was sent to President Tucker for approval.

> We visited the president, Robert Tucker, when we visited the university.

3. After Names

Do not capitalize a title that follows the name of a person unless it is the title of a high government official. Following are titles that remain capitalized.

National: President, Vice President, Cabinet members, Senator, Representative, Ambassador, Chief Justice, and heads of agencies.

State: Governor, Lieutenant Governor

Queen, King, and Prime Minister also retain the capitalization.

```
Bob Roberts, president of Central
University, wrote the paper.

Jimmy Carter, President of the
United States, is a tennis fan.
```

4. With Ex-, Former, and Late

Never capitalize *ex-*, *-elect*, *former*, or *late* when used with a title.

```
The article was written about ex-
Mayor Johns and Representative-elect
Wagner.

Harry Truman, late President of the
United States, liked to play the
piano.
```

5. In Direct Address

Capitalize any title that is used by itself in direct address except *miss* or *sir*. Sometimes these words are capitalized to show respect or emphasis or in very formal writing, for example, formal minutes.

```
Will you check my work,
Professor? Thank you, sir.
```

6. In Company and Official Titles

Official and department titles of one's own company usually are capitalized; those of other companies generally are not.

> Our Word Processing Department has an opening.

> Please have your vice president call me tomorrow.

7. With Words That Show Family Relationship

Capitalize words that show relationship only when they are used as a substitute for a name or are used preceding a name.

> I think Dad is the person whom I admire most of all.

> My aunt's plane will arrive at 7:07 p.m. I wonder if Uncle Art will be with her?

8. As Substitutes for Names

Do not capitalize a word or title that is used as a substitute for a specific name of a person, place, or thing unless it is used in place of the name of a high-ranking international, national, or state government official.

> The President gave his State of the Union address last night.

> The president of their company is a man in his thirties.

9. In Proper Nouns

Often it is necessary to distinguish between common and proper nouns by the use of capitalization.

> He is enrolled in Typing 110.

> She takes typing.

She will register for the fall
quarter.

The next time that course will be
taught will be Fall Quarter, 1984.

Titles of Artistic and Literary Works

Capitalize all words except articles, prepositions, and conjunctions of three or fewer letters in titles of books, magazines, newspapers, articles, reports, movies, programs, songs, plays, paintings, and so on. Also capitalize the first word, last word, and a word following a colon or dash.

The How to Do It Book
Down by the Old Mill Stream

Dates, Historical Events, and Seasons

Capitalize the names of the days of the week, months, holidays, and historical events and periods. Do not capitalize the names of seasons or of decades and centuries.

EXCEPTION: Capitalize such expressions as "the Gay Nineties." Also capitalize seasons which are personified or are specific titles, for example, Spring Quarter, 1983.

Each November the President proclaims
the fourth Thursday in November as
Thanksgiving Day.

Old Man Winter doesn't bother me; I'm
going to Florida in the spring.

Points of the Compass

When points of the compass are used to designate specific geographic regions, capitalize them; do not capitalize them when they are used to indicate direction. Also capitalize words derived from points of the compass when they are used to designate people.

```
throughout the          out West
   South
                        the Near East
northwest of
   Columbus             the Northerners

go west on First        Western
   Street                  civilization

westerly winds
```

Place Names

Capitalize the official and imaginative names of cities, states, countries, rivers, and so on. Capitalize *city* only when it follows the name of a city.

```
the Keystone            city of New York
   State
                        Ohio River
New York City
                        Euclid Avenue
the Windy City
```

The same rule applies to *state*.

```
Ohio State              state of Ohio
```

Do not capitalize the words "state" or "city" when used as substitutes for the names of states or cities.

```
Pay your water bill at the city office.
```

Proper Noun Derivations

Capitalize words that are derived from proper nouns. However, some words, due to usage, are not capitalized. If in doubt, check a recent dictionary.

```
Floridian               roman numerals

Canadian                Xerox, but
                           xerography
```

Academic Subjects and Degrees

Capitalize titles of specific academic courses, but do not capitalize general subjects unless they are foreign languages.

```
Marge took Botany 100 last year; this
year she will need another botany
course and one in English.
```

Academic degrees are generally not capitalized unless they are used as a specific title.

```
In his undergraduate days, he thought
he never would attain his bachelor of
arts degree.
```

Nouns Preceding Letters or Numbers

Nouns that precede letters or numbers are capitalized when they indicate sequence with the exception of small units, such as line, page, paragraph. If *No.* is used, that also is capitalized.

```
Book 12                    verse 2

page 107                   Document 73
```

Religious Titles and Supreme Beings

Capitalize religious titles such as holy days, names of saints and denominations, and references to supreme beings. Do not capitalize words derived from religious works.

```
the Bible                  biblical

God                        godlike

Saint Francis              saintly

Presbyterian
```

Music

When typing music key signatures, use capital letters for the key and lower case for the *major* or *minor*.

```
key of C
D major
```

Use the *pound symbol* (#) up one-half space for sharp and the lower-case *b* up one-half space for flat.

$$F^{\#}$$
$$E^{b}$$

Grammar

a, an

are articles (adjectives). The choice of *a* versus *an* is determined by sound—not spelling. Use *a* before all words beginning with a consonant sound. Also use *a* before words beginning with *h*, if the *h* is heard; long *u*; and *o* if the *o* sounds like *w*.

> <u>a</u> history lesson; <u>a</u> hotel, <u>a</u> holiday
>
> <u>a</u> unit, <u>a</u> uniform, <u>a</u> utility
>
> <u>a</u> one-sided game

Use *an* before words beginning with vowels unless the vowel has a consonant sound and before letters, words, or expressions that begin with a vowel sound.

> <u>an</u> apple, <u>an</u> estimate, <u>an</u> invention, <u>an</u> orange, <u>an</u> umbrella
>
> <u>an</u> hour (sounds like *our*), <u>an</u> heirloom (sounds like *eirloom*)
>
> <u>an</u> S (sounds like *es*), <u>an</u> FICA tax report (sounds like *eF*ICA)

above

is a preposition often misused as an adjective. It may be used as part of a compound adjective.

> The jet airliner flew <u>above</u> the clouds. (correct usage as a preposition)
>
> The <u>above</u> rules are easy to understand. (incorrect usage as an adjective)

41

The <u>above-mentioned</u> rules
are easy to understand.
(correct usage as part of a compound
adjective)

ACRONYMS are coined expressions derived from the initials of their completely written-out form.
They are pronounced as words.

ZIP (Zoning Improvement Plan)

CORE (Congress of Racial Equality)

(See: Abbreviations, Acronyms and Initialisms, p. 97 for more examples)

ACTIVE VOICE indicates the subject is the doer of the action specified in a verb.

Students <u>earn</u> their
tuition. (active voice)

Tuition <u>is earned</u> by
students. (passive voice—subject
receives action rather than performs
the action of earning)

ADJECTIVES modify or limit (describe) nouns or pronouns. They may be a single word, or the
adjective may be a phrase or clause.

The <u>big</u> boat cannot
navigate the river. (single
word modifier)

The boat <u>from overseas</u>
cannot navigate the river.
(prepositional phrase modifier)

The boat <u>arriving from
overseas</u> cannot navigate
the river. (participial phrase
modifier)

The boat <u>to be unloaded
next</u> is from overseas.
(infinitive phrase modifier)

The boat, <u>which is quite
big</u>, cannot navigate the
river.
(adjective clause modifier)

(See also: DEGREE, p. 54; PHRASES,
p. 77; and CLAUSES, p. 54)

ADVERBS   modify or limit verbs, adjectives, or other
adverbs. (They answer the questions: how,
when, where, why.) Often they end in *ly*.

The fog lifted <u>swiftly</u> once
the sun appeared. (modifies a
verb)

The current becomes
<u>unusually</u> swift in this
river. (modifies an adjective)

The water runs <u>very</u> swiftly
down the mountains. (modifies
an adverb)

(See also: DEGREE, p. 54; PHRASES,
p. 77; and CLAUSES, p. 50)

all   is an indefinite pronoun that may be used
to take the place of a singular or a plural
noun.

<u>All</u> was accounted for by
the auditor. (singular
antecedent)

Have <u>all</u> (the children)
received a vaccination?
(plural antecedent)

(See also: INDEFINITE PRONOUNS,
p. 63)

all of   The *of* can be omitted since *all* can be used
as an adjective.

<u>All</u> the trees are turning
color. (Not: *All of* the trees are
turning color.)

Grammar **43**

all right

is always two words. Sometimes this expression is used as an idiom, but it still is spelled as two words.

> The answers are <u>all right</u> in your test.

> <u>All right</u>, you may go. (idiomatic usage)

almost
all most

Almost is an adverb meaning nearly. All most is an indefinite pronoun used with most—an adverb in this case.

> We <u>almost</u> missed our train. (adverb modifying missed)

> You are <u>all most</u> welcome to visit our store. (pronoun plus adverb modifying the adjective welcome)

already
all ready

Already is an adverb meaning now. All ready is an indefinite pronoun plus an adjective construction.

> The assignments have <u>already</u> been posted. (adverb modifying have been posted)

> The employees are <u>all ready</u> to take their new assignments. (pronoun plus an adjective modifying all)

also
all so

Also is an adverb meaning too. All so is an indefinite pronoun plus an adverb construction.

> They <u>also</u> will be performing. (adverb modifying will be performing)

> <u>All so</u> artistically performed in the ballet. (pronoun plus adverb modifying artistically)

altogether
all together

Altogether is an adverb meaning entirely. All together is an indefinite pronoun plus an adjective or an adverb construction.

> The classroom was altogether too noisy. (adverb modifying too)

> We assembled the questionnaires all together in one pile. (pronoun plus an adverb modifying assembled)

> The papers are all together. (pronoun plus an adjective modifying papers)

always
all ways

Always is an adverb meaning forever or at all times. All ways is an adjective plus a noun construction.

> Always try to please your customers. (adverb modifying try)

> Do you have directions for all ways to get to the city? (Ways is a noun object of the preposition for and all is an adjective modifying ways.)

among

is a preposition. When speaking of three or more, use *among* rather than between.

> The candy was divided among the four children.

(See also: between, p. 48)

and, etc.

is a redundant expression. Etc. means *and so forth*; *and etc.* means *and and so forth*. Therefore, omit the *and* before etc.

> Books, pamphlets, leaflets, etc., are published by our company.

anxious
eager

Anxious is an adjective implying worry or concern; eager implies anticipation of something good or fortunate.

> I am <u>anxious</u> to know the outcome of my hospital tests.
>
> The staff members are <u>eager</u> to know what their raises will be.

anyone
any one

Anyone is an indefinite pronoun. Any one is a noun plus an adjective construction.

> <u>Anyone</u> may join the club. (pronoun)
>
> You may choose <u>any one</u> of the items as your prize. (One is a noun object of the verb choose; any modifies one.)

anyway
any way

Anyway is an adverb. Any way is a noun plus an adjective construction.

> Come <u>anyway</u>. (adverb modifying come)
>
> Come in <u>any way</u> you choose to dress. (Way is the object of the preposition in; any modifies way.)

ARTICLES

A, an, and *the,* frequently used adjectives, are known as articles. Use *the* to indicate a definite modifier; use *a* or *an* for an indefinite modifier.

> <u>A</u> time for the meeting has not been set. (indefinite)
>
> <u>The</u> time of the meeting is 8 p.m. (definite)

as, as
so, as

Use the correlative conjunctions *as, as* for positive correlation, but use the *so, as* combination for negative correlation.

> Bob is <u>as</u> tall <u>as</u> his brother. (positive correlation)

Sue is not <u>so</u> tall <u>as</u> her sister. (negative correlation)

awhile
a while

Awhile is an adverb. A while is a noun plus an adjective (article) construction.

Stay <u>awhile</u>. (adverb modifying stay)

It will be <u>a while</u> before the cake is baked. (While is a noun predicate nominative; a modifies while.)

bad
badly

Bad is an adjective; badly, an adverb. Use the adjective form after a copulative (linking) verb. If an adverb is required, use badly.

The spoiled fruit smells <u>bad</u>. (adjective required after copulative verb *smells*)

I feel <u>bad</u> that I cannot help you. (adjective required after copulative verb *feel*)

New typewriters are <u>badly</u> needed in our office. (adverb required—modifies needed)

The secretary types <u>badly</u>. (adverb required—modifies types)

because

(See: due to, p. 58; reason is, p. 79)

being that

cannot be substituted for the word because.

<u>Because</u> we were late, our salaries were docked. (Not: Being that we were late, our salaries were docked.)

beside
besides

Beside indicates location; besides means in addition to.

The table is <u>beside</u> the chair.

Who, <u>besides</u> you, is
leaving for lunch now?

**between
among**

Between is a preposition and takes the objective case of a pronoun. Use it when referring to a relationship between two nouns. If more than two are meant, use the preposition among.

> The choice is <u>between</u> you and me. (Not: Between you and I—use the objective case as object of the preposition between.)

> Competition is keen <u>between</u> the two candidates.

> Competition is keen <u>among</u> the many candidates.

bid

has two verb conjugations, each with a particular meaning. Bid, bid, bid means to offer an amount or price. Bid, bade, bidden means to ask, command, or greet.

> A high price was <u>bid</u> for the antique.

> My partner <u>bid</u> no-trump after our opponents had bid spades. (bid, bid, bid verb)

> I was <u>bidden</u> not to divulge the secret.

> They <u>bade</u> us welcome to their home. (bid, bade, bidden verb)

blame it on

Avoid this phrase except in very informal conversation. Say instead who or what is blamed.

> <u>Blame me</u> for the error. (Not: Blame the error on me.)

both alike

is redundant. Omit the both.

The twins are <u>alike</u> in appearance. (Not: The twins are both alike in appearance.)

broadcast
Broadcast, broadcast, broadcast are the correct principal parts of this verb. There is no word broadcasted.

The news was <u>broadcast</u> last week. (not broadcasted)

burst
Burst, burst, burst are the correct principal parts of this verb. There are no words bursted or busted.

When I was 12 years old, my appendix <u>burst</u>. (not bursted or busted)

but
can be used as a conjunction, a preposition, or an adverb.

It is raining now, <u>but</u> the weather should clear. (conjunction)

All <u>but</u> Kay and Ken have arrived. (preposition meaning except)

I have <u>but</u> $1 left in my checking account. (adverb meaning only)

(As an adverb *but* expresses negation. Therefore do not use: I have not but $1 left in my checking account unless the meaning intended is that there is more than $1 in the account.)

can, could may, might
Can and could imply ability. May and might indicate permission.

<u>May</u> I do the payroll report today? (You seek permission.)

<u>Can</u> you figure the payroll?
(Do you know how?)

CASE   signifies the relationship of a word to the other parts of the sentence. In the English language there are three cases: *nominative, possessive,* and *objective. Nominative* case is the term applied to words, phrases, or clauses used as subjects, predicate nouns, predicate adjectives. *Possessive* case implies ownership. *Objective* case is the term applied to words, phrases, or clauses used as direct objects, indirect objects, objects of prepositions, or complements of infinitives.

choose   Choose, chose, chosen are the principal parts of this verb. Choose is present tense. Chose is past tense. Choose and chose are often confused in spelling.

The team will <u>choose</u> a captain. (present tense)

The team <u>chose</u> a captain yesterday. (past tense)

circa   is to be used only with dates, indicating about.

Miniskirts were popular a few years ago, <u>circa</u> 1965.

CLAUSES   are groups of words containing both a subject and a predicate. *Independent (main, principal)* clauses are complete sentences. *Dependent (subordinate)* clauses, although they contain a subject and a predicate, cannot stand alone but are part of an independent clause functioning as nouns, adjectives, or adverbs.

(See: INDEPENDENT CLAUSE, p. 64 and DEPENDENT CLAUSE, p. 56)

come to
come and   The verb come followed by an infinitive

construction is correct. *Come and* is incorrect.

> <u>Come to</u> see the football game. (Not: Come and see the football game.)

common
mutual

Common is an adjective meaning shared or belonging to equally; mutual is an adjective meaning reciprocal or having the same relationship toward.

> That is a <u>common</u> spelling error. The public has <u>common</u> ownership of the playgrounds in our city.

> Insurance companies and their clients have a <u>mutual</u> interest in auto safety.

> We have a <u>mutual</u> friend.

COLLECTIVE NOUNS

are those nouns that specify a group or collection of persons, places, or things. Determining whether they are singular or plural is necessary, for the verb must agree with the noun in number.

These nouns are always used as singular nouns and therefore take a singular verb: *audience, board, class, club, committee, community, corporation, council, crowd, department, faculty, staff, team, union.*

These nouns are always used as plurals and must be followed by a plural verb: *goods, pants, pliers, proceeds, remains, riches, savings, scissors, shears, thanks.*

These nouns may be either singular or plural depending upon the meaning they are intended to convey: *counsel, deer, majority, minority, moose, number, series, sheep, species, swine.*

To determine number for other collective nouns, consult a dictionary.

COMPARATIVE DEGREE

(See: DEGREE, p. 54)

compare to/with
contrast

Use compare to to show likeness, to regard as similar; compare with to show both similarities and differences; and contrast to show differences.

> The discount-store prices <u>compare to</u> mail-order prices.

> The consumer's council <u>compared</u> discount-store prices <u>with</u> mail-order prices.

> Discount-store prices <u>contrast</u> greatly <u>with</u> mail-order prices.

COMPLEMENTS are words or phrases that complete the sense of a verb. Predicate nouns and adjectives are termed *complements*. Infinitives often require complements.

> The room is <u>dark</u>.

> That room is <u>my study</u>.

> The supervisor chose him to perform the <u>task</u>.

(See also: INFINITIVES, p. 64)

COMPOUND ADJECTIVES are a combination of two or more words that form a single modifier or descriptor. Before nouns or pronouns they are always hyphenated. Generally, if the expression comes after the noun, each word becomes part of the sentence structure (adjective, verb phrase, prepositional phrase) and is not hyphenated.

> up-to-date style   style is up to date

duty-free imports	imports are duty free
once-in-a-lifetime chance	chance comes once in a lifetime
20-floor building	building has 20 floors

If the combination of words remains strictly an adjective in the sentence structure, retain the hyphen.

My new car is company-owned.

I drive a new, company-owned car.

CONJUNCTIONS join words, phrases, and clauses. *Coordinating* conjunctions, which join words, phrases, or clauses of equal rank, are: *and, but, or, nor, for, yet, so, whereas* (whereas is used only in formal and legal writing).

Correlative conjunctions, which are used in pairs to join sentence elements, include: *as/as, both/and, either/or, neither/nor, not only/but also, so/as.*

Subordinate conjunctions, which join to the sentence elements of unequal rank, are: *after, although, as, because, before, if, since, that, though, unless, until, when, where, while,* and the relative pronouns *who, which,* and *that.*

CONJUNCTIVE ADVERBS although not classified as conjunctions, have the effect of conjunctions because they relate the preceding sentence to the sentence in which they appear. They include: *consequently, furthermore, however, moreover, nevertheless, then, therefore.*

**DANGLING
PARTICIPLES** (See: PARTICIPLES, p. 74)

datum, data *Datum* is a singular word; *data* is plural.

> The <u>data are</u> gathered each month. (plural verb)

DEGREE indicates quality, quantity, or manner of adjectives and adverbs; word form changes show degree.

Positive degree is used when a simple adjective or adverb is desired.

Comparative degree is used to show more or less quality, quantity, or manner between two nouns or pronouns. The comparative degree often ends in *er* or is formed by using more or less before the positive form.

Superlative degree is used to show more or less quality, quantity, or manner between one noun or pronoun and three or more other nouns or pronouns. The superlative degree is reflected in the *est* ending or is formed by using most or least before the positive form.

<u>Positive</u>	<u>Comparative</u>	<u>Superlative</u>
cute	cuter	cutest
beautiful	more (less) beautiful	most (least) beautiful ·
fast	faster	fastest
rapidly	more (less) rapidly	most (least) rapidly

> The baby is <u>cute</u>. (positive adjective)

> The baby is <u>cuter</u> now than last year. (comparative adjective)

The baby is <u>cutest</u> of all
entered in the contest.
(superlative)

The deer is a <u>beautiful</u>
animal.

The deer is <u>more beautiful</u>
than the horse, I think.

The deer is the <u>most
beautiful</u> of all animals.

The clerk types <u>fast</u>.
(positive adverb)

The clerk types <u>faster</u> than
the secretary. (comparative
adverb)

The clerk types <u>fastest</u> of
all our employees.
(superlative adverb)

The clerk works <u>rapidly</u>.

The clerk works <u>more rapidly</u>
than her assistant.

The clerk works <u>most rapidly</u>
of all our employees.

**DEMON-
STRATIVE
PRONOUNS**   point out persons, places, or things. They
are: *this, that, these, those.*

<u>This</u> is my home town.
<u>Those</u> are my new shoes.

Do not overuse the demonstrative pronoun
so that its antecedent becomes unclear. Instead use the demonstrative pronoun with
a noun.

This $10 is your
overpayment. (Not: This is your
overpayment.)

Those books are the library
selections. (Not: Those are the
library selections.)

**DEPENDENT
CLAUSES**

contain a subject and a predicate and are
used as nouns, adjectives, or adverbs.

What caused the explosion
remains a mystery. (noun
subject)

The judge stated that the
case would be continued.
(noun direct object)

The beach is two blocks
from where we live. (noun
object of preposition)

Your suggestion is what I
had in mind. (noun predicate
nominative)

The story that I wrote was
rejected by the publisher.
(adjective)

Since I have been on
vacation, my mail has
accumulated. (adverb)

(See: CONJUNCTIONS, p. 53, for a list of
words that are used to introduce dependent
clauses.)

differ from
differ with

Use differ from to indicate that one noun
is different from another; use differ with to
indicate a difference in opinion.

My political party differs
from yours.

Your party differs with
mine on states' rights
issues.

different from
different than

Do not use different than. Rather, use *different from*.

The result was <u>different
from</u> what was expected. (not
different than)

**DIRECT
ADDRESS** is the term applied to a direct reference to
another person by the person speaking or
writing.

Will you do it, <u>Howard</u>?

<u>Jane</u>, can you call me
tomorrow?

done is the perfect tense form, not the past tense,
of the verb do.

They <u>did</u> their assignments.
(Not: They done their assignments.)

don't is the contraction of do not. With he, she,
it, and third-person singular nouns, use
does not or *doesn't*, not *don't*.

Bill <u>doesn't</u> drive a new
car. (Not: Bill don't drive a new
car.)

She <u>doesn't</u> either. (Not:
She don't either.)

**DOUBLE
NEGATIVES** The use of two negative words in one
clause (principal or subordinate) converts
the meaning of that particular clause to a
positive expression. In the English
language such words as no, not, never,
nothing, none, and prefixes in-, un- express
negation.

Our city has elected no new
council members this year.
(Not: Our city hasn't elected no new
council members this year. This
sentence says the city has elected
some members.)

The double negative is occasionally used as a means of emphatically making a positive statement, and such usage is correct.

> It is not unlikely that a Southerner will be our next president. (It is likely.)

Several adverbs with negative meaning are particularly troublesome.

(See: but, p. 49; hardly, p. 62)

due to   should be followed by an adjective phrase. The phrase usually follows a form of the verb *to be* (is, are, was, were, etc.).

> The crop failure is <u>due to</u> drought.

If a clause or an adverbial phrase is being used, introduce it with *because of* or *on account of*.

> Because of drought, the crop failed. (adverbial phrase)

> Because drought conditions prevailed this summer, the crop failed. (adverbial clause)

eager   (See: anxious, p. 45)

either   followed by a prepositional phrase requires the use of a singular verb.

> <u>Either</u> of them <u>is</u> available. (singular subject, singular verb)

either/or   These words are correlative conjunctions. If the two words they relate are singular, use a singular verb. If the two words they relate are plural, use a plural verb. If one of the two words is singular and one is plural, make the verb agree with the word closer to it.

Either the <u>president</u> or his <u>representative</u> <u>is</u> to attend the ceremony. (two singular words—singular verb)

Either the <u>officers</u> or their <u>representatives</u> <u>are</u> to attend the ceremony. (two plural words—plural verb)

Either the <u>president</u> or his <u>representatives</u> <u>are</u> to attend the meeting. (one singular, one plural noun with plural closer to the verb—plural verb)

Either the <u>representatives</u> or the <u>president</u> <u>is</u> to attend the ceremony. (one singular, one plural noun with singular word closer to the verb—singular verb)

farther
further

Farther implies distance; further means in addition to.

You must go <u>farther</u> west to reach their house. (distance)

They have completed their typing; <u>further</u>, they are almost done with their shorthand assignments. (in addition to)

Further is often combined with *more*—furthermore.

fewer, less

Use fewer when describing number or with plural nouns. Use less to indicate degree or amount and with singular nouns.

Kelly made <u>fewer</u> typing errors than Millie. (number)

I have <u>fewer</u> quarters than dimes. (plural nouns)

It is <u>less</u> humid today.
(degree)

John's suit cost <u>less</u> than
Harry's. (amount)

I have <u>less</u> money than you.
(singular noun)

former, latter   These are the comparative degree and will be used when comparing one noun with another. If speaking or writing of more than two, use the superlative forms—first and last.

Of the <u>two</u> outfits shown in
the style show, my friend
preferred the <u>former</u>; I
liked the <u>latter</u>.

Of the <u>many</u> outfits shown,
I prefer the <u>first</u>; my
friend liked the <u>last</u>.

from   Use the preposition from with persons rather than the preposition off.

The hospital report was
obtained <u>from</u> the
physician. (not off the physician)

GENDER   indicates whether a·noun or pronoun is masculine, feminine, or neuter. Pronouns agree with their antecedents in gender.

John took <u>his</u> umbrella;
Mary wore <u>her</u> raincoat.

Traditionally, the masculine gender has been used when the gender of a group was unknown. Many writers still use this distinction.

Each employee must fill out
<u>his</u> own W-2 statement.

However, if sex bias might be suggested, the rule may be altered by using his and her or by using plurals.

Each employee must fill out
his or her own W-2
statement.

All employees must fill out
their W-2 statements.

NOTE: Though the singular use of *their* is colloquial and unacceptable to strict grammarians, its use is becoming widespread.

Everyone can pick up <u>their</u>
paycheck on Friday.

GERUNDS are words or phrases that are used partly as verbs and partly as nouns. As nouns they may be the subject, predicate noun, direct object, or object of a preposition. As nouns they may have modifiers (adjectives). Usually gerunds end in *ing*.

<u>Reading</u> is my favorite
hobby. (gerund subject)

One of my favorite hobbies
is <u>reading</u>. (gerund predicate
noun)

Television has made <u>reading</u>
less popular. (gerund direct
object)

Language skills can be
improved by reading. (gerund
object of a preposition)

Gerunds often have possessive pronoun modifiers.

The teacher was impressed
by <u>his</u> reading the novel.
(not him)

<u>Their</u> accepting the
contract prevented a
strike. (not they)

get, got,
got or gotten   is a verb meaning to obtain. It is often over-
                 worked in idiomatic usage:

                     get well, get along with,
                     get on with, get even with,
                     get away with, get going,
                     and so on.

good, well   Good is usually an adjective meaning of a
                 favorable character. Well may be an adjec-
                 tive referring to a condition of health.
                 However, well is usually an adverb.

                     She is a <u>good</u> girl.

                     I feel <u>good</u>.

                     I am not <u>well</u>. (adjective)

                     The job was <u>well</u> done.
                     (adverb)

                     (See: well, p. 87.)

had ought   Omit the had.

                     I <u>ought</u> to get to work on
                     time. (not had ought)

hang   has two verb conjugations. Hang, hung,
                 hung and hang, hanged, hanged. Hang,
                 hanged, hanged means to put to death.
                 Hang, hung, hung is used for all other
                 meanings.

                     Persons were <u>hanged</u> for
                     crimes in early times.

                     The curtains <u>hung</u> unevenly
                     on the windows.

hardly   is a negative word. Do not use another neg-
                 ative with it unless you wish to convey a
                 positive meaning.

                     They had <u>hardly</u> begun the
                     round of golf before the
                     rain came. (not: They had not
                     hardly begun.)

his	Masculine possessive form third person singular personal pronoun.

(See also: GERUNDS, p. 61 and PERSONAL PRONOUNS, p. 75)

-ics endings	require a singular verb if the noun indicates a study or an activity. With matters of behavior or operations, use a plural verb.

> <u>Athletics is</u> subsidized at our college.

> <u>Graphics is</u> a new course in the curriculum.

> <u>Politics</u> makes strange bedfellows.

> Those <u>tactics were</u> not approved ·by the committee.

> <u>Hysterics are</u> often the result of fear.

IMPERATIVE MOOD

is used to command, request, or give direction.

> <u>Feed</u> the dog before you sit down to supper. (command)

> Please <u>put</u> your coat and hat in the closet. (request)

> <u>Fold</u> the letter in thirds and insert it in the envelope. (direction)

INDEFINITE PRONOUNS

are pronouns whose antecedents are unknown or not definitely defined. Some are singular; some are plural; some may be used as singular or plural.

Singular forms that take a singular verb include: another, anybody, anyone, anything, each, either, every, everybody, everyone, everything, much, neither, nobody, nothing, one, somebody, someone, something.

Plural forms that take a plural verb include: both, few, many, others, several.

Singular or plural forms, depending upon their use in the sentence, include: all, any, more, none, other, some, such.

> <u>Anyone is</u> free to buy a ticket to the circus. (singular)

> <u>Few have</u> purchased tickets. (plural)

> <u>All is</u> lost. (singular meaning everything)

> <u>All are</u> here today. (plural meaning several)

(See: GENDER, p. 60)

INDEPENDENT CLAUSES

An independent clause is a group of words containing a subject and a predicate that form a complete thought. A sentence is an independent clause.

(See: SENTENCE, p. 81)

INDICATIVE MOOD

is used to make a statement or ask a question.

> The clock just chimed 10 o'clock. (statement)

> Will the guests be here by noon? (question)

INFINITIVES

are words or phrases containing qualities of verbs and qualities of nouns, adjectives, or adverbs. They are introduced by the word *to*. As nouns they may have modifiers or complements. A complement answers the question "what" after the infinitive.

To travel is his aim in
life. (infinitive subject)

Her aim in life is
to make money. (infinitive
predicate noun with a complement)

She decided to travel to
fulfill her ambitions.
(infinitive direct object)

She traveled to fulfill her
ambitions. (infinitive adverb—
tells why she traveled)

About to begin a new job,
he hoped to make money.
(infinitive object of preposition)

Music to dance to has
changed in recent years.
(infinitive adjective)

INTENSIVE OR REFLEXIVE PRONOUNS

Add the self ending to a personal pronoun.

I, myself, will drive you to
the airport. (intensive)

They made themselves a big
breakfast over the campfire.
(reflexive)

Do not use the reflexive pronoun as a substitute for the nominative or objective case
personal pronoun.

Give your time sheet to me.
(Not: Give your time sheet to
myself.)

You should take charge, or
You yourself should take
charge. (Not: Yourself should
take charge.)

INTERJECTIONS

are words that could stand alone or are in-
jected into a sentence but do not become

a part of the sentence structure.

They include such words as *oh, o.k., wow, yes, no.*

INTERROGATIVE PRONOUNS

(who, which, what) are used in asking questions. They may be used as singular or plural forms. Their case depends upon their relationship to other words in the clause in which they appear.

> <u>Who</u> is going to make the coffee? (singular, nominative case)

> She asked <u>whom</u> about the problem? (singular, objective case)

(See: who, p. 87; which, p. 87; what, p. 87)

INTRANSITIVE VERBS

or copulative verbs are verbs that take a complement or a predicate adjective. Examples include: appear, become, feel, look, seem, smell, sound, taste.

> The food tastes <u>bad</u>. (not badly)

> The music sounds <u>strange</u>. (not strangely)

> The perfume smelled <u>sweet</u>. (not sweetly)

> Your new outfit looks <u>nice</u>. (not nicely or well)

is

(See: to be, p. 85)

its, it's

Its is a possessive pronoun. It's is a contraction of it is.

> The animal shed <u>its</u> fur. (A possessive pronoun is required if a prepositional phrase—of it—can be substituted. The animal shed the fur of it.)

It's a fine day! (A contraction is required if words—it is—can be substituted. It is a fine day!)

kind, sort, type, variety

These words are singular nouns that are often overworked. They should be used only in informal writing. Their plurals are kinds, sorts, types, varieties.

> That **kind** of music is difficult to understand. (informal)

> That music is difficult to understand. (formal)

> Opera is difficult to understand. (formal and more specific)

kind of a

Omit the *a* from informal expressions such as kind of, type of.

> That **kind** of shirt is what was advertised. (Not: That kind of *a* shirt is what was advertised.)

less

(See: fewer, p. 59)

learn, teach

Learning is the act of acquiring knowledge. Teaching is the act of imparting knowledge. Students learn. Instructors teach. Conjugations are: learn, learned, learned, and teach, taught, taught.

> They **learned** their multiplication tables in elementary school.

> The teacher **taught** them well.

let, leave

Let implies permission. Leave indicates departure. Conjugations for these verbs are: let, let, let, and leave, left, left.

<u>Let</u> them all come to the party.

The visitors will <u>leave</u> before noon. Our personnel <u>left</u> at 10 a.m.

liable, likely

Liable means responsible for; answerable to someone or for something. Likely implies a tendency to do something or to do it in a certain way.

He was <u>liable</u> for damages to his neighbor's property.

I am <u>likely</u> to attend the IWP conference next June.

lie, lay

The verb *lie* means to rest or recline. It is an intransitive copulative verb that does not take an object. The past tense is *lay*; the participle is *lain*. To test to see if the verb lie is correct, substitute the words *rest* or *recline* for lie and be sure there is no object for the verb.

I <u>lie</u> (rest or recline) in bed every Saturday morning. (no object)

I <u>lay</u> (rested or reclined) in bed yesterday. (no object)

I <u>have lain</u> (rested or reclined) in bed every morning this week. (no object)

Lay means to put or place. It is a transitive verb that takes an object. The past tense is laid; the participle is laid. To test to see if the verb lay is correct, substitute the words *put* or *place*. Also look for an object if the verb is in active voice.

A good secretary will always <u>lay</u> (put or place) her

reference book beside her
typewriter. (lay has an object—
book)

I <u>laid</u> (put or placed) it there
this morning. (object—it)

I <u>have laid</u> (put or placed) it
there during all the years
that I have been a
secretary. (object—it)

Note that lay, because it is a transitive
verb, may be used in passive voice. Then
the object of the action becomes the subject
of the verb.

The reference book <u>was laid</u>
by my typewriter each day.

<table>
<tr><td>like, as</td><td>Like can be an adjective. Usually it is a preposition. Sometimes it is a verb. It is not a conjunction. As is a conjunction.</td></tr>
</table>

Do all the letters in <u>like</u>
manner. (like—adjective)

I look <u>like</u> my mother.
(like—preposition)

I <u>like</u> to dance. (like—verb)

The band performed their
formations <u>as</u> they had
rehearsed them. (Not: like they
had rehearsed them)

<table>
<tr><td>loose, lose</td><td>Lose means to mislay or misplace. Its principal parts are lose, lost, lost. Loose means not tight. Its most frequent use is as an adjective.</td></tr>
</table>

The teacher who <u>loses</u> her
grade book is in a
predicament.

A <u>loose</u> screw caused the
machine breakdown.

–ly words are usually adverbs. However, occasionally an adjective such as friendly or timely will end in -ly.

> She has a <u>friendly</u> smile. (adjective)

> That is a <u>timely</u> report. (adjective)

> We shall be home <u>shortly</u>. (adverb—when)

> They <u>quickly</u> found a substitute speaker. (adverb—how)

may be, maybe *May be* is a verb construction. *Maybe* is an adverb meaning perhaps.

> Someone <u>may be</u> home by the time we arrive.

> <u>Maybe</u> someone will be home by the time we arrive.

MOOD indicates the manner of action of a verb. In the English language there are three moods—*indicative, imperative,* and *subjunctive.*

(See: IMPERATIVE MOOD, p. 63; INDICATIVE MOOD, p. 64; SUBJUNCTIVE MOOD, p. 83)

myself (See: REFLEXIVE PRONOUNS, p. 65)

NEGATIVE ADVERBS include such words as but, hardly, never, not, only, scarcely. Do not use another negative word with them unless you intend to convey a positive meaning.

> The parent said to the child, "<u>Don't never</u> do that again." (Do not never do

something again means do it
sometime.)

(See: but, p. 49; hardly, p. 62)

neither   followed by a prepositional phrase still requires a singular verb.

> Neither of the lawyers
> wants to handle the case.
> (Wants is singular; want would be
> the plural verb.)

neither, nor   These words are correlative conjunctions. If the two words they relate are singular, use a singular verb. If the two words they relate are plural, use a plural verb. If one of the related words is singular and one is plural, the verb agrees with the word nearer it.

> Neither my uncle nor my
> aunt is as young as my
> mother. (two singular words—
> singular verb)

> Neither my uncles nor my
> aunts are as young as my
> mother. (two plural words—plural
> verb)

> Neither my uncle nor my
> aunts are as young as my
> mother. (one singular and one
> plural word—aunts [plural] closer to
> verb, plural verb)

> Neither my uncles nor my
> aunt is as young as my
> mother. (one singular and one
> plural word—aunt [singular] closer
> to verb, singular verb)

**no body,
nobody**   No body is a noun plus an adjective construction. Nobody is an indefinite pronoun.

<u>No body</u> was found following the drowning.

<u>Nobody</u> will be able to determine how the accident occurred.

NOUNS are parts of speech that name persons, places, or things. A noun, whether it be a single word, a phrase, or a clause, can be used as a subject, object, predicate noun, or verb complement.

<u>Mary</u> showed <u>John</u> a <u>map</u> of <u>St. Louis</u>. (Mary is a noun subject; John is a noun indirect object; map is a noun direct object; St. Louis is a noun object of a preposition.)

Her brother is <u>John</u>. (John is a noun predicate noun.)

She asked him to follow the <u>map</u> closely. (Map is the noun complement of the infinitive to follow.)

Nouns may be classified as common (general names of persons, places, or things) or proper (specific names of persons, places, or things).

The <u>city</u> is a great place to live. (City is a common noun.)

<u>New York City</u> is a great place to live. (New York City—proper noun)

number may have either a singular or a plural meaning depending upon the article used with it.

A number is plural. *The* number is singular.

A number of our employees are in the bowling league. (plural verb)

The number of bowlers has increased this year. (singular verb)

of   Do not substitute of for have.

You should have found the error. (Not: You should of found the error.)

off of   Omit the word of in prepositional phrases using off.

They picked the fruit off the trees. (Not: They picked the fruit *off of* the trees.)

PARALLEL STYLE

should be maintained in relating similar ideas.

The board of directors will arrive at the hotel, eat lunch, and then go into session. (Not: the board of directors will arrive at the hotel, eat lunch, and are going into executive session. Use the same tense for all verbs in the series.)

The typist who is fast, who is accurate, and who does neat work will be considered for promotion. (Not: The typist who is fast, who is accurate, and is doing neat work will be considered for promotion. Use three who clauses to maintain parallel style.)

The pages of my manual are old, used, and frayed at

the edges. (Not: The pages of my manual are old, used, and fraying at the edges. Use three adjectives to maintain parallel style.)

PAREN-THETICAL EXPRESSIONS are words, phrases, or clauses that are not essential to the sentence. They are often referred to as nonessential words, phrases, or clauses and are set off by commas.

There will be, <u>incidentally</u>, a fee for this service. (parenthetical word)

The fee, <u>by the way</u>, will be determined at the time of service. (parenthetical phrase)

The fee, <u>which will be set later</u>, must be paid when the service is rendered. (parenthetical clause)

PARTICIPLES are words or phrases that are used partly as verbs and partly as adjectives. Because they have the qualities of adjectives, participles must modify nouns or pronouns.

<u>Tossed</u> about by the wind, the sailboat lost its bearings. (Tossed modifies sailboat, and it also shows action.)

<u>Having driven</u> 500 miles of their trip, the vacationers were ready to stop for the night. (Having driven modifies vacationers and it shows an action—driving.)

The common error in the use of participles is that no appropriate noun or pronoun is used for the participle to modify.

Tossed about by the wind,
our bearings were lost.
(This statement says bearings were
tossed about.)

Having driven 500 miles,
the campsite was near. (This
statement says the campsite drove
500 miles.)

These constructions are called *dangling
participles*.

**PASSIVE
VOICE**
indicates that the subject of the verb is the
receiver of the action specified by the verb.

Tuition <u>is earned</u> by the
students. (Active voice indicates
that the subject receives the action.
Students earn tuition would be
active voice for this example.)

**PERSONAL
PRONOUNS**
can be substituted for the names of persons. The form of the pronoun varies in
some instances for case, number, and gender. Personal pronoun forms are:

	First Person		Second Person		Third Person	
	Sing.	Pl.	Sing.	Pl.	Sing.	Pl.
Nominative Case	I	we	you	you	he she it	they
Possessive Case	my mine	our ours	your yours	your yours	his hers its	their theirs
Objective Case	me	us	you	you	him her it	them

Use the *nominative* case for the subject of a sentence, a predicate noun, and the complement of the infinitive *to be* when *to be* does not have a subject.

They are studying law.
(subject)

It was she whom I saw.
(predicate noun)

The man appeared to be he.
(complement of to be when to be has no subject)

Use the *possessive* case for pronoun modifiers of nouns or gerunds.

Our bowling banquet is next month. (modifies banquet)

We will appreciate your making the reservations. (modifies making)

If a pronoun modifier does not immediately precede the noun it modifies, use mine, yours, his, hers, its, ours, theirs.

The pencil is not mine.
Those papers are theirs.

Use the *objective* case for the object of a verb, an indirect object, an object of a preposition, the subject of an infinitive, and the subject of the infinitive *to be* when *to be* has a complement.

Our guide met us at the terminal. (direct object)

We gave him our passports. (indirect object)

She has her camera with her. (object of a preposition)

I asked her to take a picture. (subject of an infinitive)

We chose <u>him</u> to be our spokesman. (subject of to be when to be has a complement)

PHRASES are groups of words without subjects and predicates that cannot stand alone as sentences. They include prepositional, adverbial, infinitive, participial, and gerund expressions.

I shall be home <u>for dinner</u>. (prepositional phrase)

<u>By the way</u>, what are we having for dinner? (adverbial phrase)

<u>To get through the traffic</u>, we left the office at 4 p.m. (infinitive phrase)

<u>Having beat the traffic</u>, we were home for dinner. (participial phrase)

<u>Beating the traffic</u> is not possible every evening. (gerund phrase)

POSSESSIVE CASE indicates belonging to or ownership. Inanimate objects cannot "possess."

The <u>cover of the book</u> (not the book's cover) is the correct expression.

EXCEPTION: Objects that are personified may be structured as owning or possessing something.

The <u>ship's forward end</u>; <u>autumn's beauty</u>.

Common idiomatic expressions acceptable in business use the possessive case with amounts of time and money.

Ten dollars' worth of
groceries; a dollar's worth
of change; a week's pay;
three weeks' vacation.

PREDICATE   is the principal verb in the sentence and all
words other than those in the complete sub-
ject. If a sentence contains two or more
principal verbs, it contains a *compound
predicate*.

The children romped and
played. (compound predicate)

While the adults watched
television, the children
romped and played in the
family room. (complete
predicate)

PREPOSITIONS   are connecting words. They show the relationship of a word or group of words to
other parts of the sentence. The group of
words is called a prepositional phrase.
These phrases may act as adjectives or adverbs.

The principal prepositions are about, above,
across, after, against, ahead of, along,
along with, around, as, at, away from, in
back of, before, behind, below, beneath,
between, but, by, down, down from, down
to, except, for, from, in, in front of, inside,
into, like, of, off, on, out, out of, out with,
outside, over, past, through, throughout,
to, under, underneath, until, up, upon,
with, within, without.

PRONOUNS   take the place of nouns because they refer
to persons, places, or things previously
mentioned, questioned, or understood by
the context of the sentence. A pronoun
must agree with its antecedent in person,
number, and gender. Case, however, is de-

termined by its relationship to other words in the sentence.

(See: DEMONSTRATIVE PRONOUNS, p. 55; INDEFINITE PRONOUNS, p. 63; INTENSIVE OR REFLEXIVE PRONOUNS, p. 65; INTERROGATIVE PRONOUNS, p. 66; PERSONAL PRONOUNS, p. 75; and RELATIVE PRONOUNS, p. 79)

real, very

Do not use real (an adjective) for the adverb very.

That is a <u>very</u> lovely poem.
(Not: That is a real lovely poem.)

reason is because

Reason is and because have the same connotation. Do not say reason is because, but rather use reason is that or just reason is.

The <u>reason is that</u> they overslept.

The <u>reason is</u> oversleeping.

regard

Regard is often used as a synonym for reference. Do not use regards for this meaning.

The telephone call was <u>in regard to</u> our appointment. (not in regards to)

RELATIVE PRONOUNS

introduce adjective clauses and refer back to another noun or pronoun in the sentence. Relative pronouns include: who, whom, whose, that, and which.

right, rightly

Use right as an adjective. Use rightly as an adverb.

That is the <u>right</u> address. (adjective)

The parents were <u>rightly</u>

proud of their children.
(adverb modifying proud. Do not
use: The parents were right proud of
their children.)

rise, raise   The verb rise means to ascend. It is an intransitive verb and does not take an object.
The past tense is rose; the participle is risen.
To determine if rise is the correct verb, substitute the word ascend and be sure it does
not take an object.

> The bread is <u>rising</u>.
> (ascending—no object)

> The kite <u>rose</u> (ascended)
> easily into the air. (no
> object)

> The airplane <u>has risen</u> (has
> ascended) above the clouds.
> (no object)

Raise means to lift up. It is a transitive verb
and takes an object. Its principal parts are
raise, raised, raised.

> Will you <u>raise</u> (lift up) your
> voice in protest? (object—
> voice)

> What <u>raised</u> (lifted up) that
> issue again? (object—issue)

> The merchants <u>have raised</u>
> (lifted up) their prices again.
> (object—prices)

Raise may be used in the passive voice.

> The issue <u>has been raised</u>
> many times before.

**RUN-ON
SENTENCES**   contain more than one complete thought.
Many run-on sentences can be eliminated
by correct punctuation.

> The age of electronics is
> here we'll have mini-

computers in our homes
soon. (run-on)

The age of electronics is
here; we'll have mini-
computers in our homes soon.

or

The age of electronics is
here. We'll have mini-
computers in our homes soon.

or

The age of electronics is
here, and we'll have mini-
computers in our homes
soon.

said   Do not use said as an adjective even in legal documents.

The property is on the
north side of the road.
(Not: The *said* property is on the
north side of the road.)

same   Do not use same as a pronoun.

Your order for three copies
of the textbook arrived
today. The books will be
sent this afternoon. (Not:
Your order for three copies of the
textbook arrived today. *Same* will be
sent this afternoon.)

SENTENCE   A group of words comprised of one or more independent clauses and possibly some dependent clauses that convey a complete thought. Every sentence must have a *subject* (noun or pronoun) and a *verb*.

**SENTENCE
STRUCTURE**   refers to the manner in which parts of speech are assembled to form sentences. Each word in a sentence should be defin-

**shall, should
will, would**

able in terms of parts of speech and its relationship to other words in the sentence.

Use of shall versus will (should versus would) at one time depended upon the personal pronoun or the degree of emphasis intended in the sentence. Few writers make those distinctions today.

sit, set

The verb sit means to rest or recline. It is an intransitive verb that does not take an object. The past tense is sat; the participle is sat. It cannot be used in the passive voice.

> Your picture <u>sits</u> (rests or reclines) on our table. (no object)

> We <u>sat</u> (rested or reclined) outside for several hours. (no object)

> The reference books <u>have sat</u> (have rested or reclined) on the library shelf for a number of months. (no object)

The verb set means to put or place. It is transitive and may take an object. The past tense is set; the perfect participle is also set.

> <u>Set</u> (put or place) the letters on the executive's desk. (object—letter)

> The lawyers <u>set</u> (put or placed) the agreement before the two parties. (object—agreement)

> These students <u>have set</u> (have put or placed) their minds to study. (object—minds)

The verb can be used in the passive voice.

The contract <u>was set</u> before the parties by their lawyers.

some one
someone

Some one is an indefinite pronoun plus an adjective construction. Someone is an indefinite pronoun.

<u>Some one</u> of the applicants will be hired.

<u>Someone</u> will be hired.

some time
sometime

Some time is a noun plus an adjective construction. Sometime is an adverb indicating when.

<u>Some time</u> will be required before all applicants can be interviewed. (Time, the subject noun, is modified by some.)

Will you give us <u>some time</u> to complete the analysis? (noun plus adjective)

It will be done <u>sometime</u> this week. (adverb)

sort

(See: kind, p. 67; kind of, p. 67)

SUBJECT

The subject of a sentence indicates who or what is being talked or written about. It performs or receives the action of the verb.

The <u>refrigerator</u> has an ice maker.

The <u>pupils</u> work diligently.

<u>They</u> will attend Homecoming next week.

SUBJUNCTIVE
MOOD

is used to express a wish or to describe a condition contrary to fact. For all verbs except *to be,* the verb form is the same as that for the indicative mood. However, *were* is used rather than *was* for all persons in the subjunctive mood.

> He wishes he <u>were</u> a pro football player. (wish)

> If the pamphlets <u>were</u> available for distribution, you could have one today. (condition contrary to fact)

Subjunctive mood can be used in formal writing in a dependent clause following a verb that expresses a request, command, or determination. The subjunctive form of the verb is the same as that of the imperative. This is also the form used in parliamentary procedure, motions, and resolutions.

> The doctor requested that the patient see him again next week. (request)

> Be it resolved that the Board of Trustees rehire all personnel. (rather than it is resolved)

> I move that the nominations be closed. (not are closed)

that, which

That is a relative pronoun that generally introduces *essential* clauses. (Which introduces *nonessential* clauses.)

> The books <u>that I ordered</u> <u>for our reference library</u> arrived today. (essential subordinate clause)

> The books, <u>which are</u> <u>invaluable references</u>, can be found in the library. (nonessential subordinate clause)

Verbs such as saying, thinking, wishing, feeling, require the word *that* to introduce a dependent clause as object of the verb.

He said <u>that</u> he could not come. (Not: He said he could not come.)

She feels <u>that</u> everyone should attend. (Not: She feels everyone should attend.)

I believe <u>that</u> I shall be able to get there early. (Not: I believe I shall be able to get there early.)

then, than

Then is an adverb indicating *a time* or *when*. Than is a conjunction. Than is not a preposition.

We shall see you <u>then</u>. (when)

Shopping took longer <u>than</u> we had anticipated it would. (conjunction)

Than is often followed by a clause in which some words are understood. Pronoun case must be decided as though the understood words were written or spoken.

The fashion model is taller than he or she. (not him or her)

The fashion model is taller than he or she <u>is tall</u>. (understood words)

to be

meaning, basically, to exist is the most commonly used verb. Forms of to be include: am, are, is, shall be, will be, was, were, have been, has been, had been, shall have been, will have been, be, should be, would be.

This linking verb joins nouns, predicate adjectives, and complements to a subject. It is always intransitive and cannot take an object. It may be used as an auxiliary or helping verb to form past tense (was running) or perfect tense (have received).

type
(See: kind, p. 67; kind of, p. 67)

**ULTIMATE
DEGREE**

Some adjectives and adverbs represent an ultimate or unsurpassable degree and therefore cannot be compared unless the writer intends to describe an approach to the ultimate. Some examples are perfect, eternal, unique, ultimate, first, and last.

> That approach is unique.
> (not most unique, more unique, less unique, least unique)

> His paper was more nearly perfect than hers. (Not: His paper was more perfect than hers.)

variety
(See: kind, p. 67; kind of, p. 67)

VERBALS

are words or phrases that have some verb qualities (they show action) and also contain certain qualities of other parts of speech.

(See: PARTICIPLES, p. 74; GERUNDS, p. 61: INFINITIVES, p. 64)

VERBS

are the parts of speech that show action performed or received by the subject of the sentence.

> The truck sped down the road. (Subject performs the action—truck sped.)

The letter <u>was written</u> by
the secretary. (Subject
receives action—letter was written.)

VOICE indicates whether the writer wishes to em-
phasize the subject (performer of the action
specified by the verb) or the object (receiver of the action specified by the verb).
Active voice stresses the performer; *passive* voice stresses the receiver.

Many American youth now
<u>play</u> soccer. (active voice)

Soccer <u>is</u> now <u>played</u> by
many American youth. (passive
voice)

The use of active voice is proper for strong,
emphatic, direct writing. The use of passive
voice is proper for less emphatic and indirect writing.

well is an adverb that often forms part of a compound adjective. As part of a compound
adjective, it is hyphenated only when the
adjective precedes the noun.

The <u>well-designed</u> building
will be a good choice for
an office.

The building, which is
<u>well designed</u>, will be a
good choice for an office.

what is an interrogative pronoun or a relative
pronoun.

which is an interrogative pronoun or a relative
pronoun.
(See: that, which, p. 84)

who, whose,
whom are either interrogative or relative pronouns. Their relationship to other words in

the sentence determines whether to use the nominative case (who), the possessive case (whose), or the objective case (whom).

Interrogative pronoun uses include:

> Who won the Olympic medals for swimming last year? (Subject requires nominative case.)

> The winner was who? (Predicate noun requires nominative case.)

> Whose tennis racket is this? (possessive case modifier of racket)

> The personnel department interviewed whom? (Direct object requires objective case.)

> To whom will the announcement be sent? (Object of a preposition requires the objective case.)

Relative pronoun uses in subordinate clauses include:

> I asked who would work overtime. (Who is the subject in the clause who would work overtime; who is not the object of the verb asked—rather the entire subordinate clause is the object of asked.)

> The person whose grades are the highest will receive the award. (Whose modifies grades in the clause whose grades are the highest.)

> The retailer from whom we purchased our supplies is

going out of business.
(Whom is the object of the
preposition from in the clause from
whom we purchased our supplies.)

The person <u>whom</u> we elected
will take office next week.
(Whom is the object of elected in the
clause whom we elected.)

Be sure parenthetical expressions are disregarded in determining the choice of who or whom.

She is the woman <u>who</u>, I
think, <u>should be</u> hired. (I
think is parenthetical. Who is the
subject of should be hired in the
clause who should be hired.)

<u>Who</u>, do you believe,
<u>will win</u> the election? (Do
you believe is parenthetical. Who is
an interrogative pronoun, the subject
of will win in the sentence who will
win the election.)

who's, whose   Whose is the possessive form of the relative or interrogative pronoun who. Who's is the contraction of who is.

<u>Whose</u> paper may I read?
(possessive case modifying paper)

<u>Who's</u> coming to dinner?
(who is)

**WORD
ELEMENTS
DEFINING
NUMBER**   uni (one); du, bi, di (two); tri (three); quadr, quart (four); quint, penta (five); sex, sext, hexa (six); sept (seven); oct (eight); non, nov (nine); deca (ten).

Spelling

Frequently, it is necessary to check the dictionary for the spelling of words. Note that the dictionary often gives a second spelling; however, the first spelling is the common and preferred one and should be used. Also check the definitions of words to assure yourself that you have selected the correct spelling.

Final Consonant Doubled

In words of one syllable ending in a single consonant, double the final consonant before a suffix beginning with a vowel.

stop	stopped
clan	clannish
drop	dropped
trim	trimming

In words of one syllable ending in a single consonant, double the final consonant before a suffix beginning with y.

skin	skinny
chum	chummy

In words of more than one syllable ending in a single consonant preceded by a single vowel and accented on the last syllable, double the final consonant.

refer	referring
compel	compelled
defer	deferred
concur	concurrent
begin	beginning
transfer	transferred

EXCEPTION: If the accent is shifted to a syllable other than the last, do not double the final consonant.

refer	reference
defer	deference

Final Consonant not Doubled

In words of one syllable ending in a single consonant preceded by a single vowel, do not double the final consonant.

ship	shipment
skew	skewness

In words of more than one syllable, if the accent does not fall on the last syllable of a root word ending in a single consonant preceded by a single vowel, do not double the final consonant before suffixes beginning with a vowel (ing, ed, etc.).

profit	profiting
credit	credited
cancel	canceled
parallel	paralleling

EXCEPTIONS: program, programmed, programming; kidnap, kidnapping, kidnapped

For root words ending in x, do not double the x before adding any suffix.

suffix	suffixes
tax	taxed
relax	relaxing

For root words ending in a double consonant, just add the suffix.

access	accessed
fill	filling

When a word of one or more than one syllable ends in a single consonant preceded by more than one vowel, do not double the final consonant.

eat	eaten
look	looking
chief	chiefly
wood	woody

When a word of one or more syllables ends in one or more consonants, do not double the final consonant.

hand	handful
warm	warmly

Final Silent E

When words end in silent e, the e is usually dropped before a suffix beginning with a vowel (ing, ism, ed).

approve	approving
commune	communism
file	filed
double	doubling
concentrate	concentration

EXCEPTIONS: dyeing, European

Words ending in silent e usually retain the e before a suffix beginning with a consonant (ment, ness).

arrange	arrangement
crude	crudeness

EXCEPTIONS: judgment, acknowledgment, wholly, ninth, gently, argument, truly, duly

Words ending in ce and ge (with a soft c or g) retain the final consonant when adding the able or ous suffix. Sometimes the e changes to an i.

notice	noticeable
advantage	advantageous
service	serviceable
outrage	outrageous
manage	manageable
knowledge	knowledgeable
enforce	enforceable
grace	gracious

Final Y Changed to I

Words ending in y preceded by a consonant change the y to i before any suffix except one beginning with i.

likely	likelihood
happy	happiness
bury	burying
thirty	thirtyish

Words ending in y preceded by a vowel usually retain the y before any suffix.

EXCEPTIONS:

pay	paid
lay	laid
day	daily
say	said

Ei and Ie Words

Put i before e except after c or when sounded like a as in neighbor and weigh.

EXCEPTIONS:

seize	weird
forfeit	height
ancient	financier

Words Ending in Able and Ible

Able is the more common ending. However, some of the most commonly used words end with ible.

advisable	collectible
probable	divisible
receivable	flexible
valuable	permissible

Words Ending in Cede, Ceed, and Sede

Only one word ends in sede: supersede.
Only three words end in ceed: exceed, proceed, succeed.
All other words ending with the seed sound are spelled cede.

Words Ending in Ify and Efy

Only four words end in efy: rarefy, stupefy, liquefy, and putrefy.
All other words ending with the ify sound are spelled ify.

Hyphenating Prefixes and Suffixes

When the first part of a word is a prefix or the last part is a suffix, a hyphen is generally not used. If three l's occur in succession, use a hyphen.

anticlimax	bell-like
bylaws	shell-less

With a prefix ending in a or i and the base word beginning with the same letter, use a hyphen to prevent misreading.

ultra-active	semi-independent

With a prefix ending in e or o and the base word beginning with the same letter, the hyphen is almost always omitted.

coordinate	preexamine
cooperate	reemploy

EXCEPTIONS: co-op; de-escalate

All *self* words are hyphenated except *selfish, selfsame,* and *self-less*.

The prefix *re* is not followed by a hyphen except to distinguish the word from another word with the same spelling but a different meaning.

to re-cover the chair	to recover from illness
to re-mark the price	to make a remark

When a prefix is added to a word that begins with a capital letter, use a hyphen after the prefix.

mid-June	anti-American

EXCEPTION: transatlantic

Meanings of Common Prefixes

com, con, co, cor, col	with, together
de	down
ex	out of, away
for	exclude, omit, neglect
fore	beforehand
im, in	in, not

1

inter	between, among
intra	within
intro	inward
pro	for, in favor of
re	again
dis	opposite
mis	bad, not
sub	under

SECTION 2
Abbreviations, Acronyms, and Initialisms Guide

This section of *The Wiley Office Handbook* first presents RULES FOR ABBREVIATIONS for personal names and titles, names of companies and organizations, names of places, and miscellaneous terms.

These rules are followed by a listing of ABBREVIATIONS, ACRONYMS, AND INITIALISMS that the transcriptionist, word processor, or correspondence secretary is likely to encounter.

Rules for Abbreviations

Personal Names and Titles

1. Before Names

Whether they appear with complete names or with last names only, abbreviate Mr., Messrs., Mrs., Ms., Mmes., and Dr. Write other titles in full when they are used with last names only; abbreviate them when they are used with complete names. A professional title takes preference over a personal title. Do not use both.

Mrs. Eleanor Jones	Ms. Palmer
Dr. Borden	Dr. J. E. Winslow
Reverend Wilkins	Rev. L. J. Wilkins
Governor Lentz	Gov. G. M. Lentz
Professor Tucker	Prof. Rita Tucker

2. After Names

Always abbreviate Esq., Jr., Sr., Ph.D., and other degrees, and S.J. and other names of religious orders when they follow names. When writing an abbreviation of an academic degree other than CPA, use a period after each part but do not leave a space between the parts: B.S., M.A., Ed.D., LL.B., and so on.

```
Julia Davis,              Barbara Jones,
   M.D.                       Ph.D.

George Jones,             John Alfred,
   Jr.                       LL.B.
```

NOTE: Personal names are not abbreviated with the exception of *Saint* which is usually abbreviated (St.) when it is part of a last name.

Names of Companies and Organizations

1. Part of a Name

Many companies or other organizations abbreviate one or more parts of their names. Follow the style used by the company or organization. If you are uncertain as to whether or not to use an abbreviation, check the letterhead or some other printed form.

2. Entire Name

Many well-known business firms, unions, associations, agencies, and so on, commonly abbreviate their names. These names are written without periods or spaces when they consist of all capital letters.

> FCC (Federal Communications Commission)
>
> AISE (Association of Iron and Steel Engineers)
>
> IWPA (International Word Processing Association)

Names of Places

1. Countries

Names of countries should not be abbreviated when they appear by themselves in sentences. In addresses, lists, and so on, such abbreviations as U.S.A. and U.S.S.R. are commonly used.

2. States

Names of states should be written in full within sentences. In addresses, state names are usually abbreviated through the use of the two-letter abbreviations devised by the United States Postal Service. In tables, or whenever abbreviations are necessary, use the regular state abbreviations. (See back cover)

> She lives in Gainesville, Florida.
> (not Fla. or FL)

3. Cities

Never abbreviate the name of a city; however, *Saint* is abbreviated when used as part of a city name. *Fort* is not abbreviated.

> They visited St. Louis and Fort Lauderdale last year.

Miscellaneous Terms

1. Compass Points

Do not abbreviate compass points unless used after a street name to designate a section of a city.

> She lived on West 27 Street most of her life, but her new address is 133 Third Street, N.W.

2. A.M., P.M., and so on

Write a.m. and p.m. in small letters with periods but no space between the letters. Always use figures with these abbreviations; use figures with the word "o'clock." Do not use both letter abbreviations and the word "o'clock."

Do not abbreviate noon or midnight.

> The movie will be shown at 10 a.m., 3:30 p.m., and 8:15 p.m.

She thought I said 12 midnight; what
I really said was 12 noon.

The appointment is for 10 o'clock.

3. Measurements

Units of weight, distance, and capacity should not be abbreviated except when they are used with numbers in technical
writing, in lists, on invoices, and so forth.

The pattern calls for 11 yards of
material.

The 225-pound athlete is in excellent
condition.

(See: Appendix, p. 447 for metric measurements and abbreviations)

4. Days and Months

Do not abbreviate names of the days of the week or months
except when necessary to conserve space in tables and lists.

We expect them to arrive the first
Saturday in June.

5. Business Terms

Common business terms such as FOB and COD are frequently abbreviated in sentences, on invoices, in lists, and
so on.

Abbreviations, Acronyms, and Initialisms

AA	Alcoholics Anonymous American Airlines
A.A.	Associate of Arts (degree)
AAA	Agricultural Adjustment Administration American Automobile Association
AACS	Airways and Air Communications Services
AAUP	American Association of University Professors
AAUW	American Association of University Women
AB	able-bodied
ABA	American Bankers Association American Bar Association
ABC	American Bowling Congress American Broadcasting Companies, Inc.
ABCD	Accelerated Business Collection and Delivery
ABM	antiballistic missile
a.c.	alternating current

AC	Air Canada
acct.	account
ACF	American Car and Foundry
ACLU	American Civil Liberties Union
ACRR	American Council on Race Relations
ACS	American Chemical Society American College of Surgeons
AC&U	Association of Colleges and Universities
A.D.	(anno Domini) in the year of Our Lord or after Christ
ADA	Americans for Democratic Action
ADP	Automatic Data Processing
ad val.	(ad valorem) according to value
AEC	Atomic Energy Commission
AF	Air France
AFDC	Aid to Families with Dependent Children
AFIPS	American Federation of Information Processing
AFL	American Football League
AFL-CIO	American Federation of Labor and Congress of Industrial Organizations
AFT	American Federation of Teachers
AIA	American Institute of Architects
AIAD	Acronyms, Initialisms, and Abbreviations Dictionary
AIB	American Institute of Banking
AIChE	American Institute of Chemical Engineers
AID	Agency for International Development
AIM	American Indian Movement
AISP	Association of Information Systems Professionals

AKA	also known as
AL	Allegheny Airlines American League
ALA	American Library Association
ALCOA	Aluminum Company of America
ALGOL	Algorithmic Language (for computer programming)
a.m.	(ante meridiem) before noon
AM	AeroMexiço
A&M	Agricultural and Mechanical (description of a college)
AMA	American Medical Association
AMAX	American Metal, Climax, Inc.
AMEX	American Stock Exchange
AMF	American Machine & Foundry Co.
AMP	Aircraft-Marine Products, Inc.
AMS	Administrative Management Society
amt.	amount
ANA	Association of National Advertisers
anon.	anonymous
A-OK	definitely all right
A-1	first-rate or first-class
AP	American Plan Aspen Airways Associated Press
APB	all points bulletin
API	American Petroleum Institute
APO	Army Post Office
AR	Aerolineas Argentinas
ARC	American Red Cross
ARMA	Association of Record Managers and Administrators

AS	Alaska Airlines
ASA	American Standards Association American Statistical Association
ASCAP	American Society of Composers, Authors, and Publishers
ASCE	American Society of Civil Engineers
ASME	American Society of Mechanical Engineers
assn.	association
asst.	assistant
ASTA	American Society of Travel Associations, Inc.
AT	Royal Air Maroc
atty.	attorney
Ave.	avenue
AWOL	absent without leave
AYC	American Youth Congress
B.A.	Bachelor of Arts (or A.B.)
bal.	balance
B.A.T.	British Aerial Transport Industries
B.B.A.	Bachelor of Business Administration
BBB	Better Business Bureau
BBC	British Broadcasting Corporation
bbl.	barrel
B.C.	before Christ
B/E	Bill of Exchange
B/F	brought forward
bldg.	building
Blvd.	boulevard

BMR	Basal Metabolic Rate
BN	Braniff International Airways
BNDD	Bureau of Narcotics and Dangerous Drugs
BOQ	Bachelor Officers' Quarters
BPD	barrels per day
BPW	Business and Professional Women's Clubs
B.S.	Bachelor of Science
BSI	British Standards Institution
Btu	British thermal unit
bx.	box
C	Centigrade hundred
CAB	Civil Aeronautics Board
CAF	cost and freight
CAI	computer-assisted instruction
CAP	Civil Air Patrol
cap.	capital letter
CARE	Cooperative for American Relief to Everywhere
CATV	Community Antenna Television
CB	Citizens' Band (radio)
CBC	Canadian Broadcasting Corporation
CBI	computer-based instruction
CBS	Columbia Broadcasting System
cc	carbon copy (copies) cubic centimeter(s)
CCC	Commodity Credit Corporation
CCTV	Closed-circuit Television
CD	Certificate of Deposit

CED	Committee for Economic Development
CEEB	College Entrance Examination Board
CEO	Chief Executive Officer
CETA	Comprehensive Education and Training Act
cf	compare
cfm	cubic feet per minute
cfs	cubic feet per second
CGS	centimeter-gram-second
ch.	chapter
CIA	Central Intelligence Agency
CIF	cost, insurance, and freight
CJ	Chief Justice
CLU	Chartered Life Underwriter
cm	centimeter
cm.	cumulative
Co.	company
CO	Continental Airlines
c/o	in care of
COBOL	Common Business Oriented Language
COD	cash on delivery
CofC	Chamber of Commerce
COL	cost of living
cont.	continued
CORE	Congress of Racial Equality
CP	Canadian Pacific Air
CPA	Certified Public Accountant
CPO	Chief Petty Officer

CPS	Certified Professional Secretary
CQT	College Qualification Test
cr.	credit
CRC	Civil Rights Commission
CRM	Certified Records Manager
CRT	cathode-ray tube
CS	Civil Service
CSC	Civil Service Commission
CST	Central Standard Time
cu.	cubic
c&w	Country and Western
CWO	cash with order
cwt.	hundredweight
CZ	Canal Zone
DA	District Attorney
D.A.	Doctor of Arts
DAT	Differential Aptitude Test
DAV	Disabled American Veterans
d.c.	direct current
D&C	dilatation and curettage
D.D.	Doctor of Divinity
D.D.S.	Doctor of Dentistry
DDT	Dichlorodiphenyltrichloroethane (insecticide)
dept.	department
dft.	draft
disc.	discount
DJ	disc jockey
DJIA	Dow Jones Industrial Average

2

DL	Delta Airlines, Inc.
D/L	demand loan
DMZ	demilitarized zone
DOA	dead on arrival
DP	data processing
DPF	Data Processing Financial & General Corp.
Dr.	Doctor
dr.	debit
DST	Daylight Savings Time
DX	diagnosis distance (radio terminology)
E	east energy
EA	Eastern Airlines
ECG	electrocardiogram
Ed.D.	Doctor of Education
Ed.M.	Master of Education
EDP	electronic data processing
EDT	Eastern Daylight Time
EEG	electroencephalogram
EEOC	Equal Employment Opportunity Commission
e.g.	(exempli gratia) for example
EG&G	Edgerton, Germeshausen & Grier
ENI	Ente Nationale Idrocarfuri
EO	executive order
EOF	end of file
EOM	end of month

EP	European Plan
EPA	Environmental Protection Agency
ERA	Equal Rights Amendment
ERDA	Energy Research and Development Administration
ERIC	Educational Resources Information Center
ESP	extrasensory perception
Esq.	Esquire
EST	Eastern Standard Time
et al.	(et alii) and others
ETA	estimated time of arrival
etc.	(et cetera) and so forth
ETD	estimated time of departure
ETS	Educational Testing Service
ETV	Educational Television
Ext.	Extension
F.	Fahrenheit
FAX	facsimile
FBI	Federal Bureau of Investigation
FCA	Farm Credit Administration
FCC	Federal Communications Commission
FCDA	Federal Civil Defense Corporation
FCIS	Fellow of the Chartered Institute of Secretaries
FDA	Food and Drug Administration
FDIC	Federal Deposit Insurance Corporation
Fed.	Federal
FEPC	Fair Employment Practice Commission
ff.	and the following pages

FHA	Federal Housing Administration
FHWA	Federal Highway Administration
FICA	Federal Insurance Contributions Act
FIFO	first in, first out
FL	Frontier Airlines
FLSA	Fair Labor Standards Act
FM	frequency modulation
FMC	Federal Maritime Commission Food Machinery Corporation
FMCS	Federal Mediation and Conciliation Service
FNMA	Federal National Mortgage Association
f.o.b.	free on board
FORTRAN	formula translation (computer language)
FPC	Federal Power Commission
FRB	Federal Reserve Board
FRS	Federal Reserve System
frt.	freight
FS	Foreign Service
FSLIC	Federal Savings and Loan Insurance Corporation
ft.	feet, foot
FTC	Federal Trade Commission
FW	Wright Airlines
FWD	front-wheel drive
FX	foreign exchange
FY	fiscal year
GAF	General Aniline and Film Corporation
gal.	gallon

GAO	General Accounting Office
GATT	General Agreement on Tariffs and Trade
GATX	General American Transportation Corporation
GAW	guaranteed annual wage
Genesco	General Shoe Company
GI	government issue
GM	General Motors
GMT	Greenwich Mean Time
GMW	gram molecular weight
GNI	Gross National Income
GNP	Gross National Product
GOP	Grand Old Party
GP	general practitioner
GPA	grade-point average
GPD	gallons per day
GPM	gallons per minute
GPO	Government Printing Office
GPS	gallons per second
gr	gross
GRE	Graduate Record Examination
GSA	General Services Administration
GT	gross ton
GTC	good till canceled (market)
GX	Great Lakes Airlines Ltd.
HA	Hawaiian Air Lines
HD	heavy-duty
HEW	Department of Health, Education, and Welfare

2

HF	high frequency
	First Air
HHFA	Housing and Home Finance Agency
HIC	Health Insurance Council
HIF	Health Information Foundation
HII	Health Insurance Institution
h.p.	horsepower
HR	House of Representatives
HST	Hawaiian Standard Time
HUD	Department of Housing and Urban Development
IAAF	International Amateur Athletic Association
IAEA	International Atomic Energy Agency
IATA	International Air Transport Association
IBA	Investment Bankers Association
ibid.	(ibidem) the same
IBM	International Business Machines
ICBM	intercontinental ballistic missile
ICC	Interstate Commerce Commission
ICFTU	International Confederation of Free Trade Unions
ICR	Institute for Cancer Research
ICU	intensive care unit
IDP	integrated data processing
i.e.	(id est) that is
IE	Industrial Engineer
IEEE	Institute of Electrical and Electronic Engineers
IF	intermediate frequency

IFC	International Finance Corporation
IFIP	International Federation for Information Processing
IFO	identified flying object
ill.	illustration
ILO	International Labor Organization
IMF	International Monetary Fund
in.	inch(es)
Inc.	Incorporated
INP	International News Photo
INS	International News Service
int.	interest
I/O	input/output
IOU	I owe you
IPA	International Phonetic Alphabet
IPS	inches per second
IQ	intelligence quotient
IR	Internal Revenue
IRA	Individual Retirement Account
IRS	Internal Revenue Service
ISBN	International Standard Book Number
IST	insulin shock therapy
ISV	International Scientific Vocabulary
ITA	Initial Teaching Alphabet
ital.	italics
ITO	International Trade Organization
ITT	International Telephone and Telegraph Company
ITU	International Typographical Union

ITV	instructional television
IUD	intrauterine device
IV	intravenous
JBS	John Birch Society
JCC	Junior Chamber of Commerce
J.D.	Doctor of Jurisprudence
JIT	job instruction training
J.M.	Master of Jurisprudence
JP	Justice of the Peace
Jr.	Junior
J.S.D.	Doctor of the Science of Law
JV	junior varsity
kg.	kilogram
KGPS	kilograms per second
KKK	Ku Klux Klan
km	kilometer
KMPS	kilometers per second
KO	knockout
KP	Kitchen Police
kt.	carat
kw.	kilowatt
l. ll.	line, lines
LASER	Light amplification by emission of radiation (also written laser)
lc	lower case
L/C	letter of credit

lb.	pound
lcl.	less than carload lot
LCM	least common multiple
LIFO	last in, first out
LL.B.	Bachelor of Laws
loc. cit.	(loco citato) in the place cited
LPN	Licensed Practical Nurse
L.S.	(locus sigilli) place of the seal
LSAT	Law School Admission Test
LSD	lysergic acid diethylamide
LSS	life support system
LT	long ton
Ltd.	Limited
ltl.	less-than-truckload lot
LTV	Ling-Temco-Vought, Inc.
m.	meter
M	thousand
M.A.	Master of Arts
MARS	Manned Astronautical Research Station
MATS	Military Air Transport Service
M.B.A.	Master of Business Administration
MBS	Mutual Broadcasting System
MC	Master of Ceremonies Member of Congress
MCAT	Medical College Admissions Test
M.C.E.	Master of Civil Engineering
M.D.	Doctor of Medicine

M.D.S.	Master of Dental Surgery
mdse.	merchandise
M.Ed	Masters in Education
memo	memorandum
METO	Middle East Treaty Organization
mfg.	manufacturing
mfr.	manufacturer
mg.	milligram
mgr.	manager
mi.	mile(s)
MIA	missing in action
MICR	magnetic ink character recognition
min.	minute(s)
MIO	minimum identifiable order
misc.	miscellaneous
mm.	millimeter
mo.	month
MO	mail order
Mol. Wt.	molecular weight
MOM	middle of month
MP	Member of Parliament
MPG	miles per gallon
MPH	miles per hour
MPM	meters per minute
MPS	meters per second
ms.	manuscript
MSAT	Minnesota Scholastic Aptitude Test
MSEC	millisecond

Msgr.	Monsignor
MST	Mountain Standard Time
MT	metric ton
Mtge.	mortgage
MT/ST	Magnetic Tape Selectric Typewriter
MV	millivolt
MX	Mexicana De Aviacion
N	net
n/10	net amount due in 10 days (invoicing)
NA	National Airlines, Inc.
	not applicable
	not available
NAACP	National Association for the Advancement of Colored People
Nabisco	National Biscuit Company
NACU	National Association of Colleges & Universities
NAM	National Association of Manufacturers
NANA	North American Newspaper Alliance, Inc.
NAS	National Academy of Sciences
NASA	National Aeronautics and Space Administration
NASD	National Association of Security Dealers
NATO	North Atlantic Treaty Organization
NB	(nota bene) note well
NBA	National Basketball Association
	National Boxing Association
NBC	National Broadcasting Company
NBS	National Bureau of Standards
NC	no charge
	no credit

NCAA	National Collegiate Athletic Association
NCC	National Council of Churches
NCCJ	National Conference of Christians and Jews
NCR	National Cash Register Nuclear Regulatory Commission
NCV	no commercial value
n.d.	no date
NE	Air New England northeast
NEA	National Education Association
NFL	National Football League
NFS	not for sale
NHI	National Health Insurance
NHL	National Hockey League
NL	National League
NLAA	National Legal Aid Association
NLF	National Liberation Front
NLRB	National Labor Relations Board
NMA	National Microfilming Association
No.	number
NOW	National Organization for Women
NPCF	National Pollution Control Foundation
NRA	National Recovery Administration National Rifle Association
NRC	National Research Council
NSA	National Secretaries Association
NSC	National Security Council

2

NSF	not sufficient funds
NU	name unknown
NVF	National Vulcanized Fibre Co.
NW	northwest Northwest Orient Airlines, Inc.
NYSE	New York Stock Exchange
OAS	Organization of American States
O/C	overcharge over-the-counter (market)
OCDM	Office of Civil Defense Mobilization
OCR	optical character recognition (or reader)
OCS	Officer Candidate School
OCTV	open-circuit television
OD	overdose (of a narcotic)
o.d.	overdraft
OECD	Organization for Economic Cooperation and Development
OEO	Office of Economic Opportunity
OIT	Office of International Trade
OJT	on-the-job training
OK	correct; approved Czechoslovak Airlines
OP	out of print
op. cit.	(opera citato) in the work cited
OPEC	Organization of Petroleum Exporting Countries
OR	operating room
OS	Ordinary Seaman
OSHA	Occupational Safety and Health Administration

2

oz.	ounce(s)
OZ	Ozark Airlines
p. pp.	page, pages
PA	Pan American World Airways public address Purchasing Agent
PABX	Private Automatic Branch Exchange
PAC	Political Action Committee
pat.	patent
PAU	Pan American Union
PBS	Public Broadcasting Service
PBX	Private Branch Exchange
PCB	polychlorinated biphenyl
PD	per diem
pd.	paid
PDD	past due date
PDT	Pacific Daylight Time
PE	printer's error
PEN	International Association of Poets, Playwrights, Editors, Essayists, and Novelists
PERT	Program Evaluation and Review Technique
pfd.	preferred
PG	parental guidance
PGA	Professional Golfers Associaton
PHA	Public Housing Administration
Ph.D.	Doctor of Philosophy
PHS	Public Health Service

PI	Piedmont Aviation, Inc.
pkg.	package
pl.	plural
P&L	profit and loss
PLSS	portable life support system
p.m.	(post meridiem) afternoon
PMH	production per man hour
PN	point of no return
PO	post office purchase order
POE	port of embarkation port of entry
POW	prisoner of war
PP	parcel post postpaid prepaid
PPFA	Planned Parenthood Federation of America
PPG	Pittsburgh Plate Glass Industries
PPI	policy proof of interest
PR	public relations
pro tem.	(pro tempore) temporarily
PS	postscript
PSAT	Preliminary Scholastic Aptitude Test
PSI	Pollution Standard Index
PST	Pacific Standard Time
pt.	pint
PTA	Parent-Teacher Association
PTO	Patent & Trade Mark Office
PTV	Public Television

PVT	pressure, volume, temperature
PX	Post Exchange
QDA	quantity discount agreement
QED	(quod erat demonstrandum) which was to be demonstrated
QEF	(quod erat faciendum) which was to be made or done
QEI	(quod erat inveniendum) which was to be found out
QF	Quantas Airways
QM	Quartermaster
qr.	quarter quire
qt.	quart
RADAR	radio detection and ranging (also radar)
RC	Roman Catholic
RCA	Radio Corporation of America
RCAF	Royal Canadian Air Force
RCMP	Royal Canadian Mounted Police
R&D	research and development
recd.	received
ref.	reference
regd.	registered
REV	reentry vehicle
RF	refunding
RFD	Rural Free Delivery
RN	registered nurse
ROTC	Reserve Officers' Training Corps

rpm	revolutions per minute
rps	revolutions per second
RR	railroad
R.R.	rural route
R&R	rest and recreation
RRB	Railroad Retirement Board
RSVP	(réspondez, s'il vous plaît) please reply
rte.	route
RW	Hughes Airwest
S	South
/S/	signed
SALT	Strategic Arms Limitations Talks
SAT	Scholastic Aptitude Test
SBA	Small Business Administration
SBN	Standard Book Number
SC	Supreme Court
SCAT	School and College Ability Test Supersonic Commercial Air Transport
SCM	Smith Corona Marchant Corporation
S/D	sight draft
S/D-B/L	sight draft with bill of lading
SDS	Students for a Democratic Society
SE	southeast
SEATO	Southeast Asia Treaty Organization
sec.	secretary section
SEC	Securities and Exchange Commission

SNCC	Student Nonviolent Coordinating Committee
SNOBOL	computer programming language
SO	Southern Airways, Inc.
s.o.	seller's option
SOS	call for help
SPCA	Society for the Prevention of Cruelty to Animals
SPCC	Society for the Prevention of Cruelty to Children
SPOT	satellite positioning and tracking
sq. ft.	square foot (feet)
Sr.	Senior
SRO	standing room only
ss	(scilicet) namely
SSA	Social Security Administration
SSI	Supplementary Security Income
SSS	Selective Service System
SSW	south, southwest
St.	Street
ST	short ton
stet	let it stand
S.T.D.	Doctor of Sacred Theology
stk.	stock
ST EX	stock exchange
STP	standard temperature and pressure
supt.	superintendent
SW	southwest

SWA	South-West Africa
SWG	standard wire gauge
TAC	Tactical Air Command
TB	tuberculosis
t.b.	trial balance
TBA	to be announced
TD	touchdown Treasury Department
TELEX	Teletypewriter Exchange
TGIF	Thank God, it's Friday.
Th.D.	Doctor of Theology
3M	Minnesota Mining & Manufacturing Co.
TI	Texas International Airlines, Inc.
TKO	technical knockout
TL	total loss
TLC	tender loving care
TNT	trinitrotoluene
Tosco	The Oil Shale Corporation
treas.	treasurer, treasury
TRW	Thompson, Ramo, Woolridge
TS	Aloha Airlines, Inc.
TU	trade union
TUC	Trades Union Congress
TV	television
TVA	Tennessee Valley Authority
TWA	Trans World Airlines, Inc.
TWX	Teletypewriter Exchange
TZ	Transair Limited, Canada

UA	United Air Lines, Inc.
UAR	United Arab Republic
UAW	United Automobile Workers
u.c.	upper case
UFO	unidentified flying object
UFT	United Federation of Teachers
UGT	urgent
UHF	Ultrahigh frequency
UK	United Kingdom
UL	Underwriters' Laboratory
UMT	universal military training
UMW	United Mine Workers
UN	United Nations
UNESCO	United Nations Educational, Scientific, and Cultural Organization
UPI	United Press International
UPS	United Parcel Service
US	United States
USA	United States of America United States Army
USAF	United States Air Force
USCG	United States Coast Guard
USDA	United States Department of Agriculture
USES	United States Employment Service
USIA	United States Information Agency
USM	United States Mail
USMC	United States Marine Corps
USN	United States Navy

USO	United Services Organizations
USPS	United States Postal Service
USS	United States Ship
USSR	Union of Soviet Socialist Republics
VA	Veterans Administration
VAT	value-added tax
VD	venereal disease
VF	video frequency voice frequency
VFW	Veterans of Foreign Wars
VHF	very high frequency
VIP	very important person
VITA	Volunteers for International Technical Assistance
viz.	(videlicit) namely
vol.	volume
VP	vice president
vs.	versus
VTR	video tape recorder
v.v.	vice versa
W	west
WA	Western Airlines, Inc.
WAC	Women's Army Corps
WATS	Wide Areas Telephone Service
WB	waybill
WC	Wien Air Alaska, Inc.
WCTU	Women's Christian Temperance Union
WFTU	World Federation of Trade Unions

whsle.	wholesale
WHO	World Health Organization
w.i.	when issued
WIA	wounded in action
wk.	week
WNW	west, northwest
w/o	without
WP	word processing
WPA	Works Progress Administration
WP/AS	word processing/administrative support
wpc	watts per candle
WP/IP	word processing/information processing
wpm	words per minute
WSW	west, southwest
wt.	weight
WVS	Women's Voluntary Services
X-C	ex-coupon (without the right to coupons—bonds)
X-D	ex-dividend (without the right to dividends—stock)
XR	ex-rights (without rights—finance)
XW	ex-warrants (without warrants—finance)
yd.	yard
YMCA	Young Men's Christian Association
yr.	year
YWCA	Young Women's Christian Association
ZIP	Zoning Improvement Plan
ZPG	zero population growth
ZV	Air Midwest
ZX	Air West Airlines, Ltd.

SECTION 3
Word Use Guides

The word use section deals with word-division rules for the machine transcriptionist, word processor, or correspondence secretary. It includes GENERAL RULES and a list of HELPFUL GUIDES that can assist in choosing the appropriate word division.

This section is of major importance. It includes a list of approximately 20,000 frequently used business words. It is a handy reference for proper SPELLING AND WORD DIVISION OF FREQUENTLY USED WORDS. Several important features should be noted. Since electric typewriter keyboards as well as magnetic typewriter keyboards provide for the typing of 7 to 10 or more strokes after the bell rings to signal the end of the line, no word of 7 or fewer strokes needs to be divided. Because word division is time-consuming on any typewriter and particularly so on the magnetic keyboard, it is suggested that words be divided only if necessary. In the words listed, a diagonal (/) indicates a preferred point for word division in terms of the general rules presented in this section, and a bullet (.) indicates other acceptable points for the division of each word. When no division is given, it means that it is possible to type the word without hyphenation.

Whether or not to hyphenate words is a decision that must be made by the machine transcriptionist, word processor, or correspondence secretary. Hyphenated words are indicated by a letter h (h) in the list, and hyphenation can occur only at that point.

Another problem is presented when one must decide whether to use a one-word or a two-word spelling. To assist the typist in making these choices, which are dependent upon grammatical construction within the sentence, words that are sometimes written as one word, sometimes hyphenated, and sometimes written as two words are listed and footnoted (i.e., all ready and already). The footnote explains the grammatical construction that determines the choice and is followed by a sentence illustrating the correct use of the word.

3

Rules for Word Division

General Rules

1. Words may be divided only between syllables. Do not divide one-syllable words.

2. Do not divide words of seven letters or less.

3. Do not divide a one-letter syllable from the rest of the word. Do not divide a word unless a syllable of at least three characters will remain on the upper line and at least three characters will be carried to the next line.

NOTE: The hyphen on the first line and a punctuation mark on the second line may be considered as one of the three characters.

4. Do not divide abbreviations or contractions.

Helpful Guides

1. Divide solid compound words between the elements of the compound.

   sales- person   time- table

2. Divide hyphenated compound words where the hyphens occur.

```
self-    control       mother-    in-law
```

3. Divide words after, rather than within, prefixes; divide words before, rather than within, suffixes.

```
intro-   duce          practi-    cable

circum-                convert-   ible
    stances
```

4. In words containing one-letter syllables within the root words, divide after the one-letter syllables.

```
sepa-    rate          simi-    lar
```

5. Divide between two separately sounded vowels that come together in a word.

```
gradu-   ation         retro-   active
```

6. Keep together word groups that are to be read together, such as page and number, month and day, surname and title.

```
Elmer Finlay, Jr.              April;
                               1983

Chapter 27                     17 inches
```

7. Dates may be divided between the day and year.

```
                     September 11,
    1983.
```

8. Addresses may be divided between the street name and *Street, Lane,* and so on.

```
                     1234 Joseph
    Street.
```

9. The city and the state may be divided.

```
                     Minneapolis,
    Minnesota.
```

10. Names of persons may be divided between the given name (including the middle initial) and the surname.

Medves.

11. Names with very long titles may be divided between the title and the name.

Vice President

Kern.

12. No more than two consecutive lines should end in hyphens.

13. The first line or the last full line in a paragraph should not end in a hyphen.

14. Do not divide the last word on a page.

15. Proper nouns should not be divided.

3

WP/IP NOTE:

Because most equipment has the word wrap feature, and therefore does not hyphenate, it is necessary to check the page for a pleasing appearance and to add hyphens as needed. Some equipment does automatic hyphenation at appropriate places as the document is keyboarded.

GRAMMATICAL CONSTRUCTIONS—FOOTNOTE REFERENCES

The footnotes in the section that follows are keyed *numerically* to the following list of rules for spelling and word breaks:

1. Compound adjective construction. Hyphenate if description precedes noun.

2. Adjective plus adverb construction. Do not hyphenate.

3. Noun or compound adjective construction. Hyphenate.

4. Noun construction. Hyphenate.

5. Verb construction. Do not hyphenate.

6. Noun construction. Written as one word.

7. Verb construction. Hyphenate.

8. Noun or pronoun plus adjective construction. Do not hyphenate.

9. Adverb construction. One word.

10. Indefinite pronoun. Do not hyphenate.

11. Compound adjective construction. Written as one word.

12. Relative pronoun. Written as one word.

13. Relative pronoun plus adverb. Two words.

14. Preposition plus object (noun).

Spelling and Word Division of Frequently Used Words

3

A

aback	ab.duc/tion	ab.nor/mally	above-mentioned (h)
abacus	ab.ductor	aboard	abra/sion
abalone	ab.er.ra/tion	abode	abra/sive
abandon	abet/ting	abolish	abreast
aban.don/ment	abettor	aboli/tion	abridge
abase	abey/ance	abomi/na.ble	abridg/ing
abate/ment	ab.hor/rence	abomi.na/tion	abridg/ment
abating	ab.hor/rent	abort	abroad
abbess	abide	aborted	ab.ro/gate
abbey	abili/ties	abor/tion	abrupt
abbot	ability	abor/tive	abrupt/ness
ab.bre/vi.ate	abject	abound	abscess
ab.bre/via/tion	ab.jectly	about	abscond
ab.di/cate	able	about-face (h)	ab.sconder
ab.di.cat/ing	able/bod.ied	above	absence
ab.di.ca/tion	ably	above/board	absent
abdomen	ab.nor/mal	[11]above/ground	ab.sen/tee
ab.domi/nal	ab.nor/mali/ties	[14]above ground	ab.sen/tee.ism

[11]Compound adjective construction. Written as one word. (The above-ground section of the building is smaller than the basement.)

[14]Preposition plus object (noun). (Telephone wires above ground are being replaced by underground cables.)

137

ab.sent/ing
ab.sent/minded
ab.so/lute
ab.so/lutely
ab.so/lu/tion
absolve
ab.solv/ing
absorb
ab.sor/bency
ab.sor/bent
ab.sorb/ing
ab.sorp/tion
ab.stainer
ab.stain/ers
ab.sten/tion
ab.sti/nence
ab.stract
ab.strac/tion
ab.stractly
ab.stract/ness
ab.strac/tor
absurd
abun/dance
abun/dant
abun/dantly
abuse
abused
abus/ers
abut
abut/ment
abut/ting
abys/mal
abyss
aca/demia
aca/demic
aca.demi/cally
aca.demi/cian
academy
accede
ac.ced/ing
ac.cel.er/ate
ac.cel.er/at/ing
ac.cel/era/tion
ac.cel/era/tor
accent
ac.cen.tu/ate
accept
ac.cepta/bil.ity
ac.cept/able

ac.cep/tance
ac.cept.ing
access
accesses
ac.ces.si/ble
ac.ces.si/bil.ity
ac.ces/sion
ac.ces.so/rial
ac.ces.so/ries
ac.ces/sory
ac.ci/dent
accident-prone (h)
ac.ci.den/tal
ac.ci.den/tally
acclaim
ac.cla.ma/tion
ac.cli/mate
ac.cli.ma/tize
ac.co/lade
ac.com.mo/date
ac.com.mo/dat/ing
ac.com.mo/da/tion
ac.com.pa/nied
ac.com.pa/nies
ac.com.pa/ni/ment
ac.com.pa/nist
ac.com/pany
ac.com.pa/ny/ing
ac.com/plice
ac.com/plish
ac.com/plishes
ac.com/plish/ing
ac.com/plish/ment
accord
ac.cor/dance
ac.cord/ing
ac.cord/ingly
ac.cor/dion
accost
account
ac.counta/bil.ity
ac.count/ancy
ac.count/ant
ac.count/ing
ac.cou/ter/ment
ac.credit
ac.credi/ta/tion
accrual
accrue

ac.cru/ing
ac.cu.mu/late
ac.cu.mu/la/tion
ac.cu.mu/la/tive
ac.cu.mu/la.tor
ac.cu/racy
ac.cu/rate
ac.cu/rately
ac.cu.sa/tion
ac.cu.sa/tory
accuse
ac.cus/tomı
ac.cut/ron
ace
acer/bate
acer/bity
acetate
acetic
acety/lene
ache
achieve
achieve/ment
achiev/ing
acid
acidi/fied
acidify
acidity
ac.knowl/edge
ac.knowl/edg/ing
ac.knowl/edg/ment
acme
acous/tic
acous.ti/cal
ac.quaint
ac.quaint/ance
ac.quaint/ance/ship
ac.quaint/ing
ac.quiesce
ac.quies/cence
acquire
ac.quir/ing
ac.qui.si/tion
ac.qui.si/tive
ac.quit/tal
ac.quit/ted
acre
acreage
ac.rid/ity
acrilan

ac.ri/moni.ous
ac.ro/batic
acronym
ac.ro/nyms
across
acrylic
act
acting
action
ac.tion/able
ac.ti/vate
ac.ti/vated
ac.ti.vat/ing
ac.ti.va/tor
active
ac.tively
ac.tiv/ism
ac.tiv/ist
ac.tivi/ties
ac.tiv/ity
actor
actual
ac.tu.al/ity
ac.tu.ali/za/tion
ac.tu.al/ize
ac.tu/ally
ac.tu/arial
ac.tu/ar.ies
actuary
actuate
ac.tu/ated
acuity
acumen
acu/punc/ture
acutely
ad
adage
adamant
adapt
adapt/abil/ity
adapt/able
adapta/tion
adapter
adapt/ing
adap/tive
adap/tive/ness
add
addenda
adden/dum

addict
ad.dic/tion
ad.dic/tive
adding
ad.di/tion
ad.di/tion/ally
ad.di/tive
address
ad.dressee
ad.dresser
ad.dresses
ad.dress/ing
adduce
ade
adenoid
ade/noidal
adept
ade/quacy
ade/quate
ade/quately
adhere
ad.her/ence
ad.her/ent
ad.he/sion
ad.he/sive
ad hoc
ad.ja/cent
ad.jec/tive
ad.join/ing
adjourn
ad.journ/ing
ad.journ/ment
adjudge
ad.ju.di/cate
ad.ju.di/ca/tion
ad.ju.di/ca.tor
adjunct
adjure
adjust
ad.just/able
ad.juster
ad.just/ing
ad.just/ment
ad.ju/tant
ad-lib (h)
ad-libbed (h)
ad-libbing (h)
ad.min.is/ter
ad.min.is/ter.ing

ad.min.is/tra/tion
ad.min.is/tra/tive
ad.min.is/tra.tor
ad.mi.ra/ble
admiral
ad.mi/ralty
ad.mi.ra/tion
admire
ad.mis/sible
ad.mis.si/bil.ity
ad.mis/sion
admit
ad.mit/tance
ad.mit/ted
ad.mit/tedly
ad.mit/ting
ad.mix/ture
ad.mon/ish
ad.mo.ni/tion
ad.oles/cence
ad.oles/cent
adopt
adopt/ing
adop/tion
adop/tive
ador/able
ado/ra/tion
adorn/ment
adrenal
ad.re.na/lin
ad.u.la/tion
adult
adul.ter/ate
adul/tery
ad valorem
ad.vance
ad.vance/ment
ad.van/tage
advent
ad.ven.ti/tious
ad.ven/ture
ad.ven/turer
ad.ven/ture/some
adverb
ad.ver/sary
adverse
ad.versely
ad.ver/sity
ad.ver/tise

ad.ver/tise/ment
ad.ver/tiser
ad.ver/tis/ers
ad.ver/tis.ing
ad.visa/bil.ity
ad.vis/able
advise
ad.vise/ment
adviser
ad.vis/ers
ad.vis/ing
ad.vi/sory
ad.vo/cate
aegis
aera/ting
aerial
aerobic
aero/com.mander
aero/dy/namic
aeor/dy/nam.ics
aero/nau/ti.cal
aero/nau/tics
aerosol
aero/space
aes/thetic
aes.theti/cally
affable
affair
affect
af.fec.ta/tion
af.fected
af.fect/ing
af.fec/tion
af.fec/tion.ate
af.fec/tion/ately
af.fi.da/vit
af.fili/ate
af.fili.a/tion
af.fin/ity
af.fir.ma/tion
af.fir.ma/tive
af.fir.ma/tively
af.firmed
affix
affixed
af.fix/ing
afflict
af.flu/ence
af.flu/ent

afford
affront
afghan
afire
afloat
afoot
afore/men/tioned
afore/said
afoul
afraid
AFRICA
AFRO-
    AMERICAN (h)
after
af.ter/math
af.ter/noon
af.ter/taste
af.ter/thought
af.ter/ward
again
against
agate
age
aged
agen/cies
agency
agenda
agent
ag.gran/dize
ag.gran/dize/ment
ag.gra/vate
ag.gra.va/tion
ag.gre/gate
ag.gre/gat/ing
ag.gres/sion
ag.gres/sive
ag.gres/sively
ag.gres/sor
ag.grieve
aghast
agile
agility
agi.ta/tion
ag.nosti/cism
ago
agony
agrar/ian
agree
agree/able

agree/ably	air/strip	alike	al.low/ance
agreed	air/tight	ali.men/tary	alloy
agree/ing	airwave	alimony	²all ready
agree/ment	airway	alive	²all together
agri/busi/ness	air/worthy	alkali	alltime
agri.cul/tural	aisle	al.ka/lies	allude
agri.cul/tur/al.ist	AKRON, OH	al.ka/line	allure
agri.cul/ture	ALABAMA	alkyl	ally
agron/omy	a la carte	all	almanac
aground	a la king	allay	al.mighty
ahead	alamode	al.le.ga/tion	almond
aid	alarm	allege	almost
aide-de-camp (h)	alarm/ing	al.leg/edly	aloft
aiding	alarm/ingly	ALLE/GHENIES	alone
ailing	ALASKA	ALLE/GHENY	along
ailment	ALBANY, NY	al.le.gi/ance	along/side
aim	album	al.le/gory	aloof
aiming	ALBU/QUERQUE,	allegro	alpha
air	NM	ALLEN/TOWN, PA	al.pha/beti/cal
airbag	alchemy	al.ler/gic	al.pha/beti/cally
air/cargo	alcohol	al.ler/gies	al.pha/nu.meric
air/coach	al.co/holic	allergy	alpine
air-condition (h)	al.co/hol/ism	al.le.vi/ated	⁹already
air-conditioned (h)	alcove	al.le.vi/ating	also
air-conditioning (h)	alert	alleys	altar
air/craft	ALEX/ANDRIA,	al.li/ance	alter
aired	VA	allied	alter ego
airflow	alfalfa	al.lo/cate	al.tera/tion
air/freight	algae	al.lo.cat/ing	al.ter.ca/tion
airlift	algebra	al.lo.ca/tion	al.ter/nate
airline	al.gor/ithm	allot	al.ter/nat/ing
air/liner	alias	al.lot/ment	al.ter.na/tion
airmail	alibi	al.lot/ted	al.ter.na/tive
airpark	ali.bi/ing	al.lot/ting	al.ter.na/tively
air/plane	alien	¹all-out (h)	al.ter.na/tor
airship	alien/ate	²all out	al.though
airshow	aliena/tion	allow	al.time/ter
air/space	align/ment	al.low/able	al.ti/tude

¹Compound adjective construction. Hyphenate if description precedes noun. (They made an all-out effort.)

²Adjective plus adverb construction. Do not hyphenate if description follows noun. (They are all out of the bus. When you are all ready, we'll leave. The machines are all together in one room.)

⁹Adverb construction. (She has learned to operate the equipment already.)

[9]al.to/gether
al.tru/ism
al.tru/is.tic
alu.mi/num
alumna
alumnae
alumni
alumnus
always
amalgam
amal.gam/ate
amal/gama/tion
AMA/RILLO, TX
amass
amateur
amaze
amaze/ment
amaz/ingly
am.bas.sa/dor
am.bi/dex.trous
am.bi/ence
ambient
am.bigu/ity
am.bigu/ities
am.bigu/ous
am.bi/tion
am.bi.ti/ous
am.biv.a/lence
am.biv.a/lent
ambler
am.bro/sia
am.bu/lance
am.bu.la/tory
amebic
ame.lio/rate
ame.lio/ra/tion
amen/able
amend
amend/ing
amend/ment
amenity
AMERICA
AMERI/CAN
AMERI/CANISM
ame/thyst
amiable

ami.ca/ble
amid
amidst
amino
amity
ammeter
am.mo/nia
am.mu.ni/tion
amnesia
amnesty
among
amoral
amor.ti/za/tion
amor/tize
amor.tiz/ing
amount
amount/ing
am.per/age
am.pheta/mine
am.phi/thea.ter
ample
am.pli.fi/ca/tion
am.pli/fied
am.pli/fier
amplify
amply
am.pu/tate
am.pu.ta/tion
amputee
AMSTER/DAM
amuck
amuse/ment
anach.ro/nism
anach.ro/nis.tic
ANAHEIM, CA
analog
analo/gous
analogy
an.aly/ses
an.aly/sis
analyst
ana/lysts
an.a.lyt/ic
an.alyt.i/cal
analyze
ana.lyz/ing
an.archic

an.arch/ies
an.arch/ist
anarchy
ana.tomi/cal
anatomy
anchor
ANCHOR/AGE, AK
ancient
an.cil/lary
an.ec/dote
anemic
an.es.the/sia
an.es.the/si/olo.gist
an.es/thetic
an.es.the/tist
anew
angel
angelic
angle
angling
angry
angular
animal
animate
ani.ma/tion
ani.mos/ity
ankle
annals
ANN ARBOR, MI
anneal
an.neal/ing
annex
an.nexa/tion
annexed
an.ni.hi/late
an.ni.ver/sary
an.no/tate
an.nounce
an.nounce/ment
an.noy/ance
annual
an.nu/ally
an.nui/tant
an.nui/ties
annuity
annul
an.nulled

an.nul/ling
an.nul/ment
annum
anode
anoint
anomaly
ano.nym/ity
anony/mous
another
answer
an.swer/able
an.swer/ing
antacid
an.tago/nis/tic
an.tago/nize
ANTARC/TIC
ANTARC/TICA
an.te.ce/dent
an.te/date
antenna
anthem
an.thol/ogy
an.thro/po/logi/cal
an.thro/polo/gist
an.thro/pol/ogy
an.ti/bal/listic
an.ti/bi/otic
an.ti/bi/ot.ics
an.ti/bod.ies
an.ti/body
an.ti/busi.ness
an.tici/pate
an.tici/pat.ing
an.tici/pa/tion
an.tici/pa/tory
an.ti/cli.max
an.ti/dis/crimi/na/tion
an.ti/di.ver/sion
an.ti/dote
an.ti/freeze
an.tip/athy
an.ti/pol.lu/tion
an.ti/pov/erty
an.ti/quate
an.tiq/uity
an.ti/sep.tic
an.ti/so.cial

[9]Adverb construction. (There are altogether too many errors.)

an.tithe/sis
an.ti/trust
antiwar
antler
anxiety
anxious
anxi/ously
any
anybody
anyhow
[9]anymore
[8]any more
[10]anyone
[8]any one
[9]any/place
[8]any place
any/thing
[9]anytime
[8]any time
[9]anyway
[8]any way
any/where
apar/theid
apart/ment
apa/thetic
apathy
aper/ture
apex
apexes
aphid
apiece
apolo/gies
apolo/gize
apology
apos.tro/phe
APPALA/CHIA
APPALA/CHIAN
ap.pall/ing
ap.para/tus

apparel
ap.par/ent
ap.par/ently
appeal
ap.peal/ing
appear
ap.pear/ance
ap.pear/ing
appease
ap.pease/ment
ap.pel/lant
ap.pel/late
ap.pend/age
ap.pen/dec/tomy
ap.pended
ap.pen/dices
ap.pen.di/ci.tis
ap.pen/dix
ap.pen/dixes
ap.pe/tite
ap.pe.tiz/ing
applaud
ap.plause
ap.pli/ance
ap.pli/ca/bil.ity
ap.pli.ca/ble
ap.pli/cant
ap.pli.ca/tion
applied
ap.pli/qué
apply
ap.ply/ing
appoint
ap.pointee
ap.point/ees
ap.point/ing
ap.point/ment
ap.por/tion
ap.por/tion/ing

ap.por/tion/ment
ap.po.si/tion
ap.praisal
ap.prais/als
ap.praise
ap.praiser
ap.prais/ing
ap.pre/cia.ble
ap.pre/ci.ate
ap.pre/cia/tion
ap.pre/cia/tive
ap.pre/cia/tively
ap.pre/hend
ap.pre/hen/si.ble
ap.pre/hen/sion
ap.pre/hen/sive
ap.pren/tice
ap.pren/tice/ship
apprise
ap.proach
ap.proaches
ap.proach/ing
ap.pro/pri.ate
ap.pro/pri.ated
ap.pro/pri.ately
ap.pro/pria/tion
ap.prov/able
ap.proval
approve
ap.prov/ing
ap.proxi/mate
ap.proxi/mately
ap.proxi/mat.ing
ap.proxi/ma/tion
ap.pur.te/nance
apricot
a priori
apron
apropos

ap.ti/tude
aptly
aptness
aquar/ium
aq.ue/duct
ARAB
ARABIAN
ARABIC
arbiter
ar.bi/trage
ar.bi/trar.ily
ar.bi/trary
ar.bi.tra/tion
ar.bi.tra/tor
arbor
arch
archaic
ar.chaeo/logi.cal
ar.chae/ol.ogy
arches
arche/type
ar.chi/tect
ar.chi/tec/tural
ar.chi/tec/ture
arch/ival
archive
ar.chives
ar.chi/vist
ARCTIC
ardent
ardor
arduous
area
area/wide
arena
ar.gu/able
argue
ar.gu/ing
ar.gu/ment

[8]Noun or pronoun plus adjective construction. Do not hyphenate. (Are there any more magnetic cards in the storeroom? Any one of the books is interesting. He could be heard from any place in the room. At any time she may call. Is there any way to do this easily?)

[9]Adverb construction. (She doesn't work in word processing anymore. Have you seen my pencil anyplace? I can be ready anytime. Marcia will go anyway.)

[10]Indefinite pronoun. Do not hyphenate. (Anyone in the office will be happy to help you.)

ar.gu.men/ta/tion
argyle
arid
aridity
ar.is.toc/racy
aris.to/crat
ARISTO/TELIAN
arith.me/tic
ar.ith/meti.cal
ARIZONA
ARKAN/SAS
ARLING/TON, TX
ar.ma/ture
ar.ma/ment
armband
arm/chair
armies
ar.mi/stice
armory
armrest
arm/strong
army
aroma
aro/matic
arose
around
arouse
arraign
ar.raign/ment
arrange
ar.rang/ing
array
ar.rear/age
arrears
arrest
arrival
arrive
ar.riv/ing
ar.ro/gant
arrow
arrow/head
arsenal
arsenic
arson
art
ar.te/rial
ar.te/ries
ar.te.rio/scle/ro.sis
artery
ar.te/sian

art.fully
ar.thrit/ic
ar.thri/tis
ar.ti/fact
ar.ti/cles
ar.tic.u/late
ar.ti.fi/cial
ar.ti.fi/cially
ar.til/lery
artisan
artish
arts
artwork
ARYAN
as.bes/tos
ascend
as.cen/dency
ascent
as.cer/tain
as.cer/tain.ing
ascribe
ash
ashamed
ashes
ASIAN
ASIATIC
aside
asinine
ask
askance
askew
as.para/gus
aspect
aspen
asphalt
as.phyxi/ate
as.phyxi/ation
as.pir/ant
as.pira/tion
aspire
aspirin
ascribe
as.sas/sin
as.sas.si/nate
as.sas.si/na/tion
assault
as.sem/blage
as.sem/ble
as.sem/blies
as.sem/bling

as.sem/bly
as.sem/bly/man
as.sem/bly/woman
assent
assert
as.ser/tion
assess
as.sesses
as.sess/ible
as.sess/ing
as.sess/ment
as.ses/sors
asset
as.sidu/ous
as.sidu/ously
assign
as.signee
as.sign/ing
as.sign/ment
as.simi/late
as.simi/la/tion
assist
as.sis/tance
as.sis/tant
as.sis/tant/ship
as.sist/ing
as.so.ci/ate
as.so.ci/ating
as.so.cia/tion
assort
as.sort/ment
assume
as.sum/ing
as.sump/tion
as.sur/ances
assure
as.sur/ing
as.ter/isk
asthma
asth/matic
astig.ma/tism
as.ton/ish
as.ton/ish/ingly
as.ton/ish/ment
astound
as.tound/ing
astray
as.trin/gent
as.tro/dome
as.trolo/ger

as.tro/logi.cal
as.trol/ogy
as.tro/naut
as.tro/nau/ti.cal
as.tro/nau.tics
as.tro/nomi/cal
astute
as.tute/ness
asylum
asym.met/ric
asym.me/try
as.ymp/totic
as.ymp.tot/i/cally
athlete
ath.letic
ath.leti/cally
ath.let/ics
ATLANTA, GA
ATLAN/TIC
atlas
at.mos/phere
at.mos/pheric
atom
atomic
atomize
atop
atro/cious
atroc/ity
attach
attaché
at.taches
at.tach/ing
at.tach/ment
attack
attain
at.tain/able
at.tain/ing
at.tain/ment
attempt
at.tempt/ing
attend
at.ten/dance
at.ten/dant
at.ten/dee
at.tend/ing
at.ten/tion
at.ten/tive
at.ten/tive/ness
at.tenu/ation
attest

attic
at.ti/tude
at.tor/ney
attorney-at-law (h)
attract
at.tract/ing
at.trac/tion
at.trac/tive
at.trac/tively
at.trac/tive/ness
at.trib/ut/able
at.trib/ute
at.tri/tion
attune
atypi/cal
auburn
auction
audible
au.di/ence
audio
audio/vis.ual
audio/vis.uals
audit
audit/ing
au.di/tion
auditor
au.di.to/rium
au.di/tors
auger
augment
AUGUST
au jus
auspice
aus.pi/cious
AUSTIN, TX
AUSTRIA
au.then/tic
author
au.thori/tar.ian
au.thori/ta/tive
au.thori/ta/tively
au.thori/ties
au.thor/ity
au.tho.ri/za/tion
au.tho/rized

au.tho/rizes
au.tho/riz/ing
auto
au.toc/racy
au.to/graph
au.to/mate
au.to/matic
au.to/mati/cally
au.to.mat/ing
au.to.ma/tion
au.toma/tize
au.toma/ton
au.to.mo/bile
au.to.mo/tive
au.tono/mous
au.ton/omy
autopsy
autumn
aux.il/ia/ries
aux.il/iary
avail
availa/bil.ity
avail/able
avail/ing
ava/lanche
avarice
avenue
aver
average
aver.ag/ing
averred
aver/ring
averse
avert
avia/tion
aviator
avo.ca/tion
avoid
avoid/ance
avoid/ing
await
await/ing
awake
award
award/ing

aware
aware/ness
away
awful
awfully
awkward
awry
ax
axiom
axi/omatic
aye
AZTEC

B

babble
babies
baby
babysit
baby/sit/ting
bac.ca/lau/re.ate
bache/lor
bacillie
ba.cil/lus
back
back/bite
back/bone
back/break/ing
back/charge
back/drop
back/field
back/fire
back/gam.mon
back/ground
back/hand
back/hoe
backing
back/lash
backlog
back/order
back/pack
back/pedal
back/side

back/slide
back/space
[5]back up
[6]backup
back/ward
back/wards
back/wash
back/waters
back/woods
back-work (h)
bac.te/ria
bac/te/riol.ogy
bad
badge
badger
badly
bad.min/ton
baffle
baf/fling
bag
baggage
bagged
bagging
bagpipe
BAHRAIN
bail
bailee
bailiff
baili/wick
bail/ment
bailor
[6]bailout
[5]bail out
bait
baiting
baker
bak.eries
bakery
balance
bal.ances
bal.anc/ing
bal.co/nies
balcony
bald
bald/headed

[5]Verb construction. Do not hyphenate. (When the plane ran out of gas the crew had to bail out. Please back up the car.)
[6]Noun construction. Written as one word. (She made a successful bailout from the plane. The job will require a backup.)

bale	BAR/BAD/OS	ba.si/cally	bearish
baleful	bar.bar/ian	ba.sil/ica	bear.ish/ness
baler	bar.ba/rous	basin	beast
BALKAN	bar.be/cue	basing	beat
ball	barber	basis	beaten
ballad	bar.ber/shop	basket	be.atific
ballast	bar.bitu/rate	bas.ket/ball	be.ati.fi/ca/tion
ballet	barb/wire	bas-relief (h)	beaten
bal.lis/tic	bard	bass	beatnik
balloon	bare	bas.si/net	BEAUMONT, TX
bal/loons	bare/faced	bassoon	beau.te/ous
ballot	bare/foot	bastion	beau.ti/cian
bal.lot/ing	bare/handed	batch	beau.ti/ful
ball/park	bargain	batches	beau.ti/fully
ball/point	bar.gain/able	batch/ing	beau.ti/fy/ing
ball/room	bar/gained	bath	beauty
bally/hoo	bar/gainer	bathe	beaver
balm.i/ness	bar/gainers	bath/house	became
balsam	bar.gain/ing	bathing	because
BALTIC	bar/gains	bathroom	beckon
BALTI/MORE, MD	barge	bathtub	become
bamboo	bari/tone	baton	be.com/ing
ban	barium	BATON ROUGE,	be.daz/zle
banal	bark	LA	bedded
banana	barley	bat/tal/ion	bed/ding
band	bar.ley/corn	batter	be.devil
bandage	barmaid	bat/ter.ies	be.deviled
ban/danna	bar mitzvah	battery	bed/fellow
bandit	barn	battle	BEDFORD, MA
bandsaw	ba.rome/ter	bat.tle/field	bedlam
band/stand	baro.met/ric	bat.tle/ground	bedpan
band/wagon	barrage	bat.tle/ship	bed/ridden
bang	barred	bauxite	bedroll
bangle	barrel	BAVAR/IAN	bedrock
ban.ish/ment	bar/reled	bay	bedroom
ban.is/ter	bar.ri/cade	bayonet	bed/sheet
banjo	barrier	bayo/nets	bedside
bank	barring	beach	bedsore
bank/book	bar.ris/ter	beach/comber	bed/spread
bank/roll	barroom	beach/head	bedtime
bank/rupt	bar/tender	beacon	bee
bank/ruptcy	barter	bead/work	beech
bann	base	beagle	beech/nut
banned	base/ball	beam	beef
banner	base/board	bean	beef/steak
banquet	base/line	bear	beehive
ban/quets	base/ment	bearer	beeline
bantam	bases	bearer bond	been
banter	bashful	bearing	beer
baptism	basic	bear/ings	beeswax

3

beet	bellboy	besides	bikini
beetle	bellhop	besiege	bi.lat/eral
befall	bel.li/cose	be.smirch	bi.lin/gual
befit	bel.lig/er/ence	bespeak	bilk
be.fitted	bel.lig/er/ent	bespeck	bilking
be.fit/ting	bell/weth.ers	best	bill/board
before	bel.ly/ache	bestir	billed
be.fore/hand	belong	bestow	billet
be.fore/time	be.long/ing	bet	bill/fold
be.friend	below	beta	billing
be.fuddle	belt	BETH/LEHEM	bill/ings
beggar	bemoan	be.trothal	billion
begin	bench	better	bi.monthly
be.gin/ner	benches	bet.ter/ment	bin
be.gin/ning	bench/mark	bettor	binary
be.grudge	bend	between	bi.na/tional
beguile	bending	bevel	bind
behalf	beneath	beveled	binder
behave	bene.dic/tion	bev.er/age	binding
be.hav/ior	bene.dic/tory	be.wil/der	binge
be.hav/ioral	bene.fac/tor	be.wil/der/ing	bin.ocu/lar
be.hav/ior/ally	bene.fi/cial	be.wil/der/ment	bino/mial
be.hav/ior.ism	bene.fi/ci/aries	bewitch	bio/chem/is.try
be.hav/ior.ist	bene.fi/ci.ary	beyond	bio/feed/back
be.he/moth	benefit	bias	bio/graphic
behind	bene/fited	biases	bio/graph/ical
behold	bene.fit/ing	bible	bio.log/ical
be.holder	be.nevo/lence	bib.li.og/raph.ies	bi.olo/gist
behoove	benign	bib.li.og/ra.phy	biopsy
beige	bent	bi.car/bon.ate	bio/rhythm
being	benzene	bi.cen/ten/nial	bi/parti/san
BEIRUT	benzine	biceps	bipolar
belabor	benzol	bicker	bi.rac/ial
belated	be.queath	bi.cus/pid	birch
be.lat/edly	bequest	bicycle	bird
be.lea/guer	be.reave/ment	bi.cy/cling	BIR.MING/HAM,
BELGIAN	beret	bid	AL
BELGIUM	BERKE/LEY, CA	bidder	birth
belie	BERLIN	bidding	birth/day
belief	berms	bi.en/nial	birth/place
be.liev/abil/ity	BERMUDA	bi.en/nium	birth/rate
be.liev/able	berry	bifocal	birth/right
believe	berserk	big	bi.sec/tion
be.lieved	berth	bigger	bi.sex/ual
be.liever	beryl/lium	biggest	bishop
be.liev/ing	beseech	bigness	bit
be.lit/tle	beset	bigot	bite
be.lit/tling	be.set/ting	bigotry	bitter
bell	beside		

bit.ter/est
bit/terly
bit.ter/sweet
bi.tu/mi/nous
bi.vari/ate
bivouac
biv/ouacked
bi-weekly (h)
bizarre
black
black/board
black/list
black/mail
black/out
black/smith
black/top
bladder
blade
blam/able
blame
blame/less
blank
blanket
blan/keted
blan/kets
blas.phe/mous
blas/phemy
blast
blasted
blast/ing
blatant
blaze
bleacher
bleak
bled
bleed
bleed/ing
blemish
blem/ishes
blend
blender
blend/ing
bless
blessed
bless/ing
bless/ings
blew
blight
blimp

blind
blind/spot
bliss
bliss/ful
blitz
bliz/zard
bloc
block
block/age
block/buster
blocker
blocking
blond
blood
blood/bath
blood/mo.bile
blood/shed
blood/stain
blood/thirsty
bloom/ing
blotter
blouse
blow
blower
blowing
blown
blowout
blue
blue-chip (h)
blue-collar (h)
blue-green (h)
blue/print
blues
bluff
bluish
blunder
blunt
bluntly
blur
blurb
blurred
blush
board
board/room
boast
boat
boating
bob
bobbin

bob/white
bodies
bodily
body
body/guard
BOER
bog
boggy
bogus
boil
boiler
boil.er/maker
boil.er/plate
BOISE, ID
bois.ter/ous
bold
bold/face
BOLIVIA
bo.lo/gna
BOLSHE/VIK
bolster
bolt
bomb
bombard
bom.bar/dier
bom.bard/ing
bombed
bomber
bombing
bona fide
bonanza
bond
bonded
bond/holder
bond/hold.ers
bonding
bonds/man
bone
bonus
bonuses
bon voyage
book/case
book/dealer
bookend
book/ings
book/keeper
book/keep.ers
book/keep/ing
booklet

book/mark
book/mo.bile
book/shelf
book/store
book/work
book/worm
boom.er/ang
boon
boost
booster
boost/ing
booth
bootleg
boot/leg.ger
boot/straps
booty
booze
border
bor.der/ing
bor.der/line
boredom
boring
born
borne
borough
borrow
bor/rowed
bor/rower
bor.row/ers
bor.row/ing
boss
bosses
BOSTON, MA
bo.tani/cal
bot.a/nist
botany
both
bother
both/ered
both.er/ing
both.er/some
bottle
bot.tle/neck
bottler
bot/tlers
bottom
bot/tomed
bot.tom/most
bough

bought
boulder
bou.le/vard
bounce
bound
bound/aries
bound/ary
bounded
boun.te/ous
boun.ti/ful
bouquet
bourbon
bout
bou/tique
bou.ton/niere
bow
bowel
bowl
bowling
box
boxcar
boxed
boxer
boxes
boxing
boy
boycott
boy/cotts
boy/friend
boyhood
boyish
brace
braced
brace/let
bracing
bracket
brack/ets
brack.et/ing
brag/gart
braid
BRAILLE
brain
brain/child
brain/storm/ing

brain/wash
brake
branch
branches
brand
bran/died
brand/ing
bran/dish
brass
brassie
bra/ssiere
bravery
brawn
BRAZIL
BRAZIL/IAN
breach
bread
bread/line
breadth
bread/win.ner
break
break/age
break/away
break/down
[1]break-even
[5]break even
break/ers
break/fast
break/ing
break/neck
break/through
breast
breast/bone
breath
breathe
breath/ing
breath/tak.ing
bred
breed/ing
breeze/way
breezy
breth/ren
bre/viary

brevity
brew
brewer
brew.er/ies
brewery
bribe
brick
brick/bat
brick/layer
brick-veneered (h)
brick/yard
bride/groom
bridge
bridge/head
BRIDGE/PORT, CT
bridge/work
brief
brief/case
briefed
brief/est
brief/ing
briefly
brigade
brig.a/dier
bright
brighten
brighter
bril/liance
bril/liant
bril/liantly
brim
brimful
brimmed
bring
bring/ing
brink
brink/man/ship
brisk
BRITAIN
BRI/TANNIA
BRITISH
BRIT/ISHER
BRITON
broach

broad
broad/band
broad/cast
broad/caster
broad/cast.ers
broaden
broad/ened
broad.en/ing
broader
broad/est
broad/loom
broadly
broad/minded
broad/side
broad/way
brocade
broc/coli
bro/chure
brogue
broiler
broke
broker
bro.ker/age
bro.ken/hearted
bromide
bromine
bron/chial
bron.chi/tis
bronze
brooch
brood
brooder
brood/ers
brook
BROOK/LYN, NY
broom
broom/stick
brother
broth.er/hood
brother-in-law (h)
brought
brow/beat
brown
browned

[1]Compound adjective construction. Hyphenate if description precedes noun. (We finally reached the break-even point.)
[5]Verb construction. Do not hyphenate. (Perhaps you will only break even.)

brown/ish
brown/out
browse
bruise
bru/nette
brunt
brush
brushes
brushup
bru.tal/ity
bubble
bubbled
bub/bling
BUCHAREST
buck
bucket
buckets
bucking
buckle
buckram
bucolic
bud
BUDDHA
BUD/DHISM
buddies
budget
bud.get/ary
bud/geted
bud.get/ing
buff
buffalo
buf/faloed
buf/faloes
buffer
buffoon
buf.foon/ery
buffet
buf/feted
buf.fet/ing
buggies
buggy
bugle
build

builder
build/ers
build/ing
build/ings
buildup
built
[3]built-in (h)
[5]built in
[1]built-up (h)
[5]built up
bulb
BUL/GARIA
BUL/GARIAN
bulge
bulging
bulk
bulky
bull
bull/dozer
bullet
bul.le/tin
bullet/proof
bullion
bullish
bullock
bumb/ling
bump
bumper
bumping
bundle
bunk
buoy/ancy
burden
bur/dened
bur.den/some
bureau
bu.reau/cracies
bu.reau/cracy
bu.reau/crat
bu.reau/cratic
burgeon
burglar
bur.glar/ies

bur.glar/proof
burglary
burial
buried
burlap
bur/lapped
BUR/LINGTON, VT
BURMA
burn
burning
burnt
bur.si/tis
burst/ing
bus
bused
buses
bush
bushel
bushes
bushing
bush/ings
busier
busiest
busi/ness
busi/nesses
busi/ness/like
busi/ness/man
busi/ness/woman
busing
bust
busy
busy/work
but
butane
butler
butt
butter
but.ter/milk
button
but.ton/holder
button/hole
but/tress

buxom
buy
buyback
buyer
buying
by
bygone
bylaw
bypass
by.pass/ing
by-products (h)
by.stander
byway
byword
BYZAN/TINE

3

C

cab
cabana
cabaret
cabbage
cabin
cabinet
cabi.net/maker
cable
ca.ble/gram
ca.ble/vi.sion
caboose
cache
cachet
cadaver
caddle
cadet
cadmium
cadre
cafe
cafe.te/ria
caf/feine
caisson

[1]Compound adjective construction. Hyphenate if description precedes noun. (The built-up section of the town is on the east side.)
[3]Noun or compound adjective construction. Hyphenate. (The cupboard is a built-in. The typewriter has a built-in memory.)
[5]Verb construction. Do not hyphenate. (Is your pool built in? Our suburb has built up rapidly in the last few years.)

cajole
cake
ca.lami/tous
ca.lam/ity
calcify
calcite
calcium
cal.cu.la/ble
cal.cu/late
cal.cu/lat/ing
cal.cu.la/tion
cal.cu.la/tive
cal.cu.la/tor
cal.cu/lus
cal.en/dar
calf
calf/skin
caliber
cali/brate
cali.bra/tion
cali.bra/tor
CALI/FORNIA
cal.is/then.ics
calk
call
call/able
caller
callig/ra/pher
calling
callow
callus
calm
calmly
caloric
calorie
calo/ries
calumny
cam
ca.ma.ra/de.rie
CAM/BODIA
cambric
CAM/BRIDGE, MA
CAMDEN, NJ
came
ca.mel/lia
cameo
cameos
camera
cam.era/man

cam.ou/flage
camp
cam/paign
cam/paign/ing
camper
camp/fire
camphor
camping
camp/park
camp/site
campus
cam/puses
CANADA
CANA/DIAN
canal
ca.nal/ize
canapé
cancel
can/celed
can.cel/ing
can.cel/la/tion
cancer
can.cer/ous
can.de.la/bra
can.de/la/brum
candid
can.di/dacy
can.di/date
can/didly
can.did/ness
candle
can.dle/light
can.dle/stick
candor
candy
cane
canine
can.is/ter
can.ker/ous
can.ker/worm
canned
cannery
CANNES
can.ni/bal
canning
cannon
cannot
canoe
ca.noe/ist

canon
can.on/ize
cano/pies
canopy
can.ta/loupe
can.tank/er.ous
cantata
canteen
canter
can/ti/cle
CANTON, OH
cantor
canvas
canvass
canyon
cap
ca.pa/bili/ties
ca.pa.bil/ity
capable
capably
ca.paci/tate
ca.paci/ties
ca.paci/tor
ca.pac/ity
caper
cap.il/lary
capita
capital
capital gain
capi.tal/ism
capi.tal/ist
capi.tal/istic
capi/tali/za/tion
capi.tal/ize
capitol
ca.pitu/late
caprice
ca.pri/cious
capsize
cap/stone
capsule
cap.sul/ize
captain
caption
cap.tion/ing
cap.ti/vate
captive
cap.tiv/ity
capture

cap/tures
cap.tur/ing
car
carafe
caramel
carat
caraway
carbide
carbine
car.bo/hy/drate
car/bolic
carbon
car.bon/ate
car.bon/ize
car.boni/zing
car.bon/less
carbu.re/tion
carbu.re/tor
carcass
car/casses
card
card/board
cardiac
car.di/gan
car.di/nal
car.dio/gram
car.dio/graph
car.di/olo/gist
cardio/vas/cu.lar
care
careen
career
care/free
careful
care/fully
care/less
care/less/ness
caress
care/taker
carfare
cargo
cargoes
carhop
CARIB/BEAN
cari.ca/ture
car.il/lon
carload
carmine
carnage

carnal
car.na/tion
car.ni/val
car.nivo/rous
car.pen/ter
car.pen/try
carpet
car.pet/bag.ger
car.pet/ing
carpool
carport
carrel
car/riage
carried
carrier
car.ri/ers
carries
carrot
car.rou/sel
carry
[6]carry/all
[5]carry all
car.ry/ing
[4]carry-over
[5]carry over
carsick
cart
cartage
carte blanche
cartel
car.teli/za/tion
car.ti/lage
car.to/graphic
carton
cartoon
car.toon/ist
car/tridge
carwash
cascade
case
case/ment
case/work

case/worker
cash
cashier
cash/mere
casing
casino
casinos
cask
casket
cas.se/role
cas/sette
cas.ta/net
cast/away
caste
caster
casti/gate
casting
castle
castoff
cast/offs
castor
casual
ca.su/ally
ca.su.al/ties
ca.su/alty
cata/clysm
catalog
cata/lyst
cata/lytic
cata/pult
cata/ract
catarrh
ca.tas/tro.phe
cata/strophic
catch
catch/all
catches
catch/ing
catchup
catch/word
catchy
cate/chism

cate/gori/cal
cate/gori/cally
cate.go/ries
cate.go/rize
cate/gory
cater
cater/cor.nered
caterer
cater/ing
cat.er/pil.lar
catfish
ca.thar/sis
ca.the/dral
cathode
catsup
cattail
cat.tle/men
catwalk
CAUCA/SIAN
caught
cau.li/flower
caulk
causal
causa/tive
cause
caustic
cau.ter/ize
caution
cau.tion/ary
cau/tious
cau/tiously
caval/cade
cava/lier
cavalry
caveat
cavern
caviar
cavi/ties
cavity
cavort
cease
cedar

CEDAR RAPIDS,
   IA
cede
ceiling
ceil/ings
cela/nese
cele/brate
cele/brat/ing
cele.bra/tion
cele.bra/tor
ce.leb/rity
celery
cel.es/tial
celi/bacy
cell
cellar
cellist
cello
cel.lo/phane
cel.lu/lar
cel.lu/loid
cel.lu/lose
cement
ceme.ter/ies
ceme/tery
cen.sor/ship
censure
census
cent
cen.ten/ary
cen.ten/nial
center
cen.ter/piece
cen.ti/grade
centi/gram
cen.ti/meter
central
cen.trali/za/tion
cen.tral/ize
cen/trifu.gal
cen/trifu/gally
centum

[4]Noun construction. Hyphenate. (The idea is a carry-over from the last meeting.)
[5]Verb construction. Do not hyphenate. (Please carry all the books to the library. That work can carry over until tomorrow.)
[6]Noun construction. Written as one word. (Her briefcase has become a carryall.)

cen.tu/ries
cen.tu/rion
century
ceramic
ce.ram/ics
cereal
cere.bel/lum
ce.re/bral
cere.mo/ni/ally
cere.mo/nies
cere/mony
cerise
certain
cer/tainly
cer/tainty
cer.tifi/cate
cer.ti.fi/ca/tion
cer.ti/fied
cer.ti/fies
certify
cer.ti/fy/ing
cer.ti/tude
cer.vi/cal
cervix
ces/sa/tion
CEYLON
chafe
chaff
chagrin
cha/grined
chain
chair
chaired
chair/lift
chair/man
chair/per.son
chair/woman
chalet
chalk/board

chal/lenge
chamber
cham/bray
chamois
cham/pagne
cham/pion
chance
chan.cel/lery
chan/cellor
chancy
chan.de/lier
change
change/abil.ity
change/able
change/less
change/over
channel
chan/neled
chan/nel/ing
chaos
chaotic
chap
chapel
chap/eron
chap/lain
chapter
char.ac/ter/is.tic
char.ac/teri/za/tion
char.ac/ter.ize
charade
char/coal
charge/able
charge/a/plate
[6]charge/back
[5]charge back
[6]charge/off
[5]charge off
[6]charge/out
[5]charge out

charge plate
charg/ing
chariot
cha/risma
char.is/matic
chari.ta/ble
chari.ta/bly
chari/ties
charity
char.la/tan
CHARLES/TON, SC
CHARLES/TON, WV
CHAR/LOTTE, NC
charm/ing
chart
charter
chart/ing
char/treuse
char/woman
chasm
chassis
chasten
chas.tise/ment
chas/tity
chat
chateau
CHATTA/NOOGA, TN
chattel
chatter
chauf/feur
chau.vin/ism
chau.vin/ist
chau.vin/is.tic
cheap
cheap/est
cheaply
cheap/skate

check/mark
check/mate
[11]checkoff
[5]check off
[11]checkout
[5]check out
check/point
check/room
checkup
check/writer
cheer/fully
cheer/ily
cheer/ing
cheer/leader
cheese
cheese/burger
chef
chem/ical
chemist
chem.is/try
chemo/ther.apy
cherish
cher/ries
cherry
che.ru/bic
CHESA/PEAKE, VA
chess
chess/board
chest
chest/nut
check
check/book
checker
check.er/board
check/ers
check/ing
check/less
check/list

[5]Verb construction. Do not hyphenate. (The expenses they charge back are minimal. He will charge off those three items. You need to charge out the materials. Check off your work in the book when you have completed it. Did you check out the books?)

[6]Noun construction. Written as one word. (A chargeback is noted on your budget sheet. The chargeoff will be 10 percent a year. A chargeout must be signed by you.)

[11]Compound adjective. Written as one word. (The checkoff list is not complete. They devised an excellent checkout system.)

chew
chic
CHICAGO, IL
chi.can/ery
CHICANO
chick
chicken
chick/ens
chicle
chicory
chide
chief
chiefly
chief/tain
chiffon
child
child/birth
child/hood
child/ish
child/like
chil/dren
CHILE
chili
chill
chilli/ness
chilly
chime
chimers
chimney
chim/neys
china
CHINA
CHINESE
chip
chip/board
chi.rog/ra.phy
chi.ropo/dist
chi.ro/prac.tic
chi.ro/prac.tor
chisel
chiseled
chis.el/ing
chiv.al/rous
chiv/alry

chlo/ride
chlo.ri/nate
chlo/rine
chlo.ro/phyll
choco/late
choice
choir
choke
cholera
cho.les/terol
choose
choos/ing
chop
chopper
chop/ping
chop/sticks
choral
chore
cho.re.og/raphy
chorus
chose
chosen
chowder
chro/mate
chrome
chro/mium
chro.mo/some
chronic
chroni/cally
chroni/cle
chro.no/logi/cal
chro.nol/ogy
chro/nome/ter
chry.san/the/mum
chuck/hole
chuckle
chummy
chump
chunk
church
church/goer
church/yard
churn
chute

chyme
cider
cigar
ciga/rette
cinch
CINCIN/NATI, OH
cinema
cine.ma/tog/raphy
cin.na/mon
cipher
circle
circuit
cir.cui/tous
cir/cuitry
cir.cu/lar
cir.cu/lar.ize
cir.cu/lar/iz/ing
cir.cu/late
cir.cu/lat/ing
cir.cu.la/tion
cir.cu.la/tor
cir.cu.la/tory
cir.cum/fer/ence
cir.cum/scribe
cir.cum/spect
cir.cum/stance
cir.cum/stan/tial
cir.cum/vent
cir.cum/ven/tion
circus
citadel
ci.ta/tion
cite
cities
citing
citizen
citi/zenry
citi.zen/ship
citrate
citric
citron
citrus
city
city/wide

civic
civil
ci.vil/ian
ci.vili/za/tion
clad
claim
claim/able
claim/ant
claim/ing
clam/bake
clam.mi/ness
clam.or/ing
clamp
[6]clampdown
[5]clamp down
clam/shell
clan.des/tine
clan/nish
clap/board
clapper
clari.fi/ca/tion
clari/fied
clarify
clari.fy/ing
clari/net
clarity
class
classes
classic
clas.si/cal
clas.si/cist
clas.si/fi/able
clas.si/fi/ca/tion
clas.si/fy
class/mate
class/room
clause
claus/tro/pho.bia
[1]clean-cut
[8]clean cut
clean/est
clean/ing
clean.li/ness
clean/ser

[1]Compound adjective construction. Hyphenate if description precedes noun. (It was a clean-cut case.)

[5]Verb construction. Do not hyphenate. (Clamp down on tardiness.)

[6]Noun construction. Written as one word. (A clampdown was ordered.)

[8]Noun plus adjective construction. Do not hyphenate. (A razor makes a clean cut.)

[6]cleanup
[5]clean up
clear
clear/ance
clear-cut (h)
clear/headed
clear/ing
clear/ing/house
clearly
cleat
cleav/age
cleave
clem/ency
clement
clergy
clergy/man
cler/ical
clerk
CLEVE/LAND, OH
clever
clev/erer
cliché
client
cli.en/tele
cliff
cli.mac/tic
climax
clinic
clini/cal
cli.ni/cian
clip
clip/board
clipper
clip/ping
clique
cloak
clobber
clock
clock/wise
clock/work
clog
clois/ter
close
closely
close/ness

close/out
closest
closet
clos/eted
closing
clos/ings
closure
clo/sures
cloth
clothe
clothes
cloth/ing
cloths
cloud/burst
cloudi/ness
clout
clover
clo.ver/leaf
club
club/bing
club/house
clum/sily
clum.si/ness
clumsy
cluster
clus/tered
clus.ter/ing
clutch
clutter
coach
coaches
coach/ing
co.ad/juster
co.ad/just/ers
co.ad.ju/tor
co.agu/late
co.agu.la/tion
coal
co.alesce
co.ales/cence
co.ales/cent
co.ali/tion
coarse
coarsen
coast

coastal
coast/ers
coast/ing
coast/line
coat
coating
coat/tail
co.au/thor
co.axial
cobalt
cobbler
cob.ble/stone
COBOL (ac.)
cocaine
cockpit
cock/roach
cocoa
coconut
cocoon
coddle
codeine
codicil
codi.fi/ca/tion
codify
coed
co.edu.ca/tional
co.ef.fi/cient
coerce
co.er/cion
co.er/cive
coexist
co.exis/tence
coffee
cof.fee/break
coffers
coffin
cogent
cogi.ta/tion
cognac
cog.ni/tive
cog.ni/zance
cog.ni/zant
cohabit
co.habi.ta/tion
co.her/ence

co.her/ent
co.he/sion
co.he/sive
co.he/sive/ness
cohort
coil
coin
coinage
co.in/cide
co.in.ci/dence
co.in.ci/dent
co.in.ci/dental
co.in.sur/ance
coke
cola
col.an/der
cold
cold/blooded
cole/slaw
coli/seum
colitis
col.labo/rate
col.labo/ra/tion
col.labo/ra/tive
col.labo/ra/tor
collage
col/lapse
col.laps/ible
col.laps/ing
collar
col.lards
col.lat/eral
col.lat/eral.ize
col.lat/ing
col.la/tor
col/league
collect
col.lecti/bil.ity
col.lect/ing
col.lec/tion
col.lec/tive
col.lec/tively
col.lec/tor
college
col.le/giate

[5]Verb construction. Do not hyphenate. (Be sure to clean up your desk.)
[6]Noun construction. Written as one word. (The cleanup was easy.)

col.li/sion
col.lo/quial
col.lo/qui.al.ism
col.lo/quium
col.lo/quy
col.lu/sion
col.lu/sive
cologne
COLOM/BIA
colon
colonel
co.lo/nial
co.lo/nies
colo/nist
colony
color
COLO/RADO
COLORADO
  SPRINGS, CO
col.or/blind
col.or/code
col.or/ful
col.or/ing
co.los/sal
co.los/sus
co.los/tomy
COLUM/BIA, SC
COLUM/BUS, OH
column
co.lum/nar
col.um/nist
coma
coma/tose
comb
combat
com.bat/ant
com/bat/ing
com.bi.na/tion
combine
com.bin/ing
com.bus/tible
com.bus/tion

come
[6]come/back
[5]come back
co.me/dian
comedy
com.fort
com.fort/able
com.fort/ably
com/forter
com.fort/ers
comic
comical
coming
 co.min/gle
 co.min/gling
comma
command
com.man/dant
com.man/deer
com.mand/ing
com.mand/ments
com.memo/rate
com.memo/rat/ing
com/mence
com.mence/ment
com.menc/ing
commend
com.mend/able
com.men/da/tion
com.men/da/tory
com.mend/ing
com.men/su/rate
comment
com.men/tary
com.men/ta/tor
com.ment/ing
com/merce
com.mer/cial
com.mer/cial/iza/tion
com.mer/cially

com.mis/er.ate
com.mis/era/tion
com.mis/sary
com.mis/sion
com.mis/sioner
com.mis/sion.ers
com.mis/sion/ing
commit
com.mit/ment
com.mit/ted
com.mit/tee
com.mit.tee/man
com.mit.tee/woman
com.mit/ting
commode
com.modi/ties
com.mod/ity
com.mo/dore
common
com.mon/al.ity
com/moner
com.mon/est
com/monly
com.mon/place
com.mon/wealth
com.mo/tion
commune
com.mu.ni/ca.ble
com.mu.ni/cant
com.mu.ni/cate
com.mu.ni/ca/ting
com.mu.ni/ca/tion
com.mu.ni/ca/tive
com.mu.ni/ca.tor
com.mu/nion
com.mu/ni/qué
com.mu/nism
com.mu/nist
com.mu.ni/ties
com.mu/nity
commute

com/muter
compact
com/pactly
com/pa/nies
com.pan/ion
com.pan/ion/ship
company
com.pany/wide
com.pa.ra/bil.ity
com.pa.ra/ble
com.para/tive
com.para/tively
compare
com.par/ing
com.pari/son
com.part/ment
com.part/men/
  ta.li/za/tion
com.pat/ible
com.pati/bil.ity
compel
com/pelled
com.pel/ling
com.pen/dium
com.pen/sa.ble
com.pen/sate
com.pen/sa/ting
com.pen/sa/tion
com.pen/sa/tory
compete
com.pe/tence
com.pe/tent
com.pe/tently
com.pet/ing
com.pe.ti/tion
com.peti/tive
com.peti/tively
com.péti/tive/ness
com.peti/tor
com.pi.la/tion
compile
com.pil/ing

[3]Noun or compound adjective construction. Hyphenate. (It was a come-on letter. The letter was a come-on.)

[5]Verb construction. Do not hyphenate. (They will come back later. Come on the next bus.)

[6]Noun construction. Written as one word. (The actress made a come-back.)

com.pla/cency
com.pla/cent
com/plain
com.plain/ant
com.plain/ing
com/plaint
com.plai/sant
com.ple/ment
com/plete
com/pletely
com.plete/ness
com.plet/ing
com.ple/tion
complex
com/plexes
com.plex.ion
com.plexi/ties
com.plex.ity
com.pli/ance
com.pli/cate
com.pli/ca/tion
com/plied
com.pli/ment
com.pli/men/tary
com.pli/ment/ing
comply
com.ply/ing
com.po/nent
com.port/ment
compose
com/poser
com/pos.ite
com.po.si/tion
com.po.si/tor
com.po/sure
com/pound
com/pound/ing
com.pre/hend
com.pre/hen/si.ble
com.pre/hen/sion
com.pre/hen/sive
com.pre/hen/sively
com/press
com/press.ible
com.pres/sion
com.pres/sor
com.prise
com.pris/ing
com.pro/mise
comp/trol/ler
com.pul/sion

com.pul/sive
com.pul/sory
com.put/able
com.pu.ta/tion
com.pu.ta/tion/ally
compute
com/puter
com.put/er/iza/tion
com.put/er/ize
com.put/ing
comrade
com.rade/ship
con
concave
conceal
concede
conceit
con.ceiv/able
con.ceiv/ably
conceive
con.cen/trate
con.cen/tra/ting
con.cen/tra/tion
concept
con.cep/tion
con.cep/tual
con.cep/tuali/za/tion
con.cern/ing
concert
con/certed
con.ces/sion
con.ces/sion/aire
con.ces/sional
con.cili/ation
con.cilia/tory
concise
con/cisely
con/clave
con/clude
con.clud/ing
con.clu/sion
con.clu/sive
con.clu/sively
concoct
con.coc/tion
con.comi/tant
concord
con.cor/dance
con/course
con/crete
con/cretely

concur
con.curred
con.cur/rence
con.cur/rent
con.cur/rently
con.cur/ring
con.dem/na/tion
con.demn/ing
con.den/sate
con.den/sa/tion
con.den/ser
con/des/cend
con/des/cen/sion
con.di/ment
con.di/tion
con.di/tional
con.di/tioner
con.di/tion/ing
con.do/lence
con.do/min.ium
condone
con.du/cive
conduct
con.duct/ing
con.duct/ive
con.duc/tor
conduit
cone
con.fec/tion.ary
confed/er.acy
con.fed/er.ate
con.fed/era/tion
confer
con/feree
con.fer/ence
con.fer/red
con.fer/ring
confess
con.fes/sion
con/fetti
confide
con.fi/dence
con.fi/dent
con.fi/den/tial
con.fi/den/ti/al.ity
con.fi/den/tially
con.fi/dently
con.figu/ra/tion
con/fig.ure
confine
con.fine/ment

con.fin/ing
confirm
con.fir/ma/tion
con.fir/ma/tory
con.firm/ing
con.fis/cate
con.fis/ca/tory
con.fla/gra/tion
conflict
con.flict/ing
con.flu/ence
conform
con.for/ma/tion
con.form/ing
con.form/ist
con.form/ity
con.forms
con/found
con/front
con.fron/ta/tion
con.front/ing
confuse
con.fus/ing
con.fu/sion
con.fu.ta/tion
con/gen.ial
con.ge/nial.ity
con.geni/tal
congest
con.ges/tion
con.glom/er.ate
con.glom/era/tion
CONGO
con.gratu/late
con.gratu/la/tion
con.gratu/la/tory
con.gre/gate
con.gre/ga/tion
con/gress
con/gresses
con.gres/sional
con.gress/man
con.gress/men
con.gress/woman
con.gress/women
con.gru/ence
con.gru/ent
con.gru/ity
con.gru/ous
conical
con.jec/tural

con.jec/ture
con/jugal
con.ju/gate
con.ju/ga/tion
con.junc/tion
conjure
connect
CONNEC/TICUT
con.nect/ing
con.nec/tion
connive
con/nois/seur
con.nota/tion
connote
con.quer/ing
con/queror
cons
con/science
con.sci/en/tious
con.sci/en/tiously
con.scious
con.sciously
con.scious/ness
con.scrip/tion
con.se/cra/tion
con.secu/tive
con.sen/sus
consent
con.se/quence
con.se/quent
con.se/quen/tial
con.se/quently
con.ser/va/tion
con.serva/tism
con.serva/tive
con.serva/tively
con.serva/tor
con.serva/tory
con/serve
con.serv/ing
con/sider
con.sid/er/able
con.sid/er/ably
con.sid/era/tion
con.sid/er/ing
consign
con/signee
con.sign/ing
con.sign/ment
consist
con.sis/tent

con.sis/tently
con.sist/ing
console
con.soli/date
con.soli/dat/ing
con.soli/da/tion
con.so/nance
con.so/nant
con.sor/tium
con/spicu/ous
con.spir/acy
con.spira/tor
con.spira/tor.ial
con/spire
con/stancy
con/stant
con/stantly
con.stel/la/tion
con.ster/na/tion
con.stitu/encies
con.stitu/ency
con/stitu.ent
con.sti/tute
con.sti/tu/tion
con.sti/tu/tional
con.sti/tu/tion/ally
con/strain
con/straint
con/strict
con/stric/tion
con/struct
con/struct/ing
con.struc/tion
con.struc/tion.ist
con.struc/tive
con.struc/tively
con.struc/tor
con/strue
con.stru/ing
consul
con/sular
consult
con.sul/tancy
con.sul/tant
con.sul/ta/tion
con.sul/ta/tive
con.sult/ing
con.sum/able
consume
con/sumer
con/sum/er/ism

con.sum/er/ist
con.sum/er/istic
con.sum/ing
con.sum/mate
con.sum/ma/tion
con.sump/tion
contact
con.tact/ing
con.ta/gious
contain
con/tainer
con.tain/ing
con.tain/ment
con.tami/nant
con.tami/nate
con.tami/na/tion
con.tem/plate
con.tem/plat/ing
con.tem/pla/tion
con.tem/pla/tive
con.tem/po.ra/
    ne.ous
con.tem/po/rar.ies
con.tem/po/rary
con/tempt
con.tempt/ible
contend
content
con.ten/tion
con.ten/tious
con/tents
contest
con.test/able
con.tes/tant
context
con.tex/tual
con.ti/gu/ity
con.tigu/ous
con.ti/nence
con.ti/nent
con.ti/nen/tal
con.tin/gen/cies
con.tin/gency
con.tin/gent
con.tinu/able
con/tinual
con.tinu/ally
con.tinu/ance
con.tinu/ation
con.tinue
con.tin/ued

con.tin/ues
con.tinu/ing
con.ti/nu.ity
con.tinu/ous
con.tinu/ously
con/tinuum
con.tor/tion
contour
con.tra/cep/tion
con.tra/cep/tive
con/tract
con.tract/ing
con.trac/tor
con.trac/tual
con.tra/dict
con.tra/dic/tion
con.tra/dic/tory
con.tra/dis/tinc/tion
con.trap/tion
con/trary
con/trast
con.tra/vene
con.tra/ven/tion
con.trib/ute
con.trib/uted
con.trib/ut/ing
con.tri/bu/tion
con/tribu/tor
con/tribu/tory
con/trive
control
con.trol/la.ble
con/trolled
con.trol/ler
con.trol/ler/ship
con.trol/ling
con.tro/ver/sial
con.tro/ver/sies
con.tro/versy
con.tu/sions
con.va/les/cent
con.ve/nience
con.ve/nient
convent
con.ven/tion
con.ven/tional
con.ven/tion/ally
con.ver/gence
con.ver/sant
con.ver/sa/tion
con.ver/sa/tional

con/versely
con.ver/sion
convert
con/verter
con.vert/ers
con.verti/bil.ity
con.vert/ible
con.vert/ing
convex
con.vex/ity
convey
con.vey/ance
con.vey/ing
con/veyor
con.vic/tion
con/vince
con.vinc/ing
con.vinc/ingly
con.vo.ca/tion
convoke
con.vo.lu/tion
convoy
con.vul/sion
cook
cookery
cookie
cooking
cookout
cool
coolant
cooler
cooling
coon
co-op (h)
co.op.er/ate
co.op.era/ting
co.op.era/tion
co.op.era/tive
co.op.era/tively
co.op.era/tor
co.or.di/nate
co.or.di/na/ting
co.or.di/na/tion
co.or.di/na/tor
co-owner (h)
co.part/ner
cope
copied
copier
coping

copper
copter
copy
copy/holder
copying
copy/reader
copy/right
cor/dial/ity
cor/dially
cor.du/roy
core
corn
cornea
corner
cor.ner/stone
cornet
cornice
cor.ol/lary
coro/nary
coro.na/tion
coro/ner
coronet
cor.po/ral
cor.po/rate
cor.po.ra/tion
cor.po/real
corps
corpse
cor.pu/lence
cor.pu/lent
corpus
CORPUS CHRISTI,
  TX
cor.pus/cle
corral
correct
cor.rect/ing
cor.rec/tion
cor.rec/tional
cor.rec/tive
cor/rectly
cor.rect/ness
cor.re/late
cor.re.la/ting
cor.re.la/tion
cor.re.la/tional
cor.re.la/tive
cor.re/spond
cor.re/spon/dence
cor.re/spon/dent
cor.re/spond/ing

cor.re/spond/ingly
cor.ri/dor
cor.robo/rate
cor.robo/ra/tion
cor/rod.ing
cor.ro/sion
cor.ro/sive
cor.ru/gated
corrupt
cor.rupt/ible
cor.rup/tion
corsage
cortege
cor.ti/sone
co.run/dum
co.signer
co.sign/ers
cos/metic
cos.me/tol.ogy
cosmos
cos.mo/naut
cos.mo/poli/tan
co.spon/sor
co.spon/sor/ship
cost
cost-benefit (h)
costing
cost.li/ness
costly
cost-plus (h)
costume
cot
cottage
cotton
cot.ton/tail
couch
cougar
cough
could
council
coun.cil/man
coun.cil/men
coun.cil/woman
coun.cil/women
counsel
coun/seled
coun.sel/ing
coun/selor
coun.sel/ors
count
count/able

count/down
counter
coun.ter/act
coun.ter/ac.tion
coun.ter/at.tack
coun.ter/bal.ance
coun.ter/claim
coun.ter/clock/wise
coun.ter/feit
coun.ter/feiter
coun.ter/meas.ure
coun.ter/move
coun.ter/of.fer
coun.ter/part
coun.ter/point
coun.ter/sign
coun.ter/sig.na.ture
coun/ties
count/ing
count/less
coun/tries
country
county
county/wide
coup d'etat
coupe
couple
coupler
couplet
cou/pling
coupon
courage
cou.ra/geous
courier
course
court
cour.te/ous
cour.te/ously
cour.te/sies
courtesy
court/house
court/ing
court/room
court/ship
court/yard
co.vari/ance
cove
cove/nant
cover
cov.er/age
cov.er/alls

3

covered
cov.er/ing
cov.er/ings
cover-up (h)
covet
co.vet/ous
cow
coward
cow.ard/ice
cow.ard/li/ness
cow/ardly
cowboy
cowl
co-worker (h)
cowpoke
coy
cozily
co.zi/ness
cozy
crack
crack/down
crack/ing
cradle
craft
craft/ily
crafts/man
crafts/woman
cram
crammed
cram/ming
cramp
cran/berry
crane
cranium
crank/case
crash
crashes
crate
crating
cravat
craving
crawl
crayon
crazily
cra.zi/ness
crazy
cream
cream/ery
creami/ness
create
cre.at/ing

crea/tion
crea/tive
crea/tively
crea.tiv/ity
creator
crea/ture
cre.dence
cre.den/tial
cre/denza
credi/bil.ity
credi/ble
credit
cred.it/able
cred/ited
cred.it/ing
credi/tor
credo
credu/lous
creed
creek
creep
creep/ing
cremate
cre.ma/tion
crept
cres/cendo
crest
crevice
crew
crewcut
crib
crib/bing
cried
crier
cries
crime
CRIMEAN
crimi/nal
crimi/nally
crimi/nol.ogy
crimp
crimson
cripple
crip/pling
crises
crisis
crisp
cri.te/ria
cri.te/rion
critic
criti/cal

criti/cally
criti/cism
criti/cize
cri/tique
crochet
crock/ery
croco/dile
crocus
cronies
crony
crook
crop
crop/ping
cross
cross-examine (h)
crosses
cross/ing
cross/road
cross-section (h)
cross/walk
cross/wise
cross/word
cross/work
crouton
crow
crowd
crown
crucial
crude
crudity
cruel
cruelty
cruise
crunch
crusade
crush
crush/ing
crust
crutch
crutches
crux
crying
cryptic
crystal
crys.tal/line
crys.tal/lize
crys.tal/liz/ing
cubage
CUBAN
cube
cube

cubic
cuckoo
cu.cum/ber
cuddle
cuddly
cue
cuff
cuisine
cul-de-sac (h)
cu.li/nary
cull
culling
cul.mi/nate
cul.mi/na/tion
cul.pa/ble
culprit
cul.ti/vate
cul.ti/va/tion
cul.ti/va/tor
cul.tural
cul.tur/ally
cul/tures
culvert
cum.ber/some
cum/brance
cu.mu/late
cu.mu.la/tive
cumulus
cun/ningly
cup
cup/board
cupful
curable
curate
curator
curb
curbing
curb/stone
cure
curfew
curing
cu.ri.os/ity
cu.ri/ous
curler
curli/ness
currant
cur.ren/cies
cur/rency
current
cur/rently
cur.ric/ula

3

cur.ricu/lar
cur.ricu/lum
cursory
curt
curtail
cur.tail/ment
curtain
curt/ness
curve
curvi/linear
cushion
cush.ion/ing
cuss
custard
cus.to/dial
cus.to/dian
custody
custom
cus.tom/ar.ily
cus/tom/ary
cus/tomer
cus.tom/ers
cus.tom/ize
cut
[6]cutback
[5]cut back
cutlery
[11]cutoff
[5]cut off
[6]cutout
[5]cut out
cutover
cut-rate (h)
cutter
cut/throat
cutting
cy.ber/net/ics
cy.cla/mate
cycle
cy.cli/cal
cy.clic/ally
cyclone

cyl.in/der
cy.lin/dri/cal
cymbal
cynic
cynical
cyni/cism
cyst
cystic
czar
CZECHO/SLO-
    VAKIA

D

dab
dabble
dacron
dad
daf.fo/dil
dahlia
dailies
daily
dain/tily
dain.ti/ness
dainty
dairies
dairy
dairy/man
dais
daisy
DAKAR
DAKOTA
dale
DALLAS, TX
dam
damage
dam.ag/ing
damask

dam/ming
damn
dam.na/able
dam.na/tion
damp
dampen
damp.en/ing
damper
damp/ness
dance
dancer
dancing
dan.de/lion
dan/druff
DANES
danger
dan.ger/ous
dan.ger/ously
dangle
dan/gling
DANISH
dapper
dare/devil
daring
dark
darken
dar.ken/ing
dark/ness
dark/room
darling
dar/lings
darn
dart
dash
dash/board
data
data/base
data.ma/tion
data/phone
date
dating
datum

daugh/ter
daughter-in-law (h)
daunt/less
daven/port
day
day/break
day/dream
day/light
daytime
DAYTON, OH
daze
daz/zling
deacon
dead
dead/beat
dead/line
dead.li/ness
dead/lock
deadly
deaf
deafen
deal
dealer
deal.er/ship
dealing
deal/ings
dealt
dean
deanery
dear
dearly
death
death/bed
death/less
death/trap
debacle
debar
debark
de.bar.ka/tion
de.barred
de.bar/ring
debase

[5]Verb construction. Do not hyphenate. (Where can we cut back. This morning the power was cut off. She cut out the pattern.)
[6]Noun construction. Written as one word. (The company suffered a cutback. The electrical cutout emptied the memory on the machine.)
[11]Noun or compound adjective construction. Written as one word. (When is the cutoff date? Where on the list is the cutoff?)

de.base/ment
de.bat/able
debate
de.bauch/ery
de.ben/ture
de.bili/tat/ing
debit
debo/nair
debrief
debris
debt
debtor
debug
de.bugged
de.bug/ging
debunk
debut
debu/tante
decade
deca/dence
decal
de.canter
de.capi/ta/tion
decay
decease
de.ce/dent
deceit
deceive
de.cel/era/tion
DECEM/BER
decency
decent
de.cent/rali/za/tion
de.cent/ral/ize
de.cent/ral/iz/ing
de.cep/tion
de.cep/tive
decibel
decide
de.cid/edly
de.cid/ing
decimal
de.ci/pher
de.ci/sion
de.ci/sional
decision making
de.ci/sive
deck
de.cla.ma/tion

dec.la.ra/tion
declare
de.clas/si/fi/ca/tion
de.clas/sify
dec.li.na/tion
decline
de.clin/ing
decode
de.com/pos/able
de.com/pose
de.com/posi/tion
de.con/cen/trate
de.con/trol
de.con/trolled
decor
deco/rate
deco/ra/tor
decorum
decoy
decree
decreed
decried
decry
dedi/cate
dedi.ca/tion
deduce
de.duct/ibil.ity
de.duct/ible
de.duc/tion
de.duc/tive
deed
deem
de.em.pha/size
deep
deep.en/ing
deepest
deeply
deer
deer/skin
de-escalate (h)
deface
de.fac/ing
de facto
de.fa.ma/tion
de.fault
de.fault/ing
defeat
de.feat/ist
de.fec/tion
de.fec/tive

de.fec/tor
defend
de.fend/able
de.fend/ant
de.fender
de.fend/ers
de.fend/ing
defense
de.fen.si/ble
de.fen/sive
defer
def.er/ence
def.er.en/tial
de.fer/ment
de.fer.ra/able
de.fer/ral
de.ferred
de.fer/ring
de.fi/ance
de.fi.cien/cies
de.fi/ciency
de.fi/cient
deficit
de.fin/able
define
de.fin/ing
defi/nite
defi/nitely
defi.ni/tion
defi.ni/tive
defi.ni/tively
deflate
de.fla/tion
deflect
de.flec/table
de.flec/tion
de.fo.li/ant
de.fo.li/ate
de.fo.li/ation
deform
de.for.ma/tion
de.form/ity
defraud
de.fraud/ing
defray
de.fray/able
defrost
de.froster
deftly
defunct

defy
de.gen.er/ate
de.gen/era/tion
degrade
de.gra.da/tion
degree
de.hu/mani/za/tion
de.hu/man/ize
de.hu.mid/ify
de.hy/drate
de.hy/drat/ing
de.jec/tion
de jure
DELA/WARE
delay
delayed
de.lay/ing
de.lec/ta.ble
dele/gate
dele.ga/ting
dele.ga/tion
delete
dele.te/ri.ous
de.le/tion
de.lib.er/ate
de.lib.er/ately
de.lib/era/ting
de.lib/era/tion
deli/cacy
deli/cate
deli.ca/tes/sen
de.li/cious
delight
de.light/ful
de.light/fully
delimit
de.line/ate
de.line/ation
de.lin/quen/cies
de.lin/quency
de.lin/quent
de.liri/ous
de.list/ing
deliver
de.liv.er/able
de.liv.er/ance
de.liv.er/ies
de.liv.er/ing
de.liv/ery
de.lo.ca/tion

3

delta
delude
deluge
de.lu/sion
deluxe
delve
delving
de.mag.ne/tize
dema/gogue
demand
de.mand/ing
de.mar.ca/tion
demean
de.meanor
de.mented
de.mili/ta/ri/za/tion
de.mili/ta/rize
demise
de.mo.bil/ize
de.moc/racy
demo/cratic
demo/crati/cally
demo.cra/tize
de.mog.ra/pher
demo/graphic
de.mog/raphy
de.mol/ish
de.mol/ish/ing
demo.li/tion
demon
de.mone/tize
dem.on/strate
dem.on/strat/ing
dem.on/stra/tion
dem.on/stra/tor
de.mor.al/ize
de.mo/tion
de.mo.ti/vate
de.mur/rage
de.murred
de.mur/rer
de.mur/ring
de.na/tured
denial
denim
DENMARK
de.nomi/na/tion
de.nomi/na/tor
denote

de.not/ing
de.nounce
dense
densely
den.si/fied
den.si/ties
density
dent
dental
den.ti/frice
dentist
den/tistry
denture
de.nun/cia/tion
DENVER, CO
deny
denying
de.odor/ant
de.odor/ize
de.odor/izer
depart
de.part/ment
de.part/mental
de.part/men/
ta/li/za/tion
de.par/ture
depend
de.penda/bil.ity
de.pend/able
de.pen/dence
de.pen/den/cies
de.pen/dency
de.pen/dent
de.per/son/al.ize
depict
de.pict/ing
deplane
deplete
de.ple/tion
de.plor/able
deplore
deploy
de.ploy/ment
de.por.ta/tion
de.port/ment
deposit
de.posi/tary
de.pos.it/ing
depo.si/tion

de.posi/tor
de.posi/to/ries
de.posi/tory
depot
de.pra.va/tion
de.pre/cia.ble
de.pre/cia/tion
depress
de.press/ing
de.pres/sion
de.pri.va/tion
deprive
de.pro/gram
de.pro/gram/ming
depth
depu.ta/tion
depu/tize
deputy
de.rail/ment
de.ranged
de.regu/la/tion
deri/va/tion
deri/va/tive
derive
der.ma.ti/tis
der.ma/tolo/gist
der.ma.to/logy
de.roga/tory
derrick
descend
de.scend/ant
de.scend/ing
descent
de.scrib/able
de.scribe
de.scrib/ing
de.scrip/tion
de.scrip/tive
de.seg.re/gate
de.seg.re/ga/tion
desert
de.ser/tion
deserve
de.servedly
de.serv/ing
design
des.ig/nate
des.ig.na/ting
des.ig.na/tion

de.signer
de.sign/ing
de.sira/bil.ity
de.sir/able
desire
de.sir/ing
de.sir/ous
desist
desk/bound
DES MOINES, IA
deso/late
deso.la/tion
despair
des.per/ate
des.per/ately
des/pera/tion
de.spi.ca/ble
despite
despoil
de.spon/dent
despot
dessert
de.sta.bi/lize
des.ti.na/tion
destine
des.ti/tute
destroy
de.stroyer
de.stroy/ers
de.stroy/ing
de.struc/ti.ble
de.struc/tion
de.struc/tive
detach
de.tach/able
de.tach/ing
de.tach/ment
detail
de.tail/ing
detain
detect
de.tect/able
de.tect/ing
de.tec/tion
de.tec/tive
de.tec/tor
détente
de.ten/tion
deter

de.ter/gent
de.te.rio/rate
de.te.rio/ra/tion
de.ter/min/able
de.ter/mi/nant
de.ter/mi/na/tion
de.ter/mine
de.ter/min/ing
de.ter/min.ism
de.ter/mini/stic
deterred
de.ter/rent
de.test/able
deto/nate
deto.na/tion
detour
detract
de.trac/tion
de.trac/tor
detrain
det.ri/ment
det.ri/men/tal
DETROIT, MI
de.valu/ation
devalue
dev.as/tate
dev.as/tat/ing
dev.as.ta/tion
develop
de.vel/oper
de.vel.op/ing
de.vel.op/ment
de.vel.op/men.tal
de.vi/ance
deviant
deviate
de.via/tion
device
devil
dev.il/ish
de.vi/ous
devise
devisee
devoid
devolve
devote
devotee
de.vot/ing
de.vo/tion

de.vo/tional
devour
devout
dex.ter/ity
dex/trose
dia/be.tes
dia/betic
di.ag/nose
di.ag.nos/ing
di.ag.no/ses
di.ag.no/sis
di.ag.nos/tic
di.ag.nos/ti/cian
di.ago/nal
diagram
dia.gram/matic
dia/grammed
dial
dialect
dialing
dia/logue
di.aly/sis
di.ame/ter
dia.met/ri/cal
dia.met/ri/cally
diamond
diaper
dia/phragm
diaries
diar/rhea
diary
dia/tribe
diazo
dice
di.choto/mize
di.choto/mous
di.chot/omy
dictate
dic.tat/ing
dic.ta/tion
dic.ta/tional
dic.ta/tor
dic.ta/to/rial
dic.ta/tor/ship
dic.tion/ary
dictum
did
di.dac/tic
die

died
diehard
die/maker
diesel
diet
dietary
die/tetic
die.tet/ics
di.eti/tial
differ
dif.fer/ence
dif.fer/ent
dif.fer/en/tial
dif.fer/en/ti.ate
dif.fer/en/ti.at/ing
dif.fer/en/tia/tion
dif.fer/ently
dif/fer/ing
dif.fi/cult
dif.fi/cul/ties
dif.fi/culty
dif.fi/dence
dif.fi/dent
diffuse
dif.fu/sion
dig
digest
di.gest/ible
di.gest/ing
di.ges/tive
digger
digging
digit
digital
dig.ni/fied
dig.ni/tary
dignity
digress
di.gress/ing
di.gres/sion
di.lapi/dated
dilate
di.la/tion
dila/tory
di.lemma
dili/gence
dili/gent
dili/gently
dilute

di.lu/tion
dim
dime
di.men/sion
di.men/sional
di.men/sion/al.ity
di.men/sion/ally
di.min/ish
di.min/ish/ing
dimi/nu/tion
dimming
dimout
dine
diner
dinette
dining
dinner
din.ner/ware
di.oce/san
diocese
diode
dioxide
dip
diph/the.ria
diph/thong
diploma
di.plo/macy
di.plo/mat
di.plo/matic
dipper
dipping
dire
direct
di.rect/ing
di.rec/tion
di.rec/tional
di.rec/tive
di.fectly
di.rec/tor
di.rec.to/rate
di.rec.to/ries
di.rec/tory
direful
dirge
di.ri/gi.ble
dirtily
dirti/ness
dirty
dis.abili/ties

dis.abil/ity
dis/abled
dis.ad/van/tage
dis.ad/van/ta/geous
dis.af/fected
dis.af/fec/tion
dis.af/firm
disa/gree
disa/gree/able
disa/gree/ment
dis/allow
dis.al/low/ance
dis.ap/pear
dis.ap/pear/ance
dis.ap/pear/ing
dis.ap/point
dis.ap/point/ing
dis.ap/point/ment
dis.ap/proval
dis.ap/prove
dis.ar/ma/ment
dis.ar/range
dis.ar/ray
dis.as/sem.ble
dis.as.so/ci/ate
dis.as/trous
disavow
disband
disbar
dis/barred
dis.bar/ring
dis.be/lief
dis/burse
dis.burse/ment
dis.burs/ing
disc
discard
discern
dis.cern/ible
dis.cern/ment
dis/charge
dis.ci/ple
dis.ci/pli/nar.ian
dis.ci/plin/ary
dis.ci/pline
dis/claim
dis/claimer
dis/close
dis.clos/ing

dis.clo/sure
dis/color
dis.color/ation
dis.com/fit
dis.com/fort
dis.con/cert
dis.con/cert/ing
dis.con/nect
dis.con/tent
dis.con/tinu/ance
dis.con/tinue
dis.con/tinu/ing
discord
dis.cor/dance
dis.co/theque
dis/count
dis.count/ing
dis.cour/age
dis.cour/age/ment
dis/course
dis.cour/tesy
dis/cover
dis.cov/er.ies
dis.cov/er/ing
dis.cov/ery
dis/credit
dis/creet
dis.crep/an/cies
dis.crep/ancy
dis/crete
dis.cre/tion
dis.cre/tion.ary
dis/crimi/nant
dis/crimi/nate
dis/crimi/nat/ing
dis/crimi/na/tion
dis/crimi/na/tory
discuss
dis/cusses
dis.cuss/ing
dis.cus/sion
disdain
disease
dis/en/chant
dis/en.chant/ment
dis/en.gage
dis/en.tan.gle
dis/equi.lib/rium
dis/fig.ure

dis/fran/chise
dis/func/tion
dis/func/tional
dis/grace
dis/grace/ful
dis.grac/ing
dis/grun.tle
dis/guise
disgust
dish
dis/hearten
dis/hon.est
dis/hon.esty
dis/honor
dis/hon.or/able
dis/il.lu/sion
dis/il.lu/sion/ment
dis/in.cli/na/tion
dis/in.cline
dis/in.fect
dis/in.fec/tant
dis/in.te/grate
dis/in.te/gra/tion
dis/in.ter/est
disjoin
dis/jointed
disk
dis/kette
dislike
dis/lo.cate
dis/lo.ca/tion
dis/lodge
dis/loyal
dis/loy.alty
dismal
dis/man.tle
dis/man/tling
dis/mem.ber
dis/mem.ber/ment
dismiss
dis/missal
dis/obe.di/ence
dis/obe.di/ent
disobey
dis/or.der
dis/or.derly
dis/or.ga/nize
dis/ori/ented
disown

dis/par.age
dis/par.ate
dis/par.ity
dis/patch
dis/patcher
dis/patch.ing
dispel
dis/pelled
dis.pel/ling
dis.pen/sary
dis.pen.sa/tion
dis/penser
dis.pen/sing
dis/per/sal
dis/perse
dis.per/sion
dis.place/ment
dis.play
dis.play/ing
dis/please
dis.plea/sure
dis/pos.able
dis/posal
dispose
dis.pos/ing
dis.po.si/tion
dis/pos.sess
dis/pro.por/tion.ate
dis/pro.por/tion/ately
dis/prove
dispute
dis/qual.ify
dis/quiet
dis/quiet/ing
dis/re.gard
dis/re.pair
dis/repu.ta/ble
dis/re.pute
dis/re.spect
disrupt
dis.rup/tion
dis.rup/tive
dis/sat.is/fac/tion
dis/sat.is/fied
dis.sect/ing
dis.sec/tion
dis.semi/nate
dis.semi/na/tion
dis.sen/sion

dissent
dis/senter
dis.ser/ta/tion
dis/ser.vice
dis.si/dence
dis.si/dent
dis/simi.lar
dis/simi.lar/ity
dis.si/pate
dis.si.pa/tion
dis.si/pator
dis.so.lu/tion
dis/solve
dis.solv/ing
dis.son/ance
dis.son/ant
dis/suade
distaff
dis/tance
distant
dis/taste
dis/taste.ful
distill
dis.till/ate
dis.till/ery
dis/tinct
dis.tinc/tion
dis.tinc/tive
dis.tinc/tive/ness
dis/tinctly
dis.tin/guish
dis.tin/guish/able
dis.tin/guish/ing
distort
dis.tort/ing
dis.tor/tion
dis/tract
dis/tract/ing
dis.trac/tion
dis/tress
dis/tress/ing
dis.trib/ute
dis.trib/ut/ing
dis.tri/bu/tion
dis.tri/bu/tional
dis.tri/bu/tive
dis.tri/bu/tor
dis.tri/bu/tor/ship
dis/trict

dis/trust
dis/trust.ful
disturb
dis.tur/bance
dis.turb/ing
ditch
dither
ditto
dive
di.ver/gence
di.ver/gen/cies
di.ver/gent
divers
diverse
di.ver/si/fi/able
di.ver/si/fi/ca/tion
di.ver/sify
di.ver.si/fy/ing
di.ver/sion
di.ver/sity
divert
divest
di.vesti/ture
di.vest/ment
divide
divi/dend
divider
divine
diving
di.vin/ity
di.visi/bil.ity
di.vi/sion
di.vi/sional
di.vi/sor
divorce
di.vor/cee
divot
divulge
do
docile
do.cil/ity
dock
docket
dock/hand
doctor
doc/toral
doc.tor/ate
doc.tri/naire
doc/trinal

doc/trine
docu/ment
docu.men/tary
docu.men/ta/tion
docu/ment/ing
does
doeskin
doff
dog
dog/house
dog/matic
dog.ma/tism
dol/drums
doleful
dollar
dollies
dolly
dolor
dolphin
domain
dome
do.mes/tic
do.mes.ti/cally
do.mes.ti/cate
do.mes/tic.ity
do.mes/tics
do.mi/cile
domi/nance
domi/nant
domi/nate
domi.na/tion
domi/neer/ing
do.min/ion
domino
don
donate
do.nat/ing
do.na/tion
done
donee
donor
doom
door
door/bell
door/knob
door/step
door/stop
doorway
dormant

dormer
dor.mi.to/ries
dor.mi/tory
dorsal
dosage
dose
dossier
dot
dotage
double
double-cross (h)
double-knit (h)
double-park (h)
dou/bling
doubt
doubt/ful
doubt/less
dough/nut
dove/tail
dowdy
dowel
doweled
dow.el/ing
down
down/cast
down/fall
down/grade
down/hill
down/pay/ment
down/right
down/stairs
down/time
down/town
down/trend
down/turn
down/ward
dowry
dozen
drab
drabber
draft
draft/ing
drafts/man
drafts/man/ship
drag
drag/ging
dragon
drain
drain/age

3

drama
dra/matic
dra.mati/cally
drama/tized
drap.er/ies
drapery
drapes
drastic
dras.ti/cally
draw
draw/back
draw/bridge
drawee
drawer
drawing
drawn
dray
dread
dread/ful
dream
dream/ily
drea.ri/ness
dreary
dredge
dredg/ing
dress
dresser
dress/ers
dress/ing
dress/ings
dress/maker
drew
dribble
drib/bling
dried
drier
drift
drill
drill/ing
drink
drink/able
drink/ing
drip
drip/pings
driven
driver
drive/way
driving
drizzle

drop
dropout
dropped
drop/ping
drought
drove
drowsy
drudge
drudg/ery
drug
drug/ging
drug/gist
drug/store
drum
drummer
drum/ming
drum/stick
drunk
drunk/ard
drunken
dry
dry-clean (h)
dryer
drying
dual
dubious
duck
ductile
due
duel
dueling
dug
duke
dull
duly
dummy
dump
dumping
dump/ling
dun
dun.ga/ree
dunned
dunning
duplex
du.pli/cate
du.pli/cat/ing
du.pli.ca/tion
du.pli.ca/tor
du.plic/ity

du.ra.bil/ity
du.ra/ble
du.ra/tion
duress
DURHAM, NC
during
dust
duties
dutiful
duty
dwell
dwell/ing
dwell/ings
dwindle
dwin/dling
dye
dyeing
dying
dynamic
dy.nami/cally
dy.na/mism
dy.na/mite
dynamo
dynasty
dys.func/tional

E_____

each
eager
eagerly
eagle
earache
eardrum
earlier
ear.li/est
early
earmark
ear.mark/ing
earn
earnest
ear/nestly
earning
earn/ings
ear/phone

ear/piece
earplug
earring
ear/rings
earshot
earth
earth/born
earth/bound
earth.en/ware
earth/quake
earth/shak/ing
earth/worm
earthy
ease
easel
ease/ment
easier
easiest
easily
easing
east
east/erly
eastern
east/wardly
easy
easy/go.ing
eat
eatable
eaten
eating
eaves/drop/ping
ebb
ebonite
ebony
ebul/lience
ebul/lient
ec.cen/tric
ec.cen/tric.ity
ec.clesi/as/ti.cal
echelon
eche/lons
echo
echoes
echoing
éclair
ec.lec/tic
eclipse
eco.logi/cal
eco.logi/cally

eco.lo/gist
ecology
econo/met.ric
econo/met/ric/ally
econo.me/tri/cian
eco/nomic
eco.nom/ical
eco.nom/ically
econo/mies
econo/mist
econo/mize
econo/miz.ing
economy
ecstasy
ec.static
ecu.men/ical
ecu.men/ism
eczema
edge
edge/wise
edging
edible
edict
edi.fi.ca/tion
edifice
edify
edit
editing
edition
editor
edi.to/rial
edi.to/rial.ize
edi.to/ri/ally
edu.ca/ble
educate
edu.cat/ing
edu.ca/tion
edu.ca/tional
edu.ca/tion/ally
edu.ca/tor
efface
effect
ef.fect/ing
ef.fec/tive
ef.fec/tively
ef.fec/tive/ness
ef.fec/tual
ef.fec.tu/ate
ef.femi/nate

ef.fer/ves/cence
ef.fer/ves/cent
ef.fi/cacy
ef.fi/cien/cies
ef.fi/ciency
ef.fi/cient
ef.fi/ciently
effigy
ef.flu/ent
effort
ef.fort/less
ef.fron/tery
ef.fu/sive
egali/tar.ian
egg
eggnog
ego
ego.cen/tric
ego.cen/trism
egotist
ego.tis/tic
egress
EGYPT
EGYP/TIAN
ei.gen/value
eight
eigh/teen
eigh/teenth
eighth
eighty
either
ejacu/late
ejec/tion
ejector
eking
elabo/rate
elabo/ra/tion
elastic
elas/tici/ties
elas.tic/ity
elat/edly
elation
elder
elderly
elect
elect/ing
elec/tion
elec/tive
elec/toral

elec.tor/ate
elec/tric
elec.tri/cal
elec.tri/cally
elec.tri/cian
elec.tric/ity
elec.tri/fi/ca/tion
elec/trify
elec.tro/car.dio/gram
elec.tro/car.dio/
  graph
elec.tro/chem.is/try
elec.tro/en.cepha.
  lo/graph
elec.tro/cute
elec.tro/cu/tion
elec/trode
elec.troly/sis
elec.tro/mag.net
elec/tron
elec/tronic
elec.troni/cally
elec.tro/plate
elec.tro/shock
elec.tro/static
elec.tro/ther.apy
elec.tro/type
elegant
elegy
element
ele.men/tary
ele/ments
ele/phant
elevate
ele.vat/ing
ele.va/tion
ele.va/tor
eleven
elev/enth
elicit
elic/ited
eli.gi/bil.ity
eli.gi/ble
elimi/nate
elimi/nat/ing
elimi/na/tion
elite
elitism
elixir

ELIZA/BETH, NJ
el.lip/sis
el.lip/ti.cal
elm
ELMIRA, NY
elo.cu/tion
elon/gate
elope
elo/quence
elo/quent
EL PASO, TX
else/where
elu.ci/date
elude
elusive
ema.ci/ate
emanate
eman.ci/pate
eman.ci/pa/tion
eman.ci/pa/tor
emas.cu/late
em.bank/ment
embargo
em.bar/goes
embark
em.barked
em.bar/rass
em.bar/rass/ing
em.bar/rass/ment
em.bassy
em.bat/t͜led
embed
em.bed/ded
em.bel/lish
em.bez/zle
em.bez/zle/ment
em.bit/ter
emblem
em.blem/atic
em.bod/ied
em.bodi/ment
embody
em.body/ing
emboss
em.bosses
embrace
em.braced
em.brac/ing
em.broi/dery

3

em.broil/ment	enact	endure	en.large/ment
embryo	en.ac/tion	en.dur/ing	en.larg/ing
em.bry/onic	en.act/ment	enema	en.light/ened
emerald	enamel	enemies	en.light/en/ment
em.er/alds	enam/eled	enemy	en.list/ment
emerge	enamor	en.er/getic	enmity
emer/gence	en.camp/ment	en.er/geti/cally	enor/mity
emer/gency	en.cap.su/late	en.er/gies	enor/mous
emerg/ing	encase	en.er/gize	enplane
emeri/tus	en.chant/ment	en.er/gizer	enrage
emi/grant	en.cir/cle	energy	en.rap/ture
emi/grate	enclave	ener/vate	enrich
emi.gra/tion	enclose	enforce	en.rich/ing
émigré	en.closed	en.force/able	en.rich/ment
eminent	en.clos/ing	en.forced	enroll
emi/nently	en.clo/sure	en.force/ment	en.rolled
em.is/sary	encode	en.forc/ing	en.rollee
emis/sion	en.cod/ing	en.fran/chise	en.roll/ees
emit	en.com/pass	engage	en.roll/ment
emitted	en.com/pass/ing	en.gage/ment	enroute
emo/tional	en.coun/ter	en.gag/ing	en.sem/ble
emo.tion/al.ism	en.coun/ter/ing	en.gen/der	en.shrine
emo.tion/ally	en.cour/age	engine	ensign
empathy	en.cour/age/ment	en.gi/neer	enslave
em.pha/sis	en.cour/ag/ing	en.gi/neer/ing	ensue
em.pha/size	en.croach	ENGLAND	ensuing
em.phati/cally	en.croach/ment	ENGLISH	ensure
em.phy/sema	en.cum/ber	engrave	entail
empire	en.cum/brance	en.graved	en.tailed
em.piri/cal	en.cyc.li/cal	en.graver	en.tan/gle/ment
em.piri/cally	en.cy.clo/pe.dia	en.grav/ing	enter
em.piri/cism	end	engross	en.ter/ing
employ	en.dan/ger	en.gross/ing	en.ter/prise
em.ployee	en.dan/ger.ing	engulf	en.ter/pris/ing
em.ployer	en.deavor	enhance	en.ter/tain
em.ploy/ing	en.deav/ored	en.hance/ment	en.ter/tain/ing
em.ploy/ment	en/deav/or/ing	en.hances	en.ter/tain/ment
empower	endemic	en.hanc/ing	en.thrall
em.powered	endless	enigma	en.throne
empties	en.doc/rine	enig/matic	enthuse
empty	endorse	enjoin	en.thused
emp.ty/ing	en.dorsed	en.joined	en.thu/si.asm
emulate	en.dorse/ment	enjoy	en.thu/si.ast
emul.si/fied	en.dors/ing	en.joy/able	en.thu/si/as.tic
emul/sify	endow	en.joy/ing	entice
emul/sion	en.dow/ment	en.joy/ment	en.tice/ment
enable	en.dur/able	enlarge	entire
ena/bling	en.dur/ance	en.larged	en.tirely

en.tirety	epitome	er.ro.ne/ously	ethical
en.ti/ties	epito/mize	error	ethi/cally
entitle	epoch	erup/tion	ETHIO/PIA
en.ti/tled	equal	es.ca/late	ethnic
en.ti.tle/ment	equal/ity	es.ca.lat/ing	eth.ni/cal
enti/tling	equali/za/tion	es.ca.la/tion	eth.ni/city
entity	equal/ize	es.ca.la/tor	ethyl/ene
entomb	equal/izer	es.ca/pade	eti/quette
en.tou/rage	equal/iz/ing	escape	ety.mol/ogy
en.trance	equally	es.cape/ment	eu.lo/gize
entrant	equa.nim/ity	eschew	eu.phe/mism
en.trants	equate	escort	eu.pho/ria
entreat	equa/tion	escrow	eu.pho/ric
en.treated	equa.to/rial	ESKIMO	Euro/dollar
entree	equi.dis/tant	ESKIMOS	Euro/mar.ket
en.trenched	equi.lat/eral	es.opha/gus	EUROPE
en.tre/pre/neur	equi.lib/rium	eso/teric	EURO/PEAN
en.tre/pre/neur.ial	equip	es.pe/cial	eu.tha/na.sia
entries	equip/ment	es.pe/cially	evacu/ation
entrust	equipped	es.pio/nage	evad/ers
en.trusted	equip/ping	es.pousal	evalu/ate
en.trust/ing	eq.ui.ta/ble	espouse	evalu/at/ing
entry	eq.ui.ta/bly	esquire	evalu/ation
entwine	equity	essay	evalu/ator
enu.mer/ate	eq.ui/ties	essence	evan/geli.cal
enu.mera/tion	equiva/lence	es.sen/tial	evan.ge/lism
enu.mera/tor	equiva/lency	es.sen/tially	evan.ge/list
enun.ci/ate	equiva/lent	es.tab/lish	evan.ge/lis.tic
en.ve/lope	equivo/cal	es.tab/lish/ing	evan.ge/lize
en.vi/able	era	es.tab/lish/ment	EVANS/TON, IL
envious	eradi.ca/ble	estate	EVANS/VILLE, IN
en.vi/ron/ment	eradi/cate	esteem	evapo/rate
en.vi/ron/mental	erasa/ble	es.teemed	evapo.ra/tion
en.vi.ron/men/tal.ist	erase	es.thetic	evasive
en.vi.ron/men/tally	eraser	es.ti/mate	even
en.vi/rons	erasure	es.ti.mat/ing	even/handed
en.vis/age	era/sures	es.ti.ma/tion	evening
en.vi/sion	erect	es.ti.ma/tor	eve/nings
envoy	erect/ing	es.top/pel	evenly
envy	erec/tion	es.trange	event
enzyme	erector	es.trange/ment	even/tual
epi/demic	ERIE, PA	et cetera	even.tu/al.ity
epi.der/mic	erode	etching	even.tu/ally
epi.der/mis	eroding	etch/ings	ever
epi.lep/tic	erosion	eternal	ever/green
episode	erotic	eter/nally	ever/last/ing
epistle	er.rati/cally	ethe/real	ever/more
epitaph	er.ro.ne/ous	ethic	every

[10]ev.ery/body
[8]every body
[11]ev.ery/day
[8]every day
[10]ev.ery/one
[8]every one
[10]ev.ery/thing
[8]every thing
ev.ery/where
evict
evic/tion
evictor
evi/dence
evident
evi.den/tial
evi.den/ti.ary
evi/dently
evil
evince
evo.lu/tion
evo.lu/tion.ary
evolve
evolv/ing
ewe
ex.ac/er/bate
exact
ex.act/ing
ex.acti/tude
ex.ag.ger/ate
ex.ag/gera/tion
ex.al.ta/tion
ex.ami.na/tion
examine
ex.am/iner
ex.am.in/ing
example
ex.am/ples
ex.as/per.ate

ex.ca/va/tion
ex.ca/va/tor
exceed
ex.ceeded
ex.ceed/ing
ex.ceed/ingly
excel
ex.celled
ex.cel/lence
ex.cel/lency
ex.cel/lent
ex.cel/lently
ex.cel/sior
except
ex.cepted
ex.cept/ing
ex.cep/tion
ex.cep/tional
ex.cep/tion/ally
excerpt
ex.cerpts
excess
ex.ces/sive
ex.ces/sively
ex.ces/sive/ness
ex.change
ex.change/able
ex.chang/ing
excise
ex.cit/able
ex.cite/ment
ex.cit/ing
ex.cit/ingly
exclaim
ex.cla.ma/tion
ex.cla.ma/tory
exclude

ex.cludes
ex.clud/ing
ex.clu/sion
ex.clu/sive
ex.clu/sively
ex.clu/sive/ness
ex.cre/tion
ex.cru.ci/ate
ex.cur/sion
ex.cus/able
excuse
execute
exe/cuted
exe.cu/ting
exe.cu/tion
ex.ecu/tive
exe.cu/tor
exe.cu/tory
ex.ecu/trix
ex.em/plar
ex.em/plary
ex.em.pli/fied
ex.em/plify
exempt
ex.empted
ex.empt/ing
ex.emp/tion
ex.er/cise
ex.er/ciser
ex.er.cis/ing
exert
ex.ert/ing
ex.er/tion
exhaust
ex.hausted
ex.haus/tion
ex.haus/tive
exhibit

ex.hib/ited
ex.hib.it/ing
ex.hi.bi/tion
ex.hibi/tor
ex.hib/its
ex.hila/rate
ex.hor.ta/tion
exhume
exi/gency
ex.is/tence
ex.is/tent
ex.is.ten/tial
ex.is.ten/tial.ism
ex.ist/ing
exit
exodus
ex.oge/nous
ex.on.er/ate
ex.or.bi/tant
ex.or/cise
exotic
expand
ex.pand/able
ex.panded
ex.pand/ing
ex.pan/sion
ex.pan/sion.ary
ex.pan/sion.ist
ex.pa.ti/ation
ex.pa.tri/ate
ex.pa.tri/ation
expect
ex.pec/tan/cies
ex.pec/tancy
ex.pec.ta/tion
ex.pected
ex.pect/ing
ex.pe.di/ency

[8]Noun plus adjective construction. Do not hyphenate. (Each and every body of water is different. The committee will meet every day until the work is done. Every one of you should be proud of that job. Each and every thing she does is neat.)

[10]Indefinite pronoun. (Everybody is going to the lecture. Everyone will be there. Everything you see will be new on the market.)

[11]Compound adjective. Written as one word. (Soon it will be an everyday occurrence.)

ex.pe.di/ent
ex.pe/dite
ex.pe/diter
ex.pe.di/tiously
expel
ex.pelled
ex.pel/ling
expend
ex.pend/able
expended
ex.pend/ing
ex.pendi/ture
expense
ex.penses
ex.pen/sive
ex.pe.ri/ence
ex.pe.ri/enc/ing
ex.peri/ment
ex.peri/men.tal
ex.peri/men/ta/tion
ex.peri/ment/ing
expert
ex.per/tise
ex.pertly
ex.pi.ra/tion
expire
ex.pir/ing
explain
ex.plained
ex.plain/ing
ex.plana/tion
ex.plana/tory
ex.ple/tive
ex.pli/ca.ble
ex.plicit
ex.plic/itly
explode
ex.ploded
ex.plod/ing
exploit
ex.ploi/ta/tion
ex.ploited
ex.ploit/ing
ex.plo.ra/tion
ex.plora/tory
explore
ex.plored
ex.plor/ers
ex.plo/sion

ex.plo/sive
ex.po/nent
ex.po.nen/tial
ex.po.nen/tially
export
ex.porter
ex.port/ers
ex.port/ing
ex.po.si/tion
ex.po.si/tory
ex post facto
ex.po/sure
expound
express
ex.presses
ex.press/ing
ex.pres/sion
ex.pres/sive
ex.pressly
ex.press/way
ex.pul/sion
expunge
ex.qui/site
extant
ex.tem.po/ra/ne.ous
ex.tem.po/rize
extend
ex.tended
ex.tend/ing
ex.ten/sion
ex.ten/sive
ex.ten/sively
extent
ex.tenu/at/ing
ex.te/rior
ex.ter.mi/nate
ex.ter.mi/na/tion
ex.ter.mi/na/tor
ex.ter/nal
ex.ter/nally
extinct
ex.tin/guish
ex.tin/guisher
extol
ex.tolled
ex.tor/tion
extra
extract
ex.tract/able

ex.tracted
ex.trac/tion
ex.trac/tor
ex.tra/cur.ricu.lar
ex.tra/dite
ex.tra/di/tion
ex.tra/ne.ous
ex.tra/or.di.nar.ily
ex.tra/or.di.nary
ex.trapo/late
ex.trapo/la/tion
ex.tra/sen.sory
ex.trava/gant
ex.trava/ganza
extreme
ex.tremes
ex.tremely
ex.trin/sic
ex.tro/vert
extrude
ex.tru/sion
exu.ber/ance
exu.ber/ant
exude
eye
eyeball
eyebrow
eyed
eyeful
eye/glass
eyeing
eye/shade
eye/sight
eyesore
eye/wit.ness
eyrie

F

fable
fabric
fab.ri/cate
fab.ri.ca/tion
fab.ri.ca/tor
fabu/lous
facade
face

face/less
face-lifting (h)
facet
fa.ce/tious
facile
fa.cili/tate
fa.cili/tat/ing
fac.cili/ta/tive
fa.cili/ties
fa.cil/ity
facing
fac.sim/ile
fact
fact-finding (h)
faction
fac/tions
fac/tious
factor
fac.to/rial
fac.to/ries
fac.tor/ing
factory
factual
fac.ul/ties
faculty
fad
fade
fail
fail/ings
failure
fail/ures
faint
faint/hearted
fair
fair/grounds
fair/minded
fair/ness
fairway
faith
faith/ful
faith/fully
fake
fall
fal.la/cies
fal.la/cious
fallacy
fallen
fal.li/bil.ity
fal.li/ble

⁶falloff
⁵fall off
⁶fallout
⁵fall out
follow
false
false/hood
fal.si.fi/ca/tion
fal.si.fy/ing
falsity
falter
fame
fa.mil/iar
fa.mil/iar.ity
fa.mil/iar.ize
fami/lies
family
famine
fam/ished
famous
fan
fanatic
fa.nat/ical
fancier
fan.ci/ers
fan.ci/ful
fancy
fanfare
fan.ta/size
fan.tas/tic
fantasy
far
farce
far.ci/cal
fare

fare/well
far/fetched
FARGO, ND
farm
farmer
farm/house
farm/land
¹far-off (h)
²far off
¹far-out (h)
²far out
far/reach/ing
far/sighted
farther
fas.ci/nate
fas.ci/nat/ing
fashion
fash.ion/able
fash/ioned
fash/ions
fast
fas/tener
fas.ten/ers
fat
fatal
fa.tal/ist
fa.tal.is/tic
fa.tali/ties
fa.tal.ity
fatally
fate
fateful
father
fa.thered
fa.ther/hood

fa.ther/land
fatigue
fatten
fatty
faucet
fault
fault/find/ing
faulty
favor
fa.vor/able
fa.vor/ably
fa.vor/ing
fa.vor/ite
fa.vor.it/ism
faze
fealty
fear
fearful
fear/some
fea.si/bil.ity
fea.si/ble
fea.si/bly
feast
feat
feather
feath.er/bed
feath.er/bed.ding
feath.er/weight
feature
fea/tured
fea.tur/ing
FEBRU/ARY
fe.cun/dity
fed
federal

fed.er.al/ism
fed.er.ali/za/tion
fed.er/ally
fed.era/tion
fee
feeble
fee.ble/minded
feed
feed/back
feed/lot
feed/stock
feed/stuff
feel
feeling
feel/ings
fees
feet
feign
fe.li.ci/ta/tion
fell
fellow
fel.low/man
fel.low/ship
fel.low/woman
felon
fe.lo.ni/ous
felony
felt
female
femi/nine
femi.nin/ity
femi/nism
femi/nist
femur
fence

¹Compound adjective construction. Hyphenate if description precedes noun. (The trip took them to a far-off country. The company moved to a far-out suburb.)

²Adjective plus adverb construction. Do not hyphenate if description follows noun. (They were far off on the estimate. The ball drifted far out into the lake.)

⁵Verb construction. Do not hyphenate. (The work load should fall off by next week. If the envelope is not sealed, the letter may fall out.)

⁶Noun construction. Written as one word. (We do not expect a falloff in sales. The radioactive fallout was slight.)

fencing	fibula	finals	first/hand
fend	fiche	finance	[1]first-rate (h)
fender	fiction	fi.nanced	[8]first rate
ferment	fic/tional	fi.nancer	fiscal
fer/mented	fic.ti/tious	fi.nan/cial	fish
fe.ro/cious	fi.del/ity	fi.nan/cially	fisher
fe.roc/ity	fidget	fi.nan.ci/ble	fish.er/ies
ferret	fi.du.ci/ary	fin.an/cier	fish.er/man
fer/reted	field	fi.nanc/ing	fishery
ferric	fiend/ish	finch	fission
fer.ro/al.loy	fifteen	find	fis.sion/able
fer.ro/mag/netic	fif/teenth	finding	fissure
ferrous	fifth	find/ings	fit
ferry	fifties	fine	fitness
ferry/boat	fif.ti/eth	finesse	fitting
fertile	fifty	finest	fit/tings
fer.tili/za/tion	fight	finger	five
fer.til/izer	fight/ing	fin.ger/nail	fix
fervent	figment	fin.ger/print	fixa/tion
fervor	figu.ra/tive	fin.ger/tip	fixa/tive
fes/ti/val	figure	finis	fixture
festive	figured	finish	fix/tures
festiv/ity	fig.ure/head	fin/ished	fizz
festoon	figu/rine	fin.ish/ing	fizzle
fetch/ing	fig.ur/ing	FINLAND	fiz/zling
fete	fila/ment	fir	flab.ber/gast
fetish	filbert	fire	flab.bi/ness
fetus	filial	firearm	flag
feud	fili/bus/ter	fire/arms	flag.el/late
feudal	FILI/PINO	firebug	flag.el/la/tion
feu.dal/ism	fill	fire/fighter	flag/pole
fever	fillet	fireman	fla/grant
fever/ish	film	fire/place	flail
few	film/strip	fire/proof	flair
fiancé	filter	fire/trap	flam.boy/ant
fiancée	filthi/ness	fire/works	flame
fiasco	filthy	firing	fla/menco
fi.as/coes	fil.tra/tion	firm	flaming
fiber	final	fir.ma/ment	fla/mingo
fi.ber/board	finale	first	flam.ma/ble
fi.ber/glass	fi.nal/ize	[1]first-class (h)	flange
fibrous	finally	[8]first class	flanger

[1]Compound adjective construction. Hyphenate if description precedes noun. (The letter must go by first-class mail. The center did a first-rate job on the contract.)

[8]Noun and adjective construction. Do not hyphenate. (She just completed her first class in word processing. What is the first rate you quoted?)

flannel	flier	fluc.tu/ate	folios
flan/nels	flight	fluc.tu/at/ing	folk
flap	flim.si/ness	fluc.tu/ation	folk/lore
flap/jack	flimsy	fluency	folkway
flare	flinch	flu/ently	follies
[4]flare-up (h)	fling	fluffy	follow
[5]flare up	FLINT, MI	fluid	fol/lowed
flash	flip	flu.id/ity	fol/lower
flash/back	flip/pant	flung	fol.low/ers
flash/bulb	flirt	fluo.res/cence	fol.low/ing
flash/cube	flir.ta/tion	fluo.res/cent	[3]follow-through (h)
flasher	float	fluo.ri/da/tion	[5]follow through
flash/ing	floa.ta/tion	fluo/ride	[3]follow-up (h)
flash/ings	float/ing	fluo/rine	[5]follow up
flash/light	flock	flush	folly
flat	flood	flutter	fond
flatter	flood/gate	flux	fondle
flat/ters	flood/ing	fly	fondly
flat/tery	flood/light	[1]fly-by-night (h)	food
flat/ware	flood/wa.ter	[5]fly by night	food/stuff
flaunt	floor	flyer	fool/har.di/ness
flavor	floor/board	flyers	fool/hardy
flaw/less	floor/ing	foam	foolish
flaws	floor/space	focal	fool/proof
flax	floor/walker	focus	foot
flax/seed	flop	focused	footage
fledg/ling	floral	focuses	foot/ball
fleet	FLORIDA	foc.us/ing	foot/can.dle
fleet/ing	florist	foe	foot/hill
flesh	flo.ta/tion	foggy	foot/hold
flew	flour	foil	footing
flexi/bil.ity	flour/ish	foible	foot/ings
flex/ible	flour/ish/ing	fold	foot/note
flex/ibly	flow	folder	foot/print
flexing	flow/chart	foliage	foot/step
flexi/time	flower	fo.li/ation	foot/wear
flicker	flu	folio	for

[1]Compound adjective construction. Hyphenate if description precedes noun. (I think it is a fly-by-night operation.)
[3]Noun or compound adjective construction. Hyphenate. (You can count on his follow-through. The follow-through report is due today. The follow-up is excellent. Did you complete your follow-up training?)
[4]Noun construction. Hyphenate. (There was a flare-up in the office.)
[5]Verb construction. Do not hyphenate. (Never fail to follow through. Did the secretary follow up on the call? It is less expensive to fly by night. The infection may flare up again.)

foray	for/feited	fort/night	fran.chis/ing
for.bear/ance	for.fei/ture	FORTRAN	fran/chisor
for/bearer	forge	for.tu/itous	frank
forbid	forg.er/ies	for.tu/nate	frank/furter
for.bid/den	forgery	for.tu/nately·	frank/furt.ers
for.bid/ding	forget	fortune	frantic
for.bod/ing	for.get/ting	FORT WAYNE, IN	fran.ti/cally
force	forging	FORT WORTH, TX	fra.ter/nal
force/ful	forgive	forty	fra.ter/nity
forceps	forgot	forum	fra.ter/nize
forc/ible	for.got/ten	forward	fraud
forc/ibly	fork	for/warded	fraudu/lent
forearm	forlorn	for/warder	fraught
fore/armed	form	for.ward/ing	freak
fore/cast	formal	fossil	freak/ish
fore/caster	form.al/de/hyde	foster	freely
fore/cast/ing	for.mal/ity	fos.ter/ing	freedom
fore/close	for.mal/iza/tion	fought	freeing
fore/clo.sure	for.mal/ize	foul	freeway
fore/front	for/mally	found	free/wheel/ing
forego	format	foun.da/tion	freeze
fore/going	for.matted	founder	freez/inğ
fore/gone	for.mat/ting	found/ers	freight
fore/ground	for.ma/tion	found/ing	freighter
fore/head	for.ma/tive	foundry	freight/ing
foreign	for/merly	foun/tain	FREMONT, CA
for/eigner	for.mi.da/ble	four	FRENCH
fore/knowl/edge	formula	four/fold	FRENCH/MAN
foreman	for/mulae	four/some	fre/netic
fore/most	for/mulas	four/teen	frenzy
fore/noon	for.mu/late	fourth	fre.quen/cies
fore/run.ner	for.mu/lat/ing	fox	fre/quency
foresee	for.mu/la/tion	frac/tion	fre/quent
fore/see/able	forsake	frac/tional	fre/quently
fore/shadow	for/swear	frac/ture	fresh
fore/sight	for/sworn	fragile	fresh/man
forest	fort	frag/ment	[11]fresh/wa.ter
fore/stall	forth	frag.men/ta/tion	[8]fresh water
for.es.ta/tion	forth/com/ing	fra/grance	FRESNO, CA
for/ester	forth/right	fra/grant	fretful
for/estry	forth/with	frail	fric/tion
fore/tell	for.ti/fied	frailty	fric/tional
fore/thought	for.ti/fies	frame	FRIDAY
forever	fortify	frame/work	friend
foreward	for.ti/tude	framing	friend/less
fore.warn/ing	FORT	fran/chise	friend.li/ness
forfeit	LAUDERDALE, FL	fran/chisee	friendly

[8]Noun and adjective construction. Do not hyphenate. (Give him a glass of fresh water.)

[11]Compound adjective. Written as one word. (Freshwater fish is my favorite.)

friend/ship
frigate
fright.en/ing
fright/ful
frigid
frill
fringe
fri.vol/ity
frivo/lous
frogman
frolic
frol/icked
frol.ick/ing
frol.ic/some
front
front/age
fron/tier
fron.tis/piece
frost
frosti/ness
frosty
frozen
frugal
fru.gal/ity
fru/gally
fruit
fruit/ful
frui/tion
frus/trate
frus/trated
frus/trat/ing
frus.tra/tion
fry
fudge
fuel
fueled
fueling
fulcrum
fulfill
ful/filled
ful.fill/ing
ful.fill/ment
full
full-blown (h)

fuller
full-fledged (h)
¹full-length (h)
⁸full length
fully
fu.mi.ga/tor
fun
func/tion
func/tional
func/tion/ally
func/tion/ing
fund
fun.da/men/tal
fun.da/men/tally
fun.da/men/tals
funeral
fu.nerals
fungi
fun.gi/cide
fungus
funnel
fun/neled
fun.nel/ing
funny
fur
furious
fu.ri/ously
furlong
fur/lough
furnace
furnish
fur/nishes
fur.nish/ing
fur.nish/ings
fur.ni/ture
furor
furrow
further
fur.ther/ance
fur.ther/ing
fur.ther/more
fur.ther/most
fuse
fuse/lage

fusible
fusion
fuss
fussi/ness
fussy
futile
fu.til/ity
future
fu.tur/istic
fu.tu/rity
fuz.zi/ness
fuzzy

G

gab.ar/dine
gable
gad/about
gadget
GAELIC
gage
gaiety
gain
gain/fully
gala
galaxy
gale
gall
gallant
gal/lantry
gal.ler/ies
gallery
galley
galleys
gallon
gal.lon/age
gal.lop/ing
gall/stone
gal.va/nize
GAMBIA

gambit
gamble
gambler
gamb/ling
game
games/man/ship
gaming
gamut
GAND/HIAN
gang
gang/plank
gap
gape
garage
garbage
garden
GARDEN GROVE,
    CA
GARLAND, TX
garlic
garner
garment
garnish
gar/nishee
gar.nish/ment
gar.ri/son
garter
GARY, IN
gas
gas/eous
gasi.fi/ca/tion
gasket
gas/light
gaso/line
gassed
gastric
gas/tron.omy
gate
gateway
gate/ways
gather
gath/ered
gath.er/ing
gauge

¹Compound adjective construction. Hyphenate if description precedes
noun. (The full-length report was 132 pages long.)
⁸Noun plus adjective construction. Do not hyphenate. (The movie is full
length.)

gaunt/let	geno/cide	get	gladden
gauze	genteel	getaway	glad/dens
gave	gentile	getting	gladi/ator
gay	gentle	⁴get-together (h)	gla.di/olus
gaze	gen.tle/man	⁵get together	glamor
gazette	gen.tle/woman	GETTYS/BURG, PA	glam.or/ize
ga.zet/teer	gently	geyser	glam.or/ous
gear	gentry	GHANA	glance
gearing	genu/flect	ghastly	gland
gear/less	genuine	ghetto	glan.du/lar
gear/shift	genu/inely	ghettos	glare
gelatin	geo/detic	ghost/like	glass
gem	geo/graphic	giant	glass/ily
gene	geo/graph/ical	gib.ber/ish	glass/ware
ge.ne.al/ogy	geo/graph/ically	giblet	glaze
general	ge.og/raphy	GIBRAL/TAR	glazing
gen.er.al/ist	geo.log/ical	gid.di/ness	gleam
gen.er.al/ity	ge.olo/gist	gift	gleam/ing
gen.er.ali/za/tion	geo.met/ric	gi.gan/tic	glean
gen.er.al/ize	geo.met/ri.cal	giggle	gleeful
gen.er/ally	geo.met/ri.cally	gig/gling	GLENDALE, CA
gen.er/ate	ge.ome/try	gigolo	glib
gen.er.at/ing	geo.mor/phic	gill	glide
gen.era/tion	geo/nu.clear	gimmick	glimmer
gen.era/tive	geo/physi.cal	gim/micks	glimpse
gen.era/tor	GEORGIA	gin.ger/bread	glisten
generic	geo/thermal	gin.ger/ly	glis/tened
gen.er.os/ity	ge.ra/nium	ging/ham	glis.ten/ing
gen.er/ous	geri.at/ric	gird	glitter
gen.er/ously	geri.at/rics	girder	global
genes	germ	girdle	glob/ally
genetic	GERMAN	girl/hood	globe
ge.neti/cal	germane	girt	gloom
ge.neti/cally	GERMANY	girth	gloom/ily
ge.neti/cist	ger.mi/cide	gist	gloomy
GENEVA	ger.mi/nate	give	glo.ri.fi/ca/tion
genial	ger.ry/man.der	¹¹give/away	glo.ri/ous
ge.nial/ity	gerund	⁵give away	gloss
genital	gestalt	giving	glos/sary
genius	gestapo	giz/zard	glos.si/ness
ge/niuses	gesture	glacier	glossy
geno/cidal	ges/tured	glad	glove

⁴Noun construction. Hyphenate. (The office has a get-together every
month.)

⁵Verb construction. Do not hyphenate. (When can we get together?
Some people give away priceless possessions.)

¹¹Noun or compound adjective construction. Written as one word. (It is
a giveaway show. Her expression was a giveaway.)

glow
glucose
glue
gluing
glum
glut
glut/ting
glutton
gnarl
gnash
gnawing
gnome
[3]go-ahead (h)
[3]go ahead
goal
gob
goddess
god/desses
god/par.ent
godsend
goes
goggle
going
goiter
golden
gold/brick/ing
gold/smith
golf
gondola
gon.do/las
gon.do/lier
good
good-bye (h)
goodly
good/ness
goods
good/will
gooey
goose
gor/geous
gossip
gotten
goulash
gourmet

govern
gov/erned
gov.ern/ing
gov.ern/ment
gov.ern/men/tal
gov/er/nor
gown
grab
grab/bing
grace
grace/ful
gra/cious
grad
gra.da/tion
grade
gra.di/ent
gradual
gradu/ally
gradu/ate
graft
grafted
grain
gram
grammar
grand
grand/child
grand/father
grand/mother
GRAND
    RAPIDS, MI
grange
granite
grant
grantee
grant/ing
grantor
granu/lated
grape
grape/fruit
grape/vine
graph
graphic
graphi/cal
graphi/cally

graph/ics
graph/ite
grapho/an.aly.sis
graphol/ogy
grapple
grap/pling
grasp
grass
grass/roots
grate/ful
grate/fully
grate/ful/ness
grati/fied
gratify
grati.fy/ing
gratis
grati/tude
gratu/ities
gratu/itous
gratu/ity
grave
gravel
grave/yard
gravi/tate
gravi.ta/tion
gravity
gray
graze
grease
great
great/ness
GREECE
greed
greedy
GREEK
green
GREENS/BORO,
    NC
GREEN/WICH
greet
greet/ing
gre.gari/ous
grey/hound
grid

grid/iron
griev/ance
grieve
grill
grille
grim
grim/ness
grin
grind
grind/stone
grin/ning
grip
gripe
gripper
grip/ping
grit
grit/ting
groan
grocer
gro.cer/ies
grocery
groggy
groom
groove
gross
grossly
gro/tesque
ground
ground/hog
ground/work
group
group/ing
grout
grove
grovel
grov/eled
grov.el/ing
grow
grown
growth
grudge
grudg/ingly
grue/some
grumble

[3]Noun or compound adjective construction. Hyphenate. (She gave the crew a go-ahead signal. When may we expect the go-ahead?)

[5]Verb construction. Do not hyphenate. (You may go ahead and plan your vacation.)

guar.an/tee	gy.ra/tion	halter	hap.pen/stance
guar.an/teed	gy.ro/scope	halting	happier
guar.an/tee/ing		halves	hap.pi/est
guar/anty		ham/burger	happily
guard		hammer	hap.pi/ness
guard/ian		ham.mer/ing	ha.rangue
guard/ian/ship	**H**_____	HAMMOND, IN	harass
gu.ber.na/tor.ial		hamper	ha.rassed
guer/rilla	habeas corpus	HAMPTON, VA	har.bin/ger
guess	hab.er/dash.ery	ham/strung	harbor
guess/work	ha.bili/tate	hand	hard
guest	habit	hand/bag	harden
guid/ance	habita/bil.ity	hand/ball	hard/ened
guide	hab.it/able	hand/book	hard.en/ing
guide/book	habitat	handful	hard/hearted
guide/line	habi/tats	handi/cap	hard/liner
guide/post	ha.bit/ual	handi/capped	hardly
guide/wire	hackney	handi/cap/ping	hard/ship
guiding	hack/neyed	handily	hard/ware
guild	hacksaw	hand.ker/chief	hard/wood
guil.lo/tine	haddock	handle	hard/work/ing
guilty	haggard	handle/bar	harm
GUINEA	haggle	han/dling	harmful
guitar	hag/gling	hand/made	harm/less
gulf	hail	hand-me-down (h)	har.mo.ni/ous
gul.li/ble	hail/storm	handout	har.mo.ni/ously
gulp	hair	hand/outs	har.mo/nize
gum	haircut	hand/picked	harmony
gummed	hairdo	hand/some	har.ness/ing
gump/tion	hair/dresser	hand/work	harp
gun	hair/piece	hand/writ.ten	harpist
gush	hair-raising (h)	hand/writing	harpoon
gusset	HAITI	handy	harried
gut	HAITIAN	handy/man	HARRIS/BURG, PA
gutter	hale	hang	harry
gutting	half	hangar	harsh
guy	half/back	hanger	HART/FORD, CT
guzzle	half/hearted	[6]hangup	harvest
guz/zling	half/way	[5]hang up	har/vester
gym	hall/mark	hap.haz/ard	har.vest/ing
gym.na/sium	hal.lu/ci.nate	hapless	has
gym.nas/tics	hallway	happen	hash
gy.ne.col/ogy	hall/ways	hap/pened	hashish
gypsum	halt	hap.pen/ings	hassle

[5]Verb construction. Do not hyphenate. (When our visitors arrive, please hang up their coats.)

[6]Noun construction. Written as one word. (Sometimes the dictation will consist of only a hangup.)

Spelling and Word Division **179**

hasten	head/quarter	¹heavy-hearted (h)	her.bi/cide
has.ten/ing	head/quar/tered	²heavy hearted	HERCU/LEAN
hastily	head/quar.ters	HEBRAIC	herd
hasti/ness	head/rest	HEBREW	here
hasty	head/start	hectic	here/abouts
hatbox	head/strong	hedge	here/after
hatch	head/way	hedging	hereby
hatch/ery	heal	heed	he.redi/tary
hatch/ing	healer	heed/less	he.red/ity
hate	health	hefty	herein
hatred	health/ful	HEIDEL/BERG	hereof
haughty	health/ful/ness	heifer	heresy
haul	health/ier	height	heretic
hauler	hear	heighten	he.reti/cal
HAVANA	heard	height/ened	hereto
have	hearing	heinous	here/to/fore
haven	hear/ings	heir	here/un.der
havoc	hearsay	he.li/cop.ter	here/with
HAWAII	heart	helipad	heri/tage
HAWAI/IAN	heart/ache	he.li/port	her.mit/age
hawk	heart/break	helium	hernia
hay	heart/burn	hello	her.ni/ate
hay/stack	hearten	helms/man	hero
haywire	heart/ened	help	heroes
hazard	heart/felt	helper	heroic
haz.ard/ous	hearth	helpful	heroin
hazel	hearth/side	help/fully	herring
hazi/ness	heart/ily	help.ful/ness	her.ring/bone
hazy	heart/land	help/less	herself
H-bomb (h)	heart/sick	help/lessly	hesi/tancy
head	hearty	hemi/sphere	hesi/tant
head/ache	heat	hemline	hesi/tate
head/board	heater	hemlock	het.ero/ge/ne.ity
head/count	heave	he.mo/glo.bin	het.ero/ge/neous
header	heaven	hem.or/rhage	heur/istic
head/gear	heav/enly	hem.or/rhoids	hew
head/ings	heavier	hence	hex
head/light	heav/iest	hence/forth	hexagon
head/line	heavily	hench/man	hex/ago/nal
head/long	heavy	hepa.ti/tis	HIALEAH, FL
head/master	¹heavy-handed (h)	herald	hiatus
head-on (h)	²heavy handed	herb	hi.ber.na/tion

¹Compound adjective construction. Hyphenate if description precedes noun. (A heavy-handed supervisor is often not effective. The heavy-hearted boy didn't do well on his test.)

²Adjective plus adverb construction. (The company was heavy handed in its dealings with other organizations. Anne was heavy hearted because she had failed.)

hiccup
hickory
hidden
hide/away
hideous
hideout
hi.er.ar/chic
hi.er.ar/chi.cal
hi.er.ar/chies
hi.er.ar/chy
high
high/ball
highest
high-fidelity (h)
high/light
high-rise (h)
highway
hijack
hi.jacker
hi.jack/ing
hike
hi.lari/ous
hi.lar/ity
hill
hill/billy
hilly
hilt
HIMALA/YAN
himself
hind
hinder
hin/dered
hin/drance
hind/sight
HINDU
hinge
hint
hipbone
hippie
hire
hiring
his.ta/mine
his.to/rian
his/toric
his.tor/ical
his.tor/ic/ally
histo/ries
history
hit

hitch
hitch/hike
hith/erto
hitting
hoard
hobbies
hobby
hockey
hold
hold/ings
holdout
hold/over
hole
holiday
ho.li/ness
ho.lis/tic
HOLLAND
hol.lan/daise
holly
HOLLY/WOOD, CA
HOLLY/WOOD, FL
holo/caust
holo/graph
ho.log.ra/phy
holster
holt
holy
homage
hombre
home
home/builder
home/com/ing
home/grown
home/land
home/less
home/like
home/made
home/mak/ing
home/owner
home/sick
home/site
home/stead
home/work
homi/cide
homily
ho.moge/ne.ous
ho.moge/nize
homonym
homo/nyms

homo/sexual
homo/sexual.ity
HONDURAS
hone
honest
hon/estly
honesty
honey/comb
honey/moon
honey/suckle
HONG/KONG
honing
honor
hon.or/able
hono.rar/ium
hon.or/ary
hon.or/ing
hood
hoodlum
hook
hoot
hop
hope
hopeful
hope/fully
hope/less
hope/less/ness
hoping
hopper
horde
horizon
ho.ri/zons
hori.zon/tal
hori.zon/tally
hormone
hor/mones
hornet
horo/scope
hor.ri/ble
horrid
horrify
horror
hors d'oeuvre
horse
horse/back
horse/less
horse/power
horse/rad.ish
horse/shoe

hor.ti/cul.tural
hor.ti/cul.ture
hose
hosiery
hos.pi/tal
hos.pi/tal.ity
hos.pi/tali/za/tion
host
hostel
hos.telry
hostess
hostile
hos.til/ity
hot
hotel
hotly
hotter
hottest
hour
hourly
house
house/clean
house/coat
house/hold
house/keep
house/mother
house/wares
house/wife
house/wives
house/work
housing
HOUSTON, TX
hovel
hover
how
howdy
however
hubbub
huck/ster
huddle
hue
huffi/ness
huge
hull
human
humane
hu.manis/tic
hu.mani/tar/ian
hu.mani/ties

hu.man/ity	hya/cinth	idea	il.lu.mi/nate
hu.man/ize	hybrid	ideal	il.lu.mi/nat/ing
humanly	hydrant	ide.al/ism	il.lu.mi/na/tion
humble	hy.drants	ide.al/ist	il.lu/mine
humerus	hy.drau/lic	ide.al/is.tic	il.lu/sion
humid	hydro	ide.al/ize	il.lu/sive
hu.midi/fi/ca/tion	hy.dro/car.bon	ideally	il.lu/sory
hu.mid/ify	hy.dro/chlo.ric	iden.ti/cal	il.lus/trate
hu.mid/ity	hy.dro/elec.tric	iden.ti/fi/able	il.lus/trat/ing
hu.mili/ate	hy.dro/foil	iden.ti/fi/ca/tion	il.lus/tra/tion
hu.mil/ity	hy.dro/gen	iden.ti/fied	il.lus/tra/tive
humor	hy.dro/ly.sis	iden/tify	il.lus/tri/ous
hu.mor/ist	hy.dro/pho.bia	iden.ti/fy/ing	image
hu.mor/ous	hygiene	iden/tity	imagi/nary
hunch	hymn	ide.o/logi/cal	imagi.na/tion
hunches	hy.per/bole	ide.olo/gist	imagi.na/tive
hundred	hy.per/ten/sion	ide.ol/ogy	imagine
hun/dreds	hyp.no/sis	idiom	imag.in/ing
hun/dredth	hyp/notic	idi.o/matic	im.bal/ance
hun.dred/weight	hyp.no/tize	idi.o/syn/crasy	imbibe
hung	hy.po/al.ler/genic	idiotic	im.bro/glio
HUNGAR/IAN	hy.po/chon/dria	idle	im.bro/glios
HUNGARY	hy.po/chon/driac	idle/ness	imbue
hunger	hy.poc/risy	idol	imi.ta/tion
hun.ger/ing	hy.po/crite	idola/try	imi.ta/tor
hun/grily	hy.po/der.mic	idolize	im.macu/late
hungry	hy.pothe/ses	igloo	im.macu/lately
hunt	hy.pothe/sis	ig.ni/tion	im.ma/nent
hunter	hy.pothe/size	ig.no/mini/ous	im.ma.te/rial
hunting	hy.po/theti.cal	ig.no/miny	im.ma/ture
HUNTING/TON, WV	hys.ter/ec/tomy	ig.no.ra/mus	im.mea/sur/able
HUNTING/TON	hys.te/ria	ig.no/rance	im.mea/sur/ably
BEACH, CA	hys.teri/cal	ig.no/rant	im.me.di/acy
HUNTS/VILLE, AL	hys.ter/ics	ignore	im.me.di/ate
hurdle		ignor/ing	im.me.di/ately
HURON		ill	immense
hurrah		illegal	im.mensely
hur.ri/cane		il.le.gal/ity	im.mense/ness
hur/riedly	**I**	il.legi/bil.ity	im.men/sity
hurry		il.legi/ble	immerse
hurt		il.le/giti/macy	im.mer/sion
hurtful	ice	il.le/giti/mate	im.mi/grant
hurting	iceberg	illicit	im.mi.gra/tion
husband	ice/breaker	ILLI/NOIS	im.mi/nence
hus/bands	ICELAND	il.lit.er/acy	im.mi/nent
huski/ness	ICE/LANDER	il.lit.er/ate	im.mo/bile
husky	ICE/LANDIC	illness	im.mo.bil/ity
hustle	icer	ill/nesses	im.mo.bi/li/za/tion
hustler	icicle	il.logi/cal	im.mo.bi/lize
hut	icing	ill-prepared (h)	im.mod.er/ate
	IDAHO		

im.mod/est
immoral
im.mo.ral/ity
im.mor/tal
im.mor/tal.ity
im.mov/able
immune
im.mu/nity
im.mu.ni/za/tion
im.mu.ta/ble
impact
impair
im.paired
im.pair/ment
impanel
im.paneled
im.par/tial
im.pass/able
impasse
im.pas.si/bil.ity
im.pas/sioned
im.pa/tience
im.pa/tient
impeach
im.peach/ment
im.pec.ca/ble
impede
im.pedi/ment
impel
im.pelled
im.pel/ling
im.pend/ing
im.pene/tra/ble
im.pera/tive
im.per/cep/ti.ble
im.per/fect
im.per/fec/tion
im.pe/rial
im.per/sonal
im.per/son.ate
im.per/vi.ous
im.petu/ous
impetus
impinge
im.pla/ca.ble
im.ple/ment
im.ple/men/ta/tion
im.ple/ment/ing
im.pli/cate
im.pli.ca/tion

im.plic/it
implied
implies
implore
imply
im.ply/ing
im.po/lite
im.poli/tic
im.pon/dera.ble
import
im.por/tance
im.por/tant
im.por/tantly
im.por.ta/tion
im.porter
im.port/ers
im.port/ing
impose
im.pos/ing
im.po.si/tion
im.pos.si/bil.ity
im.pos.si/ble
im.po/tence
im.po/tent
impound
im.pounded
im.pound/ment
im.pov.er.ish
im.prac/ti/ca.ble
im.prac/ti.cal
im.prac/ti/cal.ity
im.pre/cise
im.preg/na.ble
im.preg/nate
im.preg/na/tion
im.pre.sa/rio
impress
im.pressed
im.pres/sion
im.pres/sion/able
im.pres/sive
imprint
im.printed
im.print/ing
im.prison
im.pris/oned
im.pris/on/ment
im.proba/bil.ity
im.prob/able
im.promptu

im.proper
im.prop/erly
im.pro/pri.ety
improve
im.proved
im.prove/ment
im.provi/dence
im.provi/dent
im.prov/ing
im.pro/vise
im.pru/dent
im.pu/dent
impulse
im.pul/sive
im.pu/nity
impute
ina.bil/ity
in.ac.ces/si/bil.ity
in.ac.ces/si.ble
in.ac.cu/ra/cies
in.ac.cu/racy
in.ac.cu/rate
in.ac/tive
in.ac.tiv/ity
in.ade/qua/cies
in.ade/quacy
in.ade/quate
in.ade/quately
in.ad.mis/si.ble
in.ad.ver/tent
in.ad.vis/able
in.ali.en/able
in.ap.pli/ca.ble
in.ap.pro/pri.ate
in.ar/ticu/late
in.as/much
in.at.ten/tion
in.au.di/ble
in.au.gu/ral
in.au.gu/rate
in.au.gu/rat/ing
in.au.gu.ra/tion
inboard
inbound
inbred
in.can/des/cence
in.can/des/cent
in.ca.pa/bil.ity
in.ca.pa/ble
in.ca.pa/ci/ta/tion

in.ca.pac/ity
in.car/cera/tion
in.cen.di/ary
incense
in.cen/tive
in.cep/tion
in.ces/sant
inch
in.ci/dence
in.ci/dent
in.ci.den/tal
in.ci.den/tally
in.cin/era/tor
in.cipi/ent
in.ci/sion
in.ci/sive
incisor
incite
in.clem/ent
in.cli.na/tion
incline
in.clined
in.clud/able
include
in.clud/ing
in.cludes
in.clu/sion
in.clu/sive
in.cog/nito
in.co.her/ence
in.co.her/ent
income
in.com/ing
in.com.mu/ni/ca.ble
in.com.pa/ra.ble
in.com/pati/bil.ity
in.com/pat/ible
in.com.pe/tence
in.com.pe/tent
in.com/plete
in.com/pletely
in.com/pre/hen/si.ble
in.con/ceiv/able
in.con/clu/sive
in.con/gru/ity
in.con/gru.ous
in.con.se/quen/tial
in.con/sid/er.ate
in.con/sist/ent
in.con/spic/u.ous

in.con/testa/bil.ity
in.con/test/able
in.con.tro/vert/ible
in.con/tro/verti/bil.ity
in.con.ve/nience
in.con.ve/nienc/ing
in.con.ve/nient
in.con/vert/ible
in.cor.po/rate
in.cor.po/rat/ing
in.cor.po/ra/tion
in.cor/rect
in.cor/rectly
in.cor.ri/gi.ble
in.cor/rupt/ible
in.crease
in.creas/ing
in.creas/ingly
in.credi/bil.ity
in.cred/ible
in.cre.du/lity
in.credu/lous
in.cre/ment
in.cre/men/tal
in.cre/men/tally
in.crim.i/nate
in.cu.ba/tor
in.cul/cate
in.cum/bent
incur
in.cur/able
in.curred
in.cur/ring
indebted
in.debt/ed/ness
in.de/cent
in.de.ci/sion
in.de.ci/sive
indeed
in.de.fen/si.ble
in.defi/nite
in.defi/nitely
in.del/ible
in.del/ibly
in.demni/fi/ca/tion
in.dem/nify
in.dem/nity
indent
in.den.ta/tion
in.den/tion

in.den/ture
INDEPEN/DENCE,
MO
in.de.pen/dent
in.de/pend/ently
in.de/scrib/able
in.de/struct/ible
in.de.ter/min/able
in.de.ter/mi/nate
index
indexed
indexes
in.dex/ing
INDIA
INDIAN
INDIANA
INDIANAP/OLIS,
IN
in.di/cate
in.di.cat/ing
in.di.ca/tion
in.dica/tive
in.di.ca/tor
indices
indict
in.dict/able
in.dict/ment
INDIES
in.dif/fer/ence
in.dif/fer.ent
in.dige/nous
in.di/gent
in.di/gest/ible
in.di.ges/tion
in.dig/nant
in.dig.na/tion
in.dig/nity
indigo
in.di/rect
in.di/rectly
in.di/rect/ness
in.dis/cern/ible
in.dis/creet
in.dis/cre/tion
in.dis/crimi/nately
in.dis/pen/sable
in.dis/posed
in.dis/put/able
in.dis/solu.ble
in.dis/tinct

in.dis/tin/guish/able
in.di.vid/ual
in.di/vidu/al.ism
in.di/vidu/al.ity
in.di/vidu/al.ize
in.di/vidu/ally
INDO/CHINA
in.doc/tri/nate
in.doc/tri/na/tion
in.do/lence
in.do/lent
INDO/NESIA
INDO/NESIAN
indoors
in.du.bi/table
induce
in.duce/ment
in.duc/ing
in.duc/tee
in.duc/tion
in.duc/tive
in.duc/tor
indulge
in.dul/gence
in.dulg/ing
in.dus/trial
in.dus/tri/al.ist
in.dus/tri/ali/za/tion
in.dus/tri/ally
in.dus/tries
in.dus/tri.ous
in.dus/try
in.dus/try/wide
ine.bri/ate
in.ed/ible
in.ef.fec/tive
in.ef.fec/tual
in.ef.fi/cien/cies
in.ef.fi/ciency
in.ef.fi/cient
in.elas/tic
in.eli.gi/ble
inept
ine.quali/ties
ine.qual/ity
in.eq.ui/ta.ble
in.eq.ui/ties
in.eq/uity
inertia
in.es.cap/able

in.evi.ta/ble
in.evi.ta/bly
inexact
in.ex.act/ness
in.ex.cus/able
in.ex.cus/ably
in.ex/haust/ible
in.exo.ra/bly
in.ex.pen/sive
in.ex.pen/sively
in.ex.pe/ri/enced
in.ex/pert
in.ex/plain/able
in.ex.pli/ca.ble
in.ex/plicit
in.fal.li/ble
in.fa/mous
infamy
infancy
infant
in.fan/tile
in.fan/try
in.fatu/ation
infect
in.fec/tion
in.fec/tious
infer
in.fer/ence
in.fer.en/tial
in.fe/rior
in.fe.ri/or.ity
inferno
in.ferred
in.fer/ring
in.fes.ta/tion
in.fi.del/ity
in.fight/ing
in.fil/trate
in.fi/nite
in.fi/nitely
in.fini/tesi/mal
in.fini/tive
in.fir/mary
in.fir/mity
inflame
in.flam/ma.ble
in.flam/ma/tion
in.flam/ma/tory
inflate
in.flated

in.fla/tion
in.fla/tion.ary
in.flec/tion
in.flex/ible
inflict
in.flic/tion
in.flicts
inflow
in.flu/ence
in.flu/en/tial
in.flu/enza
influx
inform
in.for/mal
in.for/mal/ity
in.for/mally
in.for/mant
in.for.ma/tion
in.for.ma/tional
in.for.ma/tive
in.formed
in.form/ing
in.fo/sys.tems
in.frac/tion
in.fra/red
in.fra/struc/ture
in.fre/quent
in.fre/quently
in.fringe/ment
infuse
in.gen/ious
in.gen/iously
in.ge.nu/ity
in.genu/ous
ingot
in.grained
ingrate
in.grati/tude
in.gre/dient
in.grown
inhabit
in.habi/tant
in.har.mo/ni.ous
in.her/ent
in.her/ently
inherit
in.heri/tance
in.her/ited
inhibit
in.hib/ited

in.hibi/tion
in.hibi/tor
in.hibi/tory
in.hospi/ta.ble
inhuman
in.human/ity
in.imi/cal
in.iquity
initial
ini/tially
ini/tials
initi/ate
initi/at/ing
initi/ation
initi/ative
inject
in.jec/tion
in.jec/tor
in.ju.di/cious
in.junc/tion
in.junc/tive
injure
in.ju/ries
in.jur/ing
in.ju/ri.ous
injury
in.jus/tice
ink
inkling
inlaid
inland
inlay
inlet
inmate
inn
innate
inner
inn.ner/spring
inning
inn/keeper
in.no/cence
in.nocu/ous
in.no/vate
in.no.va/tion
in.no.va/tive/ness
in.no.va/tor
in.nu.mer/able
in.ocu/late
in.ocu.la/tion
in.op.era/ble

in.op.era/tive
in.op.por/tune
in.or.di/nate
in.or.di/nately
in.or/ganic
in.pa/tient
input
in.put/ting
inquest
inquire
in.quired
in.qui/ries
in.quir/ing
inquiry
in.quisi/tive
in.quisi/tive/ness
ın.quisi/tor
inroad
in.san/ity
in.sa.ti/able
inscribe
in.scrip/tion
in.scru.ta/ble
insect
in.sec.ti/cide
in.se/cure
in.semi/na/tion·
in.sen.si/tive
in.sen.si/tiv.ity
in.sepa/ra.ble
insert
in.sert/able
in.serted
in.sert/ing
in.ser/tion
inside
insider
in.sidi/ous
insight
in.sights
in.sig/nia
in.sig/nifi/cance
in.sig/nifi/cant
in.sin/cere
in.sinu/ation
insist
in.sist/ing
insofar
in.so/lence
in.solu/ble

in.sol/vency
in.sol/vent
inspect
in.spected
in.spect/ing
in.spec/tion
in.spec/tor
in.spi.ra/tion
in.spi.ra/tional
inspire
in.spired
in.spir/ing
in.sta/bil.ity
install
in.stal/la/tion
in.stalled
in.staller
in.stall/ing
in.stall/ment
in.stance
instant
in.stan/ta/ne.ous
in.stan/ta/ne/ously
in.stantly
instants
instead
in.sti/gate
in.sti.ga/tor
instill
in.stinct
in.stinc/tive
in.sti/tute
in.sti.tu/tion
in.sti.tu/tional
in.sti.tu/tional.ize
in.struct
in.struct/ing
in.struc/tion
in.struc/tional
in.struc/tive
in.struc/tor
in.stru/ment
in.stru/mental
in.stru/men/tal.ity
in.stru/men/ta/tion
in.sub/or/di/nate
in.sub.or/di/na/tion
in.suf.fi/ciency
in.suf.fi/cient
insular

3

in.su.lar/ity
in.su/late
in.su.la/tion
in.su.la/tor
in.sura/bil.ity
in.sur/able
in.sur/ance
insure
insured
in.sureds
insurer
in.surers
in.sur/gent
in.sur/ing
in.sur/mount/able
in.sur/rec/tion
intact
intake
in.tan.gi/ble
integer
in.te/gral
in.te/grate
in.te.gra/tion
in.teg/rity
in.tel/lect
in.tel/lec/tual
in.tel/lec/tu.al.ize
in.tel/lec/tually
in.tel.li/gence
in.tel.li/gent
in.tel.li/gently
in.tel.li/gi.ble
in.tem/per/ance
intend
in.ten/dant
in.tend.ing
intense
in.tensely
in.ten.si/fi/ca/tion
in.ten.si/fied
in.ten/sify
in.ten/sity
in.ten/sive
in.ten/sively
intent
in.ten/tion
in.ten/tional
in.ten/tion/ally
inter
interact

in.ter/acted
in.ter/ac.tion
in.ter/ac.tive
in.ter/agency
in.ter/bank
in.ter/branch
in.ter/cede
in.ter/cept
in.ter/cep/tion
in.ter/ces/sion
in.ter/change
in.ter/change/able
in.ter/change/abil.ity
in.ter/city
in.ter/coastal
inter/com
in.ter/com.pany
in.ter/con.nected
in.ter/con.nec/tion
in.ter/con.ti/nen/tal
in.ter/co.re/la/tion
in.ter/cor.po/rate
in.ter/course
in.ter/de.nomi/na/
    tional
in.ter/de.pen/dence
in.ter/de.pen/dent
in.ter/dict
in.ter/dis.ci/plin.ary
in.terest
in.ter/ested
in.ter/est/ing
in.ter/face
in.ter/fac/ing
in.ter/fere
in.ter/fered
in.ter/fer.ence
in.ter/fer/ing
in.ter/firm
in.ter/govern/mental
in.ter/group
interim
in.ter/indus.try
in.te/rior
in.ter/ject
in.ter/jec/tion
in.ter/lac/ing
in.ter/leave
in.ter/lock/ing
in.ter/locu/tory

in.ter/me.di/ar.ies
in.ter/me.di/ary
in.ter/me.di/ate
in.ter/ment
in.ter/mis/sion
in.ter/mit/tent
in.ter/modal
intern
in.ter/nal
in.ter/nally
in.ter/na.tional
in.ter/na.tion/al.ize
in.ter/na.tion/ali/
    za/tion
in.ter/nist
in.tern/ment
in.tern/ship
in.ter/of.fice
in.ter/or.gani/za/tion
in.ter/or.gani/za/tional
in.ter/per/sonal
in.ter/play
in.ter/po.late
in.ter/po.la/tion
in.ter/pret
in.ter/pret/able
in.ter/pre/ta/tion
in.ter/pre/ta/tive
in.ter/preter
in.ter/preted
in.ter/pret/ing
in.ter/ra.cial
in.ter/rater
in.terred
in.ter/re.late
in.ter/re.la/tion
in.ter/re.la/tion/ship
in.ter/ring
in.ter.ro/gate
in.ter.ro/ga/tion
in.ter.ro/ga/tor
in.ter/rupt
in.ter/rupt/ing
in.ter/rup/tion
in.ter/sec/tion
in.ter/sperse
in.ter/state
in.ter/sys.tem
in.ter/twine
in.ter/val

in.ter/vene
in.ter/ven.ing
in.ter/ven/tion
in.ter/view
in.ter/viewer
in.ter/view.ing
inter vivos trust
in.ter/woven
in.tes/tate
in.tes/tine
in.ti/macy
in.ti/mate
in.ti/mately
in.timi/date
into
in.tol.er/able
in.tol.er/ance
in.tol.er/ant
in.to.na/tion
in.toxi/cant
in.toxi/cate
in.trac/ta.ble
in.tra.mu/ral
in.tra/state
in.tra.ve/nous
in.tri/cacy
in.tri/cate
in.trigue
in.trigu/ing
in.trin/sic
in.trin/sic.ally
in.tro/duce
in.tro/duc/ing
in.tro/duc/tion
in.tro/duc/tory
in.tro/spec/tion
in.tro/spec/tive
in.tro/vert
intrude
in.truder
in.trudes
in.tru/sion
in.tui/tion
in.tui/tive
in.tui/tively
in.un/date
in.un.da/tion
invade
invaded
invader

invalid
in.vali/date
in.valu/able
in.vari/ably
in.vari/ant
in.va/sion
invent
in.vented
in.ven/tion
in.ven/tive
in.ventor
in.ven.to/ries
in.ven/tory
inverse
in.versely
invest
in.ves.ti/gate
in.ves.ti/gat/ing
in.ves.ti/ga/tion
in.ves.ti/ga/tive
in.vest/ing
in.vest/ment
in.ves/tor
in.vigo/rate
in.vin.ci/ble
in.vio/late
in.vis/ible
in.vi.ta/tion
in.vi.ta/tional
invite
in.vit/ing
in.vo.ca/tion
invoice
in.voices
in.voic/ing
invoke
in.vol.un/tar.ily
in.vol.un/tary
involve
in.volved
in.volve/ment
in.volv/ing
inward
iodine
ion
ionize
ioni.za/tion
iono/sphere
iota
IOWA
ipso facto

IRAN
IRANIAN
IRAQ
irate
IRELAND
iri.des/cent
iris
IRISH
irk/some
iron
ironed
ironic
ironi/cally
ironing
irony
ir.ra/tional
ir.regu/lar
ir.regu/lari/ties
ir.rele/vance
ir.rele/vancy
ir.rele/vant
ir.re.li/gious
ir.repa/ra.able
ir.re/press/ible
ir.re/proach/able
ir.re/sist/ible
ir.reso/lute
ir.re/spec/tive
ir.re/spon/si.ble
ir.re/spon/sive
ir.re/triev/able
ir.re/versi.ble
ir.revo/ca.ble
ir.ri.ga/tion
ir.ri.ta/ble
ir.ri/tant
ir.ri/tate
ir.ri/tat/ing
ir.ri.ta/tion
IRVING, TX
ISLAM
island
isolate
iso/lated
iso.lat/ing
iso.la/tion
iso.la/tion.ist
iso.met/rics
iso.ther/mal
ISRAEL

ISRAELI
ISRA/ELITE
is.su/ance
issue
issued
issuer
issuing
isthmus
it
ITALIAN
itali/cize
ITALY
itch
item
itemi.za/tion
itemize
item/ized
item.iz/ing
iterate
it.era/tion
in.era/tive
itin/er/ant
itin/er/ary
itself
ivory
ivy

J_____

jack
jackass
jacket
jack/ham.mer
jack/knife
jackpot
JACKSON, MI
JACKSON/VILLE,
    FL
jail
jail/break
jam
JAMAICA
jammed
janitor
jani.to/rial
JANUARY

JAPAN
JAPA/NESE
jar
jargon
jarred
jaun/dice
jaunt
javelin
jaw
jawbone
jazz
jealous
jeans
jell
jelly
jeop.ar/dize
jeop.ar/diz/ing
jeop/ardy
jersey
JERSEY CITY, NJ
jet
jet/liner
jetport
jetsam
jet.ti/son
jewel
jeweler
jew.el/ers
jewelry
jig
jigsaw
jingle
jin/gling
jinx
jitney
jitters
jittery
job
jobber
jobbing
job/holder
jobless
job.less/ness
job/seeker
jobsite
jock
jockey
jog
jogger
jogging

3

JOHAN/NESBURG	juicy	keen	kind.er/garten
join	JULY	keep	kindest
joining	jumble	keep/sake	kind/ness
joint	jumbo	keg	kindred
jointly	jump	KEN/TUCKY	kinetic
joist	jumper	KENYA	king
joke	junc/tion	kernel	kingdom
joker	junc/ture	kero/sene	kink
jolt	jungle	kettle	kinsman
jon/quil	junior	ket.tle/drum	kit
JORDAN	junk	key	kitchen
josh	junk/yard	key/board	kitch.en/ette
jot	junta	keyed	kite
jot/tings	juries	key/hole	knack
journal	ju.ris/dic/tion	KEYNES	knap/sack
jour.nal/ism	ju.ris/dic/tional	KEYNE/SIAN	knead
jour.nal/ist	ju.ris/pru/dence	keynote	knee
jour.nal/is.tic	jurist	key/noted	kneecap
journey	juror	key/noter	kneel
jour.ney/man	just	key/punch	knew
joy	justice	keysort	knick/knack
joyful	jus.ti.fi/able	key/stone	knife
joy.ful/ness	jus.ti.fi/ably	key/stroke	knight
joyous	jus.ti.fi/ca/tion	khaki	knit
joy/ously	jus.ti/fied	kick	knit/ting
joyride	jus.ti/fies	kick/back	knob
ju.bi/lant	justify	kickoff	knock
ju.bi/lee	jus.ti.fy/ing	kid	[6]knock/down
judge	justly	kidded	[5]knock down
judge/ship	ju.ve/nile	kidding	[6]knock/out
judging	jux.ta/po.si/tion	kidnap	[5]knock out
judg/ment		kid/napped	knoll
judg/mental		kid.nap/ping	knot
ju.di/cial		kill	knotted
ju.di/ciary		killing	knotty
ju.di/ci.ous	**K**	kiln	know
jug		kilo	[4]know-how (h)
juggle	ka.lei/do/scope	kilo/cy.cle	knowl/edge
jug/gling	KANSAS	ki.lo/gram	knowl/edge/able
jugular	KANSAS CITY,	ki.lo/me.ter	KNOX/VILLE, TN
juice	MO KA	ki.lo/watt	knuckle
juici/ness	keel	kind	kook

[4]Noun construction. Hyphenate. (The engineers had the know-how to get the project done.)

[5]Verb construction. Do not hyphenate. (They will knock down two walls to enlarge the office. All the plaster will be knocked out in the remodeling.)

[6]Noun construction. Written as one word. (The judge scored a knockdown for the novice fighter. He won the fight with a knockout.)

KOREA
KOREAN
kowtow
KREMLIN
KUWAIT
kudos

L

lab
label
labeled
label/ing
labor
labo.ra/to/ries
labo.ra/tory
laborer
la.bor/ers
la.bor/sav/ing
laby/rinth
lace
lac.era/tion
lack
lack/lus.ter
lacquer
lac/quered
la.crosse
lad
ladder
laden
ladies
lading
lady/like
lag
laggard
lagged
lagging
lagoon
laid

lain
laity
lake
lake/side
LAKE/WOOD, CA
lamb
lambert
lame
lament
la.men/ta.ble
lami/nate
lami.nat/ing
lami.na/tion
lamp
lampoon
lamp/shade
LANCAS/TER, PA
lance
land
land/fill
landing
land/lady
land/locked
land/lord
land/mark
land/owner
land/scape
land/scap/ing
land/slide
lane
lan/guage
lan/guish
lanolin
LANSING, MI
lantern
lap
lapped
lapping
lapse
lapsing
larceny

large
largess
larvae
lar.yn/gi.tis
larynx
laser
lash
lass
lasso
lassoed
las.so/ing
lassos
last
lasting
lastly
LAS VEGAS, NV
latch/key
late
latency
latent
later
lateral
lat.er/ally
latex
lath
lathe
lather
LATIN
LATIN AMERICA
LATIN
    AMER/ICAN
lati/tude
latter
lattice
laud
laud/able
lauda/tory
laugh
laugh.ing/stock
laugh/ter
launch

launch/ing
launder
laun/dered
laun/dress
laun/dries
laundry
lava.to/ries
lava/tory
lav.en/der
lavish
lavishly
lav.ish/ness
law
lawful
law/fully
law/maker
lawn
lawn/mower
lawsuit
law/suits
lawyer
lax
laxity
lay
layer
laying
layman
layoff
layout
layover
lazily
lazi/ness
lazy
leach
lead
leader
lead.er/ship
[3]lead-in (h)
[5]lead in
[11]leadoff
[5]lead off

[3]Noun or compound adjective construction. Hyphenate. (The lead-in wire was broken. This pipe will be the lead-in from the street.)

[5]Verb construction. Do not hyphenate. (The marshals will lead in the graduates. The keynote address will lead off the seminar.)

[11]Noun or adjective construction. Written as one word. (The speaker is an excellent leadoff for the seminar program. The leadoff batter struck out.)

[7]lead-time (h)
leaf
leaflet
league
leak
leakage
leak/proof
leaky
lean
leaner
learn
learner
learn/ers
learn/ing
leap
lease
lease/back
lease/hold
lease/holder
leash
least
leather
leath.er/neck
leath/ers
leave
leaven
lectern
lecture
lec/turer
led
ledger
leery
leeway
left
left-handed (h)
left/over
leg
lega/cies
legacy
legal

legal/ism
legal.is/tic
legal/ity
legally
le.ga/tion
legend
legen/dary
legible
legi/bil.ity
legibly
legion
leg.is/late
leg.is/la/tion
leg.is/la/tive
leg.is/la.tor
leg.is.la/ture
le.giti/macy
le.giti/mate
le.giti/mize
legume
leisure
lei/surely
lemon
lem.on/ade
lend
length
lengthen
length/ens
length/wise
lengthy
le.niency
lenient
lens
lenses
leprosy
lesion
less
lessee
lessen
less/ened

less/en/ing
lesser
lesson
lessor
let
[6]letdown
[5]let down
lethal
le.thar/gic
leth/argy
letter
let.ter/head
let.ter/ing
letter-perfect (h)
let.ter/shop
letters
   tes.ta/men/tary
letting
lettuce
[6]letup
[5]let up
levee
level
leveled
level/headed
level/ing
lever
le.ver/age
levied
levies
Levis
levity
levy
LEXING/TON, KY
lia.bili/ties
lia.bil/ity
liable
li.ai/son
lib
li.bel/ous

liberal
lib.er/ali/za/tion
lib.er/al.ize
lib.er/ate
lib.era/tion
lib.era/tor
LIBERIA
liberty
li.brarian
library
LIBYA
LIBYIAN
license
li.censee
li.censes
li.cens/ing
li.cen/tious
lick
lico/rice
lid
lien
lieu
lieu.ten/ant
life
life/blood
life/less
life/line
life/long
life/style
life/time
lift
liga/ment
light
lighten
light.en/ing
lighter
light/ning
light/weight
likable
like

[4]Noun construction. Hyphenate. (Be sure to give the data processing department enough lead-time.)

[5]Verb construction. Do not hyphenate. (Your magnetic card will let up the entrance gate. Your driving over the magnetic strip will let down the gate.)

[6]Noun construction. Written as one word. (There is no letup of the winter weather in sight. The team experienced a letdown after their exhausting tour.)

like.li/hood	[6]linkup	live.li/hood	lofty
like/wise	[5]link up	live/stock	log
lilac	li.no/leum	LIVONIA, MI	log/a.rithm
lily	linseed	load	loga/rith.mic
LIMA	lintel	loader	loges
limb	lion	loaf	logging
limber	lip	loafer	logic
limbo	liquefy	loan	logical
lime	li/queur	loathe	logi/cally
lime/light	liquid	loaves	lo.gis/tics
lim.er/ick	liq.ui/date	lobbies	logo
lime/stone	liq.ui.da/tion	lobby	logo/type
limit	liq.ui.da/tor	lob.by/ing	log/roll/ing
limi.ta/tion	li.quid/i.ty	lob.by/ist	loin
limited	liquor	lobster	lol.li/pop
lim.it/ing	list	local	LONDON
lim.it/less	listen	locale	lone
lim.ou/sine	lis/tener	lo.cali/ties	lone.li/ness
limp	list/less	lo.cal/ity	lone/some
LINCOLN, NE	lit	lo.cali/za/tion	LONG BEACH, CA
linden	lit/eracy	lo.cal/ize	lon.gev/ity
line	literal	locally	lon.gi/tude
lineage	lit.er/ally	locate	lon.gi.tu/di.nal
lineal	lit.er/ary	lo.ca/tion	long/shore.man
linear	lit.era/ture	lo.ca/tional	long/wall
lin.ear/ity	litho/graphic	lock	look
lin/early	lithog/ra.phy	lockbox	lookout
linen	LITHU/ANIA	locker	loom
liner	liti/gant	[6]lockout	loop
[6]lineup	liti/gate	[5]lock out	loop/back
[5]line up	liti.ga/tion	lock/step	looper
linger	litter	lo.co.mo/tive	loop/hole
lin.ge/rie	little	locus	loose
lingual	LITTLE ROCK, AR	locust	loose/leaf
lin.guis/tic	li.tur/gi.cal	lodge	loosen
lining	liturgy	lodger	loos.en/ing
link	live	lodging	loot
linkage	lively	lodg/ings	looting

---

[5]Verb construction. Do not hyphenate. (Please line up the file cabinets on the wall. The company will link up the offices via telecomputer services. Management intends to lock out the workforce.)

[6]Noun construction. Do not hyphenate. (The lineup for the game remains unchanged. We now have computer linkup among all our branches. Management countered the threatened strike with a lockout.)

lop/sided	LUBBOCK, TX	lynch	mag.nani/mous
lord	lube	ly.on/naise	magnate
lore	lu.bri/cant	lyre	mag.ne/sia
LOS ANGE-	lu.bri/cate	lyric	mag.ne/sium
LES, CA	lu.bri/cat.ing	lyrical	magnet
lose	lu.bri/ca/tion	lyri/cism	mag/netic
loser	lucid		mag.net/ism
loses	lu.cid/ity		mag.ne/tize
losing	luck		mag.ni/fi/ca/tion
loss	luckier	**M**	mag.ni/fi/cent
losses	lucky		magnify
lost	lu.cra/tive	maca/roni	mag.ni/tude
lot	lug	maca/roon	ma.hog/any
lotion	luggage	MA.CHIA/VEL/-	maid
lot.ter/ies	lumber	LIAN	mail
lottery	lum.ber/man	ma.chin/able	mail/abil.ity
loud	lum.ber/yard	machine	mail/able
LOUISI/ANA	lumen	ma.chin/ery	mailbag
LOUIS/VILLE, KY	lu.mi/naire	ma.chin/ing	mailbox
lounge	lu.mi/nance	ma.chin/ist	mailer
louse	lu.mi/nary	mack/erel	mail/gram
lousy	lu.mi/nous	macki/naw	mailing
love	lump	MACON, GA	mail/ings
love.li/ness	lumpy	macro	mailman
love/lorn	lunacy	mac.ro/econo/	[6]mailout
love/mak/ing	lunar	met.ric	[5]mail out
love/sick	lunch	mac.ro/eco.nomic	mail/room
low	lunch/eon	mad	main
[1]low-cost (h)	lunch/room	madam	MAINE
[8]low cost	lung	mad.den/ing	main/frame
lower	lure	made	main/land
lowered	lurk	MADISON, WI	main/line
low.er/ing	lus/cious	mad.ri/gal	mainly
[1]low-grade (h)	lush	mael/strom	main/spring
[8]low grade	luster	maga/zine	main/stay
low/handed	lus.ter/less	magenta	main/stream
low.li/est	lus/trous	magic	main/tain
lows	LUXEM/BOURG	magical	main/tain/ing
loyal	luxu.ri/ous	mag.is/trate	main.te/nance
loyally	luxury	MAGNA CHARTA	ma.jes/tic
loyalty	lying	mag.na/nim.ity	majesty

[1]Compound adjective construction. Hyphenate if description precedes noun. (The utility is burning low-grade coal. Profits depend upon the sale of low-cost items.)

[5]Verb construction. Do not hyphenate. (When shall we mail out the catalog?)

[8]Noun plus adjective construction. Do not hyphenate. (The quality of coal is low grade. The low cost of the item attracted customers.)

[6]Noun construction. Written as one word. (The mailout was taken to the post office today.)

major	man.age/abil.ity	man.ner/ism	mark/edly
ma.jori/ties	man.age/able	manning	marker
ma.jor/ity	man.age/ment	mannish	market
make	manager	man/power	mar.ket/able
maker	mana.ge/rial	mansion	mar.keta/bil.ity
make/shift	man.ag/ing	man/slaugh.ter	mar/keter
[6]makeup	MANAGUA	manual	mar.ket/ing
[1]make-up (h)	man.da/mus	man/ually	mar.ket/place
[5]make up	mandate	manu.fac/ture	marking
mal/ad.just	man.da/tory	manu.fac/turer	mark/ings
mal/ad.just/ment	man.do/lin	manu.fac/tur/ing	[6]markup
malady	ma.neu/ver	manu/script	[5]mark up
malaise	ma.neu/ver/ing	many	mar.ma/lade
malaria	man.ga/nese	map	maroon
MALAY	mangle	mapped	marred
MALAY/SIA	man/handle	mapping	mar/riage
MALAY/SIAN	MAN/HATTAN	maple	mar/riage/able
mal/con.tent	manhole	mar	married
mal/dis.tri/bu/tion	man-hour (h)	mara/schino	marring
male	manhunt	mara/thon	marrow
mal/fea/sance	mania	marble	marry
mal/for.ma/tion	maniac	MARCH	mar.ry/ing
mal/func.tion	mani/fest	march/ing	marsh
malice	mani.fes/ta/tion	MARDI GRAS	marshal
ma.li/cious	mani/festo	mar.ga/rine	mar/shaled
malign	mani/fold	mar.ga/rita	mar.shal/ing
ma.lig/nancy	manikin	margin	marsh/land
ma.lig/nant	manila	marginal	marsh/mal.low
mall	ma.ni.pu/late	MARI/ETTA, OH	martial
mal.lea/bil.ity	ma.ni.pu/lat/ing	mari/juana	martian
mal.lea/ble	ma.ni.pu/la/tion	marina	martyr
mallet	ma.ni.pu/la/tive	mari/nade	martyr/dom
mal.nu/tri/tion	MANI/TOBA	marine	marvel
mal/prac.tice	mankind	mariner	mar/veled
malt	man.li/ness	marital	mar.vel/ing
mammoth	man-made (h)	mari/time	mar.vel/ous
man	manned	mark	MARXIAN
manage	manner	mark/down	MARY/LAND

[1]Compound adjective construction. Hyphenate if description precedes
noun. (A make-up session will be held next week.)

[6]Noun construction. Written as one word. (The makeup of the committee has not been determined. The markup on the merchandise is 25
percent.)

[5]Verb construction. Do not hyphenate. (The store will mark up prices
next month. Will they make up a new pay schedule?)

mascot
mas.cu/line
mas.cu/lin.ity
mask
masked
mason
masonite
masonry
mas.quer/ade
mass
MASSA/CHUSETTS
mas.sa/cre
massage
masses
massive
mast
master
mas/tered
mas.ter/ful
mas.ter/ing
mas.ter/mind
mas.ter/piece
mast/head
mas.ti/cate
mastoid
mat
match
match/book
matches
match/ing
match/less
match/making
mate
ma.te/rial
ma.te/rial.ism
ma.te/rial/istic
ma.te/ri/al.ize
ma.te/ri/ally
ma.ter/nity
math
mathe.ma/ti/cally
mathe.ma/ti/cian
mathe/mat.ics
matinee
mating

ma.tri/archy
mat/rices
ma.tricu/late
ma.tricu/la/tion
ma.ri/mo/nial
mat.ri/mony
matrix
mat/rixes
ma.tronly
matter
mat/tered
mat/tress
mat/tresses
ma.tu.ra/tion
mature
ma.tu.ri/ties
ma.tu/rity
mav.er/ick
maxi/mize
maxi/mi.za/tion
maxi.miz/ing
maximum
MAY
may
⁹maybe
⁵may be
mayhem
may.on/naise
mayor
mayoral
may.or/alty
maze
meadow
meager
meal
meal/time
mean
meaning
mean.ing/ful
mean.ing/fully
mean.ing/ful/ness
mean.ing/less
meant
mean/time
mean/while

mea.sur/able
mea.sur/ably
measure
mea/sured
mea.sure/ment
mea/surer
mea/sures
mea.sur/ing
meat
meat/ball
meat/cut.ter
meat/cut/ting
meat/pack/ing
me.chanic
me.chan/ical
me.chani/cally
me.chan/ics
mecha/nism
mecha/nis.tic
mecha.ni/za/tion
medal
med.al/ist
med.dal/lion
med.dle/some
med/dling
media
median
mediate
me.dia/tion
me.dia/tor
Med.ic/aid
medical
medi/cally
Medi/care
medi/cate
medi/ca/tion
me.dici/nal
medi/cine
me.dio/cre
me.di.oc/rity
medi/tate
medi.ta/tion
medi.ta/tive
MEDITER/
    RANEAN

medium
medley
meet
meeting
meet/ings
mega/cy.cle
mega/phone
mega/watt
mel.an/cholia
mel.an/choly
melee
me.lio/rate
me.lio/ra/tion
mellow
melt
member
mem.ber/ship
mem/brane
memento
me.men/tos
memo
memo.ra/bi.lia
memo.ra/ble
memo.ran/dum
me.mo/rial
memo/ries
memo/rize
memory
MEMPHIS, TN
men
mend
mending
menial
men.in/gi/tis
men/strual
men.stru/ate
mental
·men.tal/ity
men/tally
menthol
mention
men/tioned
men/tions
menu
mer.can/tile

⁵Verb construction. Do not hyphenate. (There may be another position
added to the staff.)

⁹Adverb construction. (Maybe management will add another position to
the staff.)

mer.can/til.ism	meta/mor.phose	midair	mili.ta/ris.tic
mer.ce/nary	meta/mor.pho.sis	mid/ci.ties	mili/tary
mer.cer/ize	meta/phor	midcity	mili/tate
mer.chan/dis/able	meta/phys.ics	mid/con.tin/ent	milk
mer.chan/dise	mete	midday	milkman
mer.chan/diser	meteor	middle	milk/shake
mer.chan/dis.ing	me.te.oro/log/ical	[1]middle-aged (h)	mill
mer/chant	me.te.oro/logy	[2]middle aged	millage
mer.ci/ful	meter	mid.dle/man	mil.len/nium
mer.ci/less	metha/done	mid.dle/weight	miller
mercury	method	mid.dling	mil.li/gram
mer.cu/rial	me.thodi/cal	MIDEAST	mil.li/meter
mer.cu/ric	meth.odo/logi.cal	mid/month	mil.li/nery
mercy	meth.od/ol.ogy	mid/night	million
mere	me.ticu/lous	mid/point	mil.lion/aire
merely	me.ticu/lously	mid/season	mil/lionth
merge	metric	mid.ship/man	mil.li/sec.ond
mer/gence	met.ri/ca/tion	midst	MIL/WAUKEE
merger	metro	mid/sum.mer	mill/work
me.rid/ian	me.tropo/lis	midterm	mime/ograph
merit	me.tro/poli/tan	midweek	mimic
meri.to/ri.ous	mettle	MIDWEST	mim/icked
mer.ri/est	MEXICAN	mid/west.ern	mim.ick/ing
merrily	MEXICO	mid/win.ter	mimicry
mer.ri/ment	MIAMI, FL	midwife	mind
merry	MICHI/GAN	mid/wives	mindful
mesa	micro	midyear	mind/less
mesh	mi.cro/ana.lytic	might	mine
mes.mer/ize	microbe	might/ily	miner
mess	mi.cro/cosm	mighty	mineral
message	mi.cro/eco.nomic	migrant	min.er/als
mes/sages	mi.cro/elec.tron.ics	migrate	mine/sweeper
mes.sen/ger	mi.cro/fiche	mi.gra/tion	mingle
messiah	mi.cro/film	mi.gra/tory	min/gling
mes.si/anic	mi.cro/form	MILAN	min.ia/ture
met	mi.crome/ter	mild	mini/com.puter
me.tabo/lism	mi.cro/met.rics	mile	minimal
metal	mi.cro/or.gan.ism	mileage	mini.mi/za/tion
me.tal/lic	mi.cro/phone	mile/stone	mini/mize
met.al/lur/gi.cal	mi.cro/printer	milieu	minimum
met.al/lur/gist	mi.cro/scope	milieus	mining
met.al/lurgy	mi.cro/sec.ond	mili/tance	min/ister
met.al/work	mi.cro/wave	mili/tancy	min.is/try
meta/mor.phic	mid	mili/tant	mini/sys.tem
		mili.ta/rism	

[1]Compound adjective construction. Hyphenate if description precedes noun. (The middle-aged person had difficulty finding employment.)

[2]Adjective plus adverb construction. Do not hyphenate if description follows noun. (All three applicants were middle aged.)

mink	mis/guide	mis/us.age	modish
MINNE/APOLIS, MN	mis/han.dle	misuse	modular
MINNESOTA	mis/han.dling	mite	modu.lar/ity
minnow	mishap	miti/gate	modu/late
minor	mis/in.form	miti.ga/tion	modu.la/tor
mi.nor/ity	mis/in.ter/pret	mix	module
minstrel	mis/in.ter/pre/ta/tion	mixed	modum
mint	mis/judge	mixer	modus vivendi
minus	mis/label	mixes	MOHAM/MEDAN
minu/scule	mis/la.beled	mixture	moist
minute	mislaid	mix/tures	moisten
mi.nutely	mislay	[4]mix-up (h)	moist/ener
min.ute/man	mislead	[5]mix up	mois/ture
miracle	mis/lead/ing	mob	mo.las/ses
mir/acles	mis/man.age	mobile	mold
mi.racu/lous	mis/match	MOBILE, AL	mole
mirage	mis/no.mer	mo.bil/ity	mo.lecu/lar
mirror	mis/place	mo.bi.li/za/tion	mole/cule
mir/rored	mis/print	mo.bi.liz/ing	molest
mirthful	mis/quote	moc.ca/sin	mo.les.ta/tion
mis/al.lo.ca/tion	mis/rep.re/sent	mockery	mol.li.fi/ca/tion
mis/ap.pre/hen/sion	mis/rep.re/sen/ta/tion	[4]mock-up (h)	mollify
mis/ap.pro/pri.ate	mis/route	mod	moment
mis/be.have	miss	modal	mo.men/tar.ily
mis/cal.cu/late	missal	mo.dal/ity	mo.men/tary
mis/car.riage	missile	mode	mo.men/tous
mis/cel.la/neous	mis/siles	model	mo.men/tum
mis/chief	mission	modeled	monarch
mis/chie.vous	mis/sions	model/ing	mon.ar/chy
mis/con.cep/tion	mis.sion/ar.ies	mod.er/ate	MONDAY
mis/con.duct	mis.sion/ary	mod.er/ately	mone.tar/ism
mis/con.strue	MISSIS/SIPPI	mod.er/at/ing	mone.tar/ist
mis/count	MIS/SOURI	mod.era/tion	mone/tary
misdeal	mis/spell	mod.era/tor	mone/tize
mis/de.meanor	mis/state	modern	money
mis/di.rect	mis/state/ment	mod.erni/za/tion	moneys
mis/er.able	mistake	mod.ern/ize	MON/GOLIA
mis/er.ably	mis/taken	mod.ern/iz/ing	monitor
miserly	mis/tak.enly	modest	moni/tored
misery	mis.tle/toe	mod/estly	moni.tor/ing
mis/fea.sance	mis/treat	modicum	moni/tors
misfire	mis/trial	modi.fi/ca/tion	monkey
mis/for.tune	mis/trust	modi/fied	mo.nog/amy
mis/giv/ing	misty	modi/fies	mono/gram
mis/gov.ern	mis/un.der/stand	modify ·	mono/graph
	mis/un.der/stood	modi.fy/ing	mono/lith

[4]Noun construction. Hyphenate. (There was a mix-up in our order. The advertising agency sent a mock-up of the ad.)
[5]Verb construction. Do not hyphenate. (Do not mix up the two orders.)

mono/logue
MONON/GAHELA
mo.nopo/lis.tic
mo.nopo/lize
mo.nop/oly
mono/rail
mono/tone
mo.noto/nous
mo.notony
mon.ox/ide
mon.si/gnor
monster
mon/stros/ity
MONTANA
MONT/GOMERY, AL
month
MONT/REAL
monu/ment
monu.men/tal
mood
moody
moon
moon/light
moor
moor/ings
moot
mop
mopping
moral
morale
mo.ral/ity
morally
morass
mora.to/rium
morbid
more
more/over
mores
morgue
mori/bund
morning
morn/ings
MOROCCO
morose
mor/osely
mor/pheme
mor/phine
morsel
mortal

mor.tal/ity
mortar
mor.tar/board
mortem
mort/gage
mort.ga/gee
mort.ga/gor
mor.ti.fi/ca/tion
mor.tu/ary
MOSCOW
mos/quito
mos.qui/toes
most
mostly
motel
moth/ball
mother
moth.er/hood
mother-in-law (h)
moth/proof
motion
mo.ti/vate
mo.ti/vat/ing
mo.ti.va/tion
mo.ti.va/tional
mo.ti.va/tor
motive
motor
mo.tor/cycle
mo.tor/cy.clist
mo.tor/ing
mo.tor/ist
mo.tor/ize
mould
mould/ing
mount
moun/tain
moun/tain.ous
mount/ing
mourn
mourn/ful
mouse
mouse/trap
mouth
mouth/ful
mouth/piece
movable
move
move/ment
mover

movie
movie/goer
movies
moving
mow
mower
MOZAM/BIQUE
much
mu.ci/lage
muck/raker
mud
muddle
muffle
mug
mugging
mulch
mulch/ing
mule
mul.ti/bil.lion
mul.ti/branch
mul.ti/fac.eted
mul.ti/fam.ily
mul.ti/lat.eral
mul.ti/lin.gual
mul.ti/mar.ket
mul.ti/media
mul.ti/mil.lion
mul.ti/na.tional
mul.ti/ple
mul.ti/plic.ity
mul.ti/plied
mul.ti/plies
mul.ti/ply
mul.ti/pro.gram/ming
mul.ti/pur.pose
mul.ti/sec.tion
mul.ti/sided
mul.ti/state
mul.ti/tude
mul.ti/tu.di/nous
mul.ti/unit
mul.ti/vari.ate
mu.nici/pal
mu.nici/pali/ties
mu.nici/pal.ity
murder
mur.der/ous
murky
murmur
mur.mur/ing

muscles
mus.cu/lar
museum
mush/room
mush/roomed
mush/room/ing
music
musical
mu.si/cian
muslin
muss
must
mus/tache
mustard
mu.ta/tion
mute
mu.ti/late
mu.ti.la/tion
mutiny
mutter
mutton
mutual
mu.tu/ally
muzzle
myopia
myopic
myriad
myself
mys.ter/ies
mys.te.ri/ous
mystery
mystic
mys.ti/cal
mys.ti/cism
mystify
mys.ti/fy.ing
mys/tique
myth
mythi/cal
my.thol/ogy

N

nag

nail
naive
naiveté
name
name/able
namely
name/plate
naphtha
napkin
nar/cotic
NARRA/GANSETT
narrate
nar.ra/tion
nar.ra/tive
nar.ra/tor
narrow
nar/rowly
narrow-minded (h)
narrow-
  mindedness(h)
nary
nasal
nascent
NASH/VILLE, TN
NASSAU
nas.ti/ness
nasty
natal
na.ta.to/rium
nation
na.tional
na.tion/al.ism
na.tion/al/istic
na.tion/al.ity
na.tion/ali/za/tion
na.tion/ally
na.tion/wide
native
natural
natu.ral/ism
natu/rali/za/tion
natu.ral/ize
natu/rally
nature
naught
naugh/tily
naugh.ti/ness
naughty
nausea
nau.se/ate
nau.se/ous

nau.ti/cal
naval
navel
navi.ga/ble
navi/gate
navi.ga/tion
navi.ga/tor
navy
near
nearby
near/ness
neat
neatly
NE.BRASKA
nebulous
nec.es/sar.ily
nec.es/sary
ne.ces/si/tate
ne.ces/si/tat/ing
ne.ces/si/ties
ne.ces/sity
neck
neck/lace
necktie
neck/wear
nectar
nec.tar/ine
need
needi/ness
needle
nee.dle/point
need/less
need/lessly
need/ling
needy
negate
ne.ga/tion
nega/tive
nega/tively
nega.tiv/ism
neglect
ne.glected
neg.li/gence
neg.li/gent
neg.li/gi.ble
ne.go.ti/able
ne.go.ti/ate
ne.go.ti/at/ing
ne.go.ti/ation
ne.go.ti/ator
NEGRO

NEGROES
neigh/bor
neigh/bor/hood
neither
nemesis
neo/classi.cal
neo/mod.ern
neon
nephew
nepo/tism
nerve
nervous
ner.vous/ness
nest
nestle
nest/ling
net
NETHER/LANDS
netted
nettle
network
neu.ri/tis
neu.rolo/gist
neu.rol/ogy
neu.ro/sis
neu.ro/tic
neutral
neu.tral/ity
neu.tral/ize
NEVADA
nev.er/the/less
new
NEWARK, NJ
newborn
new/comer
NEW/FOUND-
  LAND
NEW HAMP/
  SHIRE
NEW HAVEN, CT
NEW JERSEY
newly
NEW MEXICO
newness
NEW ORLEANS,
  LA
NEWPORT NEWS,
  VA
news/caster
news/let.ter
newsman

news/pa.per
news/pa.per/man
NEWPORT, RI
news/print
news/reel
news/stand
news/worthy
NEW YORK
NIAGARA
nibble
NICA/RAGUA
nice
nicety
niche
nickel
nico/tine
niece
NIGERIA
night
night/club
night/mare
night/time
ni.hil/ism
nil
nine
nine/teen
nine.ti/eth
ninety
ninth
nitrate
nitric
nitride
ni.tri.fi/ca/tion
nitrite
ni.tro/gen
ni.troge/nous
ni.tro/glyc.erin
no.bil/ity
noble
nobly
nobody
noc.tur/nal
noc/turne
nod
node
nodded
nodding
nog
noise
noise/less
noisily

no.madic
no.men/cla/ture
nomial
nominal
nomi/nate
nomi.nat/ing
nomi.na/tion
nominee
non/ab.sor/bent
non/aca.demic
non/ad.di/tive
non.ad.mis/sible
non/ag.gres/sive
non/al.co/holic
non/as.sess/able
nonbank
non/be.liever
non/bio.de/grad/able
non/cer.ti/fied
non/cha.lant
non/com.mer/cial
non/com.mit/tal
non/com.peti/tive
non/con.form/ing
non/con.form/ist
non/crit.ical
non/de.duct/ible
non.de.script
non/dis.crimi/na/tion
non/dis.crimi/na/tory
non/drink.ing
non/dis.pos/able
non/dur.able
none
non/eco.nomic
non/es.sen/tial
none/the/less
non/ex.clu/sive
non/ex.is/tent
nonfarm
non/fea.sance
non/fed.eral
non/fer.rous
non/in.sured
non/in.ter/fer/ence
non/in.ter/ven/tion
non/ju.ris/dic/tional
non/lin.ear
non/listed
non/mag.netic
non/mem.ber

non/mone.tary
non/par.ti/ci/pa/tion
non/par.tisan
non/pay.ment
non/per.sonal
non/pro.fes/sional
non/profit
non/pub.lic
non/re.ceipt
non/re.cur/ring
non/regu.la/tory
non/re.newal
non/resi.dent
non/re.turn/able
non/sched.uled
nonsense
non/sen.si/cal
nonskid
non/smoker
non/smok.ers
nonstop
non/sur.gi/cal
non/tax.able
non/teach/ing
non/tech.ni/cal
non/tra.di/tional
non/trans.fer/able
non/union
non/urban
nonuse
nonuser
non/verbal
non/vio.lence
non/vio.lent
non/white
non/work/ing
noon
noonday
noon/time
nor
NORFOLK, VA
normal
mor/malcy
nor.mal/ity
nor.mal/ize
nor/mally
nor.ma/tive
north
NORTH
  CARO/LINA
NORTH DAKOTA

north/east
north/east.ern
north/erly
north/ern
north/ward
north/west
north/west.ern
NORWAY
NORWE/GIAN
nose
nose/dive
nos.tal/gia
nostril
not
notable
no.ta/rize
notary
no.ta/tion
notch
note
note/book
note/card
note/pa.per
note/tak/ing
note/wor.thy
nothing
notice
no.tice/able
no.tice/ably
no.ti.fi/ca/tion
no.ti/fied
no.ti/fies
notify
no.ti/fy/ing
noting
notion
no.to.ri/ety
no.to.ri/ous
not/with/stand/ing
nourish
nour.ish/ment
novel
nov.el/ties
novelty
NOVEM/BER
novena
novice
no.vi.ti/ate
now
nowa/days
nowhere

noxious
nozzle
nuance
nuclear
nu.cle/ation
nucleus
nudge
nudity
nui/sance
null
nul.li.fi/ca/tion
nullify
number
num/bered
num.ber/ing
numeral
nu.mer/als
nu.mera/tion
nu.mera/tor
numeric
nu.meri/cal
nu.meri/cally
nu.mer/ous
nuptial
nurse
nursery
nursing
nurture
nut
nutmeg
nu.tri/ent
nu.tri/tion
nu.tri/tion.ist
nu.tri/tious
nu.tri/tive
nut/shell
nylon

O

oak
OAKLAND, CA
oarsman
oasis
oath
oats
ob.du/rate

obe.di/ence	ob.stet/ri.cal	ocular	often
obe.di/ent	ob.ste/tri/cian	oculist	often/times
obese	ob.stet/rics	oddity	OHIO
obesity	ob.sti/nate	oddly	oiler
obey	ob.struct	oddness	oili/ness
obiter dictum	ob.struc/tion	ode	oilman
obi.tu/ary	obtain	odious	oilseed
object	ob.tain/able	odor/less	oily
ob.jected	ob.tained	odorous	oint/ment
ob.ject/ing	ob.tain/ing	offbeat	okay
ob.jec/tion	ob.tru/sive	offcast	okayed
ob.jec/tion/able	obtuse	off-color (h)	okaying
ob.jec/tive	obviate	offend	OKLA/HOMA
ob.jec/tively	obvious	of.fended	OKLA/HOMA
ob.jec/tiv.ity	ob.vi/ously	of.fender	CITY, OK
ob.la/tion	oc.ca/sion	of.fend/ers	old
ob/li/gate	oc.ca/sional	offense	oldest
ob.li.ga/tion	oc.ca/sion/ally	of.fenses	[1]old-fashioned (h)
ob.li.ga/tional	oc.ci.den/tal	of.fen/sive	[2]old fashioned
ob.li/ga/tory	oc.clu/sion	offer	oldster
oblige	occult	offered	oleo
obliger	oc.cult/ist	of.fer/ing	oleo/mar.ga/rine
oblig/ing	oc.cu/pancy	offeror	oli/gar/chy
oblique	oc.cu/pant	offhand	oli.gop/ol.ies
ob.lit/er.ate	oc.cu.pa/tion	office	oli/gopo/lis.tic
ob.liv/ion	oc.cu.pa/tional	of.fice/holder	oli.gop.oly
oblong	oc.cu/pied	officer	olive
ob.nox/ious	oc.cu/pies	of.fi/cers	OMAHA, NE
oboe	occupy	of.fice/worker	om.buds/man
obscene	oc.cu.py/ing	of.fi/cial	omelet
ob.scen/ity	occur	of.fi/cial/dom	ominous
obscure	oc.curred	of.fi/cially	omi.nously
ob.scu/rity	oc.cur/rence	of.fi.ci/ate	omis.si/ble
ob.serv/able	oc.cur/ring	of.fi/cious	omis/sion
ob.ser/vance	ocean	offing	omit
ob.ser.va/tion	ocean/go.ing	offline	omitted
ob.serva/tory	ocean/og.ra/pher	off-season (h)	omit/ting
observe	ocean/og.raphy	offset	omnibus
ob.server	o'clock	off.set/ting	om.nipo/tence
ob.ses/sion	oc.tago/nal	off/shoot	om.ni/scient
ob.so.les/cence	OCTOBER	off/shore	on.com/ing
ob.so/lete	oc.to.ge/nar.ian	off/site	oneness
ob.sta/cle	octopus	off/spring	onerous

[1]Compound adjective construction. Hyphenate if description precedes noun. (The old-fashioned piece of equipment hinders productivity.)
[2]Adjective plus adverb construction. Do not hyphenate if description follows noun. (That style for addressing envelopes is old fashioned.)

ongoing	op.ti/cally	or.ga/nize	outcry
on.ion/skin	op.ti/cian	or.ga/nizer	out/dated
online	optimal	or.ga.niz/ing	out/dis.tance
on.looker	op.ti/mally	orient	outdo
on.look/ing	op.ti/mism	ori.en/tal	outdoor
only	op.ti/mist	ori.en.ta/tion	out/doors/man
on.rush/ing	op.ti/mistic	orifice	outer
on.slaught	op.ti.mis/ti/cally	origin	out.er/most
ONTARIO	op.ti/mize	origi/nal	out.er/wear
onto	op.ti.miz/ing	origi/nal.ity	outfit
on.tol/ogy	optimum	origi/nate	outflow
onward	opting	origi.na/tor	out/go.ing
onyx	option	ORLANDO, FL	out/growth
opaque	op.tional	or.na/ment	out/guess
open	op.tome/try	or.na.men/tal	outing
open/ings	opu/lence	or.na.men/ta/tion	outlaw
open-minded (h)	opulent	ornate	out/lawed
open/ness	oracle	orphan	outlay
opera	oral	or.tho/dox	outlet
op.er/able	orally	or.tho/doxy	outline
operant	orange	or.tho/pe.dic	out/lin/ing
operate	or.ange/ade	os.cil/late	outlive
op.er/ated	orator	os.cil/lat/ing	outlook
op.er/atic	oratory	os.cil.la/tion	out/ly/ing
op.er.at/ing	orbit	os.cil.la/tor	outmode
op.era/tion	orbital	os.cil.lo/scope	out/moded
op.era/tional	orchard	OSLO	out/num.ber
op.era/tion/al.ize	or.ches/tra	os.ten.si/ble	outpace
op.era/tion/ally	or.ches/tra/tion	os.ten.si/bly	out/pa.tient
op.era/tive	ordain	os.ten.ta/tious	out/per.form
op.era/tor	ordeal	os.teo/path	out/per.form/ance
op.er/etta	order	os.tra/cize	outpost
oph.thal/mol.ogy	or.der/ing	other	out/pour/ing
opinion	or.der.li/ness	oth.er/wise	output
opin.ion/ated	orderly	OTTAWA	outrage
opin/ions	ordinal	ought	out/ra.geous
opium	or.di/nance	ounce	out/reach
op.po/nent	or.di.nar/ily	our	out/right
op.por/tune	or.di/nary	our/selves	outrun
op.por.tu/nist	or.di.na/tion	ousted	out/run/ning
op.por.tu/nis.tic	ord/nance	out	outsell
op.por.tu/ni/ties	ore	outage	outset
op.por.tu/nity	OREGON	out/board	outside
oppose	organ	out/bound	out/sider
op.pos/ing	organic	out/break	out/sized
op.po/site	or.gan/ism	out/burst	out/skirt
op.po.si/tion	or.gan/ist	outcast	out/skirts
op.pres/sive	or.ga.ni/za/tion	outcome	outsold
op.pres/sor	or.ga.ni/za/tional	outcrop	out/spent
optical	or.ga.ni/za/tion/ally	out/crop/ping	out/spo.ken

out/stand/ing
out/stand/ingly
out/state
outward
out/wardly
out/weigh
outwit
oval
ovary
oven
over
overage
over/ages
overall
over/am.bi/tious
over/bal.ance
over/bear/ing
overbid
over/blown
over/board
over/bur.den
over/charge
over/coat
over/come
over/crowd
over/de.velop
overdo
over/draft
over/drawn
overdue
over/eager
over/esti.mate
over/ex.pan/sion
over/ex.pen.di/ture
over/ex.tend
over/flow
over/grown
over/hand
over/haul
over/head
over/heat
over/joyed
over/kill
over/land
overlap
over/lap/ping
overlay
over/load
over/look
overly

over/man.age
over/night
over/paid
over/pass
over/pay/ment
over/play
over/power
over/print
over/pro.duce
over/rate
over/ride
over/rule
overrun
over/run/ning
over/save
over/seas
oversee
over/seer
over/sell
over/shadow
over/sight
over/sim.pli/fi/ca/tion
over/sim.pli/fied
over/sim.plify
over/sized
over/spend
over/staff
over/state
over/state/ment
over/stock
over/sub.scribe
over/sup.ply
overt
over/take
over/throw
over/time
over/tone
over/ture
over/value
over/view
over/weight
over/whelm
over/whelm/ing
over/whelm/ingly
over/work
over/zealous
owe
owed
owing
owl

own
own.er/ship
oxford
oxi.da/tion
oxide
oxidize
oxygen
oyster

P

pace
pace/maker
pace/set.ter
pacific
paci.fi/ca/tion
paci/fist
pack
package
pack/aged
pack/ager
packer
packet
pack.ing/house
pact
pad
padded
padding
paddle
paddler
padlock
page
pagi.na/tion
paid
pail
pain
pain/fully
pain/less
pain/lessly
pains/tak/ing
pains/tak/ingly
paint
painter
paint/ers
paint/ings
pair

paired
pajamas
PAKI/STAN
palace
pal.at/able
palate
pa.la/tial
pale
palette
pali/sade
pallet
pal.lia/tive
pallor
palm
pal/metto
pal.pi/tate
pal.pi/ta/tion
palsy
paltry
pamper
pam/phlet
pan
panacea
PANAMA
PANA/MANIAN
PAN-AMERICAN
  (h)
pana/sonic
pan/cakes
pan.chro/matic
pan/creas
panel
paneled
panel/ing
pan.el/ist
panic
pan.icked
pan.ick/ing
panning
pano/rama
pansy
pan.to/mime
pantry
pants
papacy
papal
paper
pa.per/back
pa.per/board
pa.per/hanger

pa.per/less	parent	par.ticu/larly	pat.ent/able
pa.per/weight	par.ent/age	parties	pat.en/tee
pa.per/work	pa.ren/the.ses	par.ti/san	pa.ter/nal
paprika	pa.ren/the.sis	par.ti/tion	pa.ter/nal.ism
par	par.en/theti/cal	partner	pa.ter.na/lis.tic
parable	par.ent/hood	part/ners	pa.ter/nity
para/chute	parfait	part.ner/ship	PATER/SON, NJ
parade	pari-mutuel (h)	¹part-time (h)	pa.thetic
para/digm	parish	²part time	patho/logi/cal
para/dise	pari/ties	party	pa.tholo/gist
paradox	parity	par value	pa.thol/ogy
para/doxi.cal	park	PASA/DENA, CA	pathos
para/doxi/cally	par/lance	pass/able	pa.tience
para/graph	parlay	passage	patient
par.al/lel	parley	pass/book	patio
par.al/leled	par.lia/ment	passé	pa.tri/arch
par.al/lel/ing	par.lia/men/tar.ian	pas.sen/ger	pa.tri/archal
pa.raly/sis	par.lia/men/tary	pass/erby	pa.tri/cian
para/lyze	parlor	passion	pa.tri/otic
para/medic	pa.ro/chial	passive	pa.tri/otism
para/medi.cal	parody	pass/port	patrol
para/meter	parole	pass/time	pa.trolled
para/met.ric	par.si.mo/ni.ous	pass/word	pa.trol/ling
para/mount	par.si/mony	past	pa.trol/man
para/noia	par.son/age	paste	patron
para/noiac	part	⁴paste-up (h)	pa.tron/age
para/noid	partake	⁵paste up	pa.tron/ize
para/pher/na.lia	par.tak/ing	pastel	pattern
para/phrase	partial	pas.teur/ize	pat/terned
para/ple.gic	par.tial/ity	pastime	patting
para/pro.fes/sional	par/tially	pastor	paucity
para/site	par.tici/pant	pas.to/ral	pauper
para/sitic	par.tici/pate	pas.tor/ate	pave
parasol	par.tici/pat/ing	pastry	pave/ment
parcel	par.tici/pa/tion	pasture	pa.vil/ion
par.celed	par.tici/pa/tive	pat	pawn
par.cel/ing	par.tici/pa/tory	patch	pawn/bro.ker
parcel post	par/ticle	patch/work	pawn/shop
pardon	par.ticu/lar	pâté	pay
par.don/able	par.ticu/lar.ize	patent	payable

³

¹Compound adjective construction. Hyphenate if description precedes noun. (The student held a part-time job.)
²Adjective plus adverb construction. Do not hyphenate. (If you can work part time, you will be able to pay your way through school.)
⁴Noun construction. Hyphenate. (The printer did a paste-up of the program.)
⁵Verb construction. Do not hyphenate. (The printer can paste up a rough draft for us.)

pay/check	ped/dling	pension	perhaps
payday	ped.es/tal	pen/sionee	peril
payee	pe.des/trian	pen/sioner	per.il/ous
payer	pe.dia/tri/cian	pen/tagon	pe.rime/ter
payload	pe.di.at/rics	pent/house	period
pay/mas.ter	peek	peon	pe.ri/odic
payment	peel	peonies	pe.ri.odi/cal
pay/ments	peeling	peony	pe.ri.odi/cally
[6]payoff	peer	people	pe.ri/pheral
[5]pay off	peg	PEORIA, IL	pe.riph/ery
[6]payout	pegged	pep	peri/scope
[5]pay out	pegging	pepper	perish
payroll	PEKING	pep.per/mint	per.ish/able
pay/rolls	pellet	per	peri.to/ni.tis
pea	pel.leti/za/tion	per/ceive	perjure
peace	pel.let/ize	percent	per/jurer
peace/able	pelt	per.cent/age	perjury
peace/ful	pelvis	per.cen/tile	per.ma/nence
peace/maker	pen	per.cep/ti.ble	per.ma/nency
peace/mak/ing	penal	per.cep/tion	per.ma/nent
peace/time	pe.nal/ize	per.cep/tive	per.ma/nently
peach	pen.al/ties	per.cep/tual	per.me/able
peak	penalty	per/chance	per.me/ate
peal	pen/chant	per.co/late	per.mis/si.ble
peanut	pencil	per.co.la/tion	per.mis/sion
pear	pen/ciled	per.co/la/tor	per.mis/sive
pearl	pen.cil/ing	per.cus/sion	per.mis/sive/ness
pearly	pendant	per diem	permit
peasant	pending	pe.ren/nial	per.mit/ted
peat	pen.du/lum	perfect	per.mit/ting
pebble	pene/trate	per/fected	per.mu.ta/tion
pe.cu/liar	pene/trat.ing	per.fect/ible	per.ni/cious
pe.cu/li.ari/ties	pene.tra/tion	per.fect/ing	per.pen/dicu.lar
pe.cu/liar.ity	penguin	per.fec/tion	per.pe/trate
pe.cu.ni/ary	peni.cil/lin	per.fec/tion.ist	per.pe/tra/tion
peda/gogic	pen.in/sula	per.fidi/ous	per.pe/tra/tor
peda/gogi/cal	peni.ten/ti.aries	per.fo/rate	per.pet/ual
peda/gogue	peni.ten/tiary	per.fo/rat/ing	per.petu/ally
peda/gogy	pen.man/ship	per.fo.ra/tion	per.petu/ate
pedal	penned	per.fo.ra/tor	per.petu/ation
pedaled	pennies	perform	per.petu/ity
ped.al/ing	pen.ni/less	per.for/mance	perplex
peddle	PENNSYL/VANIA	per/former	per/plexed
peddler	penny	per.func/tory	per.plex/ing

[5]Verb construction. Do not hyphenate. (Do not pay out all your cash. The company intends to pay off its bonded indebtedness.)
[6]Noun construction. Written as one word. (The payout was more than the group had cash in its account. The payoff for study will come later.)

per.plexi/ties
per.plex/ity
per.qui/site
per.se/cute
per.se/ver/ance
per.se/vere
PERSIAN
persist
per.sis/tence
per.sis/tency
per.sis/tent
per/sists
person
per.son/able
personal
per.son/ali/ties
per.son/al.ity
pers.on/al.ize
per.soni/fi/ca/tion
per.son/ify
per.son/nel
per.spec/tive
per.spi/ra/tion
per/suade
per.sua/sion
per.sua/sive
per.sua/sive/ness
pert
pertain
per.tain/ing
per.ti/nence
per.ti/nent
perturb
PERU
perusal
peruse
PERU/VIAN
pervade
per.va/sive
per/verse

per/versely
per.ver/sity
pervert
peso
pesos
pes.si/mism
pes.si/mist
pes.si/mis.tic
pest
pester
pes.ti/cide
pes.ti/lence
pes.ti/lent
pet
petite
pe.ti/tion
pe.ti/tioner
pet.ri.fi/ca/tion
petrify
pet.tro/chemi.cal
pe.tro/leum
petty
petunia
pewter
phantom
phar.ma/ceu/ti.cal
phar.ma/cist
phar.ma/colo/gist
phar.ma/col.ogy
phar/macy
phase
[6]phase/out
[5]phase out
pheas/ant
phenol
phe/nomena
phe.nome/nal
phe.nome/nally
phe.nome/non
phial

PHILA/DELPHIA,
  PA
phil.an/thropic
phi.lan/thro/pist
phi.lan/thropy
PHILIP/PINE
PHILIP/PINES
phi.loso/pher
philo/sophi/cal
philo/sophi/cally
phi.loso/phize
phi.loso/phy
phlegm
phobia
PHOENIX, AR
phone
pho/netic
phonics
pho.no/graph
phony
phos/phate
phos.pho/res/cent
phos.pho/ric
phos.pho/rous
phos.pho/rus
photo
pho.to/copier
pho.to/copy
pho.to/elec.tric
pho.to/en.grave
pho.to/en.grav.ing
pho.to/ge.nic
pho.to/graph
pho.tog/ra/pher
pho.to/graphic
pho.tog/ra.phy
photos
pho.to/sen.si/tive
pho.to/stat
pho.to/stated

pho.to/static
pho.to/syn.the.sis
pho.to/type
pho.to/type/set.ter
phrase
phrase/ol.ogy
physic
physi/cal
physi/cally
phy.si/cian
physi/cist
physics
physi/olo/gi.cal
physi/olo/gist
physi/ol.ogy
physio/thera/pist
physio/ther.apy
phy/sique
pianist
piano
piazza
pica
pica/yune
pick
picket
[6]pickup
[5]pick up
picnic
pic/nicked
pic/nicker
pic.nick/ing
pic.to/rial
pic.to/rially
picture
pic/tured
pic.tur/esque
pic.tur/ing
pie
piece
piece/meal

[5]Verb construction. Do not hyphenate. (The corporation will phase out
its operations in that state. Please pick up the mail on your way to the
office.)
[6]Noun construction. Written as one word. (The final stage of the phase-
out will be completed next year. The last mail pickup is at 4 p.m.)

piece/wise

piece/work

PIED/MONT

pier

pierce

pigeon

pi.geon/hole

pig.gy/pack

pig/ment

pig.men/ta/tion

pig/ments

pigskin

pigtail

pig/tails

pike

pile

pilfer

pil.fer/age

pil.fer/ing

pil.grim/age

pill

pillage

pil.lag/ing

pillar

pillow

pilot

pin

pinch

pinch-hit (h)

pine

pine/ap.ple

pink

pin.na/cle

pinned

pi.nochle

pin/point

pin/stripe

pint

⁶pinup

³pin up

pin/wheel

pioneer

pio/neered

pious

pip

pipe

piped

pipe/line

piper

piping

pipped

pipping

pique

piracy

pirate

pi.rat/ing

pistol

piston

pit

pitch

pitch-black (h)

pitch-dark (h)

pitcher

pitch/fork

pitch/ing

pitch/man

pitfall

pit/falls

piti/able

pitiful

pit/tance

PITTS/BURGH, PA

PITTS/FIELD, MA

pity

pivot

pivotal

pizza

piz.ze/ria

placard

pla/cards

placate

place

placebo

place.bos

place/mat

place/ment

placid

pla.gia/rism

pla.gia/rist

pla.gia/rize

plague

plagued

pla/guing

plain

plain/clothes/man

plainly

plain/tiff

plan

plane

planet

plane/tar.ium

plane/tary

plank

plank/ing

plank/ton

planned

planner

plant

planta/tion

planter

plant/ers

plant/worker

plaque

plasma

plaster

plas/terer

plastic

plas.tic/ity

plas.ti/cize

plas/tics

plat

plate

plateau

pla/teaus

platen

plat/form

plating

plati/num

plati/tude

pla/tonic

platted

plat/ting

plau.si/ble

plau.si/bil.ity

play

⁶play/back

⁵play back

playbill

playboy

play/boys

player

play/field

playful

play/ful/ness

play/goer

play/ground

playing

play/mate

⁴play-off (h)

⁵play off

play/room

play/thing

⁴Noun construction. Hyphenate. (The play-off between the tied teams will be tomorrow.)

⁵Verb construction. Do not hyphenate. (The dictator should play back his dictation to know how his voice sounds. The two teams will play off for the championship. The secretary is going to pin up the announcement on the bulletin board.)

⁶Noun construction. Written as one word. (The playback of the tape was not clear. The child has pinups of all his favorite players.)

plaza
plea
plead
plead/ings
pleas
pleas/ant
pleas/anter
please
pleas/ing
plea.sur/able
plea/sure
pleat
ple.be/ian
pledge
pledg/ing
plen.ti/ful
plenty
pleth/ora
pleu/risy
plexi/glass
pli.abil/ity
pliable
pliant
pliers
plight
plod
plodder
plod/ding
plot
plot/ting
plow
plow/share
ploy
pluck
plug
plugged
plug/ging
plum
plumber
plumb/ing
plummet
plum/meted
plum/met/ing
plump
plump/ness
plunder
plunge
plunger
plung/ing
plural

plur.al/ism
plur.al/is.tic
plu.ral/ity
plus
pluses
plush
plu.to/nium
ply
plywood
pneu/matic
pneu.mo/nia
pocket
poc.ket/book
poc.ket/ful
po.di/atry
podium
poem
poetry
poi/gnancy
poi/gnant
poin.set/tia
point
point-blank (h)
point/ers
point/ing
point/less
poise
poison
poi.son/ing
poi.son/ous
poke
poker
POLAND
po.lar/ity
po.lar/ize
pole
POLE
police
po.lic/ing
police/man
po.lice/woman
poli/cies
policy
poli.cy/holder
poli.cy/maker
poli.cy/mak/ing
poli.cy/owner
polio
polish
POLISH

pol/ishes
polite
po.lite/ness
po.liti/cal
po.liti/cally
poli.ti/cian
poli/tick.ing
poli/tico
poli/tics
polka
poll
polled
pol.li.na/tion
poll/ster
pol.lut/ant
pollute
pol.lut/ing
pol.lu/tion
poly.es/ter
poly/ethyl.ene
poly/glot
polygon
poly/graph
poly/nomial
poly/sty.rene
poly/tech.nic
poly/un.satu/rated
pom.pos/ity
pompous
poncho
ponchos
ponder
pon.der/ing
pon.der/ous
pontiff
pon.tifi/cal
pon.tifi/cate
pontoon
poodle
pool
pooled
poor
poorest
poorly
pop
popcorn
pope
popgun
poplar
popover

poppies
poppy
popu/lace
popular
popu.lar/ity
popu.lar/ize
popu/late
popu.la/tion
popu/lous
por.ce/lain
porch
porches
pore
pork
por.no/graphic
por.nog/ra.phy
porous
port
por.ta/bil.ity
por.ta/ble
portage
por/tages
portal
portend
por.ten/tous
porter
port/fo.lio
port/fo.lios
port/hole
portion
por/tions
PORT/LAND, OR
portly
por/trait
portray
por/trayal
por/trayed
por/tray/ing
por/trays
PORTS/MOUTH,
   VA
PORTU/GUAL
PORTU/GUESE
pose
posit
posited
pos.it/ing
po.si/tion
po.si/tional
po.si/tioned

po.si/tion/ing	potash	praise	pre/con.ceive
posi/tive	po.tas/sium	praise/wor.thy	pre/con.cep/tion
posi/tively	potato	prattle	precook
posse	po.ta/toes	pray	pre/cur.sor
pos/sess	potency	prayer	pre/cur.sory
pos.sesses	potent	prayer/ful	predate
pos.sess/ing	po.ten/tial	preach	pre/dated
pos.ses/sion	po.ten.ti/al.ity	preacher	pre/de.cease
pos.ses/sive	pot/pourri	preach/ers	prede/ces.sor
pos.ses/sor	potted	preach/ing	pre/des.tine
pos.si/bili/ties	potter	pre/ad.dressed	pre/de.ter/mine
pos.si/bil.ity	pot.ter/ies	pre/am.ble	pre.dica/ment
pos.si/ble	pottery	pre/ar.range	predi/cate
pos.si/bly	poul/tice	pre/as.sem.ble	predict
post	poultry	pre/au.thor.ize	pre/dicta/bil.ity
postage	pound	pre/can.cel	pre.dict/able
postal	pour	pre.cari/ous	pre.dict/ably
post/card	pourer	precast	pre/dicted
post/date	poverty	pre/cau.tion	pre.dic/tion
poster	¹poverty-stricken (h)	pre/cau.tion.ary	pre.dic/tive
pos.te/rior	²poverty stricken	precede	pre.dic/tor
post/gradu.ate	powder	prece/dence	pre.di/lec/tion
post/hu.mous	pow/dered	prece/dent	pre/dis.pose
post/hu.mously	power	pre/ced/ing	pre.domi/nance
post/in.dus/trial	pow.er/ful	precept	pre.domi/nant
postman	pow.er/fully	pre/cinct	pre.domi/nantly
post/mark	pow.er/less	pre/cious	pre.domi/nate
post/mas.ter	power plant	pre.cipi/tate	pre/elec.tion
post/mis.tress	prac.ti/ca/bil.ity	pre.cipi/ta/tion	pre.emi.nence
post/mor.tem	pra.ti/ca.ble	pre.cipi/ta/tor	pre.emi.nent
¹post-office (h)	prac.ti/cal	pre.cipi/tous	pre/ex.ist/ing
⁸post office	prac.ti/cal.ity	pre.cipi/tously	prefab
post/paid	prac.ti/cally	precise	pre/fabri/ca/tion
post/pon/able	prac/tice	pre/cisely	prefer
post/pone	prac.tic/ing	pre.cise/ness	pref.er/able
post/pone/ment	prac.ti/tioner	pre.ci/sion	pref.er/ably
post/re.tire/ment	prag/matic	pre/clude	pref.er/ence
post/se.con/dary	prag/mati/cally	pre.clud/ing	pref.er/en/tial
pos.tu/late	prag.ma/tism	pre.co/cious	pre/ferred
post/war	prag.ma/tist	precode	pre.fer/ring
pot	prairie	pre/col.lege	preg/nant

¹Compound adjective construction. Hyphenate if description precedes noun. (The post-office box number has been changed. The poverty-stricken family needs assistance.)

²Adjective plus adverb construction. Do not hyphenate if description follows noun. (The family is poverty stricken.)

⁸Noun plus adjective construction. Do not hyphenate. (A new post office is being built in the city.)

preg/nancy	pre/punched	pre.sum/able	price
preheat	pre/quali.fi/ca/tion	pre.sum/ably	price/less
pre/judge	pre/qualify	presume	pricing
preju/dice	pre/re.cord	pre.sum/ing	prick
preju/di/cial	pre/reg.is/ter	pre.sump/tion	prickly
preju/dic/ing	pre/reg.is/tra/tion	pre.sump/tu.ous	pride
pre.limi/nar.ies	pre/req.ui/site	pre/sup.pose	pride/ful
pre.limi/nary	pre/roga/tive	pre/sup.po.si/tion	priest
prelist	pre/school	pretax	primacy
prelude	pre.sci/ence	pretend	prima facie
pre/mari.tal	pre.sci/ent	pre/tender	primal
pre/ma.ture	pre/scribe	pre/tense	pri.mar/ily
pre/medi.cal	pre.scrip/tion	pre.ten/tions	primary
pre/medi/tate	pre/scrip/tive	pre.ten/tious	prime
pre/miere	pres/ence	pretest	primed
premise	present	pre/tested	primer
premium	pre.sent/able	pretext	primi/tive
pre/miums	pre.sen/ta/tion	pre/ticket	prim/rose
pre.mo/ni/tion	[1]present-day (h)	pre/timed	prince
pre/natal	[8]present day	pre/tran/scrip/tion	prin.ci/pal
pre/nurs/ing	pre.sent/ment	pre/trial	prin.ci/pal.ity
pre/oc.cu.pa/tion	pres/ents	pretty	prin.ci/pally
pre/oc.cu/pied	pres.er/va/tion	pret/tier	prin.ci/pal/ship
prepack	pre/serva/tive	pret/tily	prin.ci/ple
pre/pack.age	pre/serve	pret.ti/ness	print
prepaid	pre/server	pretzel	print/able
prepa/ra/tion	pre.serv/ers	prevail	printer
pre.pa.ra/tory	pre.serv/ing	pre/vailed	print/ers
prepare	preset	pre.vail/ing	print/ing
pre/pared/ness	preside	preva/lence	print/out
pre.par/ing	presi/dency	preva/lent	print/shop
prepay	presi/dent	prevent	print/work
pre.pay/ment	presi/den/tial	pre.vent/able	prior
preplan	pre.sid/ing	pre.venta/tive	pri.ori/ties
pre.plan/ning	press	pre/vented	pri.or/ity
pre.pon/der/ance	press/board	pre.vent/ing	prism
prepo.si/tion	press/ing	pre.ven/tion	prison
prepo.si/tional	pres/sure	pre.ven/tive	pris/oner
pre.pos/ter.ous	pres.sur/ize	preview	pris/on.ers
pre/print	pres.sur/iz/ing	pre.vi/ous	privacy
pre/pro.fes/sional	pres/tige	pre.vi/ously	private
pre/pro.grammed	pres.tig/ious	prewar	pri/vately
pre/punch	presto	prey	pri.va/tion
	pre/stressed		

[1]Compound adjective construction. Hyphenate if description precedes noun. (Present-day transportation facilities are far superior to those of the past.)

[8]Noun plus adjective construction. Do not hyphenate. (In the present day, transportation facilities are greatly improved.)

privi/lege
privy
prize
pro
proba/bil.ity
prob/able
prob/ably
probate
pro.ba/tion
pro.ba/tion.ary
probe
problem
prob.lem/ati.cal
pro.ce/dural
pro.ce/dure
proceed
pro/ceeded
pro.ceed/ing
pro.ceed/ings
pro/ceeds
process
pro/cessed
pro/cesses
pro.cess/ing
pro.ces/sion
pro.ces/sor
pro/claim
proc.la/ma/tion
pro.cras/ti/nate
pro.cras/ti/na/tion
pro/cre.ate
pro/cre.ation
proctor
procure
pro/cured
pro.cure/ment
pro.cur/ing
prod
prodded
prod/ding
prodigal
pro.di/gious
pro.di/giously
prodigy
produce
pro/ducer
pro.duc/ers
pro.duc/ing
product
pro.duc/tion

pro.duc/tive
pro.duc/tiv.ity
profane
pro.fan/ity
profess
pro.fes/sion
pro.fes/sional
pro.fes/sion/al.ism
pro.fes/sion/ally
pro.fes/sor
pro.fes/sor/ship
pro.fi/ciency
pro.fi/cient
profile
profit
profi.ta/bil.ity
prof.it/able
prof.it/ably
pro/fited
pro.fi/teer
prof.it/ing
prof.li/gate
prof.li/ga/tion
pro/found
pro/foundly
profuse
pro.fu/sion
progeny
prog.no/sis
prog.nos/ti/ca/tion
program
pro.gram/matic
pro/grammed
pro.gram/mer
pro.gram/ming
pro/gress
pro.gress/ing
pro.gres/sion
pro.gres/sive
pro.gres/sively
pro/hibit
pro.hi.bi/tion
pro.hibi/tive
project
pro/jected
pro.ject/ing
pro.jec/tion
pro.jec/tor
pro.le/tar.ian
pro.le/tar.iat

pro.lif/er.ate
pro.lif/er/ation
pro/lific
pro/logue
prolong
pro/longed
prom
prome/nade
promi/nence
promi/nent
promi/nently
promise
prom.is/ing
prom.is/sory
pro.mot/able
promote
pro/moted
pro/moter
pro.mot/ing
pro.mo/tion
pro.mo/tional
prompt
prompt/ing
promptly
prompt/ness
pro.mul/gate
pro.mul/ga/tion
prone
prone/ness
prong
pronoun
pro/nounce
pro/nounce/ment
pro.nun/ci/ation
proof
proof/ing
proof/read
propa/ganda
propa/gate
propa.ga/tion
propane
propel
pro.pel/lant
pro/pelled
pro.pel/ler
pro.pel/ling
pro.pen/sity
proper
prop.erly
prop.er/ties

prop/erty
proph/ecy
proph/esy
pro/phetic
pro.po/nent
pro.por/tion
pro.por/tional
pro.por/tion/ally
pro.por/tion.ate
por.por/tion/ately
pro/posal
propose
pro.pos/ing
propo.si/tion
pro/pound
pro.pri/etary
pro.prie/tor
pro.prie/tor/ship
pro.pri/ety
props
pro.pul/sion
pro rata
prorate
pro/rated
pro.rat/ing
pro.ra/tion
prosaic
pro/scribe
prose
prose/cute
prose.cu/tion
prose.cu/tor
prose/lyt.ize
pros/pect
pro.spec/tive
pro.spec/tus
pros.per/ity
pros.per/ous
pros/tate
pros.ti/tute
pros.ti/tu/tion
pros/trate
pro.tago/nist
protect
pro/tected
pro.tect/ing
pro.tec/tion
pro.tec/tion.ism
pro.tec/tion.ist
pro.tec/tive

3

pro.tec/tor	psy.chi/at/rist	punish	pyre
pro.tec/tor.ate	psy.chi/atry	pun.ish/able	py.ro/ma/niac
protégé	psychic	pun.ish/ment	
protein	psy.cho/analy.sis	puni/tive	
pro tem	psy.cho/ana.lyst	pupil	
protest	psy.cho/ana.lyze	pur.chas/able	**Q**
pro.tes/ta/tion	psy.cho/logic	purchase	
pro/tested	psy.cho/logi.cal	pur/chaser	quack
pro.test/ing	psy.cholo/gist	pur.chas/ers	quack/ery
pro.to/col	psy.cho/so.mat.ic	pur.chas/ing	quad/ran.gle
pro.to/plasm	psy.cho/ther.apy	pure	quad/rant
pro.to/type	public	purely	quad/ratic
pro/tract	pub.li/ca/tion	pur.ga/tive	quad.ri/lat.eral
pro/trude	pub.lic/ity	pur.ga/tory	quad.ri/ple.gic
pro.tru/sion	pub.li/cize	purge	qua.dru/ple
proud	pub/licly	pu.ri.fi/ca/tion	qua.dru/pli/cate
prov/able	publish	purify	quaff
prove	pub/lisher	puritan	quag/mire
proven	pub.lish/ing	pu.ri/tani/cal	quail
proverb	pudding	purity	quali.fi/ca/tion
pro.ver/bial	puddle	purloin	quali/fied
provide	pudgy	purple	quali/fier
pro/vided	PUEBLO, CO	pur/plish	qualify
provi/dence	PUERTO RICAN	purport	quali.fy/ing
PROVI/DENCE, RI	PUERTO RICO	pur/ported	quali.ta/tive
provi/den/tial	puff	pur.port/edly	quali.ta/tively
provider	pu.gi/list	purpose	quali/ties
pro.vid/ing	pug.na/cious	pur.pose/ful	quality
prov/ince	pull	pur.pose/ful/ness	qualm
pro.vin/cial	puller	pur.pose/less	quan/dary
proving	pulley	pur.pose/less/ness	quan.ti/fi/able
pro.vi/sion	pul.mo/nary	pur/posely	quan.ti/fi/ca/tion
pro.vi/sional	pulp	purse	quan.ti/ta/tively
proviso	pulp/mill	pursual	quan.ti/ties
pro.voca/tive	pulp/wood	pur.su/ance	quan/tity
pro.vok/ing	pulsate	pur.su/ant	quantum
prowess	pulse	pursue	quar.an/tine
proxies	pumice	pur.su/ing	quarrel
proxi/mate	pummel	pursuit	quar/reled
proxi/mately	pum/meled	purvey	quar.rel/ing
prox.im/ity	pum.mel/ing	pur/veyor	quar.rel/some
proxy	pump	push	quarry
pru/dence	pumping	push-button (h)	quart
prudent	pun	put	quarter
pru.den/tial	punch	putrid	quar.ter/back
prune	punch/line	putty	quar/terly
pry	punc.tu/al.ity	puzzle	quar.ter/mas.ter
psalm	punc.tu/ate	puzzler	quartet
pseud/onym	punc.tu/ation	pyramid	quar/tile
psy.chi/at.ric	punc/ture	pyra/mided	quartz

quasar	quin/tu/plet	raceway	rafter
quasi	quin/tu.pli/cate	racial	rag
[1]quasi-autonomous (h)	quip	rac/ially	rage
[2]quasi autonomous	quipped	racing	raging
[1]quasi-public (h)	quip/ping	racism	raglan
[2]quasi public	quire	racist	ragtime
quay	quirk	rack	ragweed
quea.si/ness	quit	racket	raid
queasy	quit/claim	racke/teer	rail
QUEBEC	quite	radar	railcar
queen	quitter	ra.dar/scope	railing
queer	quit/ting	radial	rail/lery
quell	quiver	ra.di/ance	rail/road
quench	quiz	radiant	rail/road/ing
queried	quizzed	ra.di/antly	railway
queries	quizzes	radiate	rail/ways
query	quiz.zi/cal	ra.di.at/ing	raiment
quest	quiz/zing	ra.dia/tion	rain
ques/tion	quorum	ra.dia/tor	rainbow
ques/tion/able	quot/able	radical	rain/coat
ques/tion/ing	quo.ta/tion	radi.cal/ism	rain/fall
ques/tion/naire	quote	radi/cally	rain/mak/ing
quibble	quo/tient	radi/cals	rain/storm
quick		radio	rain/water
quicken		ra.dio/ac.tive	rain/wear
quicker		ra.dio/gram	raise
quick/est		ra.dio/iso.tope	raisin
quick/sand		ra.di.olo/gist	rake
quiet	**R**	ra.di.ol/ogy	raking
quieter		ra.dio/phone	[4]rake-off (h)
quietly	rabbi	ra.dio/tele.phone	[5]rake off
quiet/ness	rabbit	ra.dio/ther.apy	RALEIGH, NC
quilt	rabble	radish	rallied
quinine	rabid	radium	rally
quintet	race	radius	ral.ly/ing
quin/tuple	race/track	raffle	ramble

[1]Compound adjective construction. Hyphenate if description precedes noun. (The quasi-autonomous workers' organization is affiliated with a state chapter. Some public utilities might be considered quasi-public corporations.)

[2]Adjective plus adverb construction. Do not hyphenate if description follows noun. (Our labor organization is quasi autonomous. The local bus company is quasi public in that it is highly regulated by state government.)

[4]Noun construction. Hyphenate. (The rake-off on the unexpected sales was more than anyone could believe.)

[5]Verb construction. Do not hyphenate. (In the spring, it is necessary to rake off all the winter debris in order that the shrubbery grow fully.)

ram/bling	rare/fied	ravine	³ready-to-wear (h)
ram.bunc/tious	rarefy	ravioli	²ready to wear
rami.fi/ca/tion	rarely	ravish	re.af/firm
ramify	rare/ness	raw	re.af.fir/ma/tion
ramp	rarity	rawhide	real
rampant	rascal	rayon	realign
rampart	rash	raze	re.align/ing
ramrod	rash/ness	razor	re.align/ment
ram/shackle	rasp/berry	reach	realism
ranch	rasping	reach/able	realist
rancher	rat	react	re.al.is/tic
ran/chero	ratable	re.act/ing	re.al.is/ti/cally
ran/cheros	rate	re.ac/tion	re.ali/ties
rancid	ratee	re.ac/tion.ary	re.al/ity
rancor	rate/mak/ing	re.ac.ti/vate	re.al.iz/able
random	rater	re.ac/tive	re.ali/za/tion
ran.dom/ize	rather	re.ac/tion	realize
ran/domly	rati.fi/ca/tion	reactor	re.al.lo/cate
ran.dom/ness	rati/fied	read	re.al.lo/ca/tion
range	rating	reada/bil.ity	really
ranger	ratio	read/able	realm
rank	ration	reader	realtime
ranking	ra.tio/nal	reader-printer (h)	realtor
ransack	ra.tio/nale	read.er/ship	real/tors
ran/sacked	ra.tion/al.ity	readied	realty
ransom	ra.tion/ali/za/tion	readies	ream
rape	ra.tion/al.ize	readily	re.ana/lyze
ra.pid/ity	ra.tion/ing	readi/ness	reap
rapidly	ratios	reading	re.ap.pli/ca/tion
rapped	rattle	re.ad/just	reapply
rapport	ravage	re.ad/just/ment	re.ap/point
rapt	ravel	⁶readout	re.ap.point/ment
rapture	raveled	⁵read out	re.ap/praisal
rap.tur/ous	ravel/ing	¹ready-made (h)	re.ap/praise
rare	raven	²ready made	rear
rarebit	rav.en/ous		rearm

¹Compound adjective construction. Hyphenate if description precedes noun. (The ready-made sweater costs less than one that is custom made.)

²Adjective plus adverb construction. Do not hyphenate if description follows noun. (The suit is ready made. The new outfit is ready to wear.)

³Noun or compound adjective construction. Hyphenate. (Ready-to-wear is their line of business. The ready-to-wear clothing is one of our best sellers.)

⁵Verb construction. Do not hyphenate. (The proofreader will read out the figures on the report.)

⁶Noun construction. Written as one word. (The computer readout is now available.)

re.ar.ma/ment
re.ar/range
re.ar/range/ment
reason
rea.son/able
rea.son/able/ness
rea.son/ably
rea.son/ing
re.as.sem/ble
re.as.sem/bling
re.as/sert
re.as/sess
re.as/sess/ment
re.as/sign
re.as/sign/ment
re.as/sure
re.as.sur/ing
rebate
rebel
re.belled
re.bel/ling
re.bel/lion
re.bel/lious
re.bel/lious/ness
rebirth
rebound
rebuff
rebuild
rebuilt
rebuke
rebut
re.but/tal
re.but/ted
re.but/ting
re.cal.ci/trant
re.cal.cu/late
re.cal.cu/la/tion
recall
re.call/ing
recant
recap
re.ca/pitu/la/tion
re.capped
re.cap/ping
re.cap/ture
recede
receipt
re.ceipts
re.ceiv/able

re.ceival
receive
re.ceiver
re.ceiv/er/ship
re.ceiv/ing
recency
recent
re.cently
re.cep/tion
re.cep/tion.ist
re.cep/tive
re.cep/tor
recess
re.ces/sion
re.ces/sional
re.ces/sion.ary
re.charg/ing
recheck
re.checked
recipe
re.cipi/ent
re.cip.ro/cal
re.cip.ro/cate
reci/proc/ity
re.cir.cu/late
re.cir.cu/la/tion
reci.ta/tion
recite
reck/less
reckon
rec.kon/able
reclaim
re.claimed
rec.la.ma/tion
re.clas/si/fi/ca/tion
re.clas/si/fied
re.clas/sify
recline
re.clin/ing
recluse
recode
rec.og.ni/tion
rec.og/niz/able
rec.og/nize
rec.og/niz/ing
recoil
rec.ol/lect
re-collect (h)
rec.ol/lec/tion

rec.om/mend
rec.om/men/da/tion
rec.om/mend/ing
rec.om/pense
rec.on/cile
rec.on/cili/ation
re.con.di/tion
re.con.di/tioned
re.con.di/tion.ing
re.con/firm
re.con/fir/ma/tion
re.con/nais/sance
re.con/noi/ter
re.con/nect
re.con/nec/tion
re.con/quer
re.con/sid/era/tion
re.con/sti/tute
re.con/struct
re.con/struc/tion
re.con/struc/tive
re.con/vene
re.con/ver/sion
re.con/vert
recopy
record
recorder
rec.ord/keep.ing
recount
recoup
re.course
recover
re.cov/ered
re.cov.er/ing
re.cov/ery
re-create (h)
rec.re/ate
rec.rea/tion
rec.rea/tional
rec.rea/tion/ally
re.crimi/na/tion
recruit
re.cruited
re.cruiter
re.cruit/ing
re.cruit/ment
rectal
rec/tangle
rec/tan/gu/lar
rec.ti/fier

rectify
rec.ti.fy/ing
rectory
rectum
re.cu.per/ate
re.cu/pera/tion
re.cu/pera/tive
recur
re.curred
re.cur/rence
re.cur/rent
re.cur/ring
re.cur/sive
recycle
re.cycled
re.cyc/ling
red
redcap
re.deco/rate
redeem
re.deema/bil.ity
re.deem/able
re.deemed
re.de/fine
re.defi/ni/tion
re.demp/tion
re.de/ploy
re.de/ploy/ment
re.de.pos/it
re.de/sign
re.de/velop
re.de.vel/op/ment
re.dis/count
re.dis/cover
re.dis/cov.ery
re.dis/trib.ute
re.dis/trict
redound
redress
re.dressed
re.dress/ing
re.duce
reducer
re.duc/ible
re.duc/ing
re.duc/tion
re.dun/dancy
re.dun/dant
redwood

3

re.edu/cate
reek
reel
reelect
re.elec/tion
re.emer/gence
re.em.pha/size
re.em/ploy
reenact
re.en/list
reenter
reentry
re.es.tab/lish
re.es.ti/mate
re.evalu/ation
re.evalu/ate
re.ex.ami/na/tion
re.ex.am/ine
refer
re.fer/able
referee
ref.er/eed
ref.er/ence
ref.er.en/dum
re.fer/ral
re.ferred
re.fer/ring
re.fig/ure
refill
refilm
re.fi/nance
re.fi/nanc/ing
refine
re.fine/ment
re.fin.er/ies
re.fin/ery
re.fin/ing
re.fin/ish/ing
reflect
re.flected
re.flect/ing
re.flec/tion
re.flec/tive
re.flec/tor
reflex
refocus
re.for.es/ta/tion
reform
ref.or.ma/tion

re.for.ma/to/ries
re.for.ma/tory
re.formu/la/tion
re.frac/tion
re.frac/tory
refrain
re.frained
re.frain/ing
re.freeze
refresh
re.fresher
re.fresh/ing
re.fresh/ingly
re.fresh/ment
re.frig/er/ate
re.frig/era/tion
re.frig/era/tor
refuge
refugee
refund
re.fund/able
re.funded
re.fund/ing
re.fur/bish
refusal
refuse
re.fus/ing
refute
re.fut/able
regain
re.gained
re.gain/ing
regal
regalia
regard
re.garded
re.gard/ing
re.gard/less
regatta
regency
re.gen.er/ate
re.gen/era/tion
re.gen/era/tive
re.gen/era/tor
regent
regents
regime
regi/ment
regi.men/ta/tion

region
re.gional
re.gion/al/ism
re.gion/al/ize
re.gion/ally
reg.is/ter
reg.is/trant
reg.is/trar
reg.is/tra/tion
reg.is/try
regress
re.gres/sion
re.gres/sive
re.gres/siv.ity
regret
re.gret/ful
re.gret/fully
re.gret/ta.ble
re.gret/ta.bly
re.gret/ted
re.gret/ting
regroup
re.grouped
re.group/ing
regular
regu.lar/ity
regu/larly
regu/late
regu.lat/ing
regu.la/tion
regu.la/tor
regu.la/tory
re.ha/bili/tate
re.ha/bili/ta/tion
re.ha/bili/ta/tive
re.han/dle
re.han/dling
rehash
re.hearsal
re.hearse
reheat
rehire
reign
re.im/burs/able
re.im/burse
re.im/burse/ment
re.im/burs/ing
re.im/pose
re.in.car/na/tion

rein/deer
re.in/force/ment
re.in/forcer
re.in/forc/ing
re.in/sert
re.in/state
re.in/state/ment
re.in/stat/ing
re.in.sti/tute
re.insur/ance
re.in/sure
re.in.ter/pret
re.in.ter/pre/ta/tion
re.in.tro/duc/tion
re.in/vest
re.in/vest/ment
re.in.vig/or.ate
re.in/voice
reissue
re.is/sued
re.it.er/ate
reject
re.jected
re.ject/ing
re.jec/tion
rejoice
re.joices
re.joic/ing
rejoin
re.join/der
re.ju.ve/nate
re.ju.ve/na/tion
re.kin/dle
re.kin/dling
relapse
relate
related
re.lat/ing
re.la/tion
re.la/tion/ship
rela/tive
rela/tively
rela.tiv/ity
relax
re.laxa/tion
relaxed
re.lax/ing
relay
re.lay/ing

Spelling and Word Division **215**

relearn
release
re.leases
re.leas/ing
rel.e/gate
relent
re.lent/less
rele/vance
rele/vancy
rele/vant
re.lia/bil.ity
re.li/able
re.li/ably
re.li/ance
reliant
relic
relied
relief
relieve
re.lieved
re.lieves
re.liev/ing
re.li/gion
re.li/gious
reline
re.lin/quish
re.lin/quish/ment
relish
reload
re.load/ing
re.lo/cate
re.lo.cat/ing
re.lo.ca/tion
re.luc/tance
re.luc/tant
rely
re.ly/ing
remain
re.main/der
re.main/der/man
remake
re.manu/fac/ture
re.manu/fac/turer
remark
re.mark/able
re.mark/ably
re.marked
re.mar/riage

re.mar/ried
remarry
re.me/dial
reme/died
reme/dies
remedy
re.mem/ber
re.mem/ber/ing
re.mem/brance
remind
re.minded
re.minder
re.mind/ers
re.mind/ful
re.mind/ing
remi/nis/cent
remiss
re.mis/sion
remit
re.mit/tance
re.mit/ted
re.mit/ting
remnant
remodel
re.mod/eled
re.mod.el/ing
re.mon/strance
remorse
re.morse/ful
remote
re.mote/ness
re.mov/able
removal
remove
remover
re.mov/ing
re.mu.ner/ate
re.mu/nera/tion
re.mu/nera/tive
re.nais/sance
rename
render
ren.der/ing
ren.dez/vous
ren.di/tion
rene/gade
renege
re.ne.go/tia.ble

re.ne.go/ti.ate
re.ne.go/tia/tion
renew
re.new/able
renewal
re.new/als
re.new/ing
re.nomi/nate
re.nomi/na/tion
re.nounce
reno/vate
reno.vat/ing
reno.va/tion
renown
re.nowned
rent
rent/able
rental
renter
re.nun/cia/tion
re.oc.cu/pancy
re.oc/cupy
reoffer
reopen
re.opened
re.opener
re.open/ing
reorder
re.or/dered
re.or.der/ing
re.or.ga/ni/za/tion
re.or.ga/ni/za/tional
re.or.ga/nize
re.or.ga/niz/ing
re.ori/ent
re.ori.en/ta/tion
repack
re.pack/age
re.pack/ing
repaid
repaint
re.painted
re.paint/ing
repaints
repair
re.paira/bil.ity
re.pair/able
re.paired

re.pair/ing
re.pair/man
re.pair/man/ship
repa.ra/tion
repast
re.pa.tri/ate
re.pa.tri/ation
repave
re.pav/ing
repay
re.pay/able
re.pay/ing
re.pay/ment
repeal
re.pealed
re.peal/ing
repeat
re.peated
re.peat/edly
re.peat/ing
repel
re.pelled
re.pel/lent
re.pel/ling
repent
re.pen/tance
re.per/cus/sion
rep.er/toire
rep.er.tor.ies
rep.er/tory
repe.ti/tion
repe.ti/tious
re.peti/tive
re.peti/tively
replace
re.place/able
re.placed
re.place/ment
re.plac/ing
re.plant/ing
replay
re.plen/ish
re.plen/ish/ment
replete
re.plevin
replica
rep/licas
rep.li/cate

rep.li.ca/tion
replied
replies
reply
re.ply/ing
report
re.port/able
re.ported
re.port/edly
re.porter
re.port/ers
re.port/ing
repose
re.posi/tion
re.posi/tory
re.pos/sess
re.pos/ses/sion
rep.re/hen/si.ble
rep.re/sent
rep.re/sen/ta/tion
rep.re/sen/ta/tive
repress
re.pressed
re.pres/sion
re.pres/sive
re.prieve
rep.ri/mand
reprint
re.printed
re.print/ing
reprisal
re.prisals
re.proach
re.pro/duce
re.pro/duc/ible
re.pro/duc/tion
re.pro/duc/tive
re.pro.graph.ic
re.pro/graph.ics
reproof
reprove
re.pub/lic
re.pub.li/can
re.pu.di/ate
re.pu.di/ation
re.pug/nance
re.pug/nant
re.pul/sion

re.pul/sive
re.pur/chase
repu.ta/ble
repu.ta/tion
repute
re.put/edly
request
re.quested
re.quest/ing
re.quests
requiem
require
re.quired
re.quire/ment
re.quir/ing
req.ui/site
req.ui.si/tion
re.quital
requite
requote
re.quoted
reread
reroute
rerun
re.sal/able
resale
re.sched/ule
rescind
re.scis/sion
rescue
re.search
re.searcher
re.searches
re.search/ing
reseed
re.seeded
re.seed/ing
resell
re.seller
re.sem/blance
re.sem/ble
re.sem/bling
resent
re.sent/ful
re.sent/ment
res.er.va/tion
reserve
re.served

re.serves
re.serv/ing
re.ser/vist
re.ser/voir
reset
reshape
re.sharpen
reshave
reship
re.ship/ping
re.shuf/fle
re.shuf/fling
reside
resi/dence
resi/dency
resi/dent
resi.den/tial
re.sid/ing
re.sid/ual
re.sidu/ary
residue
resi/dues
resign
res.ig.na/tion
re.signed
re.sil/ience
re.sil/ient
resin
resist
re.sis/tance
re.sis/tant
re.sist/ing
re.sis/tor
resold
reso/lute
reso/lutely
reso.lu/tion
resolve
reso/nance
reso/nant
resort
re.sort/ing
resound
re.sound/ing
re.source
re.source/ful
re.source/ful/ness
respect

re.specta/bil.ity
re.spect/able
re.spect/ably
re.spected
re.spect/ful
re.spect/fully
re.spect/ing
re.spec/tive
re.spec/tively
res.pi.ra/tion
res.pi.ra/tor
res.pi.ra/tory
respite
re.splen/dent
respond
re.sponded
re.spon/dent
re.spond/ing
re.sponse
re.spon/si/bili/ties
re.spon/si/bil.ity
re.spon/si.ble
re.spon/si.bly
re.spon/sive
re.spon/sive/ness
rest
restate
re.state/ment
res.tau/rant
res.tau/ra/teur
res.ti.tu/tion
restive
res.tive/ness
rest/less
rest/less/ness
restock
re.stock/ing
res.to.ra/tion
restore
re.stored
re.stor/ing
re.strain
re.straint
re.strict
re.stric/tion
re.stric/tion.ist
re.stric/tive
rest/room

re.struc/ture
restyle
re.sub/mit
re.sub/mit.ted
re.sub/mit/ting
result
re.sult/ant
re.sulted
re.sult/ful
re.sult/ing
resume
resumé
re.sum/ing
re.sump/tion
re.sur/face
re.sur/fac/ing
re.sur/gence
re.sur/gency
re.sur/gent
res.ur/rect
res.ur/rec/tion
re.sus.ci/tate
re.sus.ci/ta/tion
retail
re.tailed
re.tailer
re.tail/ers
re.tail/ing
retain
re.tained
re.tain/ing
re.tali/ate
re.tali/ation
re.tar.da/tion
re.tarded
re.tard/ing
re.ten/tion
rethink
reti/cence
reti/cent
retina
retire
retiree
re.tir/ees
re.tire/ment
re.tir/ing
retool
retort
retouch

retrace
re.trace/ment
re.traces
retract
re.tracted
re.trac/tion
re.tracts
retrain
re.trained
re.train/ing
re.trains
retread
retreat
re.treated
re.treat/ing
re.treats
re.trench
re.trench/ment
re.triev/able
re.trieval
re.trieve
re.tro/ac.tive
re.tro/ac.tively
re.tro/gress
re.tro/spect
re.tro/spec/tive
return
re.turn/able
re.turned
re.turn/ing
retype
re.typ/ing
reunion
re.un/ions
reuse
re.us/able
re.valu/ate
revalue
revamp
reveal
re.vealed
re.veal/ing
reve.la/tion
revenge
re.venged
re.venge/ful
revenue
reve/nues
re.ver/ber.ate

re.ver/bera/tion
revere
rev.er/ence
rev.er/ent
rev.er/end
reverie
re.ver/sal
reverse
re.versed
re.vers/ible
re.vers/ing
revert
review
re.viewed
re.view/ing
revise
re.vis/ing
re.vi/sion
revisit
re.vi/tali/za/tion
re.vi.tal/ize
revive
re.vo/ca.ble
re.vo.ca/tion
revoke
revo.lu/tion
revo.lu/tion.ary
revo.lu/tion.ist
revo.lu/tion.ize
revolve
re.volver
re.volves
re.volv/ing
re.vul/sion
review
reward
re.warded
re.ward/ing
rewind
re.wind/ing
rewire
reword
re.worded
rework
re.worked
re.work/ing
rewound
rewrite
re.writ/ten

REYKJA/VIK
rhap/sody
rhe/toric
rhe.tori/cal
rheu/matic
rheu.ma/tism
RHO/DESIA
rhyme
rhythm
rhyth/mic
rib
ribbon
rice
rich
RICH/MOND, VA
rich/ness
rick/shaw
rico/chet
riddle
ride
rider
rid.er/less
rid.er/ship
ridge
ridi/cule
ri.dicu/lous
riding
rife
rifle
rifle/man
rift
rig
rigged
rigging
right
right/eous
right/ful
right/fully
rightly
right/ness
right-of-way (h)
rigid
ri.gid/ity
rigidly
rigor
rig.or/ous
rim
ring
ring/leader

ring/mas.ter	roadbed	ROME	rou.tin/ize
ring/side	road/block	roof	routing
riot	roadmap	rookie	row
ri.ot/ous	road/side	room	rowboat
rip	road/ster	room/mate	row/boats
ripe	roadway	roomy	row.di/ness
ripen	ROANOKE, VA	root	rowdy
[4]rip-off (h)	roar	rope	royal
[5]rip off	roast	rose	roy.al/ties
ripped	rob	rosebud	royalty
ripping	robbed	roster	rubber
ripple	robber	rostrum	rub.ber/ize
rise	robbery	rotary	rubbing
risen	robe	rotate	rubies
rising	robin	ro.tat/ing	ruby
risk	robot	ro.ta/tion	rudder
riski/ness	robust	ro.tis/serie	ru.di/ment
risk/less	ROCHES/TER, NY	ROTTER/DAM	ru.di.men/tary
risky	rock	rotund	rue
risqué	rocker	rough	rue/fully
rite	rocket	rough/ened	rug
ritual	roc.ketry	rough.en/ing	rugged
rival	ROCK/FORD, IL	rough/shod	rug.ged/ness
rivaled	rocky	rou/lette	ruin
ri.val/ing	rod	round	ruinous
ri.val/ries	rode	round/about	rule
rivalry	rodent	round/ing	ruling
river	rodeo	[11]round/table	RUMANIA
ri.ver/boat	rogue	[8]round table	rumble
ri.ver/front	roguish	[11]roundup	rum/bling
ri.ver/side	role	[5]round up	rummage
RIVER/SIDE, CA	roll	rout	rumor
ri.ver/view	roll/back	route	run
rivet	rolling	route/man	run/about
riveted	romance	routine	run/away
road	ro.man.ti/cism	rou/tinely	rundown

[4]Noun construction. Hyphenate. (The exorbitant prices were considered a rip-off.)

[5]Verb construction. Do not hyphenate. (Rip off the used pages in the notebook. Does your calculator round up to the next hundred?)

[8]Noun plus adjective construction. Do not hyphenate. (Because I have a round table, I have difficulty finding tablecloths to fit it.)

[11]Noun or adjective construction. Written as one word. (The roundup of all the interoffice envelopes provided an ample supply. The roundup feature of my calculator is not found on all models. A roundtable discussion was held to consider the alternatives.)

running
"runoff
⁵run off
⁶runout
⁵run out
runway
rupture
rural
rush
RUSSIA
RUSSIAN
rust
rustic
rustle
rust/proof
ruth/less
ruth/lessly
rye

3

S

sab.bat/ical
saber
sabo/tage
sabo/teur
sac
sac.cha/rin
sachet
sa.cheted
sack
sack/cloth
sac.ra/ment
sac.ra/men.tal
SACRA/MENTO,
  CA
sacred
sac.ri/fi/cial

sac.ri/fice
sac.ri/fic/ing
sac.ri/lege
sac.ri/le/gious
sac.ro/sanct
sacrum
sad
sadden
saddle
sad.dle/cloth
sadism
sadist
sa.dis/tic
sadly
sadness
sad/nesses
safari
safe
safe/guard
safe/guard/ing
safe/keep/ing
safety
sag
saga
sa.ga/cious
sa.gac/ity
SAHARA
said
SAIGON
sail
sail/able
sail/boat
sail/cloth
sailing
sail/ings
sailor
saint
saint.li/ness
sake
sala/bil.ity

salable
salad
salami
sala/ried
sala/ries
salary
sale
SALEM, MA
SALEM, OR
sales/clerk
sales/force
sales/man
sales/man/ship
salesmen
sales/people
sales/woman
sales/women
salient
saline
sa.lin/ity
saliva
salmon
salon
saloon
salt
salt/cel.lar
saltine
salti/ness
SALT LAKE CITY,
  UT
salt/shaker
salt/water
salty
salu/tary
salu.ta/tion
salute
salvage
sal/vaged
sal.va/tion
salve

same
same/ness
sample
sampler
sam/pling
SAN ANTONIO,
  TX
sana.to/rium
SAN
  BERNARDINO, CA
sanc.ti/fi/ca/tion
sanc/tify
sanc.ti/mo/ni.ous
sanc/tion
sanc.tu/ary
sanctum
sand
sandal
sandbar
sand/blast
sandbox
SAN DIEGO, CA
sandlot
sandman
sand/pa.per
sand/stone
sand/wich
sandy
san.for/ized
SAN FRANCISCO,
  CA
sang
san/guine
sani.tar/ium
sani/tary
sani.ta/tion
sani/tizer
sani/tiz.ers
sanity
SAN JOSE, CA

⁵Verb construction. Do not hyphenate. (Let the water run off the plants. The operator will run out the results on the computer.)

⁶Noun construction. Written as one word. (The runout from the computer will be ready soon.)

"Noun or adjective construction. Written as one word. (There will be a runoff to break the deadlocked vote. The runoff election will be tomorrow.)

SANTA ANA, CA
sap/phire
sarcasm
sar.cas/tic
sardine
sar/donic
sash
SAS/KATCHE/
  WAN
sas.sa/fras
sat
satan
satanic
sat.el/lite
satiate
satin
satire
sa.tiri/cal
sat.is/fac/tion
sat.is/fac/to/rily
sat.is/fac/tory
sat.is/fied
sat.is/fies
satisfy
sat.is/fy/ing
satu/rate
satu.ra/tion
SATUR/DAY
sauce
saucer
SAUDI
sau.er/bra.ten
sauer/kraut
SAULT SAINTE
  MARIE, MI
sauna
saunter
sausage
sau/sages
sauté
sau/terne
savage
sav/agery
SAVAN/NAH, GA
save
savings
savor
savory
savvy

saw
sawdust
sawmill
saxo/phone
say
saying
scaf/fold
scala/bil.ity
scalar
scale
scaling
scallop
scalpel
scan
scandal
scan.dal/ize
scan.dal/ous
SCANDI/NAVIA
SCANDI/NAVIAN
scanner
scan/ning
scant
scant/ily
scape/goat
scar
scarce
scarcely
scar.ci/ties
scar/city
scare
scarlet
scarred
scar/ring
scarves
scath/ing
scatter
scat.ter/brain
scat/tered
scat/ter/ing
scav/enge
scav/enged
scav.en/ger
scav.eng/ing
scen/ario
scen.ar/ios
scene
scenery
scenic
scent

sceptic
scep.ti/cism
sched/ule
sched/ul/ing
schem/ata
schem/atic
scheme
schism
schizo/phre.nia
schizo/phrenic
scholar
schol/arly
schol/ars
schol.ar/ship
scho.las/tic
school
school/house
school/ing
school/mate
school/room
school/teacher
schoo/ner
sciatic
science
sci/ences
sci.en/tific
sci.en/tifi/cally
sci.en/tist
scin.til/late
scion
scis/sors
scle.ro/sis
scoff
scoop
scope
scorch
scorcher
score
score/board
score/card
score/keeper
scoring
scorn
scotch
SCOT/LAND
scoun/drel
scour
scourge
scout

scram/ble
scram/bler
scrap
scrape
scraped
scrap/ing
scrapped
scrap/ping
scratch
scratched
scratchi/ness
scratch/ing
scream
screech
screen
screen/ing
screw
scrib/ble
scribe
scrim/mage
script
scrub
scrub/ber
scrub/bing
scruple
scru.pu/lously
scru.ti/nize
scru/tiny
scuff
scuffle
sculp/tor
sculp/ture
scurry
scuttle
sea
sea/board
sea/coast
seafood
sea/foods
seagull
seal
seal/skin
seam
seaman
seam/less
seam/stress
séance
sear
search

3

search/able	sector	seizing	senate
searched	secular	seizure	senator
search/ing	secu.lar/ism	seldom	sena.to/rial
sea/scape	secure	select	sena/tors
sea/shell	se.cur/ing	se.lected	send
sea/shore	se.cu/ri/ties	se.lect/ing	sender
seasick	se.cu/rity	se.lec/tion	⁴send-off (h)
season	sedan	se.lec/tive	⁵send off
sea.son/able	sedate	se.lec/tively	SENEGAL
sea/sonal	se.da/tion	se.lec/tiv.ity	senile
sea.son/ally	se.da/tive	se.lec/tor	se.nil/ity
sea/soned	sedi/ment	self	senior
seat	sedi.men/ta/tion	*self-appointed (h)	se.nior/ity
SEATTLE, WA	sedi.men/tary	selfish	sen.sa/tion
seaway	se.di/tion	selfless	sen.sa/tional
seaweed	se.di/tious	self/same	sen.sa/tion/ally
sea/worthy	seduce	sell	sense
secede	se.duc/tion	seller	sense/less
se.ces/sion	se.duc/tive	se.man/tic	senses
seclude	see	sem/blance	sen.si/ble
se.clu/sion	seed	se.mes/ter	sensing
second	seeded	semi/an.nual	sen.si/tive
sec.on/dar.ily	seed/ling	semi/an.nu.ally	sen.si/tiv.ity
sec.on/dary	seedy	semi/au.tono.mous	sen.si/tize
sec/onded	seeing	semi/cir.cle	sensory
sec.ond/hand	seek	semi/colon	sensual
sec/ondly	seem	semi/con.duc.tor	sen.su/ous
secrecy	seem/ingly	semi/fi.nal	sent
secret	seemly	semi/monthly	sen/tence
sec.re/tar.ial	seen	seminal	sen.ti/ment
sec.re/tar.ies	seep	seminar	sen.ti/mental
sec.re/tary	seepage	semi/nars	sen.ti/nel
secrete	seer/sucker	semi/nary	sentry
se.cre/tion	seesaw	semi/pre.cious	sep.a.ra/ble
se.cre/tive	segment	semi/pri.vate	sep.a/rate
sect	seg.men/ta/tion	semipro	sep.a/rately
sec.tar/ian	seg/mented	semi/pub.lic	sep.a/rat/ing
sec.tari/an.ism	seg/ments	semi/re.tired	sep.a.ra/tion
section	seg.re/gate	semi/re.tire/ment	sep.a.ra/tism
sec/tional	seg.re/ga/tion	semi/skilled	sep.a.ra/tor
sec.tion/al/iz/ing	seg.re/ga/tion.ist	semi/trailer	sepia
sec/tioned	seis.mo/graph	semi/weekly	SEPTEM/BER
sec/tions	seize	semi/yearly	septic

*All self words except selfish, selfless, and selfsame are hyphenated and are divided only at the hyphen. For spelling, refer to root word.
⁴Noun construction. Hyphenate. (They gave the retirees a big send-off.)
⁵Verb construction. Do not hyphenate. (Send off our reservations to-day.)

sequel
se.quence
se.quen/tial
sequin
sere/nade
serene
se.ren/ity
ser/geant
serial
se.ri/al.ize
series
serious
se.ri/ously
se.ri/ous/ness
sermon
serrate
ser.ra/tion
serum
servant
serve
service
ser.vice/able
ser/viced
ser.vice/man
ser.vice/men
ser/vices
ser/vic/ing
servile
ser.vil/ity
serving
ser.vi/tude
session
ses/sions
sct
setback
set/backs
set/screw
settee
setter
setting
settle
set.tle/ment
settler

set/tling
settlor
[6]setup
[5]set up
seven
sev.en/teen
seventh
sev.en/ties
sever
several
sev.er.al/fold
sev.er/ance
severe
se.verely
se.ver/ity
sew
sewage
sewer
sew.er/age
sewn
sex
sexes
sexist
sextet
sexton
sexual
shabby
shackle
shade
shadow
shaft
shaft/ing
shag
shah
shake
shake/down
[6]shake/out
[5]shake out
shaker
[6]shakeup
[5]shake up
shakily
shaky

shale
shall
shallow
shal/lower
sham
shamble
shame
shame/ful
shame/less
shampoo
sham/pooed
sham/rock
shape
shape.li/ness
share
share/crop.per
share/holder
share/hold.ers
share/owner
share/own.ers
sharp
sharpen
sharp/ened
sharp/ener
sharp/en/ing
sharp/ens
sharp/est
SHARPS/BURG, PA
sharp/shooter
shatter
shat/ter/ing
shat.ter/proof
shave
shaven
shaver
shaving
she
sheaf
shear
shears
sheath
sheath/ing
shed

shed/ding
sheep
sheer
sheet
sheet/ing
shelf
shell
shellac
shel/lacked
shel/lack/ing
shelter
shel/tered
shelves
shelv/ing
shep/herd
sherbet
sheriff
sher/iffs
Shet/land
shield
shield/ing
shift
shifti/ness
shift/ing
shift/less
shim
shim/ming
shimmy
shine
shined
shingle
shining
shiny
ship
ship/build/ing
ship/mate
ship/ment
shipped
shipper
ship/pers
ship/ping
ship/shape
ship/wreck

[5]Verb construction. Do not hyphenate. (Set up a new file. Shake out the dust cloth. Shake up the correction fluid before using it.)

[6]Noun construction. Written as one word. (That is a good setup. We need a shakeout of out-of-date customers. They had a shakeup in management.)

shirt	[8]short circuit	showy	shut/down
shirt/tail	short/com.ing	shrap/nel	[6]shutoff
shish ke.bob	short/cut	shred	[5]shut off
shock	shorten	shred/ded	shutter
shock/proof	[1]short-order (h)	shred/der	shuttle
shod/dily	[1]short-range (h)	shred/ding	shuttled
shod.di/ness	[8]short range	SHREVE/PORT,	shut/tling
shoddy	[1]short-sighted (h)	LA	shy
shoe	[2]short sighted	shrewd	shyster
shoed	[1]short-tempered (h)	shriek	SIBERIA
shoe/string	[2]short tempered	shrill	sick
shook	[1]short-term (h)	shrimp	sick/ened
shoot	[8]short term	shrink	sick/li/ness
shooter	short/wave	shrink/age	sickly
shoot/ing	shot	shrink/ing	sick/ness
shop	shotgun	shrivel	side
shop/keeper	shot/guns	shriv/eled	side/light
shop/lift/ing	should	shriv/el/ing	side/line
shopped	shoul/der	shroud	side/step
shopper	shovel	shrug	side/step/ping
shop/ping	shov/eled	shrugged	side/track
shop/worn	shov/el/ing	shrug/ging	side/walk
shore	show	shuck	side/wall
shore/line	show/case	shudder	side/ways
shore/man	show/down	shuffle	siding
shore/side	shower	shuf/fling	siege
short	show/ings	shun	siesta
short/age	showman	shunned	sieve
short/change	show.man/ship	shun/ning	sift
[7]short-circuit (h)	show/room	shut	sigh

[1]Compound adjective construction. Hyphenate if description precedes noun. (a short-range plan, a short-sighted policy, a short-tempered executive, a short-term loan, a short-order cook)

[2]Adjective plus adverb construction. Do not hyphenate if description follows noun. (policy that is short sighted, executive who is short tempered)

[5]Verb construction. Do not hyphenate. (Electricity may be shut off because of the energy shortage.)

[6]Noun construction. Written as one word. (We experienced a power shutoff.)

[7]Verb construction. Hyphenate. (The damp plug short-circuited the electric typewriter.)

[8]Noun plus adjective construction. Do not hyphenate. (We had a short circuit in our electrical lines. They adopted a plan that is short range. Can you get a loan for a short term?)

sight	simmer	sin.is/ter	skele/tal
sight.li/ness	simple	sink	skele/ton
³sight-seeing (h)	simpler	sinking fund	skeptic
sigma	sim/plest	sinus	skep.ti/cal
sign	sim.plic/ity	SIOUX FALLS, SD	skep.ti/cism
signal	sim.pli/fi/ca/tion	siphon	sketch
signaled	sim.pli/fied	si.phon/ing	sketched
sig/nal.ing	sim.pli/fies	sir	sketches
sig.na/tory	sim/plify	sire	sketch/ily
sig.na/ture	sim.plis/tic	siren	sketchy
signer	simply	sirloin	skew
sig.nifi/cance	simu/late	sissies	skewed
sig.nifi/cant	simu.la/tion	sissy	skew/ness
sig.nifi/cantly	simu/lator	sister	ski
signify	si.mul.ta/neous	sister-in-law (h)	skid
silence	si.mul.ta/neously	sit	skidded
si.lencer	sin	³sitdown	skid/ding
si.lences	since	⁵sit down	skier
silent	sincere	site	skies
sil.hou/ette	sin/cerely	⁴sit-in (h)	skiing
silica	sin.cer/est	⁵sit in	skill
sili/cate	sin.cer/ity	sitting	skillet
silicon	sine	situate	skil/lets
sili/cone	sinewy	situ/ated	skill/ful
sili/cons	sing	situ/ation	skill/fully
sili/co.sis	SINGAPORE	situ/ational	skim
silk	singe	six	skimpy
silken	singe/ing	sixteen	skin
silo	singer	sixth	skinned
silos	singing	sixties	skip
silver	single	six.ti/eth	skipped
sil.ver/plate	single-mindedness (h)	sixty	skipper
sil.ver/smith	¹single-spaced (h)	sizable	skip/ping
sil.ver/ware	²single spaced	size	skir/mish
similar	single/ton	sizzle	skir/mishes
simi.lar/ity	singly	siz/zling	skirt
simi/larly	sin.gu/lar	skein	skull

¹Compound adjective construction. Hyphenate if description precedes noun. (Single-spaced lines may be difficult to read.)

²Adjective plus adverb construction. Do not hyphenate if description follows noun. (All copy is single spaced in this office.)

³Noun or compound adjective construction. Hyphenate. (We went sight-seeing. They took a sight-seeing trip across the country.)

⁴Noun construction. Hyphenate. (Sit-ins were popular in the 60s.)

⁵Verb construction. Do not hyphenate. (Please sit down. Will you sit in for me at the meeting?)

⁸Noun or Pronoun plus adjective construction. Do not hyphenate. (Students held a sitdown strike.)

skull/cap	sledge/ham.mer	snubbed	soft/ball
skunk	sleep	snub/bing	[1]soft-boiled (h)
sky	sleeper	sung	[2]soft boiled
sky/coach	sleepi/ness	snugger	soften
sky/crane	sleep/ing	snug/gest	sof/tened
skyline	sleep/less/ness	snuggle	soft/ware
sky/roc.ket	sleeve	snug/gling	sog.gi/ness
sky/roc.ket/ing	sleigh	soap	soggy
sky/scraper	slender	soar	soil
skyward	sleuth	sober	sojourn
slab	slew	so.ber/ing	solace
slack	slice	so.bri/ety	solar
slacken	slick	so-called (h)	sold
slack/ened	slicker	soccer	solder
slag	slide	so.cia/bil.ity	soldier
slalom	sliding	so.cia/ble	sol/diers
slam	slight	social	sole
slammed	slighted	so.cial/ism	solely
slam/ming	slight/est	so.cial/ist	solemn
slander	slightly	so.cial/is.tic	solicit
slan/der.ous	slim	so.cial/ite	so.lici/ta/tion
slang	slime	so.ciali/za/tion	so.lic/ited
slant	slimy	so.cial/ize	so.lic/it/ing
slap	sling	so.cially	so.lici/tor
slapped	slip	so.ci/etal	so.lici/tous
slap/ping	[3]slip-on (h)	so.ci/eties	solid
slap/stick	[5]slip on	society	soli/dar.ity
slash	slip/page	so.cio/eco.nomic	so.lidi/fi/ca/tion
slat	slipper	so.cio/logi.cal	so.lid/ify
slate	slip/pers	so.cio/ol.ogy	[1]solid-state
slaugh/ter	snow/blower	sock	[8]solid state
slave	snow/fall	socket	so.lil.o/quy
slavery	snow/mo.bile	sod	soli/taire
slavish	snow/plow	soda	soli/tary
sled	snow/storm	sodding	soli/tude
sled/ding	snowy	sodium	solo
sledge	snub	soft	soloist
			solos

[1]Compound adjective construction. Hyphenate if description precedes noun. (Soft-boiled eggs are on the menu. The solid-state construction of the television set insures a better picture.)

[2]Adjective plus adverb construction. Do not hyphenate if description follows noun. (Are your eggs soft boiled?)

[3]Noun or compound adjective construction. Hyphenate. (Slip-ons are popular in men's shoes. My new slip-on sweater is comfortable.)

[5]Verb construction. Do not hyphenate. (Be careful not to slip on the highly waxed floor.)

[8]Noun plus adjective construction. Do not hyphenate. (Ice is water in the solid state.)

solu.bil/ity	soothe	south/east.ern	spate
soluble	sooth/ing	south/erly	spatial
so.lu/tion	so.phis/ti/cate	south/ern	spa/tially
solv/able	so.phis/ti/ca/tion	south/land	spatter
solve	sopho/more	south/west	spatula
sol/vency	sordid	south/west.ern	spawn
solvent	sore	sou.ve/nir	speak
sol/vents	sorely	sov.er/eign	speaker
solver	sorghum	sov.er/eignty	speak/ers
solving	sor/ghums	soy	speak/ing
SOMALIA	sorely	soybean	spear/head
somber	so.ror/ity	soy/beans	spear/mint
some	sorrow	spa	special
some/body	sor.row/ful	space	spe.cial/ist
[9]someday	sorry	space/craft	spe.ciali/za/tion
[8]some day	sort	space/flight	spe.cial/ize
somehow	soufflé	spacer	spe.cial/iz/ing
[10]someone	sought	space/ship	spe/cially
[8]some one	soul	spacial	spe.ci.al/i.ties
[9]some/place	[3]soul-searching (h)	spa/cious	spe.ci.al/ity
[8]some place	sound	spade/work	specie
som.er/sault	sounder	spa/ghetti	species
[10]some/thing	sound/est	SPAIN	spe/cific
[8]some thing	sound/ing	span	spe.cifi/cally
[9]some/time	sound/ness	SPANISH	speci.fi/ca/tion
[8]some time	sound/proof	spangle	speci/fied
some/what	soup	span/gled	speci/fier
some/where	source	spanned	speci/fies
son	sou.sa/phone	span/ning	specify
song	south	spare	speci/fy/ing
sonic	SOUTH BEND, IN	spark	speci/men
son-in-law (h)	SOUTH	sparkle	specs
sonnet	CARO/LINA	spar/kling	spec.ta/cle
so.nor/ous	SOUTH DAKOTA	sparse	spec/tacu/lar
soon	south/east	sparsely	spec/tacu/larly

[3]Noun or compound adjective construction. Hyphenate. (They engaged in some soul-searching activities. They did some soul-searching before making the decision.)

[8]Noun plus adjective construction. Do not hyphenate. (We should meet at some place close to the office. He must excel in some one thing. I have wanted to change jobs for some time now. We should have lunch on some day next week. The typing must be done by some one of us.)

[9]Adverb construction. One word. (I shall see you someday soon. It must be someplace here. We will meet sometime soon.)

[10]Indefinite pronoun. (Someone will transcribe your notes. Something must be done about employee absences.)

Spelling and Word Division **227**

spec.ta/tor
specter
spec/tral
spec/trum
specu/late
specu.la/tion
specu.la/tive
speech
speech/less
speed
speed/ily
speed/ing
speed/ome.ter
speed/way
spell
spell/bound
spell/ing
spend
spend/able
spend/ing
spend/thrift
spent
sphere
spheri/cal
spice
spider
spigot
spike
spill
spill/over
spinach
spinal
spindle
spine
spinet
spinner

spin/ners
spin/ning
[6]spinoff
[5]spin off
spin/ster
spiral
spi/raled
spi.ral/ing
spirally
spirit
spir/ited
spir.it/less
spiri/tual
spiri/tual.ism
spiri.tu/al.ity
spite
spite/ful
splash
splash/down
splash/ing
splen/did
splen/didly
splen/dor
spline
splint
splin/ter
split
[3]split-level (h)
split/ting
splurge
spoil/age
spoil/sport
SPOKANE, WA
spoke
spoken
spokes/man

spokes/per.son
spokes/woman
sponge
spongy
sponsor
spon/sored
spon.sor/ing
spon.sor/ship
spon.ta/ne.ity
spon.ta/ne.ous
spoon/ful
spool
spoon
spor/adic
sport
sport/ing
sports/cast
sports/man
sports/man/ship
sports/wear
spot
[4,7]spot-check (h)
spot/less
spot/lessly
spot/light
spotted
spot/ting
spotty
spouse
spout
sprain
sprawl
sprawled
spray
spray/ing
spread

spread/ing
spree
spring
spring/board
SPRING/FIELD,
MA
SPRING/FIELD,
MO
spring/time
sprin/kle
sprin/kler
sprocket
sprock/ets
sprout
spruce
spur
spu.ri/ous
spurred
spur/ring
spurt
sputter
sputum
spy/glass
squab/ble
squab/bling
squad
squad/ron
squalid
squall
squalor
squan/der
square
squarely
squash
squat/ter
squaw

[3]Noun or compound adjective construction. Hyphenate. (Split-levels are popular among home builders these days. Our new split-level house has a great deal of floor space.)

[4]Noun construction. Hyphenate. (We ran a spot-check to judge the quality of the product.)

[5]Verb construction. Do not hyphenate. (The yarn will spin off the huge cone.)

[6]Noun construction. Written as one word. (Full employment will result in a spinoff of increased department store sales.)

[7]Verb construction. Hyphenate. (Will you spot-check the order to see if all items are included?)

squawk
squeaky
squeam/ish
squee/gee
squeeze
squeezed
squeez/ing
squirm
squir/rel
squirt
sta.bil/ity
sta.bili/za/tion
sta.bi/lize
sta.bi/lizer
sta.bi/liz/ing
stable
stac/cato
stack
stack/ing
stadium
sta/diums
staff
staffer
staff/ing
staff/men
stage/craft
stage/hand
stagger
stag/gered
staging
stag/nant
stag.nate
stag.na/tion
stain
stain/less
stair
stake
staking

stale
stale/mate
stal/wart
stamen
STAM/FORD, CT
stamina
stam/mer
stamp
stam/pede
stamp/ing
stance
stand
stan/dard
stan/dardi/za/tion
stan/dard.ize
stan/dard/iz/ing
[5]standby
[6]stand/by
[6]stand/bys
[4]stand-in (h)
[5]stand in
stand/ing
[6]stand/off
[5]stand off
[6]standout
[5]stand out
stand/pipe
stand/point
[6]stand/still
[5]stand still
staple
stapler
sta/plers
sta/pling
star
star/board
starch
stardom

stare
start
starter
start/ers
star/ting
startle
star/tled
star/tling
[4]start-up (h)
[5]start up
star.va/tion
stat
state
state/hood
state/house
stately
state/ment
state/room
state/side
states/man/ship
state/wide
static
station
sta.tion/ary
sta/tioner
sta.tio/nery
sta/tions
sta.tis/ti.cal
sta.tis/ti/cally
stat.is/ti/cian
sta.tis/tic
statue
statu/esque
stature
status
statute
stat/utes
statu/tory

staunch
stave
stay
staying
stead/fast
stead/ier
stead/ily
steady
steak
steal
steal/ing
steam
steam/boat
steamer
steam/ers
steam/ship
steel
steel/mak/ing
steel/plate
steel/worker
steep
steeple
steer
steer/ing
stem
stemmed
stem/ming
stencil
sten/ciled
sten.cil/ing
sten/cils
steno
ste.nog/ra/pher
ste.nog/ra/phic
ste.nog/raphy
step
step/brother
step/child

3

[4]Noun construction. Hyphenate. (He acted as my stand-in at the meeting. Factory start-ups increased last month.)

[5]Verb construction. Do not hyphenate. (Please stand by in case there is a seat for you. Will you stand in for me at the election? Do not stand off to that side of the platform. The child will not stand still for the examination. They will start up a new factory. They stand out in a crowd.)

[6]Noun construction. Written as one word. (There are a number of standbys for this flight. The negotiations in the labor dispute are at a standoff. Our new salesperson is a standout. Things are at a standstill.)

step/daugh.ter	stimu/late	stop/page	strap
[4]step-down (h)	stimu/lat/ing	stopped	strapped
[5]step down	stimu/la.tor	stopper	strap/ping
step/father	stimu/lus	stop/pers	stra.te/gic
step/mother	stingy	stop/ping	stra.te/gi/cally
step/par.ent	stint	storage	strat.eg/ies
step/ping	stipend	stor/ages	strate/gist
step/sis.ter	stipu/late	store	strategy
stepson	stipu/lat/ing	store/keeper	strat/ify
stereo	stipu.la/tion	store/room	strati/fi/ca/tion
stereo/type	stir	store/wide	strato/sphere
sterile	stirred	stories	stratum
ste.ril/ity	stir/ring	storm	straw
steri/li/za/tion	stitch	stormy	straw/berry
ster.il/ize	stitched	story	streak
ster.il/iz/ing	stitch/ing	sto.ry/board	stream
ster/ling	ST. LOUIS, MO	sto.ry/book	streamer
stern	stock	stout	stream/ers
stetho/scope	stock/holder	stout/hearted	stream/line
ste.ve/dore	stock/hold.ers	stoutly	stream/liner
ste.ve/dor/ing	stock/ing	stove	street
steward	stock/man	stow	street/car
stew.ard/ess	stock/pile	stow/away	strength
stew.ard/esses	stock/pil/ing	ST. PAUL, MN	strengthen
stew/ards	stock/room	ST. PETERSBURG,	strength/ened
stew.ard/ship	stock split	FL	strength/en/ing
stick	STOCKTON, CA	straddle	strenu/ous
sticker	stock/yard	strad/dling	strep.to/coc.cus
stick/ers	stodgy	straggly	strep.to/my.cin
stick/ing	stole	straight	stress
stiff	stolen	straighten	stress/ing
stiffen	stomach	straight/en/ing	stretch
stiff/ener	stom.ach/ache	straight/ens	stretched
stiff/en.ers	stomp	straight/for.ward	stretcher
stiffens	stone	strain	stretch/ers
stifle	stone/mason	strainer	stricken
stif/ling	stood	strait	strict
stigma	stool	strange	strict/est
stig.ma/tize	stoop	strangely	stric/ture
stile	stop	stranger	stride
still	stopgap	stran.gu/late	strife
stimu/lant	stop/over	stran.gu/lat/ing	strike

[4]Noun construction. Hyphenate. (His step-down from the presidency was a surprise.)

[5]Verb construction. Do not hyphenate. (She will step down from the presidency.)

strike/breaker	stuffer	sub/jects	sub.stan/ti.ate
[6]strike/out	stuffi/ness	sub.ju.ga/tion	sub.stan/ti/ation
[5]strike out	stul/tify	sub.junc/tive	sub.stan/tive
striking	stumble	sub/lease	sub.stan/tively
string	stum/bling	sub.li/mate	sub.sti/tute
strin/gent	stun	sub.ma/rine	sub.sti/tut/ing
strip	stung	sublime	sub.sti/tu/tion
stripe	stun/ning	sub/merge	sub/sys.tem
striped	stunt	sub.mer/sion	sub.ter/fuge
strip/ing	stupefy	sub.mis/sion	sub/ter.ra/nean
stripped	stu.pen/dous	submit	subtle
strip/ping	stupid	sub.mit/tal	sub/tlety
strive	stu.pid/ity	sub.mit/ted	subtly
striv/ing	stupor	sub.mit/ting	sub/tract
stroke	stur/dier	sub/nor.mal	sub.trac/tion
strok/ing	stur.di/ness	sub.or.di/nate	sub/tropi.cal
strong	sturdy	sub/para.graph	subunit
stronger	stutter	sub/poena	suburb
strong/est	style	sub/re.gion	sub/ur.ban
strong/hold	styling	sub.ro/ga/tion	sub/ur.bia
strongly	stylish	sub/sam.ple	sub/ver.sion
struck	stylus	sub/scribe	sub.ver/sive
struc/tural	stymie	sub/scriber	subway
struc/tur/ally	stymied	sub/scrib.ers	subzero
struc/ture	styrene	sub/scrib/ing	succeed
struc/tur/ing	suave	sub.scrip/tion	suc.ceeded
struggle	sub/agent	sub/sec.tion	suc.ceed/ing
strug/gling	sub/cate.gory	sub.se/quent	success
strut	sub/chap.ter	sub.se/quently	suc/cesses
stub	subcode	subset	suc.cess/ful
stub/born	sub/com.mit.tee	subside	suc.cess/fully
stucco	sub/con.scious	sub/sides	suc.ces/sion
stuck	sub/con.tract	sub.sidi/ar.ies	suc.ces/sive
student	sub/con.trac.tor	sub.sidi/ary	suc.ces/sively
stu/dents	sub/cul.ture	sub.si/dies	suc.ces/sor
studied	sub/di.vide	sub.sid/ing	suc/cinct
studies	sub/di.vi.sion	sub.si/dize	suc.co/tash
studio	subdue	subsidy	suc.cu/lent
studios	sub/group	sub.sis/tence	succumb
stu.di/ous	subject	sub/stance	suc/cumbs
study	sub/jected	sub/stan.dard	such
study/ing	sub.ject/ing	sub.stan/tial	sucker
stuff	sub.jec/tive	sub.stan/tially	suction

[5]Verb construction. Do not hyphenate. (The agent decided to strike out on his own.)

[6]Noun construction. Written as one word. (The pitcher had three strikeouts in one inning.)

suc/tioned
sudden
sud/denly
sue
suede
suffer
suf/fered
suf/ferer
suf.fer/ing
suffice
suf.fi/ciency
suf.fi/cient
suf.fi/ciently
suffix
suf.fo/cat/ing
suf/frage
sugar
sug.ar/cane
sug.ar/coat
suggest
sug/gested
sug.gest/ing
sug.ges/tion
sui/cidal
suicide
suing
suit
suita/bil.ity
suit/able
suite
suiting
suitor
sulfide
sulfur
sullen
sul/phite
sulphur
sultan
sultry
sum
sum.ma/ries
sum.mar/ily
sum.ma.ri/za/tion
sum.ma/rize
sum.ma/riz/ing
summary
sum.ma/tion
summer
sum.mer/time
summing

summit
summon
sum/moned
summons
sun
sunbath
sun/bathe
sun/bath/ing
sunburn
SUNDAY
sunder
sundial
sundown
sun/dries
sundry
sunfast
sunfish
sung
sun/glasses
sunken
sunny
SUNNYVALE, CA
sun/shine
sunspot
super
superb
su.perbly
su.per/fi/cial
su.per/fine
su.per/flu.ous
su.per/human
su.per/im.pose
su.per/in/tend.ency
su.per/in/tend.ent
su.pe/rior
su.pe/ri/or.ity
su.per/la/tive
su.per/mar.ket
su.per/natu.ral
su.per/sales.man
su.per/script
su.per/sede
su.per/sonic
su.per/star
su.per/sti/tious
su.per/tanker
su.per/vise
su.per/vis/ing
su.per/vi/sion
su.per/vi.sor

su.per/vi.sory
sup/plant
supple
sup.ple/ment
sup.ple/mental
sup.ple/men/tary
sup.ple/men/ta/tion
sup.pli/cant
sup.pli/cate
sup/plied
sup/plier
sup/plies
supply
sup.ply/ing
support
sup/ported
sup/porter
sup.port/ers
sup.port/ing
suppose
sup/posed
sup.posi/to.ries
sup.posi/tory
sup/press
supra
su.prem/acy
supreme
sur/charge
sure
surely
surest
sure/ties
surety
surf
surface
sur/faced
sur.fac/ing
surfer
surfing
surge
surgeon
sur/geons
surgery
sur.gi/cal
surging
surly
surmise
sur/mount
surname
surpass

sur/passes
surplus
sur/pluses
sur/prise
sur.pris/ing
sur.pris/ingly
sur.ren/der
sur.ro/gate
sur/round
sur/round/ing
surtax
sur.veil/lance
survey
sur/veyed
sur/veyor
sur/vival
survive
sur/vives
sur.viv/ing
sur/vivor
sur.vi/vor/ship
sus.cep/ti.ble
sus.cep/ti/bil.ity
suspect
sus/pected
sus.pect/ing
suspend
sus/pended
sus.pend/ing
sus/pense
sus.pen/sion
sus.pi/cion
sus.pi/cious
sustain
sus.tain/able
sus/tained
sus.tain/ing
sus/tains
sus.te/nance
suture
swallow
swal/lowed
swamp
swamp/land
swan
swap
swarthy
swatch
swatches
swear

swear/ing	sym.pa/thetic	tabled	tail/spin
sweat	sym.pa/thize	ta.ble d'hôte	taint
sweater	sym.pa/thy	table-hop (h)	TAIWAN
sweat/ers	sym/phony	ta.ble/spoon	take
SWEDEN	sym.po/sia	tablet	taken
sweep	sym.po/sium	ta.ble/top	[6]takeoff
sweeper	symptom	ta.ble/ware	[5]take off
sweep/ers	symp/toms	ta.bling	[6]take/over
sweep/ing	syn.chro/nize	tabloid	[5]take over
sweep/stakes	syn.di/cate	taboo	taker
sweet	syn.di/ca/tion	taboos	talent
sweet/ener	syn/drome	tabular	tal.is/man
sweet/en.ers	syn.er/gism	tabu/late	talk
swell	syn.er/gis.tic	tabu.lat/ing	talk/ative
swelter	synergy	tabu.la/tion	[11]talk/down
swift	synod	tabu.la/tor	[5]talk down
swim	synonym	ta.chis/to/scope	TALLA/HASSEE,
swim/ming	syn.ony/mous	ta.chome/ter	FL
swindle	syno/nyms	tacit	tallow
swin/dling	syn.op/sis	taci/turn	tamale
swine	syntax	tack	tamely
swing	syn.the/sis	tackle	TAMPA, FL
swinger	syn.the/size	tack/ling	tamper
switch	syn/thetic	TACOMA, WA	tan
switch/blade	syn.thet/ics	taco/nite	tandem
switch/board	SYRA/CUSE, NY	tact	tangent
switches	syringe	tactful	tan/gents
switch/ing	syrup	tactic	tan.ger/ine
swivel	system	tac.ti/cal	tan.gi/bil.ity
swoop	sys.tem/atic	tac.ti/cian	tan.gi/ble
sworn	sys.tem/ati/cally	tactile	tangle
syca/more	sys.tema/tize	tact/less	tangled
syl/labic		taffeta	tank
syl.labi/cate		tag	tankage
syl.la/ble		tag/board	tankard
syl.la/bus		tagged	tanker
syl.lo/gism		tagging	tannery
symbol	**T**	tail	tannic
sym/bolic		tail/gate	tan.ta/mount
sym.bol/ism	tab	tail/light	TANZA/NIA
sym.bol/ize	table	tailor	tap
sym/metry	ta.ble/cloth	tai/lored	tape

[5]Verb construction. Do not hyphenate. (The plane will take off at 5 p.m. Sue will take over for you while you are on vacation. They hope to talk down the idea.)

[6]Noun construction. Written as one word. (Coffee will be served soon after takeoff. When the takeover occurred, it was a complete surprise.)

[11]Adjective construction. Written as one word. (The talkdown tone on the recorder would not cease.)

taper	²tax exempt	tedium	tem.pera/men.tal
tape-record (h)	taxi	teem	tem.per/ate
tape recorder	taxicab	teen	tem.pera/ture
tap.es/try	taxi.der/mist	teenage	tempered
taping	taxi/dermy	teen/ager	tempest
tapping	taxied	teeth	tem.pes/tu.ous
taproom	tax.on/omy	tee.to/taler	tem/plate
tar	tax/payer	TEHRAN	temple
tardily	tax/pay/ing	tele/cast	tempo
tar.di/ness	T-bone	telecom	tem.po/ral
tardy	tea	tele.com/mu/ni/	tem.po/rar.ily
tar.geted	teach	ca/tion	tem.po/rary
tar.get/ing	teach/able	tele/copier	tem.po/rize
tariff	teacher	tele/gram	tempt
tarism	teach/ers	tele/graph	temp.ta/tion
tarnish	teach/ing	tele/graphic	ten
tar.pau/lin	team	tele/lec/ture	tenable
tartan	team/mate	tele/me.ter	te.na/cious
task	team/ster	te.lepa/thy	te.na/ciously
task/mas.ter	team-teach (h)	tele/phone	te.nac/ity
tassel	team/work	tele/phon/ing	ten.an/cies
taste	teapot	tele/print	tenancy
taste/ful	tear	tele/printer	tenant
taste/less	tear sheet	tele/pro/cess/ing	tend
taster	tease	tele/prompter	ten.den/cies
tasting	tea/spoon	tele/pur/chas/ing	ten/dency
tatters	tea/spoon/ful	tele/scope	tender
tattoo	tech.ni/cal	tele/scopic	ten/dered
tat.too/ing	tech.ni/cali/ties	tele/scop/ing	tenet
taught	tech.ni/cal.ity	tele/thon	tene/ment
taunt	tech.ni/cally	tele/tic/ket/ing	TENNES/SEE
taut	tech.ni/cian	tele/type	tennis
tavern	tech.ni/color	tele/type/writer	tenor
tax	tech/nique	tele/vise	tens
taxa.bil/ity	tech.no/crat	tele/vi.sion	tense
taxable	tech.no/lo/gi.cal	tell	tensile
taxa/tion	tech.no/lo/gi/cally	teller	tension
¹tax-deductible (h)	tech/nolo/gist	tel.ler/less	tent
²tax deductible	tech.nol/ogy	tell/tale	ten.ta/tive
taxed	tedious	te.mer/ity	ten.ta/tively
taxes	te.di/ously	temper	tenth
¹tax-exempt (h)	te.di.ous/ness	tem.pera/ment	tenuous

¹Compound adjective construction. Hyphenate if description precedes noun. (The contribution is a tax-deductible donation. The church is a tax-exempt organization.)

²Adjective plus adverb construction. Do not hyphenate if description follows noun. (Will the cost be tax deductible? They believe their group should be tax exempt.)

tenu.ously	tetanus	there/after	thirsty
tenure	tether	thereby	thir/teen
tenured	teth/ered	there/for	thir/ties
tepid	TEXAS	there/fore	thirty
te.quila	text	there/from	this
term	text/book	therein	thistle
ter.mi/na.ble	textile	thereof	tho/racic
ter.mi/nal	tex/tiles	thereon	thorax
ter.mi/nate	textual	thereto	thor/ough
ter.mi/nated	texture	there/upon	thor/ough/bred
ter.mi/na/tion	tex/tured	there/with	thor/ough/fare
ter.mi/nol.ogy	tex.tur/ing	thermal	thor/ough/ness
ter.mi/nus	than	ther.mo/cou.ples	those
termite	thank	ther.mo/dy/namic	though
terrace	thank/ful	ther.mo/dy/nam.ics	thought
terrain	thank/ing	ther.mɔ/elec.tric	thought/ful
ter.rar/ium	thanks	ther/mome/ter	thought/fully
ter/razzo	thanks/giv/ing	ther.mo/nu.clear	thought/ful/ness
TERRE HAUTE, IN	theater	ther.mo/pane	thou/sand
ter.res/trial	the.at/ri.cal	ther.mo/plas.tic	thrall
ter.ri/ble	theft	ther.mo/stat	thrash
ter.ri/bly	their	the.sau/rus	thrash/ing
ter/rific	them	these	thread
ter.ri/fied	theme	theses	thread/bare
ter.ri/to/rial	them/selves	thesis	thread/ing
ter.ri/to/ri/ally	then	they	threat
ter.ri/to/ries	thence	thick	threaten
ter.ri/tory	thence/forth	thicket	threat/ened
terror	theo.lo/gian	thick/ness	threat/en/ing
ter.ror/ism	theo/logi.cal	thick/nesses	three
ter.ror/ist	the.ol/ogy	thief	three/fold
ter.ror/ize	theorem	thiev/ery	three/some
terse	theo/retic	thieves	thresh/old
ter.ti/ary	theo.ret/ical	thigh	threw
test	theo/reti/cally	thin	thrift
tes.ta/ment	theo/ries	thing	thrift/ily
tes.ta/men/tary	theo/rist	think	thrift/less
tes.ta/tor	theo/rize	thinker	thrifty
tes.ti/cle	theory	think/ers	thrill
tes.ti/fied	thera/peu.tic	think/ing	thrilled
testify	thera/pist	thinner	thrill/ing
tes.ti/fy/ing	therapy	third	thrive
tes.ti/mo/nial	there	¹third-rate (h)	thriv/ing
tes.ti/mo/nies	there/abouts	²third rate	throat
tes.ti/mony			

¹Compound adjective construction. Hyphenate if description precedes noun. (The third-rate movie wasn't worth seeing.)
²Adjective plus adverb construction. Do not hyphenate if description follows noun. (Their service is third rate.)

throb
throb/bing
throm.bo/sis
throng
throt/tle
through
through/out
through/put
through/way
throw
throw/ing
thrown
thrust
thumb
thumb/nail
thumb/print
thunder
thun.der/ous
thun.der/storm
THURSDAY
thus
thwart
thyroid
thy.roid/ec.tomy
tick
ticker
ticket
tick/eted
tick.et/ing
tickler
tick/lish
tidal
tidbit

tide
tidily
tie
[4]tie-in (h)
[5]tie in
tier
tiered
[4]tie-up (h)
[5]tie up
tight
tight/ened
tight.en/ing
[11]tight/fisted
[2]tight fisted
[11]tight/mouthed
[2]tight mouthed
tight/rope
tight/wad
TIJUANA
tile
till
tilt
timber
tim.ber/land
tim.ber/line
time
[1]time-consuming (h)
time/keeper
time.li/ness
time lock
timely
time/piece
timer

time-saver (h)
time/sav.ing
time-sharing (h)
time/ta.ble
timid
ti.mid/ity
timing
timo/rous
tin
tinc/ture
tingle
tiniest
tinker
tin.ker/ing
tin/plate
tinsel
tin/seled
tint
tiny
tip
[4]tip-off (h)
[5]tip off
tipped
tipping
tipple
tipster
tirade
tire
tire/lessly
tire/some
tiring
tissue
titan

ti.ta/nium
tithe
tithing
tither
tit.il/late
tit.il/lat/ing
title
titled
titular
toast
toaster
toast/mas.ter
tobacco
to.bog/gan
today
toe
toehold
to.gether
to.geth/er/ness
toil
toilet
toi.let/ries
token
to.ken/ism
TOKYO
told
TOLEDO, OH
tol.er/able
tol.er/ance
tol.er/ant
tol.er/ate
tol.era/tion
toll

[1]Compound adjective construction. Hyphenate if description precedes noun. (Proofreading is a time-consuming process. Studying is time-consuming.)

[2]Adjective plus adverb construction. Do not hyphenate if description follows noun. (That person is tight fisted or tight mouthed.)

[4]Noun construction. Hyphenate. (Your work has a tie-in with mine. The snow caused a traffic tie-up. The informer gave us a tip-off.)

[5]Verb construction. Do not hyphenate. (It's a surprise party, so do not tip off the guests of honor. Your talk should tie in the importance of training. Tie up the package securely.)

[11]Adjective construction. Written as one word. (a tightfisted or tight-mouthed individual)

toll/booth	top/pling	tourism	trades/peo.ple
toll/gate	topsoil	tourist	tra.di/tion
toma/hawk	topsy-turvey (h)	tour/ister	tra.di/tional
tomato	topwork	tour.ma/line	tra.di/tion/ally
to.ma/toes	top/work/ing	tour.na/ment	traffic
tomb	torch	tourney	trage/dies
tomboy	torch/light	tour.ni/quet	tragedy
tomb/stone	torment	toward	tragic
to.mor/row	tor.men/tor	towage	trail
ton	tornado	towel	trail/blazer
tonal	tor.na/does	tow.el/ing	trailer
tone	torpedo	tower	trail/ers
tongue	tor.pe/doed	town	train
tonic	tor.pe/does	town/house	traina/bil.ity
tonight	torpid	town/ship	train/able
tonnage	torpor	towns/peo.ple	trainee
tonsil	torque	toxic	train/ees
ton.sil/lec/tomy	TORRANCE, CA	toxi/city	train.ee/ship
too	torrent	toxi.co/lo/gi.cal	trainer
took	tor.ren/tial	toxi.col/ogy	train/ing
tool	torrid	toxin	trait
tooled	torso	toy	traitor
tooling	tort	trace	trai/tors
tooth	torture	trace/able	tra.jec/tory
tooth/ache	tor/tured	tracer	tra.jec/tor.ies
tooth/brush	total	trachea	tramp
tooth/pick	totaled	tracing	trample
top	to.tal/ing	track	tram/ples
topaz	to.tal/ity	track/age	tram.po/line
topcoat	totally	track/less	tran/quil
top/coats	tote	tract	tran/quil/izer
TOPEKA, KS	totem	tract/able	tran/quil/lity
top/heavi/ness	touch	trac/tion	trans/act
top/heavy	touch/able	tractor	trans/ac.tion
topic	touch/down	trac/tors	trans/ac.tional
top/notch	touché	trade	trans/ac.tor
to.pog/ra/pher	touch/ing	[3]trade-in (h)	trans/at.lan.tic
topo/graphi/cally	touch/stone	[5]trade in	trans/cei.ver
to.pog/raphy	tough	trade/mark	trans/cend
topped	tougher	[6]trade/off	trans/cen/dent
topple	toupee	[5]trade off	trans/con/ti/nen.tal
toppled	tour	trades/men	tran/scribe

[3]Noun or compound adjective construction. Hyphenate. (What is the trade-in value? Is your old car a trade-in?)

[5]Verb construction. Do not hyphenate. (I will trade in the old typewriter for a new one. They trade off turns driving to work.)

[6]Noun construction. Written as one word. (Do you think it is a fair tradeoff?)

tran/scriber
tran/scrib.ers
tran/scrib/ing
tran/script
tran/scrip/tion
trans/fer
trans/fer/able
trans/fera/bil.ity
trans/feree
trans/ferred
trans/fer/ring
trans/fig.ure
trans/form
trans/for/ma/tion
trans/former
trans/fu/sion
trans/gress
trans/gres/sion
tran/sient
tran.sis/tor
tran.sis/tor.ize
tran.sis/tor.ized
transit
tran.si/tion
tran.si/tional
tran.si/tory
trans/late
trans/lat/ing
trans/la/tion
trans/la/tor
trans/lo/ca/tion
trans/lu/cent
trans/mis/si.ble
trans/mis/sion
trans/mit
trans/mit.tal
trans/mit.ted
trans/mit.ter
trans/mit/ting
trans/mu/ta/tion
trans/mute
trans/oce.anic
trans/par/en/cies
trans/par/ency
trans/par.ent
tran/spire
tran/spir/ing
trans/plant
trans/port

trans/por/ta/tion
trans/port/ing
trans/pose
trans/po.si/tion
tran/sub/stan/ti/ation
trans/verse
trans/versely
trans/ves/tite
trans/ves/tity
trap
trapeze
trapped
trap/ping
trash
trauma
trau/matic
travel
trav/eled
trav/eler
trav.el/ers
trav.el/ing
tra/verse
trav/esty
trawler
trawl/ers
tray
treach/er.ous
treach/ery
tread/mill
treason
trea/sure
trea/surer
trea/sury
treat
trea/ties
treat/ing
trea/tise
treat/ment
treaty
treble
tree
trem/bling
tre.men/dous
tre.men/dously
tremor
trench
trend
TRENTON, NJ
trepi.da/tion

tres/pass
tres/passer
trestle
triad
trial
tri.an/gle
tri.an/gu.lar
tribal
tribe
tribes/man
tribu.la/tion
tri.bu/nal
tribu/tar.ies
tribu/tary
tribute
trib/utes
trick
trick/ier
trickle
trick/ling
tri/color
tri/cy.cle
tried
trifle
tri/focal
trigger
trig/gers
trigo/nome.try
tril/lion
trilogy
trim
trimmed
trim/ming
trinity
trinket
trio
trip
tri.par/tite
triple
triple-space (h)
trip.li/cate
trip/ling
tripod
triumph
tri.um/phant
tri.um/vi/rate
trite
trivia
trivial

trivi.al/ity
troika
trolley
trol/leys
trom/bone
trooper
troop/ship
tro/phies
trophy
trop/ical
trot
trotted
trot/ting
trouble
trou/bled
trou.ble/maker
trou/bles
trou.ble/shooter
trou.ble/shoot/ing
trou.ble/some
trough
troupe
trou/sers
trout
trowel
truancy
truant
truck
trucker
truck/ers
truck/ing
truck/line
truck/load
tru.cu/lent
true
true/blood
truism
truist
truly
trumpet
trum/pets
trun/cate
trundle
truss
trusses
trust
trustee
trust/ees
trust.ee/ship

trusting	tunnel	twen.ti/eth	tyrant
trust/wor.thy	tun/neled	twenty	
trusty	tun.nel/ing	twice	
truth	turbine	twi/light	
truth/ful	tur.bo/charger	twin	**U**
truth/fully	tur.bo/jet	twine	
try	tur.bu/lent	twinge	
trying	turkey	twist	ubiq.ui/tous
6tryout	tur/meric	two	ubiq/uity
5try out	turmoil	twofold	UGANDA
T-shirt (h)	tur/moils	twosome	ug.li/ness
tub	turn	tycoon	ugly
tube	1turn-around (h)	tying	uku/lele
tu.ber/cu.lar	5turn around	type	ulcer
tu.ber/cu/lo.sis	turnip	type/face	ul.cera/tion
tubing	turnkey	typer	ul.cer/ous
tubular	11turnout	type/script	ul.te/rior
TUCSON, AZ	5turn out	type/set.ter	ul.ti/mate
TUESDAY	turn/outs	type/writer	ul.ti/mately
tuition	11turn/over	type/writ.ers	ul.ti.ma/tum
tui/tions	5turn over	type/writ/ing	ultra
tulip	turn/pike	type/writ.ten	ultra/con.ser/va.tive
tulle	turn/stile	typhoid	ultra/mod.ern
TULSA, OK	turn/ta.ble	typhoon	ultra/sonic
tumbler	tur.pen/tine	typical	ultra/vio.let
tum/blers	tur.pi/tude	typi/cally	um.bil/ical
tum/bling	tur/quoise	typify	um.bi.li/cus
tumor	tussle	typist	um.brella
tumult	tu.te/lage	ty.pog/ra/pher	umpire
tu.mul/tu.ous	tutor	typo/graphi.cal	un.abashed
tuna	tu.tor/ial	ty.pog/ra.phy	un.abated
tune	twain	ty.pol/ogy	unable
3tune-up (h)	twelfth	ty.ran/ni.cal	un.abra/sive
5tune up	twelve	tyr.an/nize	un.ac/cept/able
tung/sten	twen/ties	tyranny	un.ac/count/able

1Compound adjective construction. Hyphenate if description precedes noun. (Our turn-around time has improved immensely.)

3Noun or compound adjective construction. Hyphenate. (Is a tune-up kit expensive? The machine needs a tune-up.)

5Verb construction. Do not hyphenate. (We'll try out the idea next week. The violinist must tune up the instrument. Turn around to the audience. They turn out nice work. The engine will not turn over.)

6Noun construction. Written as one word. (Will there be a tryout for the team?)

11Noun or adjective construction. Written as one word. (The turnout for the rally was disappointing. Turnover in our office is low. Turnover rate in our office is high.)

un.ac/cred/ited
un.ac.cus/tomed
un.ad/justed
un.adorned
un.adul/ter/ated
un.ad.ver/tised
un.ad.vis/able
un.af/fected
un.af/fili/ated
un.afraid
un.agree/able
unaided
un.al.lo/cated
un.al.low/able
un.ai.ter/ably
un.am/bigu/ous
un-American (h)
una.nim/ity
unani/mous
unani/mously
un.an/swered
un.ap/peal/ing
un.ap/plauded
un.ap/proved
un.as/sail/able
un.as.sem/bled
un.as/simi/lated
un.as.sum/ing
un.at/tain/able
un.at/tended
un.at/trac/tive
un.au/dited
un.au.tho/rized
un.availa/bil.ity
un.avail/able
un.avoid/able
un.avoid/ably
unaware
un.aware/ness
un.bal/ance
un.bal/anced
un.bear/able
un.beat/able
un.be/liev/able
un.be/liev/ably
un.bend/ing
un.bi/ased
un.bounded
un.brid/led

un.busi/ness/like
un.but/ton
uncanny
un.cer/tain
un.cer/tain.ties
un.cer/tainty
un.cen/sored
un.cere/moni/ously
un.chal/lenged
un.changed
un.chari/ta.ble
un.checked
uncle
unclean
unclear
un.clut/tered
un.coated
un.col/lected
un.col/lec/ti.ble
un.com/fort/able
un.com/mit.ted
un.com/mon
un.com.mu/ni/ca/tive
un.com/pli/men/tary
un.com/pro/mis/ing
un.con/cerned
un.con.di/tional
un.con.di/tion/ally
un.con/scio/na.ble
un.con/scious
un.con/tra/dicted
un.con/trol/la.ble
un.con/trolled
un.co.op/era/tive
uncouth
uncover
un.cov/ered
uncrate
undated
un.de.liv/er/able
un.de.liv/ered
un.de.ni/able
un.de/pend/able
un.der/age
un.der/arm
un.der/brush
un.der/charge
un.der/class.man
un.der/clothes

un.der/cur/rent
un.der/cut
un.der/de.vel/oped
un.der/dog
un.der/em.ploy/ment
undergo
un.der/goes
un.der/go/ing
un.der/gone
un.der/gradu.ate
un.der/ground
un.der/handed
un.der/lies
un.der/line
un.der/lined
un.der/lin/ing
un.der/ly/ing
un.der/mine
un.der/neath
un.der/pass
un.der/privi/leged
un.der/rate
un.der/score
un.der/sell
un.der/signed
un.der/sized
un.der/stand
un.der/stand/able
un.der/stand/ably
un.der/stand/ing
un.der/stood
un.der/study
un.der/take
un.der/taken
un.der/taker
un.der/tak/ing
un.der/tone
un.der/took
un.der/tow
un.der/value
un.der/water
un.der/way
un.der/wear
un.der/weight
un.der/world
un.der/write
un.der/writer
un.der/writ.ers
un.der/writ/ing

un.der/writ.ten
un.de.sir/able
un.de/tected
un.dis/trib/uted
un.dis/turbed
un.di/vided
undo
undoing
un.doubt/edly
undue
un.du.la/tion
unduly
un.earned
un.easi/ness
uneasy
un.em/ploy/able
un.em/ploy/ables
un.em/ployed
un.em/ploy/ment
un.en/force/able
unequal
un.err/ing
uneven
un.ex/celled
un.ex/pected
un.ex/pect/edly
un.ex/pended
un.fail/ing
unfair
un.fa.mil/iar
un.fa.vor/able
un.filled
un.fin/ished
unfold
un.fold/ing
un.fore/see/able
un.fore/seen
un.for/get/ta.ble
un.for.tu/nate
un.for.tu/nately
unfurl
un.gainly
ungodly
unguent
un.gummed
un.hap/pily
un.hap.pi/ness
unhappy
un.healthy

unheard
un.hesi/tat/ingly
un.hon/ored
uni/cel/lu.lar
un.iden/ti/fied
uni.fi.ca/tion
unified
uniform
uni/for/mity
uni/forms
unify
uni.lat/eral
un.im/proved
un.in.hab/ited
un.in.hib/ited
un.in/sured
un.in.tel/li/gi.ble
un.in.ter/ested
un.in.ter/est/ing
un.in.ter/rupted
union
union/ize
unique
uniquely
unison
unit
unite
unit/ized
unity
uni.ver/sal
uni.ver/sal.ity
uni.ver/sally
uni/verse
uni.ver/si/ties
uni.ver/sity
unjust
un.jus.ti/fi/able
un.jus.ti/fi/ably
unkempt
unknown
un.law/ful
un.leash
unless
unlike
un.likely
un.lim/ited
unload
un.loaded
un.loader

un.load/ing
un.man/age/able
un.mar/ket/able
un.mar/ried
un.matched
un.mind/ful
un.mis/tak/able
un.mis/tak/ably
un.natu/ral
un.nec.es/sar.ily
un.nec.es/sary
un.needed
un.ob.li/gated
un.ob/tain/able
un.oc.cu/pied
un.of.fi/cially
un.opened
un.op/posed
un.or/tho/dox
unpack
unpaid
un.par.al/leled
un.par/don/able
un.pleas/ant
un.prece/dented
un.pre/dict/able
un.preju/diced
un.pre/medi/tated
un.pre/pared
un.prin/ci/pled
un.prof/it/able
un.pro/tected
un.proven
un.quali/fied
un.quali/fiedly
un.ques/tion/able
un.ques/tion/ably
un.ques/tioned
unravel
un.rav/eled
un.rav/el/ing
unreal
un.re.al/is.tic
un.rea/son/able
un.rea/son/ably
un.re/lated
un.re/leased
un.re.mit/ting
un.re/serv/edly

unrest
un.re/stricted
unruly
un.sal/able
un.sat.is/fac/tory
un.scathed
un.schooled
un.scru/pu/lous
unsealed
un.se/cured
un.seemly
un.self/ish
un.set/tled
un.set/tling
un.shipped
un.skilled
un.so.cia/ble
un.so.lic/ited
un.so/phis/ti/cated
un.sound
un.speak/able
un.sub/scribed
un.sub.si/dized
un.suc/cess.ful
un.sur/passed
un.taxed
un.ten/able
untidy
untie
untied
until
un.timely
un.tir/ing
untying
unto
untold
un.touch/able
un.touched
un.trained
un.trimmed
un.truth/ful
un.turned
un.tu/tored
un.us/able
unused
unusual
un.usu/ally
un.uti/lized
un.wanted

un.wel/come
unwell
un.whole/some
un.wieldi/ness
un.wieldy
un.will/ing
un.will/ing/ness
unwise
un.wit/tingly
un.work/able
un.worthy
unwrap
un.writ/ten
up
upbeat
up.bring/ing
up.com/ing
update
updated
up.dat/ing
upgrade
up.graded
up.grad/ing
up.heaval
upheld
uphill
uphold
up.hold/ing
up.hol/ster
up.hol/stered
up.hol/ster/ing
up.hol/stery
upkeep
upland
uplands
uplift
upon
upper
up.per/class/man
up.per/most
uppers
upright
up.ris/ing
uproar
up.roari/ous
upset
upshot
upstage
up.stairs

3

upstart
up.stream
upsurge
upturn
upward
ura/nium
urban
urbane
ur.bani/za/tion
urchin
urge
urgency
urgent
urging
uric
uri.naly/sis
urinary
urine
urolo/gist
usable
usage
use
useful
use/fully
use.ful/ness
useless
user
usher
usual
usually
usurer
usu.ri/ous
usurp
usur.pa/tion
usurper
usury
UTAH
utensil
uten/sils
uterine
utili/tar.ian
utili/ties
utility
uti.li.za/tion
utilize
uti/lized
uti/lizes
uti.liz/ing
utmost

utopia
utopian
uto.pi.an/ism
ut.ter/ance
ut.ter/ing

V

va.can/cies
vacancy
vacant
vacate
va.cat/ing
va.ca/tion
va.ca/tion.ist
vac.ci/nate
vac.ci.na/tion
vaccine
vac.il/late
vacuum
va.grancy
vagrant
vague
vaguely
vain
valance
vale
vale.dic/to.rian
vale.dic/tory
valence
val.en/tine
valet
valid
vali/date
vali/da/tion
va.lidi/ties
va.lid/ity
valise
valley
valor
val.or/ous
valu/able
valu/ation
value
valve
van

van/dal.ism
vane
van/guard
vanilla
vanish
van/quish
vantage
vapor
va.por/iza/tion
vari/able
vari/ance
vari/ation
vari/cose
varied
var.ie/gate
va.rie/ties
variety
various
vari/ously
varnish
var/nishes
varsity
vary
varying
vas.cu/lar
va.sec/tomy
vast
vastly
vaude/ville
vault
vege/table
vege.tar/ian
vege/tate
vege/ta/tion
ve.he/mence
ve.he/ment
vehicle
ve.hi/cles
ve.hicu/lar
veil
vein
vellum
ve.loc/ity
velour
velvet
vel.ve/teen
velvety
vend
vendee

ven/detta
vendor
veneer
ven.er/able
ven.er/ate
ven.era/tion
ve.ne/tian
venge/ance
venial
venison
ven.om/ous
vent
ven.ti/late
ven.ti/lat/ing
ven.ti/la/tion
ven.ti/la.tor
ven.tri/cle
ven/trilo/quist
vents
venture
ven/tured
ven.ture/some
venue
ve.rac/ity
veranda
verbal
ver.bali/za/tion
ver/bally
ver.ba/tim
ver/biage
verbose
verdant
verdict
veri.fi/ca/tion
veri/fied
veri/fier
verify
veri/fy/ing
veri/table
verity
vermin
VERMONT
ver.nacu/lar
ver.sa/tile
ver.sa/til.ity
version
ver/sions
versus
ver.te/bra

ver.te/brae
ver.te/brate
vertex
ver.ti/cal
ver.ti/cally
very
vesicle
vespers
vessel
vest
vested
ves.ti/bule
vestige
ves.ti/gial
vesting
vest/ment
veteran
vet.er/ans
vet.eri/nar.ian
vet.eri/nary
veto
vetoed
vetoes
vex
vexa/tion
vexed
vexing
via
viable
viaduct
vial
vibrant
vibrate
vi.bra/tion
vi.bra/tor
vicar
vi.cari/ous
vice
vice versa
vi.cini/ties
vi.cin/ity
vicious
vi.cis.si/tude
victim
vic.tim/ize
victor
vic.to.ri/ous
victory
victual

video
vid.eo/cas.sette
vid.eo/re.cord
vid.eo/tape
vie
VIENNA
VIETNAM
VIETNA/MESE
view
view/point
vigil
vigi/lance
vigi/lant
vigi/lante
vigor
vig.or/ous
vig.or/ously
vile
vilify
villa
village
vil/lages
villain
vil.lain/ous
vim
vin.di/cate
vin.di/ca/tion
vin.dic/tive
vinegar
vine/yard
vintage
vin/tages
vinyl
viol
violate
vio.lat/ing
vio.la/tion
vio/lence
violent
violet
violin
virgin
VIR/GINIA
VIRGINIA BEACH,
    VA
virile
vi.ril/ity
vir/tually
virtue

vir.tu.os/ity
vir.tu/oso
vir.tu/ous
viru/lence
viru/lent
virus
visa
vis-a-vis (h)
vis/ceral
vis.cos/ity
viscous
vise
visi.bil/ity
visible
vision
vi.sion/ary
visit
visi.ta/tion
vis.it/ing
visitor
visi/tors
visor
vista
visual
vi.su.al/ize
vi.su/ally
vita
vitae
vital
vi.tal/ity
vi.tal.iz/ing
vitally
vitamin
vi.ta/mins
vitiate
vit.re/ous
vitrify
vi.tu/pera/tion
vi.va/cious
vi.vac/ity
vivid
vivi/sec/tion
vo.cabu/lary
vocal
vo.cal/ist
vo.cal/ize
vo.ca/tion
vo.ca/tional
vo.cif.er/ous

vodka
vogue
voice
void
void/able
vola/tile
vola.til/ity
vol.ca/nic
volcano
vo.li/tion
volley
vol.ley/ball
volt
voltage
volt/ages
volume
vo.lu.mi/nous
vol.un/tar.ily
vol.un/tary
vol.un/teer
vo.lup.tu/ous
vomit
vo.ra/cious
vo.rac/ity
vortex
vote
votive
vouch
voucher
vouch/ers
vow
vowel
voyage
vul.ca/nize
vulgar
vul.gar/ity
vulture
vul.ner/abil.ity
vul.ner/able
vying

W

wad
wadded

wadding	war	wary	wa.ter/line
wade	ward	was	wa.ter/melon
wafer	warden	wash	wa.ter/power
waffle	ward/robe	wash/able	wa.ter/proof
wage	ware/house	washer	[1]water-repellent (h)
wager	ware/house/man	WASHING/TON	[2]water repellent
wagon	ware/hous/ing	WASSAU, WI	wa.ter/shed
wain/scot	ware/room	wash/room	wa.ter/tight
waist	warfare	washtub	wa.ter/way
waist/band	warm	waste	wa.ter/works
waist/line	[1]warm-blooded (h)	waste/bas.ket	watt
wait	[2]warm blooded	waste/ful	wattage
wait/ress	warm/hearted	waste/land	wave
waive	warmth	waste/pa.per	waver
waiver	[3]warm-up (h)	wasting	wavy
wake	[5]warm up	watch	wax
walk	warn	watch/band	waxes
walkie-talkie (h)	warning	watch/dog	way
[3]walk-in (h)	warn/ings	watches	waybill
[5]walk in	warp	watch/ful	way/billed
walkout	warrant	watch/ing	way/bills
walkway	war/ranted	watch/maker	waylay
wall	war.ran/tee	watch/word	wayside
wall/board	war/rant/ing	water	way/sides
wallet	war.ran/tor	WATER/BURY, CT	wayward
wallop	war/ranty	wa.ter/color	weak
wall/pa.per	WARREN, MI	wa.ter/cress	weaken
wander	warrior	wa.ter/flow	weak/ened
wan/derer	WARSAW	wa.ter/fowl	[1]weak-kneed (h)
wan.der/ers	warship	wa.ter/front	[2]weak kneed
want	war/ships	wa.ter/ing	weak/ling
wanton	wartime		weak/ness

[1]Compound adjective construction. Hyphenate if description precedes noun. (Our warm-blooded president has his window open in January. They sell water-repellent coats. My weak-kneed friend collapsed from excitement.)

[2]Adjective plus adverb construction. Do not hyphenate if description follows noun. (Not all of us are so warm blooded as he! The material is water repellent. The recipient of the award became weak kneed during the presentation.)

[3]Noun or compound adjective construction. Hyphenate. (All walk-ins are given application blanks. The walk-in applicant was the one who was hired. A warm-up before a timed writing can be very helpful. The warm-up jacket was lettered with our company name.)

[5]Verb construction. Do not hyphenate. (Don't walk in when the executive is dictating. A typist should warm up before beginning a timed writing.)

wealth	weighted	¹well-off (h)	wheeler
wealthy	weighti/ness	²well off	wheel/house
weapon	weight/ing	¹well-read (h)	wheel/ing
wear	weight/less/ness	²well read	when
wear/able	weighty	¹well-thought-of (h)	whence
wearily	weird	²well thought of	when/ever
weari/ness	welcome	¹well-timed (h)	when.so/ever
wea.ri/some	wel/comed	²well timed	where
weary	wel.com/ing	¹well-to-do (h)	where/abouts
weather	weld	²well to do	whereas
weath/ered	welder	¹well-worn	whereby
weath.er/proof	welfare	²well worn	where/for
weave	wel.far/ism	welt	where/fore
weaving	well	went	wherein
web	¹well-advised (h)	were	whereof
webbing	²well advised	west	where.so/ever
web/bings	⁴well-being (h)	WESTCHESTER, NY	where/upon
wed	¹well-disposed (h)	western	wher/ever
wedding	²well disposed	*West/ern	where/withal
wed/dings	¹well-done (h)	west/erner	whether
wedge	²well done	WEST VIRGINIA	whew
wedlock	¹well-fixed (h)	west/ward	which
WEDNES/DAY	²well fixed	wet	which/ever
wee	¹well-founded (h)	wet/ta/ble	while
weed	²well founded	whale	whimper
week	¹well-grounded (h)	whammy	whims
weekday	²well grounded	wharf	whim.si/cal
weekend	¹well-handled (h)	wharf/age	whip
week/ender	²well handled	what/ever	whip/lash
week/end.ers	¹well-healed (h)	what.so/ever	whip/ping
weekly	²well healed	wheat	whirl
weigh	¹well-known (h)	wheel	whirl/pool
weighed	²well known	wheel/bar.row	whirl/wind
weigh/ing	¹well-meaning (h)	wheel/base	whiskey
weight	²well meaning	wheel/chair	whis/keys

*A type of movie or play.

¹Compound adjective construction. Hyphenate if description precedes noun. The well-advised student; the well-founded statement; well-off clientele; well-read students; well-thought-of representatives; a well-handled situation, etc.)

²Adjective plus adverb construction. Do not hyphenate if description follows noun. (The student is well advised; the statement is well founded; the situation is well handled; clientele that is well off; students who are well read; representatives who are well thought of, etc.)

⁴Noun construction. Hyphenate. (The well-being of the employees is an important consideration.)

whisper	whose	wild	wine/press
whistle	why	wildcat	winery
whis/tled	WICHITA, KS	wildest	wine/skin
[3]whistle-stop (h)	wick	wild/life	wing
whist/ling	wicked	wile	wing/span
white	wick.ed/ness	will	wing/spread
white-collar (h)	wicket	willful	winner
whites	wide	will/fully	win/nings
white/wall	[1]wide-angle (h)	will/ingly	winsome
white/wash	[8]wide angle	will.ing/ness	WINSTON-SALEM,
whither	[1]wide-awake (h)	will/power	NC (h)
whittle	[2]wide awake	win	winter
whit/tles	[1]wide-eyed (h)	wind	win.ter/green
who	[2]wide eyed	wind/blown	win.ter/ize
[12]whoever	widely	wind/burn	wintry
[13]who ever	widen	wind/fall	wipe
whole	wid/ened	wind/mill	wiper
whole/hearted	wid/en/ing	window	wire
whole/heart/edly	wider	win.dow/pane	wire/less
whole/sale	wide/spread	win.dow/sill	wiretap
whole/saler	widow	wind/pipe	wire/tap.per
whole/sal/ing	widower	wind/shield	wiring
wholesome	width	wind/storm	WISCON/SIN
wholly	wield	wind/swept	wisdom
wholly-owned	wife	[3]wind-up (h)	wise
sub.sidi/ary (h)	wig	[5]wind up	wise/acre
whom	wiggle	wine	wise/crack
whoop	wigwag	wine/glass	wish

[1]Compound adjective construction. Hyphenate if description precedes noun. (The wide-angle diagram will not fit on the page. The wide-awake salesman took advantage of the opportunity to make a sale. The wide-eyed look indicated surprise.)

[2]Adjective plus adverb construction. Do not hyphenate if description follows noun. (The salesman was wide awake. He looked wide eyed in amazement.)

[3]Noun or compound adjective construction. Hyphenate. (The wind-up will be at 2 p.m. Wind-up activities are expected to take about an hour. Will the next whistle-stop be in Cleveland? The politician conducted a whistle-stop campaign.)

[5]Verb construction. Do not hyphenate. (When do they intend to wind up that project?)

[8]Noun plus adjective construction. Do not hyphenate. (The geometry student, using his protractor, drew a wide angle.)

[12]Relative pronoun. (Whoever arrives first usually unlocks the files.)

[13]Relative pronoun plus adverb. (Who ever would have expected that the company would experience such growth.)

wishes	wom.an/li/ness	worka/day	wrench
wishful	women	work/bas.ket	wrenches
wistful	won	work/bench	wrestle
wit	wonder	work/book	wres/tling
witch	won/dered	workday	wretched
[4]witch-hunt (h)	won.der/ful	work force	wriggle
with	won.der/fully	work.ing/man	wring
withal	won/der/ing	work/ings	worsted
with/draw	won.der/land	work/load	wor/steds
with/draw/able	wood	work.man/like	worth
with/drawal	wood-carver (h)	work.man/ship	worth/while
with/draw/ing	wood/craft	workmen	worthy
with/drawn	wooded	work/sheets	would
wither	wooden	work/shop	wound
with/held	wood/land	workup	woven
with/hold	wood/pile	world	wrangle
with/hold/ing	wood/stock	world.li/ness	wran/gler
within	woodsy	worldly	wrap
without	wood/work	[1]world-shaking (h)	wrap/around
with/stand	wood/work/ing	[2]world shaking	wrapped
witness	woody	world/wide	wrapper
wit/nessed	wool	worm	wrap/ping
wit/nesses	woolly	wormed	wrap/pings
wit.ti/cism	WOR/CESTER, MA	worm/wood	[3]wrap-up (h)
wit/tingly	word	worn	[5]wrap up
witty	worded	worried	wrath
wives	wording	wor.ri/some	warth/ful
woe.be/gone	[1]word-of-mouth (h)	worry	wreath
woeful	[8]word of mouth	worry/wart	wreathe
woman	wore	worse	wreck
wom.an/hood	work	worship	wreck/age
wom.an/kind	work/able	worst	wrecked

3

[1]Compound adjective construction. Hyphenate if description precedes noun. (Word-of-mouth news travels fast. The world-shaking news affected stock market activities.)

[2]Adjective plus adverb construction. Do not hyphenate if description follows noun. (The event was world shaking.)

[3]Noun or compound adjective construction. Hyphenate. (A wrap-up is planned to close the convention. A wrap-up session is a good way to end a conference.)

[4]Noun construction. Hyphenate. (Good personnel managers do not engage in witch-hunts.)

[5]Verb construction. Do not hyphenate. (Do not wrap up the package yet.)

[8]Noun plus adjective phrase construction. Do not hyphenate. (The news spread by word of mouth.)

wringer
wring/ers
wrinkle
wrin/kles
wrin/kling
wrist
wrist/band
wrist/watch
write
[1]write-in (h)
[5]write in
[6]write/off
[5]write off
[6]writeup
[5]write up
writhe
written
wrong
wrong/do/ing
wrong/ful
wrongly
wrote
wrought
wrung
wry
wryly
WYOMING

X

xe.rog/ra.phy
Xerox
X-rated (h)
x-ray (h)
X-ray
xylo/phone

Y

yacht
yachts/man
yak
yam
yard
yardage
yard/mas.ter
yard/stick
yarn
yea
year
year/book
year-end (h)
year/long
yearly
yearn
year-round (h)
yellow
yen
yeoman
yeo/manry
yes
yes-man (h)
yes.ter/day
yes.ter/year
yet
yield
yielded
yield/ing
yodel
yoga
yogurt
yoke
yokel
yolk
yonder
YONKERS, NY

yore
you
young
younger
young/ster
YOUNGS/TOWN,
    OH
your
your/self
your/selves
youth
youth/ful
yule/tide

Z

zag
zany
zealot
zealous
zebra
zenith
zephyr
zep.pe/lin
zero
zeroed
zeros
zest
zigzag
zinc
zip
zipped
zipper
zipping
zippy
zodiac
zonal
zone

zoo
zoo.logi/cal
zo.olo/gist
zoology
zuc/chini
zygote
zygotic

[1]Compound adjective construction. Hyphenate if description precedes noun. (The write-in candidate was elected.)

[5]Verb construction. Do not hyphenate. (Write in the exact amount of the check. Write off the expense as a tax deduction. Write up the information for the newspaper.)

[6]Noun construction. Written as one word. (The tax writeoff will reduce our final payment. The newspaper writeup was good publicity for the firm.)

SECTION 4
Words Frequently Confused and Misused

This section is a list of FREQUENTLY CONFUSED AND MIS-USED WORDS that the machine transcriber should find of special assistance in the interpretation of voice dictation. To assist in choosing the appropriate word, both meanings and parts of speech are specified for each word in the list.

It is important, when transcribing, to listen closely to the pronunciation of the words and also to think in terms of the idea that the author is presenting. While the goal of a good machine transcriptionist or word processor is to work independently, there may be times when it will be necessary to contact the author of the dictation for clarification.

abjure	(v) to renounce under oath, forswear, retract
adjure	(v) to entreat, beg
accede	(v) to assent, yield
exceed	(v) to go beyond, surpass
accelerate	(v) to speed up, hasten progress
exhilarate	(v) to cheer, gladden, refresh, stimulate
accent	(n) emphasis, mark showing syllable emphasis
ascend	(v) to go up, rise
ascent	(n) act of rising, climbing
assent	(n) agreement, concurrence (v) to agree to
acetic	(adj) sour, acidy
ascetic	(adj) austere, practicing self-denial
accomplish	(v) to successfully conclude, complete
accomplice	(n) an associate in a wrongdoing
adapt	(v) to make fit, adjust
adept	(adj) highly skilled, expert
adopt	(v) to choose, take up, accept
accept	(v) to receive, take
except	(prep) other than (v) to leave out, omit
access	(n) approach, right to enter, use
assess	(v) to set a value, impose fine, tax, etc.
excess	(n) superfluity, overindulgence (adj) extra or surplus
ad	(Latin prefix) motion toward, near (n) short for advertisement
add	(v) to join, unite, combine, increasing size, number, quantity
adherence	(n) act of adhering; devotion, support for
adherents	(n pl) supporters, followers
adherent	(adj) sticking fast, attached
addenda	(n pl of addendum) something added

agenda	(n) program of things to be done
adverse	(adj) opposite in direction; unfavorable, harmful
averse	(adj) unwilling, opposed to, reluctant
addition	(n) summing; joining of parts, part added
edition	(n) published work
advice	(n) an opinion, counsel, information
advise	(v) to give an opinion, counsel; recommend
advert	(v) to call attention to, refer, allude
avert	(v) to turn away from, prevent
affect	(v) to influence, change; to feign
effect	(n) result (v) to bring about, accomplish
aggravate	(v) to make worse (colloquial only: to annoy)
aggregate	(n) group or mass considered in total (adj) considered as a whole, totaled (v) act of grouping
aid	(n) helper or assistant (v) to give help or relief
aide	(n) French derivative used in military expressions; aid, helper, assistant
air	(n) atmosphere (v) to let air in; to publicize
heir	(n) person who inherits or is entitled to inherit property
aisle	(n) passageway
isle	(n) small portion of land in a sea
allowed	(v) (past tense of allow) permitted
aloud	(adv) with normal voice; loudly
allusion	(n) indirect reference; casual mention
illusion	(n) false idea, impression of what one sees
elusion	(n) an escape, avoidance, evasion
delusion	(n) false belief not substantiated by objective evidence

4

Words Frequently Confused and Misused **251**

| altar | (n) raised platform, sacred table |
| alter | (v) to make different, change, vary |

| anecdote | (n) account of a happening; story |
| antidote | (n) remedy, that which counteracts an unwanted condition |

| alternate | (v) to do by turns
(adj) occurring by turns |
| alternative | (n) one of two or more options
(adj) providing a choice |

alumnus	(n—Latin) male graduate or former attendee of a particular school
alumni	(n pl—Latin) male graduates or former attendees
alumna	(n—Latin) female graduate or former attendee
alumnae	(n pl—Latin) female graduates or former attendees

| ante | (Latin prefix) before |
| anti | (Latin prefix) against |

antecedence	(n) act or fact of going before
antecedents	(n pl) happenings or things prior to others
antecedent	(adj) previous

| appraise | (v) to set a price for, estimate |
| apprise | (v) to inform, notify |

apt	(adj) appropriate or fit; quick to learn
liable	(adj) legally bound or obligated
likely	(adj) apparently true; reasonably to be expected

are	(v) form of the verb to be
hour	(n) period of time
our	(adj or possessive pronoun) belonging to us

| area | (n) place, surface, scope |
| aria | (n) melody |

| arraign | (v) to bring to court; to accuse |
| arrange | (v) to rank, put in order, prepare |

arrant	(adj) errant
errant	(adj) given to travel; straying from a standard
assay	(n) analysis, results
	(v) to examine, test
essay	(n) short literary composition
attendance	(n) act of attending; total number attending
attendants	(n pl) persons who attend or serve
attendant	(adj) attending or serving
aught	(n) zero; anything, whatever
	(adv) at all
ought	(v—auxiliary, used with infinitives) used to express obligation
aural	(adj) relating to the ear
oral	(adj) spoken; of the mouth
avail	(v) to be of use
	(n) effectiveness, use, help
avow	(v) to acknowledge, admit openly
bad	(adj) not good, evil
bade	(v—past tense of bid) asked, implored
bail	(n) money or credit to get an arrested person released; release
	(v) to deliver in trust; to set free; to dip out
bale	(n) a bundle; evil, disaster, woe
	(v) to make into a bundle
bare	(adj) without usual covering; no more than
bear	(v) to carry; take on; bring forth
	(n) an animal
base	(n) foundation
	(adj) lacking decency or quality
bass	(n) species of fish; lowest male voice, low tone
	(adj) having low, deep sound

4

bases	(n pl) foundations
basis	(n) chief supporting factor, main ingredient
bazaar	(n) marketplace; a sale
bizarre	(adj) odd, queer, grotesque
beach	(n) sandy area along a lake, river, and so on
	(v) to run aground
beech	(n) hardwood tree with nuts
beat	(n) series of movements
	(v) to strike, defeat
beet	(n) genus of vegetable plant
berry	(n) small, juicy fruit
bury	(v) to put into the earth; to hide
beside	(prep) alongside, near
besides	(prep) in addition, except
better	(adj) comparative degree of good; with verbs, means ought
bettor	(n) person who gambles
biannual	(adj) twice a year; semiannual
biennial	(adj) every two years
bibliography	(n) list of sources of information
biography	(n) account of a person's life
birth	(n) act of bringing forth; native background
berth	(n) built-in bed; ship's place to anchor
bloc	(n) a political alliance
block	(n) large, solid piece of material
	(v) to form into a block; obstruct
	(adj) formed in a block
board	(n) plank, council
	(v) to close up with planks; get on; provide meals
bored	(v—past tense) drilled or cut through
	(adj) uninterested

boarder	(n) one who gets meals and lodging; one who gets on a ship, train, and so on
border	(n) edge or margin (v) to provide with a border (adj) adjoining
born	(v—perfect participle of bear) to have brought forth
borne	(v—perfect participle of bear) to have carried
bolder	(adj—comparative degree of bold) more brave, daring; more sharp, clear
boulder	(n) large rock
bouillon	(n) broth
bullion	(n) gold or silver ingots
boy	(n) male youth
buoy	(n) floating marker (v) to keep afloat; lift up
bough	(n) branch of a tree
bow	(n) bending of head, body (v) to bend head, body in respect, salutation, recognition
brake	(n) device for stopping motion or progress (v) to slow down or stop with a brake
break	(n) a breach, fracture; sudden move (v) to breach; cause to come apart
breach	(n) violation, opening, breakthrough (v) to break open or through; violate
breech	(n) lower or back part of a thing; part of a gun (v) to clothe with breeches; to provide a gun with a breech
bread	(n) food made of dough
bred	(v—past tense of breed) to have brought forth
breadth	(n) distance from side to side, width
breath	(n) air taken in and let out of lungs; respiration; puff of air

4

breathe	(v) to inhale and exhale air; to live
briar	(n) tobacco pipe
brier	(n) a plant with thorns; root used for making pipes
bridal	(adj) of a bride or wedding
bridle	(n) harness for a horse, anything that restrains
bring	(v) to carry or lead toward (here)
take	(v) to carry or lead away (there); seize, capture, grasp
fetch	(v) to go for and come back with
carry	(v) to hold or support while moving; to transport
broach	(v) to bring up, introduce; make a hole in (n) pointed rod
brooch	(n) ornamental pin or piece of jewelry worn at the neck
burger	(n) fried or grilled patty, usually a hamburger
burgher	(n) inhabitant of a town
burned	(v—past tense, perfect participle of burn) consumed by fire; used up (adj) quality of having been burned
burnt	(v and adj—alternate forms of burned) generally use burned
buy	(v) to purchase
by	(prep) expressing relationship in space, time, direction; expressing manner, mode, sanction
bye	(n) something secondary or incidental
cache	(n) hiding or storage place
cash	(v) to pay money or obtain money for a check
calendar	(n) system for arranging the year; schedule
calender	(n) machine for processing paper or cloth (v) to process through a calender

colander	(n) a strainer
callous	(adj) hardened, thickened; without feeling or sympathy
callus	(n) hard skin or bark
Calvary	(n) hill near Jerusalem
cavalry	(n) army component that moves on horses or in vehicles
cannon	(n) piece of artillery; weapon
canon	(n) body of rules, basic principle; member of a clerical group
canyon	(n) long, narrow valley between cliffs
canvas	(n) coarse cloth made of hemp
canvass	(v) to examine in detail; seek votes
capital	(n) official city of a state; money; accumulated wealth (adj) most important, serious
capitol	(n) a building housing a state legislature or Congress
carat	(n) unit of weight for precious stones
caret	(n) punctuation mark showing an insertion
carrot	(n) a vegetable
karat	(n) unit of weight for gold
carton	(n) cardboard or wooden box
cartoon	(n) a caricature, satirical drawing
casual	(adj) not planned, random, incidental
causal	(adj) relating to cause or reason
cast	(n) a throw or throw off; actors; something formed in a mold (v) to throw; throw off; assign actors parts; to pour into a mold
caste	(n) social class or system
cede	(v) to surrender formally
seed	(n) plant part; origin or source (v) to let fall, sow
ceiling	(n) top part of a room opposite the floor; limit

4

sealing	(v—present perfect of seal) engraving; securing contents by wax, mucilage, tape, and so on
censer	(n) container for burning incense
censor	(n) official who examines materials to determine moral fitness
	(v) to subject to censorship
censure	(n) resolution or condemnation as wrong
	(v) to express disapproval of, condemn as wrong
census	(n) official counting
senses	(n pl) feelings, reactions to stimuli, perceptions
	(v) perceives, comprehends, feels
cent	(n) 1/100th of a dollar, penny
scent	(n) odor or smell
	(v) to smell; give odor; suspect
sent	(v—past tense and perfect participle of send) dispatched
certainty	(n) being certain on the basis of evidence
certitude	(n) freedom from doubt, feeling certain
childish	(adj) of or befitting a child; suggests immaturity
childlike	(adj) of or befitting a child; suggests innocence, trust
chord	(n) harmonious combination of tones; instrument string
	(v) to harmonize
cord	(n) thick string, tie
	(v) to bind or tie
cite	(v) to summon; quote; refer to
sight	(n) that which is seen; act of seeing
	(v) to observe, see
site	(n) piece of land; location
climb	(v) to go up
clime	(n) weather

close	(n) termination
	(v) to block up; bring edges together; terminate
	(adj) near, guarded, confining
clothes	(n pl) wearing apparel
cloths	(n pl) fabrics
coarse	(adj) rough, not smooth
course	(n) an onward movement; path; a series of studies
collision	(n) a coming together with force, crash
collusion	(n) secret illegal or fraudulent agreement
colonel	(n) military officer
kernel	(n) seed; core
coma	(n) prolonged unconsciousness
comma	(n) mark of punctuation
command	(n) an order, direction
	(v) to order, direct, control
commend	(v) to entrust; commit to one's charge
complacent	(adj) self-satisfied, unconcerned
complaisant	(adj) inclined to please or comply, amiable
commence	(v) to begin, start, initiate
comments	(n pl) notes of explanation, remarks
	(v) makes remarks
complement	(n) that which completes or brings to perfection
	(v) to complete
compliment	(n) expression of courtesy, praise, respect
	(v) to pay a compliment, congratulate
connote	(v) to imply
denote	(v) to stand for, signify
comprehensible	(adj) intelligible
comprehensive	(adj) all-inclusive
confidant	(n) close, trusted friend (may be used for male or female)
confidante	(n) close, trusted female friend

4

consul	(n) governmental representative to a foreign country
council	(n) group of people who administer, legislate, advise; legislative body
counsel	(n) advice; deliberation (v) to advise; exchange ideas
conscience	(n) sense of right and wrong
conscious	(adj) having feeling, awareness
contemptuous	(adj) scornful, full of contempt
contemptible	(adj) deserving scorn
continual	(adj) happening repeatedly
continuous	(adj) happening without interruption
cooperation	(n) joint effort
corporation	(n) type of business organization
core	(n) center or innermost part (v) to remove core
CORE	(n—proper) Congress of Racial Equality
corps	(n) body of people; military group (may be singular or plural)
corporal	(n) military rank
corporeal	(adj) personal, of or pertaining to body (adj) tangible, substantial, not spiritual
correspondence	(n) conformity; letters exchanged; letter communication
correspondents	(n pl) letter writers; things that correspond
correspondent	(n) letter writer; one named jointly in a legal action
costume	(n) style of clothing; set of clothes (v) to put on or provide a costume
custom	(n) usual practice or habit
crape	(n) sign of mourning (v) to cover or shroud with crape
crepe	(n) food; crinkled fabric, paper; a thin pancake

creak	(n) squeaking, harsh sound
	(v) to make a squeaking, harsh sound
creek	(n) small stream
credible	(adj) believable, reliable, plausible
creditable	(adj) deserving of credit
credulous	(adj) too easily convinced
cue	(n) signal, suggestion, hint
queue	(n) pigtail (British usage—a line or file of people)
quay	(n) wharf
currant	(n) small fruit; berry
current	(adj) now going on, progressing
cymbal	(n) musical instrument
symbol	(n) something that stands for or represents something else; sign
decease	(v) to die
disease	(n) an illness; destructive process
	(v) to cause disease in; infect
decent	(adj) reasonably good; not immodest, befitting
descent	(n) a coming down; lineage; decline or fall
dissent	(n) act of dissenting, disagreeing
	(v) to differ in belief, opinion; disagree
decree	(n) an official order, edict, decision
	(v) to order, decide, appoint
degree	(n) a successive step, stage; a rank
deference	(n) a yielding to opinion, wish, judgment; respect
difference	(n) condition, quality, fact of being different
deferential	(adj) showing deference; very respectful
differential	(adj) showing or making a difference
definite	(adj) free of uncertainty, precise, explicit
definitive	(adj) final, conclusive

4

depositary	(n) person entrusted with something for safekeeping
depository	(n) place where things are put for safekeeping
deposition	(n) deposing or putting down; testimony
disposition	(n) arrangement; settlement of affairs; temperament
depraved	(v—past and perfect participle of deprave) corrupted, debased
	(adj) corrupt, perverted
deprived	(v—past tense and perfect participle of deprive) took away; dispossessed
	(adj) underprivileged
deprecate	(v) to plead against; belittle
depreciate	(v) to reduce in value
desert	(n) dry, barren region; deserved reward or punishment
	(v) to forsake, leave
dessert	(n) last course of a meal, sweets
desolate	(v) to lay waste, abandon, devastate
	(adj) lonely, deserted, uninhabited
dissolute	(adj) loose, unrestrained; immoral
device	(n) plan, scheme; mechanical contrivance
devise	(v) to contrive, plan, invent
dice	(n pl of die) numbered cubes, gambling device
dies	(n) tools or devices for stamping, molding
	(v) passes away
dyes	(n) coloring agent, tint
dinghy	(n) boat
dingy	(adj) shabby, dirty, discolored
disapprove	(v) to consider wrong, condemn; not approve
disprove	(v) to prove false, refute
disassemble	(v) to take apart
dissemble	(v) to disguise; conceal the truth

disburse	(v) to pay out, expend
disperse	(v) to break up, scatter
disc	(n) phonograph record; part of a plow
disk	(n) part of a flower; anatomical structure; computer storage unit
disinterested	(adj) impartial, unbiased
uninterested	(adj) not interested, indifferent
divers	(adj) several, various
diverse	(adj) different, dissimilar
do	(v) to perform
due	(adj) owed or owing; scheduled to arrive
dew	(n) condensed moisture
dominate	(v) to rule by superior power, tower over
domineer	(v) to rule tyranically, arrogantly
done	(v—perfect participle of do) completed
dun	(v) to ask for payment; annoy
	(adj) dull grayish brown in color
dose	(n) amount of medicine; extent of treatment
	(v) to give doses of medicine to
doze	(v) to sleep lightly, nap
drier	(adj) more dry
dryer	(n) appliance
dual	(adj) of two, double
duel	(n) formal fight or contest
	(v) to fight a duel
dyeing	(v) coloring or tinting
dying	(v) expiring, deceasing
elegy	(n) song or poem expressing sadness or mourning
eulogy	(n) funeral oration or statement of praise
elicit	(v) to draw out, extract
illicit	(adj) unlawful, improper, prohibited
eligible	(adj) fit to be chosen
illegible	(adj) difficult to read

4

illogical	(adj) not reasonable
elude	(v) to avoid
allude	(v) to hint
elusive	(adj) hard to grasp, baffling
illusive	(adj) unreal
emerge	(v) to rise from; become visible
immerge	(v) to plunge into or disappear
emigrant	(n) one who moves out or away
immigrant	(n) one who comes into a new area
emigrate	(v) to move out or away from an area
immigrate	(v) to come or move into an area
eminent	(adj) outstanding, famous, distinguished
imminent	(adj) threatening, impending
emanate	(v) to issue from, emit
entomology	(n) study of insects
etymology	(n) study of history of words
envelop	(v) to wrap, cover; to surround; to conceal
envelope	(n) wrapper or cover, container for a letter
equable	(adj) steady, uniform
equitable	(adj) fair, just
equivocal	(adj) uncertain, undecided, questionable, doubtful
erasable	(adj) capable of being wiped out
irascible	(adj) easily angered, quick-tempered
eraser	(n) instrument for erasing
erasure	(n) the result of erasing, a rubbing out
ere	(prep) poetic for before
e'er	(adv) poetic contraction for ever
err	(v) to be wrong, mistaken
eruption	(n) a bursting forth
irruption	(n) an abrupt increase in size
especially	(adv) particularly, mainly, unusually
specially	(adv) in a special manner

ensure	(v) to make sure, certain, safe
insure	(v) to take out or to issue insurance
assure	(v) to convince, give confidence
ensue	(v) to follow immediately; result from
exalt	(v) to elevate, praise
exult	(v) to rejoice
expand	(v) to spread out; to increase in size or scope
expend	(v) to spend, use up
expanse	(n) wide area
expense	(n) financial cost
exercise	(n) practice; bodily exertion (v) to use, exert, practice
exorcise	(v) to expel an evil spirit, to get rid of
expansive	(adj) widely extended, broad
expensive	(adj) high-priced
expatiate	(v) speak or write in great detail
expatriate	(n) one who is expelled or withdraws from fatherland (v) to expel or withdraw from fatherland
expiate	(v) to make satisfactory, atone
explicit	(adj) clearly stated; not implied
implicit	(adj) suggested, implied
extant	(adj) not extinct, still existing
extent	(n) range, limit, scope, size, length, breadth
facet	(n) any of a number of sides, aspects
faucet	(n) device for regulating flow of liquid, tap
facetious	(adj) witty at an inappropriate time
factious	(adj) causing dissension
factitious	(adj) not genuine, artificial
fictitious	(adj) imaginary, not real
facilitate	(v) to make easy
felicitate	(v) to make happy; to congratulate
facility	(n) ease of doing; ability, skill
felicity	(n) happiness, bliss, good fortune

4

faint	(n) condition of loss of consciousness
	(v) to fall into temporary unconsciousness
	(adj) weak, feeble
feint	(n) a sham, pretense
fair	(n) festival, carnival, market
	(adj) according to the rules; light in color
fare	(n) money paid for transportation
	(v) to happen
farther	(adj) more distant or remote
further	(adv) in addition; moreover
faze	(v) to disturb, embarrass
phase	(n) any state in a cycle of change; aspect
	(v) to plan, carry out in stages
feat	(n) remarkable deed or accomplishment
feet	(n pl) end parts of the legs; units of length
finale	(n) conclusion, last part, end
finally	(adv) in conclusion, irrevocably
finely	(adv) in a fine manner
fineness	(n) quality or state of being fine
finesse	(n) ability to handle delicate situations with skill; adroitness
fir	(n) type of evergreen tree
fur	(n) hair covering the body of an animal; garment made of skin with animal hair
fiscal	(adj) financial; pertaining to public revenues
physical	(adj) of nature; pertaining to the body
flair	(n) natural aptitude
flare	(n) flame, light, sudden outburst
	(v) to burn; shine; violently break out
flaunt	(v) to display ostentatiously or defiantly
flout	(v) to show scorn
flew	(v—past tense of fly) soared through the air
flu	(n) short for influenza; viral infection
flue	(n) air passage, part of a chimney

flour	(n) finely ground grain
	(v) to put flour in or on
flower	(n) blossoming plant
for	(prep) in place of, representative of, in favor of
fore	(adj) situated in front of, previous
'fore	(adj) poetic for before
four	(n) cardinal number
forbear	(v) to restrain oneself, refrain
forebear	(n) an ancestor
forego	(v) to go before
forgo	(v) to do without; relinquish
formally	(adv) in a formal manner
formerly	(adv) at an earlier time, in the past
fort	(n) enclosed place; place of defense
forte	(n) special accomplishment; strong point
	(adj) musical direction; loud
forth	(adv) forward or onward
fourth	(n) the one following third
	(adj) preceded by one, two, and three
freeze	(v) to form into ice
frieze	(n) decoration, ornamental band; heavy woolen cloth
forced	(adj) not voluntary
forceful	(adj) powerful, vigorous
forcible	(adj) done or effected by force
gaff	(n) pole supporting a sail
gaffe	(n) blunder; faux pas
gait	(n) way of walking or moving on foot; sequence of foot movements
	(v) to train foot movements of a horse; to lead a dog in a show (judging)
gate	(n) an entrance or exit; opening in a wall or fence
gamble	(n) act of risk or chance
	(v) to play games of chance, take risks
gambol	(n) a jumping about, frolic
	(v) to jump about, skip, frolic

4

gap	(n) a hole or opening
gape	(v) to yawn; to stare in wonder or surprise
genial	(adj) cheerful, friendly, amiable
genius	(n) great natural ability
genus	(n) class, kind, or sort
gibe	(v) to jeer, taunt, scoff at
jibe	(v) to change the course of a ship; colloquial—to be in harmony with, agree
gild	(v) to overlay gold
guild	(n) an association; medieval association of men
gist	(n) essence or main point
jest	(n) jibe, joke
	(v) to jeer, mock, joke
grate	(n) part of a fireplace
	(v) to grind or scrape
great	(adj) of more than ordinary size, quantity, scope
grill	(n) griddle for cooking food
grille	(n) an open screen, often of wrought iron, used as a divider
guarantee	(n) pledge that a purchase is as represented
	(v) to give a guarantee or guaranty; to promise
guaranty	(n) commitment to assume debt or responsibility of another
guerrilla	(n) one who engages in irregular warfare
gorilla	(n) ape
guessed	(v—past tense and perfect participle of guess) judged or estimated
guest	(n) visitor who is entertained or entertains
	(adj) for guests; entertaining by special invitation

hail	(n) precipitation in form of balls of ice
	(v) to precipitate hail; to pour down or strike like hail; salute, greet, summon
hale	(adj) sound, healthy
hall	(n) large room; passageway
haul	(v) to pull with force, transport, tug, drag
handsome	(adj) good-looking, gracious, considerable
hansom	(n) two-wheeled covered carriage
hangar	(n) shelter, shed for airplanes
	(v) to place into a hangar
hanger	(n) one who hangs, causes something to be hung; or something that hangs; device by which something is hung
heal	(v) to make healthy, restore
heel	(n) back part of foot; part of a shoe; unscrupulous person
	(v) to follow at the rear
healthful	(adj) promoting or maintaining health
healthy	(adj) having good health
hear	(v) to perceive or sense sound through the ear
here	(adv) at or in this place
heard	(v—past tense and perfect participle of hear) sensed sounds
herd	(n) a group of animals; crowd; the masses
	(v) to drive together into or as a group
hearsay	(n) rumor, gossip
heresy	(n) opinion or belief contrary to established doctrine
hew	(v) to chop, hack with ax, knife
hue	(n) color, shade; loud shout or cry
higher	(adj—comparative degree of high) loftier
hire	(n) amount paid for services; a hiring
	(v) to employ
hoard	(v) to store in reserve
horde	(n) supply stored away; large, moving crowd or throng

4

Words Frequently Confused and Misused **269**

hole	(n) hollow place, cavity, opening
whole	(adj) entire, intact, complete
holey	(adj) having a hole or holes
holly	(n) genus of shrub with glossy leaves and red berries
holy	(adj) sacred, hallowed
wholly	(adv) completely, entirely
human	(n) a person
	(adj) pertaining to mankind
humane	(adj) civilized; having the best qualities of mankind
hypercritical	(adj) too critical, severe
hypocritical	(adj) pretending to something one is not
ideal	(n) perfect model, archetype, goal
idle	(v) to move aimlessly; loaf
	(adj) useless, unemployed, not working
idol	(n) image of a god; object of ardent admiration
idyll	(n) poem depicting rural life; an extended narrative poem
impassable	(adj) incapable of being passed, traveled, surmounted
impassible	(adj) incapable of suffering or feeling pain, impassive
impasse	(n) an impassable road or way; a deadlock
inane	(adj) foolish, silly
insane	(adj) mentally ill, deranged
inapt	(adj) not apt; inappropriate
inept	(adj) awkward, clumsy
incidence	(n) act of falling upon or influencing
incidents	(n pl) occurrences, happenings
incinerate	(v) to burn to ashes
insinuate	(v) to introduce, hint, suggest
incite	(v) to stir to action; arouse
insight	(n) clear understanding; ability to clearly understand

indict	(v) to charge with or accuse of a crime
indite	(v) to compose or write; to dictate
indigenous	(adj) naturally produced, native to a region; inborn
indigent	(n) a needy, poor person (adj) in poverty, poor
indignant	(adj) expressing scorn, anger
infarction	(n) diseased body tissue
infection	(n) act or result of contamination with a disease-producing substance
infraction	(n) a violation
ingenious	(adj) having genius, clever, resourceful
ingenuous	(adj) frank, open, candid
insoluble	(adj) that which cannot be dissolved
insolvable	(adj) that which cannot be solved
insolvent	(adj) bankrupt; not able to pay debts
instance	(n) example, case, illustration
instants	(n pl) particular moments
interment	(v) burial
internment	(n) confinement
intestate	(adj) having made no will
interstate	(adj) between or among states
intrastate	(adj) within a state
intelligent	(adj) having intelligence; bright, perceptive
intelligible	(adj) understandable, clear
intense	(adj) strong, violent, earnest
intents	(n pl) aims, purposes
judicial	(adj) to judge; the judiciary or justice, critical
judicious	(adj) characterized by sound judgment
knew	(v—past tense of know) perceived, understood
new	(adj) not old, never existing before
know	(v) to clearly perceive, understand

4

no	(adj) not any, not a (adv) not in any degree, opposite of yes
lapse	(v) slip of the tongue, mind, moral standard; termination of a right or privilege
elapse	(v) to slip by, pass
relapse	(v) to fall back into a former condition
last	(n) block for repairing shoes; the end (v) to continue or endure (adj—superlative degree of late) coming after all others, final (adv) finally
latest	(adv—superlative degree of late) most recent, newest
lath	(n) framework for plaster (v) to cover with laths
lathe	(n) machine used for shaping (v) to shape on a lathe
lead	(n) a malleable metal (v) to guide
led	(v—past tense and perfect participle of lead) guided
leak	(v) to enter or escape through an opening (n) crack or hole
leek	(n) vegetable
lean	(v) to bend or incline (adj) thin, slender
lien	(n) claim or property as security for a debt
leased	(v—past tense and perfect participle of lease) contracted for rental
least	(n) smallest in size, amount, importance (adj—superlative degree of little) smallest, slightest
lest	(conj) for fear that, in case
legislator	(n) member of a lawmaking body
legislature	(n) a lawmaking body

lessen	(v) to make less, decrease
lesson	(n) something to be learned; instruction
lend	(v) to give out temporarily (past tense is lent)
loan	(n) act of lending; something lent
lone	(adj) standing apart, by oneself, alone
lesser	(adj—comparative degree of less) smaller, less important
lessor	(n) one who gives a lease, landlord
levee	(n) bank along a river
levy	(n) tax imposed; compulsory military enlistment
	(v) to impose a tax, to enlist troops
liable	(adj) legally bound, obligated
libel	(n) false written statements
	(v) to publish false statements
liable	(adj) legally bound or obligated
likable	(adj) genial, pleasant
like	(n) preference, taste, affection
	(v) to please, have a fondness for
	(adj) having similar qualities
	(prep) similar to
likely	(adj) credible, probable
lie	(n) untruth
	(v) to tell an untruth; to rest or recline (See: GRAMMAR, p. 68 for proper use of the verb lie)
lye	(n) strong alkaline solution
lightening	(v) making less heavy; gladdening; making pale
lighting	(n) illumination
lightning	(n) atmospheric electricity
linage	(n) sample of lines; printed or written matter; method of payment for literary material
lineage	(n) descent; derivation of ancestry

4

liqueur	(n) sweetened and flavored alcoholic beverage
liquor	(n) distilled alcoholic beverage
load	(n) burden; something carried
	(v) to put upon or into a carrier
lode	(n) vein of ore
loath	(adj) unwilling, reluctant
loathe	(v) to detest, hate
local	(adj) confined to a particular place
locale	(n) setting for a story, play, and so on
loose	(v) to set free (See: GRAMMAR, p. 69 for proper use of loose)
	(adj) free, unbound
lose	(v) to mislay; to suffer a loss
magnate	(n) important, influential person
magnet	(n) person or thing that attracts
magnificent	(adj) grand, stately
munificent	(adj) very generous, lavish
manner	(n) mode, procedure, method
manor	(n) estate, residence
mantel	(n) shelf of a fireplace
mantle	(n) loose sleeveless garment, cloak
	(v) to cover or cloak
marshal	(n) an official, officer
	(v) to arrange, dispose, direct
martial	(adj) of war, pertaining to the military
marital	(adj) pertaining to marriage or matrimony
mask	(n) face cover or disguise; pretense
	(v) to assume a mask; disguise
masque	(n) dramatic entertainment
material	(n) substance, matter
matériel	(n) weapons, equipment of the armed forces as opposed to its personnel
mean	(n) average, middle
	(v) to have in mind, intend
	(adj) common, lowly; bad-tempered

mien	(n) way of carrying oneself, bearing, appearance
meat	(n) animal flesh used as food
meet	(n) an assembly; a race
	(v) to come together
mete	(v) to allot, distribute
medal	(n) an award; inscribed or designed piece of metal
meddle	(v) to tamper with; interfere
middle	(n) mid-point
metal	(n) an alloy; chemical element
mettle	(n) high quality, character, spirit
militate	(v) to work against
military	(n) the army
	(adj) of the armed forces, martial
miner	(n) one who digs coal, ores from mines
minor	(n) person under legal age
	(adj) under legal age; lesser, small
missed	(v—past tense and perfect participle of miss) failed to hit, meet, obtain; overlooked
mist	(n) water vapor, light fog
	(v) to become or make misty, obscure
might	(n) superior power, force
	(v—past tense and perfect participle of may) implies a possibility
mite	(n) very small sum of money
monetary	(adj) pertaining to money; financial
monitory	(adj) containing an admonition
modal	(adj) indicating mode or mood
model	(n) a small copy or reproduction; a person who poses
	(v) to pose
module	(n) unit of measure
mood	(n) mental disposition; an aspect of verbs
mode	(n) manner of acting, method

moral	(adj) relating to right and wrong
morale	(n) mental condition of an individual or group
morality	(n) moral quality, rightness or wrongness
mortality	(n) condition of being mortal or having to die; death rate
morning	(n) early part of the day—midnight to noon
mourning	(n) the expression of grief (v) expressing grief (adj) pertaining to grieving
motif	(n) main element, theme
motive	(n) inner drive or intention
naval	(adj) of or relating to a navy
navel	(n) depression in the middle of the abdomen; middle
official	(n) one who officiates (adj) authorized, formal
officious	(adj) meddlesome, overbearing
one	(n) a cardinal number; a single unit (pron) some or any person or thing (adj) united, single
won	(v—past tense and perfect participle of win) gained victory, triumphed
ordinance	(n) direction or command, a law
ordnance	(n) military weapons and ammunition
overdo	(v) to do in excess
overdue	(adj) tardy, past-due
packed	(v—past tense and perfect participle of pack) bundled; grouped, pressed together
pact	(n) an agreement
pail	(n) a container, bucket
pale	(adj) pallid, wan; faint, dim
pain	(n) sensation of hurting; strong discomfort (v) to cause pain

pane	(n) a sheet of glass, window part
pair	(n) two similar things joined or used together
	(v) to match two things
pare	(v) to cut or trim; reduce
pear	(n) a fruit
parameter	(n) reference for determining other values; constant with variable values
perimeter	(n) outer boundary of an area; circumference
partiality	(n) state of being partial; bias
partially	(adv) in a biased, prejudiced manner
partly	(adv) not completely; in some measure or degree, in part
passed	(v—past tense and perfect participle of pass) moved forward, crossed, lead
past	(n) time gone by; history
palate	(n) roof of the mouth
palette	(n) painter's board or tablet
pallet	(n) bed
parlay	(v) to transform into something of great value
parley	(n) meeting, conference, discussion
patience	(n) endurance, perseverance
patients	(n pl) persons receiving care or treatment
peace	(n) state of calm; freedom from war
piece	(n) a part or fragment; one thing
	(v) to join or unite
peak	(n) tapering part that projects; summit
	(v) to bring to the highest point
	(adj) maximum
peek	(n) a glance
	(v) to glance at; to look quickly
peal	(n) ringing of a bell
peel	(n) the skin or rind
	(v) to cut away, strip off, skin

4

pedal	(n) lever operated by the foot
	(v) to operate a pedal
	(adj) of the foot
peddle	(v) to sell
petal	(n) part of a flower
piddle	(v) to trifle
peer	(n) person or thing of equal rank, value; an equal
pier	(n) landing place, dock
perfect	(v) to bring to completion
	(adj) without defect, flawless
prefect	(n) administrative official
perquisite	(n) some expected additional amount to pay; profit; a tip, a privilege, or a benefit
prerequisite	(n) something required beforehand
	(adj) required beforehand
perpetrate	(v) to do or perform; to be guilty of
perpetuate	(v) to cause to continue or to be remembered
persecute	(v) to afflict, harass, annoy constantly
prosecute	(v) to carry on; to institute legal proceedings
personal	(adj) peculiar to one person; of the person, body, human beings
personnel	(n) persons employed, workers
perspective	(n) appearance, point of view
prospective	(adj) expected, likely
perspicacity	(n) keenness, shrewdness
perspicuity	(n) clarity
peruse	(v) to read, study
pursue	(v) to follow, overtake, seek after
physic	(n) a medicine, laxative
physique	(n) appearance of the body
physiology	(n) branch of biology dealing with living organisms

psychology	(n) science dealing with the mind, mental and emotional processes
pinnacle	(n) a lofty summit; peak, acme
	(v) to surmount with or raise or rear on a pinnacle
pinochle	(n) a card game
pique	(n) resentment at being slighted, ruffled pride
	(v) to provoke
piqué	(n) woven cotton fabric (need accent)
piquet	(n) a card game
pistil	(n) part of a flower
pistol	(n) handgun
plain	(n) broad, flat field
	(adj) clear, obvious, simple, ordinary
plane	(n) even, flat surface; short for airplane
	(v) to shave wood
plaintiff	(n) a person who sues
plaintive	(adj) mournful, sad
plait	(n) braid or pigtail
plat	(v) to braid
plate	(n) dish, layer of metal; denture
	(v) to cover equipment with a plate
plurality	(n) multitude; number of votes the leading candidate receives over the one with the next highest number of votes
majority	(n) over half of a group; more than half of total votes
pole	(n) long, slender piece of metal or wood
poll	(n) a counting, listing, registering of persons; voting place
	(v) to canvass, count
poor	(adj) lacking material possessions; needy
pore	(n) tiny opening
	(v) to think or study carefully, to ponder
pour	(v) to emit steadily; flow freely

4

populace	(n) the common people, masses
populous	(adj) thickly populated, crowded with people
portend	(v) to foreshadow; to be an omen of
portent	(n) an omen, warning, indication
portion	(n) part or share of something
	(v) to divide into parts
proportion	(n) comparative relation between parts; symmetry
	(v) to cause to be in proper relation, harmony, balance
apportion	(v) to divide according to a plan; to allot
practicable	(adj) that which can be put into practice; feasible
practical	(adj) useful, workable
pray	(v) to supplicate, implore; to recite a prayer
prey	(n) human or animal victim of another
	(v) to hunt animals for food; to weigh heavily upon
precede	(v) to be, come, go before
proceed	(v) to advance; go on
precedence	(n) act or fact of preceding; priority
precedents	(n pl) previous statements; legal cases that serve as examples
president	(n) highest executive officer
preposition	(n) a part of speech; a connecting word
proposition	(n) a plan, proposal
prescribe	(v) to set down in writing a rule or direction
proscribe	(v) to outlaw; to banish; to forbid
prescience	(n) foreknowledge
presence	(n) existence, occurrence, attendance
presents	(n pl) gifts; writings (legal term)
presentiment	(n) a premonition, foreboding
presentment	(n) an exhibition; the producing of a negotiable instrument for payment

pretend	(v) to allege, claim falsely, make believe, assume
principal	(n) chief presiding officer, head (adj) chief, first in rank
principle	(n) rule, law, cause of something
profit	(n) monetary gain; a benefit
prophet	(n) one who predicts future events
prone	(adj) lying or leaning face downward, prostrate
supine	(adj) lying on the back, face upward; sluggish, listless
prophecy	(n) prediction
prophesy	(v) to predict
propose	(v) to put forth, offer
purpose	(n) intention, resolution (v) to intend, resolve
psyche	(n) the mind
psychic	(n) a spiritualist (adj) of the mind; sensitive to forces beyond the physical world
quiet	(n) calmness, stillness (adj) silent, noiseless
quite	(adv) completely, truly, considerable
quit	(v) to abandon, stop, give up
rain	(n) water falling to earth (v) to fall, pour down
rein	(n) harness (v) to control, guide
reign	(n) royal power, sovereignty, rule (v) to rule, dominate, prevail
raise	(v) to lift, elevate (See: GRAMMAR, p. 80, for proper usage of verb raise)
rays	(n pl) beams of light
raze	(v) to demolish, destroy
rap	(v) to tap; knock sharply
wrap	(n) an outer covering; outer garment (v) to cover, envelop

rapt	(adj) wholly absorbed, transported with emotion; engrossed
wrapped	(v—past tense of wrap) covered, enveloped, enfolded, embraced
real	(adj) in fact, actual, genuine, true
reel	(n) a dance; a spool
reality	(n) quality or fact of being real
realty	(n) real estate
read	(v) to interpret characters or signs for meaning
reed	(n) a grass or stem of a long, slender grass
receipt	(n) written acknowledgment
	(v) to write an acknowledgment
recipe	(n) list of ingredients and directions
recent	(adj) just before the present time; modern, new
resent	(v) to feel or show indignation
reference	(n) a referring to; the directing of attention to
reverence	(n) deep respect, awe
relaid	(v) laid again
relayed	(v) sent on, transmitted
repairable	(adj) capable of repair—a material object
reparable	(adj) capable of repair—an immaterial object such as an error
residence	(n) dwelling; a residing in or at
residents	(n pl) those who reside or live in or at a place
respectability	(n) quality or state of being respected
respectably	(adv) to a degree worth respect or esteem
respectful	(adj) characterized by respect, deference
respectfully	(adv) in a respectful or deferential manner
respective	(adj) as relates individually to each of two or more persons or things; several

respectively	(adv) in the order named
right	(n) that which is fact, law, privilege; not left
	(adj) in accordance with fact, law, justice
rite	(n) formal ceremony
wright	(n) one who works at construction, repair
write	(v) to inscribe; to communicate in writing
role	(n) part, character, function, office
roll	(n) something rolled up; a register or list; a cake or bread
roomer	(n) person who rents a room, lodger
rumor	(n) gossip, hearsay
	(v) to spread gossip or hearsay
root	(n) part of a plant; origin, source
	(v) to begin to grow; to originate
route	(n) a road or course of travel, path
	(v) to establish a course or order
rote	(n) routine (by rote: by memory)
wrote	(v—past tense of to write) inscribed, communicated
rye	(n) a grass, used for grain
wry	(adj) having a bent or twisted shape or condition; wrongheaded
sac	(n) a pouch within an animal or plant, usually containing fluid
sack	(n) rectangular-shaped bag; a unit of measure; a loose-fitting dress; a dismissal; a bed or bunk
	(v) to put into a bag; to dismiss; to plunder, loot, or ravage
sail	(n) the canvas part of a boat
	(v) to move by means of sails
sale	(n) act of exchanging property for consideration
scene	(n) setting; place something occurs
seen	(v—perfect participle of to see) observed

4

Words Frequently Confused and Misused **283**

scent	(n) a smell, odor
	(v) to smell
sent	(v—past tense and perfect participle of send) dispatched, conveyed, transmitted
sense	(n) received impression; good judgment
scull	(n) an oar or set of oars; a racing shell
	(v) to propel with oars
skull	(n) skeleton of a head; mind
seam	(n) the line where two pieces are sewed together
	(v) to join, sew together
seem	(v) to appear to be
seize	(v) to take; assume ownership, grasp
seige	(n) an attempt to gain control; period of distress
serial	(n) novel, movie, and so on; produced in parts
	(adj) arranged or appearing in continuous parts
cereal	(n) a food made from grain
sell	(v) to trade, exchange goods or property
cell	(n) a small room; small complex unit of tissue
seller	(n) one who trades, exchanges
cellar	(n) room below ground level
selvage	(n) edge of a fabric; border
salvage	(n) that which is saved or rescued
	(v) to save or rescue
serf	(n) member of a servile or feudal class
surf	(n) swell of the sea that breaks ashore
	(v) to ride the waves
serge	(n) a fabric
	(adj) made of serge fabric
surge	(n) wave, billow of water
	(v) to move violently; increase suddenly
session	(n) a meeting of a group

4

cession	(n) a giving up or ceding to another
cessation	(n) a ceasing or stopping
settler	(n) person or thing that settles, colonizes
settlor	(n) person who makes a property settlement
sew	(v) to fasten with stitches
so	(adv) in such manner; thus
sow	(n) female pig
	(v) to scatter or plant
shear	(v) to cut or dip; to remove hair
sheer	(v) to swerve, to deviate from a course
	(adj) very thin; pure
simple	(adj) not complex, mere, plain, easy
simplistic	(adj) oversimplified
sleight	(n) cunning or craftiness; dexterity
slight	(n) disrespectful treatment
	(v) to neglect; to treat with indifference
	(adj) slender, frail; not great or intense
soar	(v) to rise, fly, sail high
sore	(adj) painful, filled with grief (colloquial: angry)
stationary	(adj) not moving, fixed
stationery	(n) writing paper and envelopes
statue	(n) carved or molded form; model
stature	(n) height of a person; level of attainment
statute	(n) a law or regulation
stile	(n) set of steps (turnstile)
style	(n) distinction, manner
	(v) to design, fashion
straight	(adj) not crooked or bent; level
strait	(n) narrow waterway; difficulty, distress
suit	(n) set of clothes; legal action; set or series
	(v) to make appropriate, fit, satisfy
suite	(n) set of rooms; matched pieces of furniture; a staff or retinue

4

sweet	(adj) having a sugary taste; agreeable to the mind or senses
superintendence	(n) the direction or act of directing something
superintendents	(n pl) people who direct, supervise
tail	(n) rear part; an appendage; men's formal attire
	(v) to follow closely behind
	(adj) at the rear
tale	(n) story or account; a falsehood
tare	(n) weight of a container, wrapper
	(v) to mark, determine the wrapper's weight
tear	(n) water flowing from eyeball
	(v) to separate, rip, puncture; to fill with tears
tier	(n) a row, layer, arranged ranks
	(v) to put in layers
taught	(v—past tense and perfect participle of to teach) instructed
taut	(adj) tightly drawn, not slack; tense
team	(n) a group, crew, gang
	(v) to form a group, crew, or gang
teem	(v) to become filled to overflowing; abound
tenant	(n) one who rents or leases
tenet	(n) a principle, belief, doctrine
terse	(adj) concise, succinct
trite	(adj) lacking in novelty, originality
than	(conj) expresses exception; connects elements in a comparison
then	(adv) soon afterward, next
their	(possessive pronoun) of, belonging to
there	(adv) at or in that place (often used as an intensive pronoun)
they're	(contraction) they are

therefor	(adv) for this, that, it (legal usage)
therefore	(adv) as a result of; hence
threw	(v—past tense of to throw) caused to move through the air
through	(prep) from one end to another (adv) to the end (adj) allowing free passage
to	(prep) in the direction of; toward
too	(adv) in addition, as well, besides
two	(n) number between one and three; a pair, couple
topography	(n) description of a place; science of mapmaking
typography	(n) the setting or arranging of type
track	(n) a mark left as evidence; a path or trail; pair of rails; athletic field (v) to follow or trace evidence
tract	(n) stretch of land
troop	(n) a group of soldiers; collection of people or things (v) to move or gather in crowds; to associate, throng
troupe	(n) a group of theatrical performers
trustee	(n) one to whom something is entrusted; legal administrator
trusty	(n) a trusted person; convict allowed special privileges (adj) trustworthy, dependable
urban	(adj) of, relating to a city
urbane	(adj) polite, polished, suave
vain	(adj) idle, worthless, useless, silly, conceited
vane	(n) device for measuring wind
vein	(n) lode, blood vessel, mode of expression, strain
vale	(n) valley, dale

4

vail	(v) to lower in submission
veil	(n) head and shoulder or face covering
	(v) to cover, conceal
vial	(n) small vessel for liquids
vile	(adj) common, mean, foul, contemptible
viol	(n) sixteenth century, stringed musical instrument
vice	(n) wickedness, foible, fault
	(prefix) one who takes the place of
vise	(n) a tool for holding work
	(v) to hold, force, squeeze
vigilant	(adj) watchful
vigilante	(n) a watchman, guard
waist	(n) the middle part of the body; a blouse
waste	(n) devastated stretch of land; useless spending; discarded material
	(adj) superfluous, leftover
waive	(v) to forego, relinquish
wave	(n) surge of water; hand signal; curl in hair
	(v) to fluctuate, swing, sway; to signal
ware	(n) piece or kind of goods for sale
wear	(v) to carry on the person; to become consumed
where	(adv) in, at, toward what place
weak	(adj) lacking in strength, feeble; easily upset
week	(n) period of seven days
weather	(n) condition of the atmosphere
	(v) to endure exposure to weather
whether	(conj) in case, if it be the case
who's	(contraction) who is or who has
whose	(pronoun) that or those belonging to whom
woman	(n) female
women	(n pl) females

wrack	(n) misery, punishment; ruin, destruction
	(v) to ruin, wreck
rack	(n) a framework for holding things; an instrument of torture
	(v) to torture, afflict; to place in or on a rack
yew	(n) evergreen shrub
you	(pronoun) one being addressed
your	(possessive pronoun) of, belonging to you
you're	(contraction) you are

4

SECTION 5
Correspondence Format Guides

In this section of the manual, guides are presented for preparing text material that word processors, machine transcribers, and correspondence secretaries are often asked to prepare in final copy. Special instructions that illustrate methods for using word processing equipment most efficiently in formatting are provided in WP/IP NOTES.

Of major importance is the CORRESPONDENCE division. It outlines information on letter style, punctuation, letter parts, stationery sizes, and address, salutation, and complimentary close formats. Actual-size illustrations are used so that format may be followed either from the outlined information or from the examples themselves. Format guides for interoffice correspondence and for addressing envelopes are outlined, and general rules as well as the most recent rules specified by the United States Postal Guide are given. Specific applications for outgoing mail, interoffice mail, special mailing notations, and return addresses are dealt with. Rules for addressing foreign mail are presented. Information concerning the placement of addresses on various size envelopes will be of value to the secretary who must occasionally use other than standard business envelopes.

5

Letter Styles for Outgoing Correspondence

5

Block (See EXAMPLE A, p. 336)

- All lines begin at the left margin.
- This style is recommended for organizations desiring a modern, efficient letter style.

Modified Block (See EXAMPLE B, p. 338)

- All lines begin at the left margin except the dateline and complimentary close.

- The dateline may be centered, typed to end at the right margin, or begun at the same point the complimentary close is begun.

- The complimentary close and signature lines begin slightly to the right of center (55 elite, 47 pica) or begin to end at the right margin.

- Paragraphs may be blocked (begun at left margin) or indented 5, 7, or 10 spaces.

- This style is recommended for organizations desiring a traditional letter style.

Simplified (See EXAMPLE C, p. 340)

- The salutation and complimentary close are omitted.

- A subject line typed in all caps and begun a triple space after the inside address and a triple space before the body is required.

- All lines including enumerated items are blocked (begun at left margin).

- The signature line is typed in all caps four lines after the body of the letter.

- Reference and enclosure notations are double spaced after the signature line.

- This letter style was developed and is recommended by the Administrative Management Society.

- It is most efficient in preparation.

WP/IP NOTE:

Block and simplified letter styles are most adaptable to word processing output.

Form Letters

- The correspondent chooses appropriate paragraphs from standardized copy.

- Form letters are appropriate for large volume or routine correspondence.

- Variable information may be inserted where necessary.

WP/IP NOTE:

In setting up standard paragraphs for magnetic media equipment, it is important to determine formatting such as tabs and line length for all documents. Each paragraph should end with the same coding, such as 2 CR and SC.

A standard setup for repetitive letters is desirable. It is suggested that as much material as possible be recorded; for example, CRs to the date location and the space(s) preceding variable information.

Executive Correspondence

- Executive correspondence includes letters of a personal or social business nature.

- They are usually prepared on Monarch size ($7\frac{1}{2} \times 10$ inches) or half-size ($5\frac{1}{2} \times 8\frac{1}{2}$ inches) stationery.

- They may be typed in any letter style.

5

Official Correspondence

- Official correspondence is that prepared in U.S. Government offices.

- Stationery is $8 \times 10\frac{1}{2}$ inches rather than $8\frac{1}{2} \times 11$ inches. Federal offices are expected soon to adopt stationery size of $8\frac{1}{2} \times 11$ inches.

- The inside address is typed four to six lines below closing lines at the left margin.

- Reference initials and other notations are omitted on the original copy, but they may be included on carbon copies or file copies.

Two-Page Letter

- The second-page heading begins 1 or 1½ inches from the top of the page.

- It includes the first line of the inside address, the page number, and the date.

- Format follows one of these arrangements.

```
ABC Company
Page 2
October 8, 1983
```
                              or
```
ABC Company          2              October 8, 1983
```

- There must be two lines of the body on each page succeeding the first page.

- Triple space after heading and before continuation of body of letter.

WP/IP NOTE:

Headings and page numbers are not recorded on the letter but are put into a header format. With older equipment, it may be necessary to type the heading and page numbers manually.

Punctuation

Open (See EXAMPLE A, p. 336)

- No colon follows salutation.
- No comma follows complimentary close.
- Only sentence punctuation is required.

Mixed (See EXAMPLE B, p. 338)

- Colon follows salutation.
- Comma follows complimentary close.
- The comma is not appropriate after the salutation even in a personal business letter.
- A colon (:) should not be confused with the semicolon (;).

Parts of a
Business Letter

Letterhead

● The letterhead includes the printed or engraved company name, address, telephone number. It may also contain other data: trademark, art work, names of officers, departments, cable address, and so on.

● As a general rule, approximately 2 inches of space at the top of the page is consumed by the letterhead.

Dateline

- The current date is typed on all letters approximately two lines below the letterhead (usually line 12, 13, or 14).

- Horizontal placement depends on letter style. (See EXAMPLES A, B, C, pp. 336–341)

Inside Address

- The inside address includes the complete name and address of the person or organization that the letter is written to.

- Generally the envelope address is prepared from the inside address.

- Both inside address and envelope address usually contain at least three lines. If there is no street address, the city and state are placed on one line, making only a two-line address. For example:

      Lakeland Community College
      Mentor, OH 44060

- An appropriate personal or professional title should be included if the letter is addressed to an individual. (See ADDRESS AND SALUTATION FORMAT, p. 313)

5

Attention Line (See EXAMPLE A, p. 336)

- An attention line is used to direct the correspondence to a specific person or department when the letter is addressed to an organization.

- It may be typed in any of the following ways:

      ATTENTION MR. COOPER

      Attention Chief Engineer

      Attention: Credit Department

- It is placed two spaces below the city, state, ZIP code line in the inside address and two spaces below the return address on the envelope.

● When an attention line is used, the salutation is "Gentlemen" since the letter is written to the company.

● An attention line should not be used if correspondence can be appropriately addressed to an individual.

Subject Line (See EXAMPLE A, p. 336)

● The subject line is a reference or introduction to the body of the letter.

● It may be typed in all caps or underscored for emphasis.

● Otherwise, the first letter of all words except articles, prepositions, and conjunctions is capitalized.

● In legal correspondence, by precedent, the subject line is placed before the salutation although modern legal style requires placement after the salutation as in other correspondence.

● The terms *Re* or *Ref.* may be used instead of the word *Subject*.

● Illustrations of ways to type subject lines include:

```
SUBJECT: LETTER STYLES

Ref. Your Order No. 349

Re: Letter Styles for Modern
    Business
```

SUBJECT: Letter Styles for Modern
Business

Body or Message

● The body is single spaced with double spacing between paragraphs.

● It should be attractively placed so that it looks like a picture in a frame.

● Very short letters may be double spaced; paragraphs in double-spaced letters must be indented; triple spacing between paragraphs may be used.

● Tabulated material is set up according to rules for tabulation. (See STATISTICAL TYPING, p. 357)

Complimentary Close

● Capitalize only the first word in the complimentary close.

● Vertical placement is always two lines following the last line of the body of the letter.

● Horizontal placement varies with letter style. (See EXAMPLES A, B, C, pp. 336–341)

Company Signature

● Although still used by some organizations, a company signature is not necessary when the company name and pertinent data are included in the letterhead.

● It is typed in all caps a double space below the complimentary close.

● Omit the complimentary close in the Simplified AMS letter style.

Typewritten Signature

- A typewritten signature is required in all business letters.

- Vertical placement depends upon letter placement. (See LETTER PLACEMENT, p. 307)

- Horizontal placement depends upon letter style. (See LETTER STYLE, p. 293)

- The official title of the dictator or writer is usually included.

- This title may be typed on the same line as the signature or on a separate line immediately below the typewritten signature.

- The personal title of dictator or writer should be omitted unless a woman intends to specify marital status. *Mr.* is not used before a man's name; *Miss* or *Mrs.* may be used before a woman's name. A woman's title may be placed in parentheses or typed without parentheses: (Miss) Mary Jones or Mrs. Mary Jones.

- Professional titles may be included before or after names and are typed without parentheses: John J. Jones, M.D.; Dr. John J. Jones; John J. Jones, Ph.D.; Professor John Jones; Dr. John Jones; Reverend John Jones; John Jones, S. J., and so on.

5

Reference Initials (See EXAMPLE A, p. 337)

- The typist's or work-station initials are always included on both outgoing and interoffice correspondence.

- Lower-case letters are used.

- The dictator's or writer's initials need not be included if his or her signature is typewritten in the signature section.

- If the dictator's or writer's initials are used, type them in all caps, but still use lower case for the typist's initials. For example: rt (typist's only); RCK/rt (dictator's and typist's).

Enclosure Notations (See EXAMPLE A, p. 337)

● If an enclosure is included with a letter, the abbreviation *Enc.* is used to indicate this fact.

● More than one enclosure is indicated by *Enc.* followed by the number of enclosures (for example, *Enc. 2* or *Enc. 3*).

● This notation is always the first notation to follow the typist's reference initials (or writer's signature if no reference initials are necessary).

● It is placed at the left margin, two spaces below the typist's reference initials (or writer's typewritten signature if no reference initials are necessary).

● If the enclosure is attached (stapled or in a binder), the *Enc.* may be replaced by the abbreviation for attachment—*Attach.*

Carbon Copy Notations (See EXAMPLE A, p. 337)

● Notations indicating other persons to whom copies of a letter have been sent are called carbon copy notations.

● They are indicated by the abbreviation *cc:* followed by the name and, if necessary, the address of those persons receiving copies. For example: cc: Mr. John Jones, or cc: Mr. John Jones, Smith Company, 415 South 14th Street, Sebring, OH 44673.

● Although photocopies and other copy processes are now used rather than carbon copies, it is still appropriate to use the *cc:* abbreviation for any type of copy. Some organizations are using *pc* rather than *cc*.

Special Mailing Notations (See EXAMPLE B, p. 338)

● Special mailing notations indicate the purchase of special postal services such as registered mail, special delivery, and so on; these markings provide directions for postal workers.

● They are placed immediately before the inside address and are followed by a double space.

● They are typed in all caps.

● They are typed on the envelope address as well. (See FORMAT GUIDES, ENVELOPES, p. 331)

● Since airmail is no longer a special service for domestic mail, airmail notation is not required.

Personal Notations (See EXAMPLE C, p. 340)

● Personal notations such as Confidential are used to alert the receiver of correspondence of some personal matter or to give special instructions such as Please Forward, Hold for Arrival, and so on.

● They are placed immediately before the inside address and are followed by a double space.

● They are typed in all caps.

● They are typed on the envelope address as well. (See: FORMAT GUIDES, ENVELOPES, p. 329)

Letter Placement

Variation in Line Length

- Spacing between parts of the letter remains constant.

- The date line begins on line 12, 13, or 14.

- Double spacing is used between all parts of the letter except:
  (a) Four to six lines are left between date and inside address.
  (b) Four lines are left between the complimentary close and the typewritten signature.
  (c) Three lines are left between the second-page heading and the continuation of the body of the letter.

- Double spacing occurs between paragraphs in the body of the letter.

- A short letter has 100 words or less; it requires a 2-inch left and right margin or a 50-space line. (Elite margins are 25 and 80; pica margins, 17 and 72.)

- A medium-length letter has between 100 and 200 words; it requires a 1½-inch left and right margin or a 60-space line. (Elite margins are 20 and 85; pica margins, 12 and 77.)

- A long letter has between 200 and 300 words; it requires a 1-inch left and right margin or a 70-space line. (Elite margins are 15 and 90; pica margins, 7 and 82.)

- Generally letters of more than 300 words will require more than one page if pica type is used; letters of more than 350 words will require more than one page if elite type is used. The extent of tabulation, statistics, quoted material, and so on, will affect letter placement.

- At least two lines of the body of the letter must be on each page succeeding the first page; the closing lines alone cannot be carried to another page.

- All pages must have at least 1-inch bottom margins.

Standard Margins

- A 60- or 70-space line is used for all letters regardless of word count. (Use 60 spaces if the majority of letters are of medium length or short; use 70 spaces if the majority of letters are long letters.)

- The space between the date and the inside address is varied to adjust for differences in letter length; variation may run from 4 to 12 lines.

- The space between the complimentary close and the type-written signature varies between 4 and 6 lines.

- Space is varied from 2 to 4 lines between typewritten signature and reference notations.

- Space is varied from 2 to 4 lines between reference notations and enclosure or other notations.

- To incorporate the use of standard margins, more space is left between parts of a short letter (expanding total space used) and less space is left between parts of a long letter (decreasing total space used).

5

WP/IP NOTE:

Whenever possible, use a standard line length in all correspondence. Many machines are set up with an automatic line length of 6 inches.

5

Stationery Sizes

Standard

● 8½ × 11 inches is used for most business correspondence.

● 8 × 10½ inches is used by all federal and some state governmental organizations for regular business correspondence. Federal offices will soon adopt stationery 8½ × 11 inches.

Special

● 7½ × 10 inches (Monarch or Executive) is used for personal business correspondence by certain executives within an organization.

● 5½ × 8½ inches (Baronial or half-sheet size) may be substituted for Monarch size.

Address and Salutation Format

General Rules

- A title is used for all persons to whom correspondence is addressed.

- If the addressee has a professional title, that title is used rather than a personal title.

- If the addressee has no professional title, a personal title is used.

- Either a personal or professional title is used; never both.

- The words *Sir, Madam, Madams, Mmes.* are considered out of date; their use should be avoided.

Personal Titles

Classification	Inside Address	Salutation
A man	Mr. James Doe	Dear Mr. Doe (formal) or Dear Jim (informal)
Two or more men, same last name	Messrs. John and James Doe	Dear Messrs. Doe (informal) or Dear John and Jim (informal)
Two or more men, different last names	Mr. John Doe and Mr. James Roe	Dear Mr. Doe and Mr. Roe (formal) or Dear John and Jim (informal)
A married woman	Mrs. or Ms. (her preference) Mary Doe	Dear Mrs. or Ms. Doe (formal) or Dear Mary (informal)
A single woman	Miss or Ms. (her preference) Mary Doe	Dear Miss or Ms. Doe (formal) or Dear Mary (informal)
A woman, marital status unknown	Ms. Mary Doe	Dear Ms. Doe (formal) or Dear Mary (informal)
A married couple	Mr. and Mrs. John Doe	Dear Mr. and Mrs. Doe
Two married women, same last name	Mrs. Mary and Mrs. Jane Doe or Ms. Mary and Ms. Jane Doe	Dear Mmes. Doe (formal) or Dear Mary and Jane (informal)

Personal Titles (Continued)

Classification	Inside Address	Salutation
Two married women, different last names	Mrs. Mary Doe and Mrs. Jane Roe or Ms. Mary Doe and Ms. Jane Roe	Dear Mrs. Doe and Mrs. Roe or Dear Ms. Doe and Ms. Roe (formal) or Dear Mary and Jane (informal)
Two single women, same last name	Misses Mary and Jane Doe or Ms. Mary and Ms. Jane Doe	Dear Misses Doe (formal) or Dear Mary and Jane (informal)
Two single women, different last names	Miss Mary Doe and Miss Jane Roe or Ms. Mary Doe and Ms. Jane Roe	Dear Miss Doe and Miss Roe or Dear Ms. Doe and Ms. Roe (formal) or Dear Mary and Jane (informal)
A company or corporation, gender of members or owners unknown	The XYZ Company	Gentlemen
A company or corporation of women	The XYZ Corporation	Ladies

5

Professional Titles—Governmental

Classification	Inside Address	Salutation
U.S. President	President (full name)	Mr. President or Dear Mr. President

Professional Titles—Governmental (Continued)

Classification	Inside Address	Salutation
U.S. Vice President	Vice President (full name)	Mr. Vice President or Dear Mr. Vice President
U.S. or State Senator	The Honorable or Honorable (full name)	Dear Senator (last name) or Dear Mr. (Mrs., Ms.) (last name)
U.S. or State Speaker of the House	The Honorable or Honorable (full name)	Mr. Speaker or Dear Mr. Speaker (last name)
U.S. or State Representa-tive	The Honorable or Honorable (full name)	Dear Representa-tive (last name) or Dear Mr. (Mrs., Ms.) (last name)
Federal or State Cabinet Members	The Honorable or Honorable (full name)	Dear Secretary, Dear Secretary (last name) or Dear Mr. (Mrs., Ms.) (last name)
Federal or State Directors of Bureaus, Commissions, and so on	The Honorable (full name) or Chief (full name)	Dear Director (Chief, Commissioner) (last name) or Dear Mr. (Mrs., Ms.) (full name)

Professional Titles—Governmental (Continued)

Classification	Inside Address	Salutation
Federal or State Chief Justice of Supreme Court	The Honorable (full name)	Dear Mr. Chief Justice
Federal or State Associate Justice of the Supreme Court	The Honorable (full name)	Dear Mr. Justice or Dear Mr. Justice (last name)
State Governor	The Honorable (full name) or Governor of the State of (full name)	Dear Governor (last name)
State Lieutenant Governor	The Honorable (full name) or Lieutenant Governor State of (full name)	Dear Mr. (Mrs., Ms.) (last name)
City Alderman or Alderwoman	Alderman (or Alderwoman) (full name) or The Honorable (full name) Alderman (Alderwoman), City of ___	Dear Alderman (Alderwoman) (last name) or Dear Mr. (Mrs., Ms.) (last name)
City Council Representative	Councilman (Councilwoman) (full name) or The Honorable (full name) Councilman (Councilwoman), City of ___	Dear Councilman (Councilwoman) (last name) or Dear Mr. (Mrs., Ms.) (last name)

5

Professional Titles—Governmental (Continued)

Classification	Inside Address	Salutation
City Attorney or Solicitor	Honorable (full name) Attorney (Solicitor), City of ___	Dear Attorney (Solicitor) (last name) or Dear Mr. (Mrs., Ms.) (last name)
District Attorney	The Honorable (full name) or District Attorney (full name)	Dear Mr. (Mrs., Ms.) (last name)
County Officials	Honorable or Chief (Commis- sioner, Supervisor) (full name)	Dear Chief (Com- missioner, Supervisor) (last name) or Dear Mr. (Mrs., Ms.) (last name)
Mayor	The Honorable (full name)	Dear Mayor (last name)

Professional Titles—Diplomatic

Classification	Inside Address	Salutation
Ambassador	The Honorable (full name), The Ambassador of the United States or American Ambassador	Dear Ambassador (last name)

Professional Titles—Diplomatic (Continued)

Classification	Inside Address	Salutation
Consul	Mr. (full name), Consul of the United States or American Consul	Dear Mr. (Mrs., Ms.) (last name)
United Nations Secretary General	His Excellency (full name), Secretary General, United Nations	Dear Secretary General or Dear Mr. Secretary General
United Nations Delegate	His Excellency (full name), Delegate, United Nations	Excellency or Dear Mr. (Mrs., Ms.) (last name)

Professional Titles—Armed Forces

Classification	Inside Address	Salutation
General, Army	General (full name), USA	Dear General (last name)
Admiral, Navy	Admiral (full name), USN	Dear Admiral (last name)
General, Marines	General (full name), USMC	Dear General (last name)
Colonel, Air Force	Colonel (full name), USAF	Dear Colonel (last name)
Captain, Coast Guard	Captain (full name), USCG	Dear Captain (last name)

Professional Titles—Armed Forces (Continued)

Classification	Inside Address	Salutation
Other officers (commissioned and noncommissioned)	(Rank) (full name), (service)	Dear (rank) (last name)
Chaplain	Lieutenant (full name), Ch.C, (service)	Dear Chaplain (last name)
Other personnel	Title and name Serial no. Station	Dear (title) (last name)

Professional Titles—Religious

Classification	Inside Address	Salutation
Catholic Pope	His Holiness, Pope ___	Your Holiness or Dear Holy Father
Catholic Cardinal	His Eminence (given name), Cardinal (last name)	Your Eminence or Dear Cardinal (last name)
Catholic Archbishop	The Most Reverend (full name), Archbishop of (diocese)	Your Excellency or Dear Archbishop (last name)
Catholic Bishop	The Most Reverend (full name), Bishop of (diocese)	Your Excellency or Dear Bishop (last name)

Professional Titles—Religious (Continued)

Classification	Inside Address	Salutation
Monsignor	The Most Right Reverend (full name), (church)	Dear Father or Dear Right Reverend (last name)
Catholic or Episcopal Priest	The Reverend (full name), (church) or	Dear Reverend Father (last name) or Dear Father
	The Reverend (full name), Ph.D. (institution)	Dear Doctor
Religious Order Priest	The Reverend (full name), (order initials, e.g., S.J.)	Dear Father
Religious Order Brother	Brother (full name), (order or order initials) or Brother (religious name), (order initials)	Dear Brother or Dear Brother (religious name)
Sister	Sister (full name), (order) or Sister (religious name), (order initials)	Dear Sister or Dear Sister (religious name)
Protestant Bishop	The Reverend (full name), Bishop of (diocese) or The Right Reverend (last name)	Dear Reverend (last name) or Dear Mr. (last name)

Professional Titles—Religious

Classification	Inside Address	Salutation
Protestant Minister	The Reverend (full name) or The Very Reverend (full name), D.D. or Dean (full name)	Dear Reverend (last name) or Dear Mr. (last name) or Dear Dean (last name)
Rabbi	Rabbi (full name)	Dear Rabbi (last name), or Dear Rabbi or Dear Dr. (last name)

Complimentary Close Format 5

General Rules

- Use a complimentary closing in all outgoing letters except those typed in the simplified AMS style.

- Do not use a complimentary close in interoffice correspondence.

- The complimentary close should agree in style with the salutation.

- A formal salutation requires a formal complimentary closing; an informal salutation requires an informal complimentary closing.

Salutation Agreement

- The following salutations are formal: Dear Mr., Dear Mrs., Dear Ms., Dear Miss (or their plurals), and all professional titles.

- Using a first name with *Dear* is considered informal.

Closings

- *Sincerely yours*, *Yours sincerely*, and *Sincerely* are used with formal salutations.

- *Cordially yours*, *Yours cordially*, and *Cordially* are used with informal salutations.

- *Respectfully yours*, *Yours respectfully*, and *Respectfully* may be used to show deference for the position of the addressee. They are used with high government positions (U.S. president), high military positions (a captain), high religious positions (monsignor), and so on.

- *Yours very truly* and *Very truly yours*, although still frequently seen in correspondence, are considered formal and somewhat out of date. They should be used sparingly, if at all.

Punctuation and Capitalization

- Only the first word of a complimentary close is capitalized.

- A comma follows the complimentary close if mixed punctuation is used; no punctuation is required if open punctuation is used.

- Open punctuation is often used with the block letter format.

Memo or Interoffice Correspondence Format

Purpose

- To prepare internal correspondence in less time than would be required if preparation were done in outgoing style.

- To reduce costs of internal correspondence through the use of less expensive stationery.

325

Style (See EXAMPLE D, p. 342)

- The headings usually included in all formats are *To, From, Subject,* and *Date*. Other headings that may be appropriate for particular situations may be added to format.

- Headings may run vertically down left margin or may be spread across the top of the form.

- Interoffice correspondence should be limited to one page if possible.

- If more than one page is required, a second-page heading may be used or pages may be numbered as in manuscript form.

- Arrangement of second-page heading is:

```
Ms. Ann Daw
Page 2
January 1, 1983
```

```
                    or
Ms. Ann Daw        2            January 1, 1983
```

Parts

- In addition to heading information, all parts of a business letter may be included except the salutation, complimentary close, and company signature.

- The penwritten signature may be omitted. If it is, the letter should be initialed by the dictator after his or her name in the *From* line, or at the end of the letter.

Placement

- Outgoing mail placement scales may be used.

- Margins may be aligned with headings in either of two ways:

TO		TO
FROM		FROM
SUBJECT	or	SUBJECT
DATE		DATE
(L.M.) _____		(L.M.) _____
_____		_____
_____		_____

Punctuation and Capitalization

- Headings require no punctuation.

- Capitalize first letter of each word (except articles, prepositions, and conjunctions) in headings.

- Type subject in all caps if emphasis is required.

5

Format Guides for Addressing Envelopes

5

General Rules for Outgoing Mail

- An address can consist of two, three, or four lines.
- All addresses should be single spaced.
- The attention line is the second line of the address.

329

● The envelope address should match the inside address of the letter. (Exception: When using the Postal Service recommended format of all caps and no punctuation, the traditional inside address is sometimes preferred.)

WP/IP NOTE:

The envelope address is played out from the recorded letter address. (*Exception:* When using U.S. postal service recommendations (requiring all caps, no punctuation), some people prepare the envelope address separately instead of using the letter style. However, this is time-consuming.)

● Placement of an address on the envelope varies with envelope size. (See RULES FOR ADDRESSING DIFFERENT SIZE ENVELOPES, p. 333)

● ZIP Codes should be used for all domestic mail.

U.S. Postal Service Recommendations for Outgoing Mail

● Capitalize everything in the address.

● Eliminate all punctuation.

● Abbreviate only those items listed in the "Address Abbreviations" section of the *National ZIP Code Directory*. (Two-letter state abbreviations are reproduced on the inside back cover.)

● Allow a maximum of 22 positions for city, state abbreviations, and ZIP Code (13 or less for city, 1 space between city and state, 2 for state abbreviation, 1 space between state and ZIP Code, and 5 for the ZIP Code). Cities with names of more than 13 characters are abbreviated according to the *National ZIP Code Directory* (for example, Geneva-on-the-Lake is abbreviated GENEVA ON LK).

● No printing can appear to the left, right, or below the address.

● The address must begin no less than 1 inch from the left edge of the envelope and must end within 1 inch of the right edge of the envelope. The last line must be more than a half inch from the bottom of the envelope.

● An illustration of an addressed envelope is:

```
EDUCATION DEPT
KSU          (Ret. Address)
KENT OH 44234
```

(Addressee Notations go here)   (Postal Notations go here)

```
              SEZON REALTORS
              ATTN MS R M SEZON
              145 BROADWAY        (Addressee)
              GENEVA ON LK OH 44089
```

General Rules for Interoffice Mail

● If the envelope requires sealing, a one-time envelope should be used.

● Usually a name, department, and room number are sufficient address information.

● If mail is to be sent to branches in bulk, the branch and location should be included.

● If the envelope does not require sealing, one should be used that is ruled for routing and reuse. This type of envelope should not be sealed.

5

Placement of Special Mailing Notations

● Postal notations are typed in all caps in the upper right-hand corner of the envelope below the postage stamp. Such notations include: SPECIAL DELIVERY, CERTIFIED MAIL, REGISTERED MAIL, and RETURN RECEIPT REQUESTED.

● For domestic mail, air mail is no longer a special service if the item weighs 10 ounces or less. However, this notation should still be included on international mail. It should be typed in all caps in the upper right-hand corner beneath the postage stamp.

- Addressee notations are typed in all caps in the upper left-hand corner beneath the return address. They include: CONFIDENTIAL, HOLD FOR ARRIVAL, PERSONAL, PLEASE FORWARD.

Foreign Mail

- The right half of the envelope should be reserved for the address, stamps, and mailing notations.

- The addressee's name and house or business number must be included.

- The name of the post office and country are written in capital letters and are not abbreviated. (Exception: U.S.S.R. Also, the two-letter province abbreviations are used for Canadian mail.) See inside back cover.

- The postal delivery zone is included if known. It is the last line of the address.

- The return address must include the U.S. ZIP Code.

- The airmail notation should be typed on foreign mail on the right side directly beneath the postage.

- Only single postal cards are acceptable for foreign mail with maximum size 6 × 4½ inches and minimum size 5½ × 3½ inches (except Canada and Mexico, where minimum is 5½ × 3¼ inches).

Return Address

- When sending mail in envelopes that do not have a printed address, type a return address in the upper left-hand corner approximately two lines below the top of the envelope and three spaces from the left side of the envelope.

- Single space the complete return address (name, company, street address, city, state abbreviation, and ZIP Code).

- When using envelopes with a printed return address, the author's name is typed above the printed company return address.

332 Section 5 Correspondence Format Guides

Rules for Addressing Different Size Envelopes

● No. 6 (6½ × 3⅝ inches)

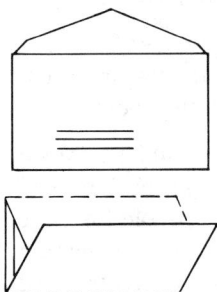

Address: Begin address 2 inches from top edge (line 12 or 13); 2½ inches from left edge (usually space 25 for pica type and 30 for elite type).

Use for: Baronial stationery, half sheets, and sometimes for one-page 8½ × 11 inch sheets.

Fold: (for half page) Page should be folded in thirds. Begin by folding right edge to left; then left edge to right. Leave a ½-inch margin between left edge and first fold.

● No. 10 (9½ × 4⅛ inches)

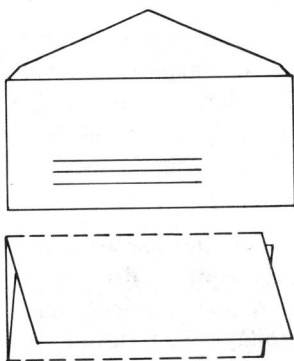

Address: Begin address 2½ inches from top edge (line 15 or 16); 4 inches from left edge (usually space 40 for pica type and 48 for elite type).

Use for: 8½ × 11-inch business stationery.

Fold: Page should be folded in thirds. Begin by folding bottom edge up; fold top edge down. Leave a ½-inch margin between top edge and first fold.

WP/IP NOTE:

Some equipment has an automatic feed feature for envelopes. However, on some machines it is faster and easier to use gummed labels than to put individual envelopes into the machine. An exception would be continuous-form envelopes.

● No. 7 (7½ × 3⅞ inches)

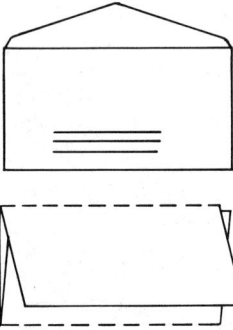

Address: Begin address 2¼ inches from top edge (line 14 or 15) and 3 inches from left edge (usually space 30 for pica type and 36 for elite type).

Use for: Monarch- or executive-size stationery only.

Fold: Page should be folded in thirds. Begin by folding bottom edge up; fold top edge down. Leave ½-inch margin between top edge and first fold.

● Window Envelopes
  (May be No. 6 or No. 10 size)

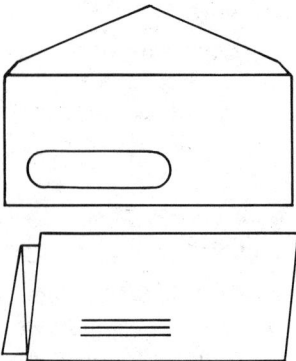

Address: No address is necessary; the inside address from letterhead shows through the window.

Use for: Statements of account and other routine forms.

Fold: Inside address must show. Place the page's printed side face down on the desk. Fold in thirds, second fold coming to within ½ inch of top back edge.

Note: With the use of computerized address lists, window envelopes are less common today than formerly. Address labels and continuous form envelopes have superseded the window envelope in many cases.

● On April 14, 1978, the United States Postal Service instituted a change in mail classification. Envelopes 3½ × 5 inches that are less than ½ inch thick will be rejected from the mail sorter.

Also cards less than $7/1000$ inch thick will be rejected. A surcharge will be levied on these nonstandard items.

● **Manila Envelopes**
Come in various sizes—from slightly larger than No. 10 to sizes large enough to carry legal documents. May be closed with a string fastener, a metal fastener, or sealed.

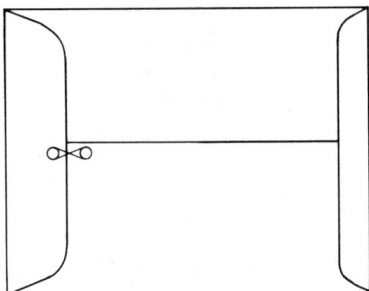

Address: Prepare a gummed label; then center it on the envelope.

Use for: Items that should not be folded, bulky items of several pages that will not fit in a No. 10 envelope.

Fold: Usually no folding is necessary (if envelope is same size or larger than stationery). If pages must be folded, they can be folded in half. If they must be folded in thirds, follow instructions for the No. 10 envelope.

● **Interoffice Envelopes**

INTER-DEPARTMENTAL MAIL
Cross out previous address. Use repeatedly until all spaces are utilized.

Address: Write or print address on the ruled line including name and location of addressee. Cross out addressee on the preceding line. Do not seal. Tuck flap in or use the string fastener.

Use for: All internal correspondence including that going to branch offices in bulk unless the item is of a personal or confidential nature.

Fold: Depending upon envelope size, fold all materials in half, thirds, or not at all.

5

November 29, 1983

Colonial Investments
6446 Seminole Trail
Pierre, SD 54501

Attention Ms. Mary D'Arco

Gentlemen

Subject: Policy No. DW 34-90752
          Property Located at 1262 East 357 Street, Pierre, SD 54501

EXAMPLE A
BLOCK STYLE LETTER
WITH OPEN
PUNCTUATION

5

The enclosed booklet contains helpful facts about the importance of reevaluating real estate on a regular basis.

Your annual premium for comprehensive coverage is now $435. Let us appraise your property to determine its current market value and adjust your insurance coverage accordingly. We shall quote you new premium rates after the appraisal.

We shall await your response to this suggestion.

Sincerely

Robert Scott, President

rt

Enclosure

cc: All-Nation Insurance Corporation
    375 Wisconsin Boulevard
    Minneapolis, MN 63344

5

August 27, 1983

BRONX COUNTY NATIONAL BANK

30 SOUTH PARK PLACE   BRONX NEW YORK 10462   (212) 352 4444

EXPRESS MAIL

Mr. Robert I. Updike
Executive Vice President
Queens Bank of New York
New York, NY 10015

Dear Mr. Updike:

Your article that appeared in the April 1983 issue of the United
States Banker was very interesting to me. One of the most difficult

5

338

EXAMPLE B
MODIFIED BLOCK STYLE
LETTER WITH
MIXED PUNCTUATION

system to anyone who [...] review them. May I have a set of your evaluation materials?

Of special interest to me is how you determine who will receive the year-end bonus given in addition to the annual salary increase. Currently, we are considering such a plan.

These timely materials will be helpful to us.

Sincerely,

W. R. Moyer
Vice President

WRM/et/5

5

EXAMPLE C
SIMPLIFIED LETTER STYLE

5

COMMERCIAL   RESIDENTIAL

Vann Realty

10 Longwood Ave.
Longwood, FL 32750
Telephone 354-2222

September 26, 1983

CONFIDENTIAL

Mr. Joseph Carpenter
300 Venice Boulevard
Key West, FL 32750

REAL ESTATE INVESTMENTS

Why are we at Vann Realty so firmly convinced that real estate is the best
investment today, Mr. Carpenter?

Here are several reasons:

...ndustr...
...ncing

3. The population increase that will need housing

4. The safety of a real estate investment

5. The steady and real appreciation of real estate

Economic history shows that a substantial percentage of the wealth acquired by people in this country came about as a result of real estate investments. Prudent investing in real estate and turning it to the best use has paid handsome dividends for many wise persons. As population and industry increase, the potential financial gain to be derived from real estate investment is even more realistic today than in the past.

We at Vann Realty believe now is the time to make a move. We would be more than happy to discuss the market and its potential at your convenience.

HAROLD VANN, BROKER

HV:bt/a

INTEROFFICE CORRESPONDENCE

Donna Jason

V. H. Cooper

Company Correspondence

July 27, 1983

In the future, company correspondence will be typed on this interoffice form. You will notice that salutation, titles, complimentary close, and signature are omitted.

Very short messages may be double spaced; however, short, average-length, and longer ones are single spaced with a

EXAMPLE D
MEMO OR INTEROFFICE
CORRESPONDENCE STYLE

initials   the
end of the message. Enclos s, copies, and other notations
occupy the same position as in other correspondence.

VHC:cz

5

343

SECTION 6
Report and Technical Typing Guides

This section gives guides for the preparation of various types of reports and technical typing that must be executed by the machine transcriber, word processor, or correspondence secretary and contains five divisions: OUTLINES, MINUTES, STATISTI-

CAL TYPING, REPORT AND MANUSCRIPT, and FOOT-
NOTES AND BIBLIOGRAPHY.

In the OUTLINES division information is presented for an alphanumeric arrangement as well as for a decimal gradation. Illustrations of the layouts provide an easy-to-follow reference.

The MINUTES division includes format guides for preparing
minutes as well as general information on summarizing discus-
sions.

Reference material for STATISTICAL TYPING shows several
methods for accurately placing tabulated material on the typewritten page.

REPORT AND MANUSCRIPT formats for periodic and formal
reports are illustrated with actual examples. Information on purpose, style, parts, spacing, and punctuation and capitalization is
outlined.

FOOTNOTE AND BIBLIOGRAPHY background data are outlined in the final division of Format Guides. Illustrations combin-
ing footnote and bibliography entries are given as well as
information and examples showing their separate arrangement.

6

Outline Formats

6

Purposes

- To indicate the structure of a report or lecture before writing.
- To order major and secondary points.
- To present information in a concise, organized manner.
- To summarize information.
- To develop a table of contents for a written report.

347

Style

- Traditional style combines roman numerals, capital letters, Arabic numerals, and lower-case letters to indicate gradation in topics presented. For example:

    I. _____
      A. _____
      B. _____
      C. _____
        1. _____
        2. _____
        3. _____
          a. _____
          b. _____
          c. _____
            (1) _____
            (2) _____
              (a) _____
              (b) _____
   II. _____
   III. _____

- Decimal arrangement is becoming more widely used. An illustration of decimal arrangement is:

    1. _____   1.
      1.1 _____   1.1
      1.2 _____   1.2
        1.21 _____ or 1.2.1
        1.22 _____   1.2.2
          1.221 _____   1.2.2.1
    2. _____   2.

- Items of equal rank (e.g., *A*, *B*, *C*) should be parallel in rank or importance.

- It is unusual to need more than four or five levels in an outline.

- All levels must include at least two elements. If there is an *A*, there must be a *B* element as well; or if there is a *1*, there must be a *2*. Otherwise, the point in the single element should be incorporated into the previous element.

- The style of writing must be parallel. For example, if words are used in item *1*, words must be used in item *2*. If phrases are used in item *A*, then phrases must be used in item *B*.

- Words, phrases, or complete sentences may be used in structuring an outline.

Punctuation and Capitalization

- Numerals and letters are aligned at the right so that periods are lined up. In decimal format the periods in the decimals are always aligned. For example:

  I.

  II.

  III.

  IV.

- Two spaces follow the periods after letters or numerals.

- End punctuation may be omitted unless a complete sentence style of writing is used, but questions should be followed by a question mark in both phrases and sentences.

- Capitalization may vary, but it should be consistent. If the first word is capitalized in an *A* section, capitalize it in the *B* section. For efficiency, avoid excessive capitalization.

- Major headings may be typed in all caps, or the first letter of all words may be capitalized for emphasis.

- It is customary to capitalize at least the first letter of the first word in secondary headings.

- It is customary to omit capitalization of even first words in minor gradations.

- All proper nouns and adjectives should be capitalized.

Placement

- The outline may be single spaced throughout.

- It may be double spaced, but an element containing two or more lines would be single spaced. For example:

      B. Placement

            1. Outlines may be single spaced.

            2. Outlines may be double spaced,
               but an element containing two or
               more lines would be single
               spaced.

            3. Etc.

- Outlines may be double spaced between major elements and single spaced between minor elements if consistency in arrangement is maintained. For example:

      B. Placement
            1. Single spaced
            2. Double spaced
            3. Etc.
      C. _____

            1. _____

            2. _____

WP/IP NOTE:

	Standard Typewriter	*WP/IP Keyboard*
Roman numerals in outline	Begin at margin. Use MAR REL and BS as necessary.	Set margin five spaces to left. T for "I"; T; (CBS) for "II"; etc.
Numbers under and over 10	Begin at margin. Use MAR REL and BS as necessary.	Sp once; type single digit; T. The "10" begins at the margin without the Sp; T.

NOTE: Some machines allow use of a margin release key to get into the left margin.

6

Numbered lists or sentences	1. Sp, Sp ____ CR	Sp1. (CT) ____ CR
	TAB ____ . CR	____ .
	2. Sp, Sp ____ CR	(CCR)
	TAB ____ . CR	Sp2. (CT) ____ CR
		____ .
		(CCR)

NOTE: Follow your machine instructions for temporary indent when paragraphs are to be typed.

Minutes Format

Purpose

6

- To create an official report of a meeting.

- To summarize transactions of a meeting including reports, motions and their disposition, and topics for discussion.

Style (See EXAMPLE G, p. 400)

- Thoroughness may vary, but minutes should include a heading (name of organizational unit, type of meeting such as regular or special, date, time, and place), a record of all reports and motions made with an explanation of their disposition, and the name and title of the person presiding.

- They usually include the names of persons making and persons seconding motions as well as the names of those in attendance (unless a large group is meeting), and a summary of the discussion.

- The exact wording of each motion is required. Other transactions and discussion may be summarized in modern business language.

- Discussion of topics can be summarized in paragraph form. The agenda can be followed to arrange topics discussed.

- Minutes become more formal in organizations having strong legal obligations. They may include a record of how each member voted, a list of those not attending, and so on. The most formal minutes are verbatim transcripts of all that transpired.

- The correct language for stating motions is: "It was moved that . . ." or "John moved and Julia seconded that . . . ." It is incorrect to say: "A motion was made that . . ." or "John made a motion that . . . ."

Placement

- The heading begins 1½ or 2 inches from the top of the page. It is usually centered, but it may be arranged attractively at the left. Triple space after the heading.

- Attendance information can be tabulated following the heading or incorporated into the report in paragraph form.

- Manuscript format should be used with either single or double spacing.

- Side headings may be used to highlight the presentation of particular topics.

Punctuation and Capitalization

● Follow rules for manuscript typing.

6

Statistical Typing Format   6

Purpose

- To present information in a concise, easy-to-interpret manner.

- To show comparative data through tables, charts, and graphs in an easy-to-interpret manner.

Style

- Any kind of statistical data, tables, charts, or graphs may be presented within the body of a letter or report if the information can be placed within the margin settings in use.

- The material may be appended or attached to the letter or report depending upon its size and relevance.

- Tables may be single or double spaced. Charts and graphs may be arranged for clarity in reading.

- The trend is toward simplicity, eliminating all unnecessary rulings.

Placement

- Any table, chart, or graph should be fitted on a single page.

- If the statistical format exceeds the one-page limit, prepare it on oversized paper and reduce it on a copy machine to the required size.

WP/IP NOTE:

Automatic formatting is available on many word processors. Standardize whenever possible for maximum efficiency. Consult the manufacturer's guide for instructions.

Centering Tabulated Material

- There are three generally accepted methods for properly centering tabulated material.

  a. Backspace-from-center placement (used for simple tabulations).

  b. Mathematical placement (used for complex tabulations with a number of columns or headings).

  c. Judgment placement (used by experienced typists for most work).

- In all methods, these three things must be determined:

a. Left margin setting.

b. Tabulator stops.

c. Center points for headings, including columnar headings.

● In determining column placement, the longest line in each column, whether it be within a column or in the column heading, is used for calculation purposes.

● Fractions or half spaces can be disregarded in calculations.

● All whole numbers are lined up on the right in tabulated material.

```
  213
4,178
   25
```

● Numbers with decimals are lined up at the decimal point.

```
  3.7
 12.701
951.322495
  6.4
```

WP/IP NOTE:

Word processing machines have an automatic centering feature. Another feature that is available on word processors is the decimal tab. This allows the operator to automatically line up decimal points on columns. Most new equipment also allows for moving columns from place to place on a page. Check the manufacturer's guide for functions on your equipment and the instructions for using them.

6

Backspace-from-Center Method

● To find the center of the paper, add two figures from the paper scale—the point where the left edge of the paper lies and the point where the right edge of the paper lies; divide the sum by two. For 8½-inch wide paper, the center point is 50 or 51 for elite type and 42 or 43 for pica type.

- Center all main and secondary headings by backspacing from the center point one time for each two letters, spaces, and punctuation marks in the headings.

- *Left-Margin Set.* Backspace one time for each two letters, spaces, and so on, in the longest line for each column. Backspace one time for each two spaces to be left between columns. Set *Left Margin* at this point.

- *Tab Stop Sets.* With the space bar, space forward one time for each letter in the longest line in the first column and space forward one time for each space to be left between columns 1 and 2. Set a *Tab Stop.* The second column will begin at this point. Space forward one time for each letter in the longest line in the second column and space forward one time for each space to be left between columns 2 and 3. Set a *Tap Stop.* The third column will begin at this point. Continue this procedure until tab stops have been set for all columns.

- After tab stops have been set for each column, columnar headings shorter than the longest column line can be centered over each column by tabbing to the point where the column will begin. To determine the center point of the column, space forward one time for each two letters, spaces, and so on, in the longest line of the column, which brings you to the center of the column. Backspace one time for every two letters and spaces within the columnar heading. Type the heading.

- When the longest line in the column is the heading, after the heading is typed the tab stop for the column may be reset in terms of the longest line other than the heading (the longest line in the column itself). Tab to the setting required for the heading. Remove this tab stop. Space forward one time for every two letters, spaces, and so on, in the heading to find the center point of the column. Backspace one time for every two letters, spaces, and so on, in the longest columnar line. Set a tab stop at this point.

Mathematical Method (exact spreading of spaces between columns and margins)

- Center all main and secondary headings by the backspace-from-center method.

- Prepare a diagram of tabulated material and enter all figures in the diagram as they are calculated.

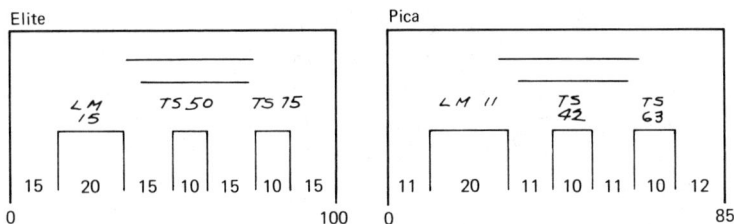

Elite

LM 15   TS 50   TS 75

| 15 | 20 | 15 | 10 | 15 | 10 | 15 |

0 _____ 100

Pica

LM 11   TS 42   TS 63

| 11 | 20 | 11 | 10 | 11 | 10 | 12 |

0 _____ 85

- Count the longest line in each column. Enter the figures in the diagram. The total spaces needed for the columns equals 40. Subtract that number from the number of horizontal spaces on the page (for standard-size paper, 8½ inches wide, 100 or 102 elite type and 85 for pica type).

Elite	*Pica*
100	85
−40	− 40
60 spaces remain	45 spaces remain

These remaining spaces are to be divided between margins and columns.

- Count the number of margins and blank columns among which remaining spaces must be divided. (The number is always one more than the number of columns in the tabulation.) Divide the remaining spaces by this number; enter the figures in the diagram.

$$\frac{15}{4\,/\,60}\qquad\qquad \frac{11}{4\,/\,45}\ (+1)$$

- Set the left margin at the point calculated for spaces between columns.

- Calculate tab stop by:

  a. Adding to the left margin the number of spaces in first column plus the number of spaces between the first and second columns. Set a tab stop at this point (in examples, at 50 for elite, 42 for pica type).

  b. Adding to the first tab stop the number of spaces in the second column plus the number of spaces between columns 2 and 3. Set a tab stop at this point (in examples, at 75 for elite, 63 for pica type).

● To check the accuracy of the calculations, add the number of spaces in the last column to the last tab stop plus spaces in the right margin. If calculations are accurate, the figure should equal the number of horizontal spaces on the page. If the calculation does not add to the width of the page, recalculate until all spaces can be accounted for.

● To place the columnar headings, look at the diagram to determine the center of each column. For lines with an even number of spaces, the midpoint will be one out of two spaces; for lines with an odd number of spaces, the midpoint will be only one space. For example:

14 spaces = longest line   15 spaces = longest line

Mathematical Method (judgment of number of spaces between columns)

● Center all main and secondary headings by the backspace-from-center method.

● Prepare a diagram of tabulated material and enter all figures in the diagram as they are calculated.

● Count the longest line in each column. Enter the figures in the diagram.

● Determine the number of spaces to be left between columns (five in the example shown below).

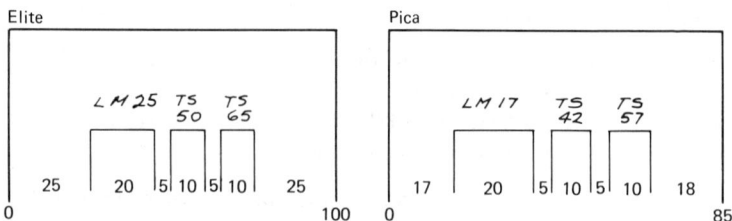

- Total all figures; subtract from the number of spaces across the page.

Elite		Pica	
	100		85
−	40	−	40
−	10	−	10
	50 spaces remain		35 spaces remain

- The remaining spaces are to be divided by two for the left and right margin. Enter figures in the diagram.

$$\frac{25}{2\,/\,50} \qquad\qquad \frac{17}{2\,/\,35}\ (+1)$$

- Set the left margin at the point calculated for it (at 25 or 17 in the example).

- Calculate tab stops by:

   a. Adding to the left margin the number of spaces in the first column plus the number of spaces between the first and second columns. Set a tab stop at this point (in examples, at 50 for elite, 42 for pica type).

   b. Add to the first tab stop the number of spaces in the second column plus the number of spaces between columns 2 and 3. Set a tab stop (in examples, at 65 for elite, 57 for pica type).

- To check the accuracy of the calculations, add the number of spaces in the last column to the last tab stop plus the spaces in the right margin. If the calculations are accurate, the figure should equal the number of horizontal spaces on the page. If the calculation does not add to the width of the page, recalculate until all spaces can be accounted for.

- Place columnar headings as in the other mathematical example.

Judgment Placement

- Select the number of spaces you wish columns to begin and end from the left and right margins. Set a left margin stop.

- Move the carriage to the right and set a tab stop for the last column so that an equivalent number of spaces will appear in the right margin as were allowed in the left. Account not only for the spaces in the right margin but also for those in the last column as well. Set the tab at the appropriate space.

- Set tab stops for other columns so that the arrangement will be well balanced and pleasing to the eye.

WP/IP NOTE:

Whenever possible, judgment placement for columns should be used. Care must be taken to give a page a pleasing appearance.

Report and
Manuscript Format

6

Purpose

- *Periodic* or *Informal Reports* are written to report routine facts or information. Often referred to as informal reports, they include such documents as sales reports, progress reports, financial reports, or any other report written on a regular basis.

- *Formal Reports* are written to report a study or investigation of a particular problem or topic. They include a thorough and scientific presentation of data concerning research, research procedures, and research findings. Classroom manuscripts and term papers as well as scientific investigations fall into the category of formal reports.

Style

- Periodic reports are often set up within a letter or memo, and such a letter or memo may follow any conventional letter or memo style.

- Although paragraphing usually delineates parts of the body of a periodic report, side headings and paragraph headings are appropriate.

- Formal reports require the presentation of preliminary information as well as discussion of the problem or purpose of the study, a description of the research procedures and techniques, presentation of findings, conclusions, and recommendations for further study. (See PARTS OF A FORMAL REPORT, p. 370)

- Because reports are objective and factual, they are written in third person. They should not be written in first or second person, which reflects personal observations or opinions of a writer. For example:

  The investigation revealed 14 cases of misused prepositional phrases. These cases are cited in Table 1.

  Not:

  I found 14 cases of misused prepositional phrases. You will see them listed in Table 1.

- An exception to the third person rule is sometimes made when periodic reports are written in first and second person. However, third person is more objective.

- Quotations of four or more lines in length are single spaced and indented from the left margin. Quotation marks may be omitted. Quotations of less than four lines are typed within the body of the report in manuscript style and quotation marks are used to indicate the beginning and the end of the quoted matter. Examples follow.

Arrangement for Less Than Four Lines

Penzer points out that, while many managers in manufacturing concerns strain to reverse the damages of the philosophy of scientific management, administrative management is moving "toward specialization of office and clerical jobs in the guise of efficiency and cost reduction."

Arrangement for Four or More Lines

The speaker said:

While many managers in manufacturing concerns strain to reverse the damages of the philosophy of scientific management, administrative management is moving toward specialization of office and clerical jobs in the guise of efficiency and cost reduction.

Then he related a number of examples in the office organization area that illustrated his point.

● Reference citations must be given for all quoted material within a manuscript as well as ideas of others that might be paraphrased throughout the writing. Several methods of making the citations are used. In the more traditional manuscript setup, direct quotations are made within the body of the report and footnoted on the page on which they appear. Paraphrased material is not set in quotation marks, but it is footnoted on the page on which it appears. Footnotes may be numbered consecutively throughout the manuscript, throughout the chapter, or throughout each page. Many writers now place all footnotes at the end of a chapter or at the end of the report—a practice that saves time and effort in manuscript preparation. An example of a direct quote, which would be footnoted at the bottom of the page, at the end of a chapter, or at the end of the manuscript follows.

> He points out that, while many managers in manufacturing concerns strain to reverse the damages of the philosophy of scientific management, administrative management is moving "toward specialization of office and clerical jobs in the guise of efficiency and cost reduction."[1]

_____

[1]William N. Penzer. "The Mechanization of Emily," Administrative Management. 1974, 1, p. 53.

● A résumé of all sources of information is presented in a bibliography at the end of the report. The bibliographic entry for this quoted matter appears as follows.

Penzer, William N. "The Mechanization of Emily," Administrative Management. 1974, 1, 52–60.

● Still another more recent style recommends the use of very few direct quotations and a combination of the footnote and bibliography citation at the end of the report. The author's name is used within the text, making it necessary to cite only a year of publication and page number if a reference is to a direct quote or a citation from a particular page.

An example of a combined bibliography and footnote reference with a quote is:

> Penzer suggests that, although managers in manufacturing concerns are making attempts to reverse damages of scientific management, "office managers are moving toward more specialization

in the guise of efficiency and cost
reduction." (1974, p. 53)

An example of a combined bibliography and footnote reference
without a quote is:

Penzer (1974) discusses the trend
toward specialization of office work
and is concerned that office managers
might be returning to the concepts of
scientific management.

● A combined footnote-bibliography entry for the citation would
be:

Penzer, W. N. The mechanization of Emily.
Administrative Management, 1974, 1, 52–60.

● The rules for typing numbers (see LANGUAGE USE
GUIDES, Numbers, p. 27) should be applied in manuscript
preparation. However, when many numbers are used within
the manuscript, the trend is toward using figures for all of
them throughout the writing.

● Pagination of a report incorporated within a letter follows the
rules for page numbering of letters and memos.

● Pagination of a formal report includes the numbering of all
pages throughout the report. The preliminary pages are numbered with small Roman numerals. (See EXAMPLE C, p. 394)
The title page is counted as page 1 although no numeral is
typed on this page. The page following the title page is *ii,* and
that numeral is typed at the bottom of the page. Beginning
with the first page of the body of the report Arabic numbers
are used and are continued throughout the body and supplementary pages. The first page of each chapter is considered
a page, but the number may be omitted or is typed at the
bottom of the page. (See EXAMPLE E, p. 397)

Parts of a Periodic Report

● Because periodic reports are written on a regular basis, preliminary information is not required. Often they are in letter
form. (See EXAMPLE A, p. 390)

- The body of a periodic report includes an introduction, which explains the authorization, purpose, scope, and organization of data; the descriptive data, which includes all factual data gathered, discussion of that data and results; and the conclusions or recommendations the writer may wish to present.

Parts of a Formal Report

- The formal report includes preliminary information, the body of the report, and supplementary data in varying detail. References are available that provide guidelines for writing various kinds of formal reports: term papers, technical reports, articles for publication, and so on.

- A complete outline of all parts of formal reports follows. However, not all formal reports require the use of all parts in the outline. The list is sequenced in the order in which the parts would appear in the report.

Preliminary Information

Cover
May be a special binder, a standard binder, or merely a page of the same quality paper on which the report is typed; it includes the report title.

Title Page
Includes the name of the report, the author and author's title, and the date. (For a term paper, this page may include course data. (See EXAMPLE B, p. 392)

Copyright Page
If the manuscript is copyrighted, that notation including the author's full name and date is made on a separate page. (See EXAMPLE C, p. 394)

Letter of Transmittal
Cover letter explaining the purpose of the report and that it is being given to the addressee of the letter.

Preface or Foreword
An explanation in more personal terms of what the report is or why it is being written.

Acknowledgments
Recognition by the writer of persons or institutions who have given assistance in the preparation of the report.

Abstract or Summary
A synopsis or concise summary of the report that presents major facts, results, recommendations, and conclusions. It aids the reader who does not have time to study the complete report. Often it is the review of the report included in published references.

Table of Contents
An outline of the report including page numbers on which sections and subsections begin. It is developed from the original report outline. (See EXAMPLE D, p. 395)

List of Illustrations, List of Tables, or Other Lists
Lists of special kinds of data used throughout the report and the page numbers on which each item appears.

Body of the Report

Statement of the Problem
A thorough discussion that explains:

1. *Need* or why the study should be done.

2. *Purpose* or what the study intends to accomplish.

3. *Hypotheses* or broad implications expected to be found through the study. (Hypotheses are stated later in the report in testable form.)

4. *Theory* or *Assumptions* or explanations of the current thinking pertinent to the subject.

5. *Limitations* or explanations of questions not to be considered, shortcomings in the scientific method, and so on.

6. *Definitions* or explanations of terminology that would not be familiar to readers.

7. *Overview* or indication of the outline of the remainder of the report.

Review of the Literature
A part or chapter that presents a discussion of previous research on the problem under investigation; it includes a summary of that research.

Design of the Study
Tells how the investigation or problem will be addressed and may require an explanation of:

1. *Sample* or select population under investigation and all vital demographic data for that population.

2. *Measures* or instruments used in the study including reliability and validity data for those measures as well as reliability of the measures for the research sample.

3. *Design* or explanation of the true experimental or quasi-experimental process, or an explanation of what predictive or descriptive data will result.

4. *Testable Hypotheses* or statements of what will be proved or disproved in the investigation, often written in symbolic form. Hypotheses may be stated in the null form or in an alternative to the null form. An example of a null hypothesis stated in words is: There will be no difference in mean wages of factory workers and mean wages of middle managers. A null hypothesis stated symbolically is: HO: $M_1 = M_2$. (M_1 represents factory workers and M_2 represents middle managers.) An alternative to the null hypothesis in words is: The mean wages of factory workers will be greater than the mean wages of middle managers. An alternative to the null form in symbols is: Ha: $M_1 \neq M_2$.

5. *Statistical Analysis* or an explanation of the statistical models that will be used to analyze the data derived from the measures.

6. *Summary* or résumé of the design of the study.

Analysis of the Results
Presents results in the order in which hypotheses were reported in previous chapters with no interpretation of the meaning of the results. (If it is necessary to interpret the meaning, this should be done under a specific heading, *Discussion*, to insure that no bias is reflected in the presentation of results.)

Summary or Conclusions
The final part or chapter in a formal report begins with a synopsis of the problem, the literature, the research design, and the results. The summary is followed by conclusions as they relate to the particular study or to the general subject field, and the recommendation of possible future research that would affect the problem being investigated.

Supplementary Information

Bibliography (or Bibliography and Footnotes Combined)
A listing of all sources of data used in the preparation of the report including sources of all directly quoted and paraphrased material as well as references contributing to ideas within the report.

Notes
Annotations of the author, further explanation of data reported, or comments on references cited.

Appendix or Appendixes
Additional data expanding or substantiating data presented in the report.

Index
Detailed alphabetic listing of all topics and subtopics included in the report together with a page reference on which the topic or subtopic is discussed.

Placement Information

- *Cover Page.* The title, if a binder is used, is usually prepared on a label, typed in all caps, centered horizontally in inverted pyramid style, and single or double spaced depending upon title length. If plain paper is used, the title may be centered horizontally and begun at least 2½ inches from the top of the paper. The title must appear above the center point of the paper.

- *Title Page.* Information should be centered horizontally. The title is typed in inverted pyramid style at least 2½ inches for left-bound manuscripts and 3 inches for top-bound manuscripts from the top edge of the paper. The author's name and title may be vertically placed at the center of the page or about 2 inches from the bottom edge of the paper. The date should be placed vertically approximately 1½ inches from the bottom edge of the page. (See EXAMPLE B, p. 392)

- *Table of Contents, Lists of Tables,* and so on. These are single or double spaced depending upon length. Headings should be centered horizontally and typed 2 or 2½ inches for left-bound manuscripts and 2½ or 3 inches for top-bound manuscripts from the top edge of the paper. A triple space follows the heading. Margins may be the same width as those used in the manuscript, or the writing line may be shortened to accommodate short entries. The minimum margin for both the right and bottom edges of the paper is 1 inch. Pages subsequent to the headed page require a top margin of 1 inch. The left edge margin is 1½ inches for left-bound manuscripts and 1 inch for top-bound manuscripts. (See EXAMPLE D, p. 395)

- *Foreword, Preface, Abstract.* These pages are typed with the same margin settings used in the body of the report. Headings are centered in all caps and followed by a triple space. They are begun 2 or 2½ inches from the top edge of the paper for left-bound manuscripts and 2½ or 3 inches from the top edge for top-bound manuscripts.

- *Body of the Report.* Margins vary at the top and left, but the right margin and the bottom margin of each page must always equal at least 1 inch after binding. Note the variations for top and left-side margins.

a. Top-bound manuscripts require a 1½ inch margin at the top of each page other than the first page of a chapter or section. For the first page of each chapter a 2½- or 3-inch margin is required to insure a 2- or 2½-inch margin after binding. The left margin is 1 inch.

b. Left-bound manuscripts require a 1½-inch left margin to insure a 1-inch margin after binding. An inch top margin is required on all pages except the first page of each chapter, which requires a 2- or 2½-inch top margin.

For left-bound manuscripts margin settings of 18 and 90 to 95 will insure inch margins on the left and right after binding if elite-size type is being used. For pica-size type, margin settings of 12 and 72 to 75 will insure inch margins on the left and right after binding. To maintain inch margins at the top of each page, begin typing on the seventh line from the top edge of the paper. To maintain inch margins at the bottom of the page, use a line guide and make line 60 the last line of typing, or make a light pencil ruling 1 inch from the bottom edge of the paper and stop typing at the ruling. Erase the ruling when the paper is removed from the typewriter. (See EXAMPLE E, p. 396)

WP/IP NOTE:

A 6-inch line setting will give inch side margins. Whenever possible, scan the pages and use the line count feature of the equipment for uniform bottom margins.

● *Footnotes.* When they are placed at the bottom of each page, they must be followed by a 1-inch bottom margin. To allow for footnoting, move the pencil line up approximately ½ to ⅔ inch (three or four lines) each time a footnote is typed in the body of the report. When the adjusted pencil ruling is reached, single space and type the 1½-inch ruling separating the body of the report and the footnotes. Double space, indent, and type the first footnote. Some typists prefer to use guide sheets indicating line numbers, but the number of lines per inch and per footnote still should be calculated in determining the proper placement of footnotes.

6

- *Page Numbers.* For left-bound reports, page numbers are usually typed at the top right approximately ½ inch from the top edge and 1 inch inside the right edge of the paper (line 4 or 5, space 88 to 90 elite type or 74 to 75 pica type). Some authors prefer that page numbers be centered ½ from the top edge of the paper. For top-bound manuscripts, it is proper to number the pages at the bottom center, ½ inch from the bottom edge (line 62 or 63). Pages with major headings, such as the first page of a chapter, are numbered at the bottom (centered, line 62 or 63), or the number may be omitted although the page is counted in the consecutive numbering of the pages.

6

- *Main Headings.* Center horizontally and type in all caps.

- *Side Headings.* Start at the left margin and begin each word (except articles, prepositions, and conjunctions) with a capital letter.

- *Paragraph Headings.* Indent if the paragraphs are indented or type at the left margin if paragraphs are not indented. Follow

the heading with a period and two spaces. Begin the opening
paragraph on the same line as the heading. Only the first letter
of the first word in the paragraph heading is capitalized.

Spacing Between Sections

● After a centered heading, always triple space. (See EXAM-
PLE E, p. 396)

● Before a side heading triple space. After the side heading,
double space. (See EXAMPLE E, p. 396)

● Before a paragraph heading, double space. Continue typing
the paragraph on the same line as the heading. (See EXAM-
PLE E, p. 396)

● Double space all formal reports or manuscript typing. Periodic
reports and some business reports may be single spaced. (See
EXAMPLE E, p. 396)

● Quotations of less than four lines are incorporated into the
double-spaced material. Quotations of more than four lines
are indented five spaces from the left margin and single
spaced. Double space before and after single-spaced quotes.
(See STYLE, p. 366)

● Statistical material may be set up as numbered tables or it may
be incorporated into the body of the report. If it is included
in the body of the report, it may be single or double spaced;
but a double space should precede and follow it. If a table
arrangement is used, it is customary to number the tables.
They may be numbered consecutively throughout the manuscript; or, if they are numerous, they may be numbered consecutively through each chapter. The table number is typed
three spaces after the manuscript line, usually in lower case
and underscored. A double space precedes the table title,
which is typed in all caps and centered. Any subtitle may be
centered and typed in lower case letters and underscored. A
triple space follows all centered headings. Columnar headings
are typed centered over the columns, followed by a double
space and the column information. (See EXAMPLE F, p. 398)

6

Standard Typewriter
With indentions a document that is double spaced requires a triple space between paragraphs.

WP/IP Keyboard
With indentions a document that is double spaced requires only a double space between paragraphs.

Standard Typewriter
Without indentions a document requires a triple space between paragraphs.

WP/IP Keyboard
Without indentions a document can be typed with two double spaces between paragraphs.
NOTE: If a triple space must be left between the double-spaced paragraphs, use the format change feature available on most equipment or enter a stop instruction and add one extra line manually.

● Complicated rulings of headings should be avoided. However, if a double ruling is required, the lines should be close enough together to appear as a bold printed ruling. For example:

● If braced headings are used, columnar headings within the braced ruling should appear equidistant from each ruling. For example:

COUNTRIES IN THE WESTERN HEMISPHERE	
North America	South America

Capitalization and Punctuation (See EXAMPLES E and F, pp. 396 and 398)

● Capitalization and punctuation within the body of the report conform to formal rules of English communication.

- Major headings and table titles are typed in all caps. Side headings, table numbers, subheadings, and columnar headings are typed in lower case with the first letter of all words (except articles, prepositions, and conjunctions) capitalized. These headings are usually underscored. Paragraph headings are typed in lower case with only the first letter of the first word capitalized.

- Leaders may appear in tables or unfinished quotations. Leaders are made by typing a period followed by a space. For example: . . . . In tables, to line up leaders, first note whether the first period is typed on an odd or even space. Then type on either all the even or all the odd spaces. In a quotation, three periods followed by spaces indicate an unfinished quotation. If the material is at the end of a sentence, a fourth space and period are added as the end punctuation of the sentence.

6

Footnote and
Bibliography Format

Purpose

- To give credit to other authors for ideas, quotations, and information used.

- To provide readers with adequate source information so that they may refer to that information.

381

Style

- Although there are several formats for presenting footnotes and the bibliography, all entries must contain adequate information so that the reader can find the source.

- Because data banks of information that can be searched by subject entry are now available, footnote and bibliography style is often simplified.

- In an informal report, the computer output arrangement of data may be satisfactory. However, in a formal report, traditional styles must be used.

- Basically, two styles are currently used for the listing of sources in manuscripts. One style requires the separate preparation of footnotes and bibliography entries. The other combines the footnote and bibliography references in one entry.

- One style of referencing should be maintained throughout a report.

Placement

- In the preparation of separate bibliography and footnote references, the footnotes may be placed on each page, at the end of a chapter, or at the end of the report. They will be numbered by page, by chapter, or throughout the report. The bibliography follows the last page of the report and comes before any appendixes.

- If the combined bibliographic and footnote reference section is used, it appears at the very end of the report; it follows any appendixes or supplementary material.

- Footnotes appearing on the page on which the reference is cited are placed at the bottom of each page so that at least a 1 inch margin remains after the typing of the footnote. A 1½ inch line (15 pica spaces, 18 elite spaces) separates the body of the report from the footnotes. After the last line of the body of the report, single space and type the separation ruling; then double space and begin the footnote, indenting the first line of the footnote five or seven spaces. (Follow the same indention pattern used in the report.) Double space between footnotes.

- An example of a footnote placed at the bottom of the page follows:

Why study punctuation? "Punctuation is a tool used to help clarify the meaning of written communications."[1] If that is not convincing,

---

[1]Lois Meyer and Ruth Moyer, <u>Machine Transcription in Modern Business</u> (New York: John Wiley & Sons, 1978), p. 3.

   1"   1"

- If footnotes are placed at the end of a chapter or the end of a report, make the ruling and begin typing the references. Footnotes at the end of a report may begin on a separate page with the heading *Footnotes*.

- The bibliography or combined bibliography-footnote reference section is begun with a heading: BIBLIOGRAPHY. It is centered and typed in all caps 2 or 2½ inches from the top edge of the paper. (Follow the same pattern used for chapter headings.) Each entry is single spaced with double spacing between entries. They are typed in inverted paragraph style; the first line of each entry begins at the left margin but remaining lines are indented five or seven spaces. It is most efficient to reset the left margin to the point of indentation; use the margin release and backspace for the beginning line of each footnote. For example:

BIBLIOGRAPHY

Meyer, Lois and Moyer, Ruth. <u>Machine Transcription in Modern Business</u>. New York: John Wiley & Sons, 1978.

6

WP/IP NOTE:

To create the "overhang" format in a bibliography, set a tab five spaces in from the left margin. On some equipment, a coded tab is needed followed by five coded backspaces to get back to the margin. On other equipment, put the cursor at the temporary margin and cursor back to the margin to begin typing. With either kind of equipment, the second line will begin at the indent point.

Combined Footnote and Bibliography Entries Illustrated (Simplified Capitalization)

- **A Book. One Author**

  Green, G. To Brooklyn with love. New York: Trident Press, 1967.

- **A Book. Several Authors**

  Herzberg, F., Mausner, B., & Snyderman, B. The motivation to work (2nd ed.) New York: John Wiley & Sons, 1959.

- **A Book. No Author, but Editor(s) Indicated**

  Bahr, G., & Bangs, K. (eds.) Foundations of business education. Reston, Virginia: National Business Education Association, 1975.

- **A Journal Article (Professional Publication)**

  Bloomfield, R. M. The changing world of the secretary. Personnel Journal, 1973, 52, 793-6.

- **A Magazine Article (Popular Publication)**

  Swett, D. D. Productivity of word processing. The Office, August, 1975, pp. 57-59.

A Newspaper Article

College core curriculum: a better
route. Cleveland Plain Dealer,
November, 1977, p. 16A.

A Monograph or Bulletin (Author or Editor Cited)

Hopkins, C. R. (ed.) Needed research in
business education. Delta Pi Epsilon
Research Bulletin. 1972, No. 3.

Publication of an Organization (No Author Cited)

International Word Processing
Association. Word processing and
employment. Willow Grove,
Pennsylvania: Author, 1975.

Publication of U.S. Government

U.S. Government Printing Office.
Dictionary of occupational titles (Vol.
2, 3rd ed.). Washington, D.C.:
Department of Labor, 1965.

A Dissertation

Wanous, J. P. An experimental test of
job attraction theory in an
organizational setting (Doctoral
dissertation, Yale University, 1973).
Dissertation Abstracts International,
1973, 33, 7-B, 3366 (University
Microfilms No. 73-381).

Footnote Entries Only Illustrated

● A Book. One Author

[1]Gerald Green, <u>To Brooklyn with Love</u> (New York: Trident Press, 1967), p. 188.

● A Book. Several Authors

[1]Frederick Herzberg, B. Mausner, and B. Snyderman, <u>The Motivation to Work</u> (2nd ed. New York: John Wiley & Sons, 1959), p. 237.

● A Book. No Author, but Editor(s) Indicated

[1]Gladys Bahr and Kenneth Bangs, eds., <u>Foundations of Business Education</u> (Reston, Virginia: National Business Education Association, 1975), p. 10.

● A Journal Article (Professional Publication)

[1]Robert M. Bloomfield, "The Changing World of the Secretary," <u>Personnel Journal</u>, 52 (September, 1973), 794.

● A Magazine Article (Popular Publication)

[1]Donald D. Swett, "Productivity of Word Processing," <u>The Office</u> (August, 1975), p. 58.

● A Newspaper Article

[1]"College Core Curriculum: A Better Route," <u>Cleveland Plain Dealer</u>, (November 12, 1977), p. 16A.

A Monograph or Bulletin (Author or Editor Cited)

[1]Charles R. Hopkins, ed.,
Needed Research in Business Education,
Delta Pi Epsilon Research Bulletin, No.
3, 1972 (St. Cloud, Minnesota: Delta Pi
Epsilon, 1972), p. 7.

Publication of an Organization (No Author Cited)

[1]International Word Processing
Association, Word Processing
and Employment (Willow Grove,
Pennsylvania: International Word
Processing Association, 1975), p. 12.

Publication of U.S. Government

[1]U.S. Department of Labor,
Dictionary of Occupational Titles, Vol.
II, 3rd ed. (Washington, D.C.:
Government Printing Office, 1965), p.
263.

A Dissertation

[1]J. P. Wanous, "An Experimental Test
of Job Attraction Theory in an
Organizational Setting" (unpublished
Ph.D. dissertation, Yale University,
1973), p. 25.

6

Bibliography Entries Only Illustrated

A Book. One Author

Green, Gerald. To Brooklyn with Love.
New York: Trident Press, 1967.

● A Book. Several Authors

Herzberg, Frederick, Mausner, B., and
Snyderman, B. <u>The Motivation to Work</u>.
2nd ed. New York: John Wiley & Sons,
1959.

● A Book. No Author, but Editor(s) Indicated

Bahr, Gladys and Bangs, Kenneth, eds.
<u>Foundations of Business Education</u>.
Reston, Virginia: National Business
Education Association, 1975.

● A Journal Article (Professional Publication)

Bloomfield, Robert M. "The Changing
World of the Secretary."
<u>Personnel Journal</u>, 52 (September,
1973), 494–798.

● A Magazine Article (Popular Publication)

Swett, Donald D. "Productivity of Word
Processing." <u>The Office</u>, August, 1975,
pp. 57–59.

● A Newspaper Article

Cleveland Plain Dealer. "College Core
Curriculum: A Better Route," November
12, 1977.

● A Monograph or Bulletin (Author or Editor Cited)

Hopkins, Charles R., ed. <u>Needed
Research in Business Education</u>. Delta
Pi Epsilon Research Bulletin, No. 3,
1973. St. Cloud, Minnesota: Delta Pi
Epsilon, 1973.

● Publication of an Organization (No Author Cited)

International Word Processing
    Association. Word Processing and
    Employment. Willow Grove,
    Pennsylvania: International Word
    Processing Association, 1975.

● Publication of U.S. Government

U.S. Department of Labor.
    Dictionary of Occupational Titles, Vol.
    II, 3rd Ed. Washington, D.C.:
    Government Printing Office, 1965.

● A Dissertation

J. P. Wanous. "An Experimental Test of
    Job Attraction Theory in an
    Organizational Setting." Unpublished
    Ph.D. dissertation, Yale University,
    1973.

6

INTEROFFICE MEMORANDUM

TO: Mrs. Ruth Densmore, Personnel Director

FROM: J. Weekly, Midwest Regional Manager

SUBJECT: Evaluation of Secretarial and Clerical Positions

DATE: November 12, 1984

Purpose
You asked for an evaluation of secretarial and clerical positions within
the Midwest Region. The job analysis/work measurement study undertaken
by our office had several objectives. . . .

Rationale for the Study

The paperwork explosion of the forties, fifties, and sixties has affected
adversely office costs in this company as it has in most industries throughout the nation. . . . In an effort to control office costs, every effort
is being made to increase productivity.

Procedures

After determining with the home office those positions classified as office
positions, meetings with the incumbents in those jobs were held to explain
... of the project an... ...eral procedu...
... the study

EXAMPLE A
PERIODIC REPORT

he p...
three phases

ss...es

{ Body

Phase I. _____

Phase II. _____

Coding System. Each person involved in the study was identified by number and by work unit. Data were entered into the computer for each work station by the code identification number._____

Results of the Study

Results of the study are reported in several categories. These include: job analysis information, productivity reports, office costs, quality of output,_____

} Conclusions and Recommendations

Conclusions and Recommendations _____

DEVELOPING AN INSTRUMENT FOR ANALYZING INTERACTION
BETWEEN PUPILS AND TEACHERS IN A BEGINNING
SHORTHAND CLASS AND THE APPLICATION OF
IT TO THREE SHORTHAND CLASSES

Analysis of Teaching Project
for
Dr. J. Arch Phillips, Jr.

by
Jane Doe
December 9, 1984

JOB ANALYSIS/WORK MEASUREMENT STUDY OF
SECRETARIAL AND CLERICAL POSITIONS

at

LAKESIDE PRODUCTS, INC.
1000 Kennedy Boulevard
Cleveland, Ohio   44114

by

Weekly and Roberts
Office Management Consultants

December 9, 1984

6

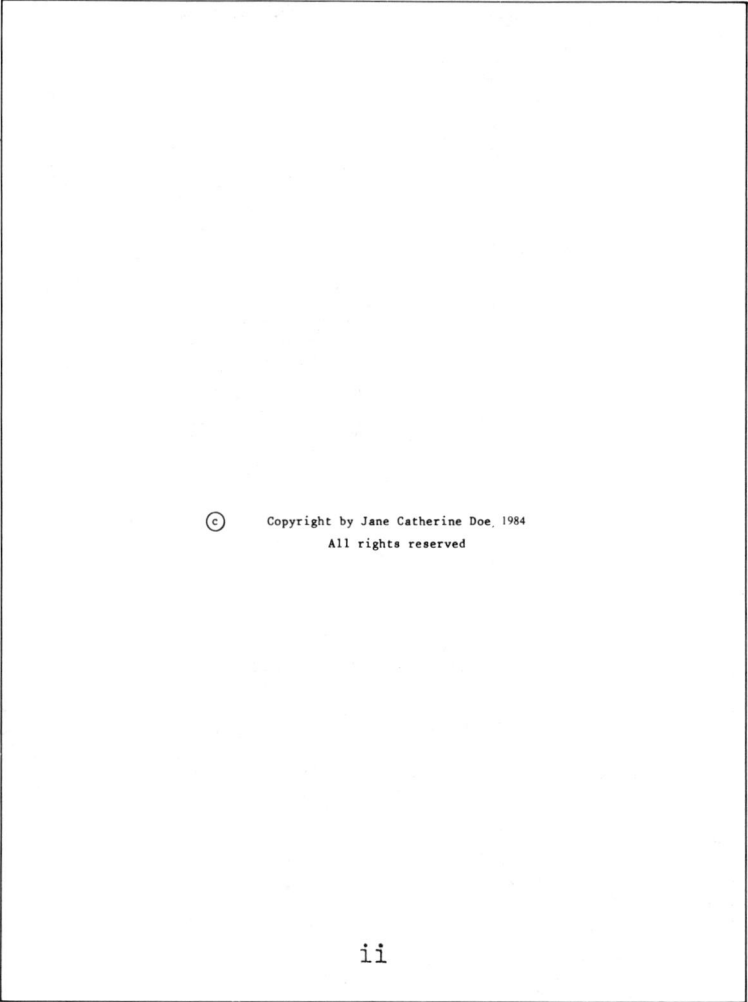

ii

EXAMPLE C
COPYRIGHT PAGE

394

TABLE OF CONTENTS

6

EXAMPLE D
TABLE OF CONTENTS PAGE

395

CHAPTER II: REVIEW OF THE LITERATURE

Since this research involved several areas of study, it was appropriate to review literature in the following fields: job design, job
satisfaction, business organization and administration, word processing,
and business education.

Job Design/Job Satisfaction Literature.

A theory of job design in relation to worker characteristics is in
the process of development. The Herzberg two-factor theory (Herzberg,
Mausner, and Snyderman, 1959) was one of the first research studies to
propose conditions on the job that will be satisfying. These conditions,
according to this theory, include opportunities . . . achievement, recognition,
. . . ment, and growth . . .

EXAMPLE E
FIRST PAGE OF A
MANUSCRIPT

6

...sponsibility, advance... ...n competence.

Recent research has shown that this theory is open to question.
Empirical evidence also does not support the two-factor theory. Major
criticism of the two-factor theory is that it fails to take into account
the variance in worker characteristics. . . .

Job characteristics. Turner and Lawrence (1965) contributed one of
the most significant and thorough investigations of job design in their
development of a measure of job characteristics and study of these
characteristics in relation to job satisfaction. They operationalized
job characteristics in terms of six "requisite task attributes."

These attributes were: variety, autonomy, interaction required,
optional interaction . . . .

12

6

397

Table 1

SUBJECTS BY ORGANIZATION AND SECRETARIAL CLASSIFICATION

Organization Type and Number Included	Tradi-tional	Wd. Pro-cessing	Admin. Support	Total
Banks (1)	4	2	0	6
Educational (1)	10	7	6	23
Governmental (2)	8	0	0	8
Hospitals (3)	6	6	7	19
Industrial (6)	35	44	0	80
Insurance (1)	0	7	0	7
Labor Unions (1)	0	9	0	9
Legal Firms (4)	11	4	0	15
Public Utilities (2)	0	19	34	52
Retail (1)	0	8	0	8
Transportation (1)	0	9	0	9
Total	74	115	47	236

From these organizations 236 secretarial personnel participated in the research study. Of these 236, 74 were classified as traditional ...ified as word pro... ...d 47

...ries

were t... b were ...ersonnel,

were classified as administrative s...rt personnel. A further brea...

down of word processing personnel and administrative support personnel

indicated that 96 word processors were operators; 11 were lead operators,

and 8 were supervisors. In the administrative support group, 40 were

administrative support secretaries while 7 were categorized as coordi-

nators. These data are presented in Table 2.

Table 2

WORD PROCESSING AND ADMINISTRATIVE SUPPORT SUBJECTS

Word Processing Groups		Administrative Support Groups	
Operators	96	Admin. Support Secretaries	40
Lead Operators	11	Coordinators	7
Supervisors	8		—
	115		47

6

BROKEN OAK FACULTY ASSOCIATION

Minutes of the Regular Executive Committee Meeting

September 2, 1984

Present: C. DiSanto, J. Adkins, R. Tomchak, and T. Hartman

Absent: J. Stocking

The Executive Committee of the Broken Oak Faculty Association held its regularly scheduled meeting on Wednesday, September 2, 1984, at 3 p.m. in the Parsons Lecture Hall.

The meeting was called to order by President Adkins. The secretary reported that the minutes of the August 5 meeting had been circulated to all members. Upon a motion duly made, seconded, and passed, those minutes were approved.

The president announced the names of new faculty members for the 1984–85 school year. Upon a motion duly made, seconded, and carried, these persons were voted to become members of the as

EXAMPLE G
MINUTES OF A MEETING

It was moved by T. Hartma... yearly social dues to ...
motion was seconded by J. Adkins. After some discussion, the motion
carried.

Negotiations Committee Report

C. DiSanto reported on the Negotiations Committee's recent meeting with
the Board of Trustees. . . .

Calendar Committee

R. Tomchak introduced a resolution to the Board of Trustees recommending
that the committee membership be increased to include staff as well as
faculty personnel. The resolution was duly seconded and carried.
Therefore, the secretary was instructed to prepare the resolution and
forward it to the Board of Trustees.

After announcing that the next regular meeting would be on September 21,
the president adjourned the meeting.

D. Winterton

Secretary

6

SECTION 7
WP/IP Guides

The first division of this section is WP/IP KEYBOARD ME-
CHANICS. This includes a table that lists common problems in
typing. In the second column, a description is given of how each
problem is solved at the standard typewriter. A third column ex-

plains how to solve the problem at the word processing keyboard. This section also includes helpful MISCELLANEOUS WP/IP NOTES arranged alphabetically by topic. The total presentation should be helpful to a secretary who makes the transition from a standard typewriter to word processing equipment.

Following this material is a general discussion of the various categories of WP/IP EQUIPMENT, including typing, playout, and dictation machines.

Completing the WP/IP Guides section is WP/IP TERMS, a glossary of common word processing terminology. The administrative secretary as well as the correspondence secretary will benefit from the use of this list.

WP/IP Keyboard Mechanics

7

405

It is often desirable to set standard tabs and line lengths on word processors. Many manufacturers have equipped their machines with these standards. If all equipment in a word processing situation is set the same way, time can be saved in input, revisions, and playout.

Key

BS	Backspace	Items within parentheses show simul-
C	Code or Required	taneous operations, for example, (CT)
CR	Carrier Return	indicates that the code is held at the
CU	Code Underline	same time as the tab, and (CSpSpSpSp)
DT	Decimal Tab	indicates that four spaces are typed
R	Reverse Index	while the code is held.
SC	Stop Code	
Sp	Space	
T	Tab	
U	Underscore.	

Problem	Standard Typewriter	WP/IP Keyboard
Underscore a long title	<u>The Prince and the Pauper</u>	<u>The</u> <u>Prince</u> <u>and</u> <u>the</u> <u>Pauper</u> (If underscores must be kept with the words for proper playout.)
Underscore several lines	Type each line; backspace and underscore solid.	Most machines are equipped with codes that cause underscores until an end-underscore instruction is given. If your machine does not have this

		code, type lines; enter SC; when machine stops, do underscores manually.
		NOTE: Where possible, use all caps rather than underscores.
Roman numerals in outline	Begin at margin. Use **MAR REL** and **BS** as necessary.	Set margin five spaces to left. (CT) for ''I''; (CT)(CBS) for ''II''; and so on.
Numbers under and over 10	Begin at margin. Use **MAR REL** and **BS** as necessary.	Sp once; type single digit; (CT). The ''10'' begins at the margin without the Sp; (CT).
Numbered lists or sentences	1.Sp,Sp ____ CR T ____.CR 2.Sp,Sp ____ CR T ____.CR	Sp1.(CT) ____ ____. (CR) Sp2.(CT) ____ R ____. (CR)
Double-spaced documents	*With* *indentions* a document that is double spaced requires a triple space between paragraphs.	*With* *indentions* a document that is double spaced requires only a double space between paragraphs.

7

Problem	Standard Typewriter	WP/IP Keyboard
	Without indentions a document requires a triple space between paragraphs.	*Without indentions* a document can be typed with two double spaces between paragraphs.
		NOTE: If this is not acceptable, use a format change or enter SC and add one extra line.

Problem	Standard Typewriter	WP/IP Keyboard
Decimal tabulations	SpSp 983.45 SpSpSpSp 83.45 SpSpSpSpSp <u>1.45</u> 1,068.35	Without decimal tab: SpSp 983.45 SpSpSpSp 83.45 SpSpSpSpSp <u>1.45</u>(CU) or 1,068.35(CBS);U
		Most equipment now has decimal tab.
		With decimal tab: DT983.45 DT83.45 DT1.45(CU) or (CBS);U DT1,068.35

Problem	Standard Typewriter	WP/IP Keyboard
Equations, Formulas, Subscripts, Superscripts	H_2O Roll down with use of variable line spaces. $$\frac{x}{y} = 4Z$$	H_2O H; ↓ ½; 2; ↑ ½; O. x; (U); (CBS) IR;y; ↑ ½; = 4Z.

7

NOTE: The underscore in this type of formula *must* be on the same level as the "equals" sign in order to retain the true meaning of the formula.

Construction of brackets	— — / / — —	
	Use diagonal and underscores.	Type diagonal, (CBS);U; ↑ ↑ U; or enter SC and do the bracket manually. Many machines have the brackets on the keyboard.
Dash	Use two hyphens with no spaces before or after.	It is necessary on some equipment to use required hyphens.
Exclamation point	If the exclamation point does not appear on your keyboard, use the apostrophe, BS, and a period.	If the exclamation point does not appear on your keyboard, use the apostrophe, (CBS), and a period.
Hyphen	No special instructions.	Determine whether or not you need to retain the hyphen if the margins adjust. Code if necessary.

7

Miscellaneous
WP/IP Notes

7

CENTERING	Word processing machines have an automatic centering feature. If the equipment does not have this feature, it is necessary to tab to center and code backspace.
ENVELOPES	The envelope address is played out from the recorded letter address.
FOOTNOTES	Preparation of footnotes on word processing equipment is done in a variety of ways depending on the machine features. Frequently, this must be a manual process; therefore, it is recommended that, when possible, footnotes should be put onto a separate sheet at the end of the document. If they must be kept with the text on a page, refer to instructions of the manufacturer during pagination.
FORMATTING	Automatic formatting is available on many word processors. Standardize whenever possible for maximum efficiency. Consult the manufacturer's guide for instructions.
HYPHENATION	Because most equipment has the word wrap feature and, therefore, do not hyphenate, it is necessary to check the page for a pleasing appearance and to add hyphens as needed. Some equipment does automatic hyphenation at appropriate places as the document is keyboarded.
LETTER STYLES	Block and simplified letter styles are most adaptable to word processing output.
LINE LENGTH	Whenever possible, use a standard line length in all correspondence. Many machines are set up with automatic line lengths.
MARGINS	A 6-inch line setting will give inch side margins. Whenever possible, scan the

7

pages and use line count or pagination for uniform bottom margins.

OVERHANG FORMAT
To create the "overhang" format in a bibliography, tab once at the beginning of line 1; code backspace to margin (five times), then type. The carrier will return to the indent position on line 2.

PAGINATION
Page numbers are not recorded on the magnetic medium but are typed manually or are put into a header or footer.

REFERENCE INITIALS
The reference initials can reflect the author, machine, day on which the document was prepared, and the job. RCK:amc = RCK (author); a (machine); m (Monday); c (job name).

TABULATIONS
Whenever possible, judgment placement for columns should be used. Care must be taken to give the page a pleasing appearance.

WP/IP Equipment

WP/IP keyboards are currently manufactured by more than 50 companies. While each piece of equipment has a variety of characteristics, for purposes of brevity the equipment will be discussed in several general categories. Each type of equipment is appropriate for certain applications and work loads.

Stand-alone text editing equipment is capable of keyboarding, revisions, and playout within one unit or pair of units; the total typing-playout function can be accomplished through its use. Revisions may be limited or virtually limitless depending on the versatility of the media employed. A number of these units are capable of communicating with other similar units.

The least versatile type of stand-alone text editor contains only one tape, cassette, or card "station." Keying is done directly to the media. This single-station unit cannot be merged with a second station and, therefore, revision capability is limited to the replacement of characters or the addition of a few words to each line. Where dual stations are used, revisions can be much greater through merging tapes, cassettes, or cards and through transfer and addition of newly keyed-in material.

When single-station units are combined with a memory, revisions are generally easier, faster, and almost limitless. Where the memory is used alone, versatility is reduced and storage is limited.

The method of input in stand-alone equipment is keyboard-to-paper or keyboard-to-video display screen. At the same time as the keying is done, recording takes place on either a magnetic medium (card, tape, etc.) or into the memory.

Playout is usually accomplished through the same Selectric or daisy wheel printer that has been used for the input; however, the IBM System 6 uses an ink jet printer, which is a separate unit, rather than one of the impact devices.

Many units have such features as dual pitch, right justification, automatic centering and underscoring, and automatic tabulation.

Shared logic equipment is highly efficient and versatile since it is made up of a number of input keyboards that share the logic of one master unit. This type of equipment has the capability of great on-line as well as off-line storage. The device for input can be as basic as a single-station keyboard direct to magnetic media; it can be keyboard-to-memory-to-media; or it can employ the keyboard-to-screen method.

Playout can be through a computer printer, or frequently the input device acts as the printer, using the Selectric element or the wheel printer.

As in the stand-alone units, shared-logic equipment has many desirable features, such as right justification, automatic setup of tables, global search, and automatic pagination.

Distributed logic equipment has a central master unit for the bulk of the stored material. In addition, it has at each terminal (keyboard) some intelligence, which allows work to continue when the master unit is down.

Optical character recognition (OCR) is a method of input through a standard Selectric or wheel-printer typewriter with the use of a special element or wheel. A typed page is entered into the OCR unit and is scanned and transferred onto a diskette. It can then be taken to a word processor for revisions and is played out as is any project prepared on the word processing equipment. The scanner is useful as an input device in many instances.

Photocomposition equipment is sometimes found in the word processing center. It has the capability to prepare professional quality documents through the use of proportional spacing and a wide variety of type sizes and styles. The keyboards are similar to standard typewriter keyboards. Some phototypesetters are stand-alone units, while others can play out from media that is typed and edited at a different keyboard. A number of vendors provide interfaces between word processing keyboards and photocomposition equipment. Documents can be stored on magnetic tapes, cards, cassettes, and diskettes.

There are service bureaus available that use diskettes or tapes from word processors or computers and translate the material into typeset form. These services are economical for companies that cannot justify having their own typesetting equipment.

Centralized dictation equipment is wired to a central location either through the public telephone or a private wire system. Through the use of a central system, the author is able to dictate from his or her office directly to the remote recorder through either the telephone or a microphone. It is possible to back up, review, correct, and give special and delayed instructions. Maximum recording time on these units is from 6 to 240 minutes; most units have rapid automatic media change features.

Central systems employ discrete (removable) or endless loop media. Discrete media include disks, belts, cassettes, minicassettes or microcassettes. The endless loop is not removable from its tank, but simultaneous dictation is available through the use of tracks. Transcription can begin while dictation is still taking place.

Portable dictation equipment is available in a wide variety of models. Some units can be used for both dictation and transcription and are complete with earphones and foot pedals. Others are simply recorders and come in a variety of sizes. Some units are small enough to be carried in a pocket. The media used in these portable units include disks, belts, cassettes, minicassettes, and microcassettes.

Whatever type of word processing equipment your organization uses, it is important that you as an operator learn the capabilities of that equipment and use its capabilities where applicable.

Checklist of Word/Information Processing System Characteristics

The following checklist of word/information processing equipment may be useful to the operator in analyzing his/her knowledge of equipment and in maximizing the use of available equipment. It may be valuable to management and supervisory personnel in matching equipment features of various manufacturers to user requirements.

A. Manufacturer _____ **Model** _____

B. Equipment Configurations

Modular design:	___ Keyboard	___ CRT	___ Printer
Integrated design:	___ Keyboard	___ CRT	___ Printer
Drive:	___ Disk	___ Diskette	
Compatible with other		___ Single	___ Dual
products of the manufacturer:		___ Yes	___ No
Upgradable:		___ Yes	___ No

C. CPU

How many K in the memory? ___

Is it software programmable? ___ Yes ___ No

D. Display

What is the CRT screen size? ___

Is the display a ___ partial page? ___ full page?

Number of horizontal characters displayed? ___

Number of vertical lines displayed? ___

What is the color of the characters? ___

What is the background color of the screen? ___

What is the size of the buffer? ___

Scrolling: How many horizontal characters? ___

How many vertical lines? ___

Page scrolling? ___ Yes ___ No

Is the screen ___ tiltable? ___ stationary?

Is the screen
brightness ___ adjustable? ___ nonadjustable?

Does it have a split
screen? ___ Yes ___ No

E. Keyboard

How many alphanumeric keys? ___

How many control keys? ___

How many function keys? ___

Are the control keys separate
from the alphanumeric keys? ___ Yes ___ No

Are the function keys separate
from the alphanumeric keys? ___ Yes ___ No

F. Storage

Storage medium: ____ card ____ tape ____ minidiskette
____ diskette ____ hard disk

Pages per storage unit: ____

Characters per storage unit: ____

G. Printers

Separate ____ Keyboard ____

Daisywheel?	____ Yes	____ No
Letter quality?	____ Yes	____ No
Draft quality?	____ Yes	____ No

Playout pitch ____ 10 ____ 12 ____ 15
____ Proportional ____ Other

Speed of output? ____

Width of paper handled? ____ Length of paper handled? ____

Document queing? ____ Yes ____ No

H. Communications

Available? ____ Yes ____ No

Formats ____

Speed ____

I. Peripheral Equipment

Sheet feeder?	____ Yes	____ No
Draft printer?	____ Yes	____ No
OCR?	____ Yes	____ No
Photocomposition?	____ Yes	____ No

J. Text Features

Word wraparound/automatic return	____
Automatic decimal alignment	____
Hyphenation	____
System scan for hyphenation	____
Automatic input underlining	____
Automatic input double underlining	____
Automatic redlining	____
Automatic super and subscripts	____
Automatic justification of right margin	____
Automatic boldfacing	____
Menus and prompts	____
Pagination	____

7

Automatic repagination   ____
Document assembly/merge   ____
Search capability   ____   ____ Character string
Delete capability   ____ Character   ____ Word
     ____ Sentence   ____ Paragraph   ____ Document
Global search and replace   ____
Automatic file sort   ____
Automatic file select   ____
Dictionary (Spelling check)   ____
Math functions   ____

K. Service

Available on call   ____   Waiting period   ____
Monthly charge?   ____

L. Training

Number of hours?   ____
On manufacturer's premises   ____
on customer's premises   ____
Free   ____   Cost?   ____

M. Delivery Date on Equipment Purchases   ____

WP/IP Terms

7

ACCESS
To get information to or from the word processor.

ADJUST
A playback mode that permits lines to be rearranged automatically.

423

ADMINI-STRATIVE SECRETARY	A secretary who carries out all clerical duties of the secretarial job with the exception of the correspondence duties.
ARCHIVING	Taking material from on-line storage and putting it onto storage medium.
AUTHOR	The originator of a document.
AUTOMATIC CARRIER RETURN	One that does not require operator action; the machine returns the carriage when the line ending is reached.
AUTOMATIC CENTERING	Centering that is performed by a keystroke command to the word processing equipment.
AUTOMATIC DECIMAL TAB	A keystroke command to the word processing equipment that causes columns to be aligned.
AUTOMATIC LINE SPACING	Line spacing (single, double, triple) input into the processing unit at the time of typing rather than during playback.
AUTOMATIC PAGINATION	Page numbers put in automatically when the desired number of lines is reached. If the document is changed or rearranged, page numbers can be changed also.
AUTOMATIC UNDERSCORE	Underscoring that is performed by the word processing equipment in reaction to a keystroke command to the equipment.
BACKGROUND PRINTING	Ability of a word processor to print while the operator inputs or edits other material.
BATCHING	Inputting an entire group of items before processing any of them.
BIDIREC-TIONAL PRINTING	Printing first from left to right and then from right to left during playout of text material.
BIT	The smallest unit recognized by a computer.

BLOCK AND MOVE	Ability of word processor to select and move a block of information to another location in the same or a different document.
BOILERPLATE	Stored material that is used to create other documents.
BYTE	A sequence of bits.
CARTRIDGE, DISK	A container holding magnetic-coated disks on which dictation is recorded.
CARTRIDGE, TAPE	A container holding magnetic tape on which typewritten characters or spoken words are recorded.
CASSETTE	A holder of magnetic tape that is used in recording typewritten characters or spoken words.
CENTRAL DICTATION SYSTEM	A system that is wired directly into a central location where the dictation is received.
CHARACTER	Any input symbol, letter, or number.
CHARACTER STRING	A consecutive group of characters.
CLEAR	To remove material from memory.
COMMAND	An instruction to the processing unit.
COMMUNI-CATING TYPEWRITER	A typewriter that can send and receive information to and from other like units through a telephone hookup.
COMPUTER	An automatic calculating machine.
CONSOLE	The part of a word processor through which one can record and play back. In computers, that part through which programs are entered and changed.
CONTROL CARD	A magnetic card that contains general instructions for the processing unit.

7

CORRESPON-DENCE SECRETARY	See: WORD PROCESSING SPECIALIST.
CPS	Characters per second; refers to playout speed of processor.
CPU	Central processing unit; a computing device.
CRT	Cathode ray tube; a picture tube on which the text is displayed as keying takes place.
CURSOR	A position indicator on a CRT.
DAISY WHEEL	A print element that is available in a variety of type styles that can be easily interchanged.
DATA BASE	A collection of libraries used by an organization and made up of files of information.
DELETE	An instruction to remove a character, word, line, and so on from the storage medium.
DISC (DISK)	A type of storage used in recording dictation on some equipment and for storage in some word processors (also called diskettes or floppy disks).
DISCRETE MEDIA	Magnetic media that are removable for storage.
DOWN TIME	Amount of time lost when equipment is not functioning properly.
DUMP	To put the contents of the memory onto storage medium.
DUPLICATE	In word processing, to copy electronically material from one card, tape, or diskette to another card, tape, or diskette.
EDIT	To change.

ELECTRONIC DICTIONARY	A large list of words contained in the software of a word processor with which the machine checks spelling of documents.
ELECTRONIC TYPEWRITER	A typewriter that is electronic rather than mechanical. It has few moving parts and operates silently.
ELEMENT	A kind of removable, replaceable print head.
ENDLESS LOOP RECORDER	A kind of central dictation unit that has within it a loop of magnetic tape as its recording medium. This revolves within a ''tank'' and allows dictation and transcription to take place simultaneously.
FACSIMILE (FAX)	The transmission of images through the use of a scanner at the point of origin and reconstruction at a receiver; the image is then produced on paper.
FLOWCHART	A diagram with lines and symbols showing step-by-step progression of a procedure.
FORMAT	The way in which a project is set up.
GLOBAL SEARCH	A feature on some word processors whereby the machine will locate a designated character string throughout the document. In some equipment, the character string can also be replaced throughout the document.
HARD COPY	Typed or printed copy.
HARDWARE	The word processing equipment.
HIGHLIGHTING	Brightening or blinking certain sections of a CRT.
HOT ZONE	The area on the right side of lines where adjusting of the margin and hyphenation decisions take place.

7

INPUT	Information entered into the system. Input can refer to material that is dictated into the system or it can refer to material that is typed into the word processor.
JUSTIFIED PLAYOUT	Material played out with flush right and flush left margins.
K	When used with a number, it represents a thousand characters (for example, 20K is 20,000 characters).
KEYBOARD	The input device for the word processing unit.
LINE	All material on a line including one carrier return.
LOAD	To enter the magnetic medium into the word processor.
MAGNETIC CARD	A card coated with a magnetic substance on which approximately one page of typewritten material or 50 to 100 lines can be recorded.
MAGNETIC CARTRIDGE	Magnetic-coated tape in a cartridge on which approximately 20 pages of typewritten material can be recorded.
MAGNETIC CASSETTE	Magnetic-coated tape in a cassette on which approximately 20 pages of typewritten material can be recorded.
MAGNETIC DISKETTE	Magnetic-coated diskette on which typewritten material can be recorded.
MAGNETIC MEDIA	Plural of magnetic medium. The various storage devices used in word processing, such as magnetic cards, cassettes, tapes, and diskettes.
MAGNETIC TAPE	Magnetic-coated tape on which recording takes place.
MATH FUNCTION	Ability of a word processor to do mathematical calculations.

MEMORY	An internal device of the word processor in which material may be stored and from which material may be recalled upon demand.
MERGING	Combining text to form a document.
MINI-COMPUTER	A small computer; in word processing, a computer made especially for the word processing function.
OFF-LINE	Equipment that is not connected to and controlled by a central master unit.
ON-LINE	Equipment that is connected to and controlled by a central master unit.
OPTICAL CHARACTER READER (OCR)	This device changes characters that have been typed with certain specific elements into a form to be used by a word processor. Thus, an ordinary typewriter can prepare input into a word processing system.
ORIGINATOR	The person who composes the document to be processed.
OUTPUT	Information played out automatically from a word processing unit.
PBX DICTATION SYSTEM	Central dictation equipment that operates through interface with the telephone system.
PERIPHERAL EQUIPMENT	Equipment that works with the central unit but is not an integral part of it. This includes keyboards, printers, and the like.
PITCH	The size of type; refers to the number of characters to the inch.
PLAYBACK	To play out automatically material from the word processing equipment.
PLAYOUT	The automatic output of the word processing equipment.

7

PLAYOUT SPEED	The rate at which the automatic output is accomplished.
PRERECORD	To type material onto some magnetic medium for playback at a later time.
PRINCIPAL	The originator; the person who authors the document.
PRINTER	The part of the output device that puts text onto paper. Common word processing printers include the Selectric element, the wheel printer, and the ink jet printer.
PROPORTIONAL SPACING	A kind of spacing whereby each character fills a number of units of space, with narrow letters (such as ''i'') using fewer units than wide letters (such as ''w'').
RECORD	To store typed material on a magnetic medium for future use.
REMOTE TERMINAL	A unit that is wired to the central computer.
SEARCH	A command given to the word processor that causes the equipment to locate a desired section.
SHARED LOGIC	A system by which two or more stations or terminals may use the memory of the main unit.
SKIP	A mode that allows the unit to bypass material automatically.
SOFTWARE	The instructions and programs used in conjunction with word processing equipment.
SORT CAPABILITY	Capability of a word processor to sort lists alphabetically or numerically.
STAND-ALONE UNIT	A word processor that is used as an independent unit. It is not dependent on another piece of equipment for either input or output.

STATION	In word processing, a work location for an operator.
STOP CODE	A code entered onto the magnetic media that causes the equipment to stop during playback.
STORE	To hold a document on magnetic media or in memory for future use.
SWITCH CODE	A code entered onto the magnetic media that causes the unit to switch playback from one section of memory or medium to another.
TERMINAL	In word processing, a device with a keyboard that can input and sometimes play out text.
TEXT EDITOR	A typewriter that has capabilities for changing and revising text through the use of memory or magnetic media.
THROUGHPUT	The volume of work processed by the word processor.
TIME-SHARING	A number of terminals using a central processing unit.
TRACK	A specific section of a magnetic card, disk, or diskette.
TRANSFER	To copy from one tape, card, or disk onto another, with the ability to revise during the process.
TURNAROUND TIME	The length of time from the input of a job into a word processing center to the completion of that job.
UNATTENDED PLAYBACK	A feature that permits documents to be printed without operator intervention.
VARIABLE	Information that is different on each document and is combined with prerecorded material.

7

WORD	A word recognized by word processing equipment as a group of characters that is followed by a space, tab, or carrier return.
WORD PROCESSING (WP/IP)	A system whereby the correspondence function is removed from the secretarial position, allowing the remaining administrative duties to be performed by fewer personnel. Usually, the typing is accomplished by highly skilled operators through the use of magnetic media equipment.
WORD PROCESSING CENTER	A centralized location where the word processing function takes place. This often includes some type of dictation system and magnetic media equipment, with procedures specialized for greater efficiency.
WORD PROCESSING SPECIALIST	A secretary who does the correspondence function of the secretarial job; a word processing operator.
WORD PROCESSING SYSTEM	A total support system for a company or department that includes word processing specialists and administrative secretaries working together with standardized procedures and controls.
WORD WRAPAROUND	A feature that causes a word that cannot fit within the right margin to go to the next line.

7

SECTION 8
Proofreading and Editing

Proofreading and editing are very important tasks in any secretarial setting. When proofreading, the secretary must look for several kinds of errors: mechanical errors such as missing, inverted, or incorrect letters; missing words or lines; and incorrect spelling. In addition, the valuable secretary will also edit the document, that is, look for author errors such as incorrect column totals, poor grammar, wrong dates, poor formats, and the like.

In the word processing setting, proofreading and editing demand special attention. Recognizing the time and skill needed for this function, some centers employ full-time proofreaders to check all operator output. The speed and cost-effectiveness of word processing are quickly reduced when documents must be rerun because of careless errors.

This section gives a number of proofreading and editing techniques. First some general guides are listed, followed by special tips for various kinds of documents. Next are some ideas primarily useful to the word processing specialist. The section also contains words and phrases to avoid and a list of proofreader's marks.

General Proofreading
and Editing Guides

435

8

1. Check for consistency of style throughout the document before you begin typing. If an outline or numerical list is used, make sure the numbers or letters are consecutive. Contact the author if you have questions.

2. Take your time and concentrate. It is impossible to proofread efficiently if your mind is on something else or if you are in a hurry.

3. Read the text first for sense. Are there words missing? Are the grammar and sentence structure correct? Does the material make sense? Check the punctuation and capitalization.

4. Read the text a second time for accuracy. Are letters inverted or omitted? Is spelling correct? Use the dictionary when in doubt.

5. When proofreading names and unfamiliar terms, check carefully letter by letter.

6. Use a dictionary and a good reference manual whenever you have questions.

7. To avoid the need to realign the work in the typewriter, proofread the material while it is still in the typewriter *if you are working on final copy.*

8. Double-check figures carefully with the handwritten or dictated document.

9. If you have trouble looking at one word at a time and thus are missing inverted or missing letters, try reading from right to left. This will force you to scrutinize each word.

10. If you frequently skip a line while typing, use a ruler or one of the mechanical devices for copy that has foot pedals to advance one or two lines of copy at a time.

11. To maintain attention and keep the eyes focused on the line being proofread, some proofreaders prefer to use the forefinger and the pen or the pen alone as a guide when a ruler is not being used. To use the pen, hold the writing instrument in the hand with which you will be making corrections. Point the pen at the far left or the far right of each line as it is proofread. To use the forefinger and the

pen, point the forefinger of the hand not holding the pen at the center of each line as you proofread.

12. When you proofread, look for more than the obvious typing errors. Does the page present a pleasing picture as arranged? Is the format consistent throughout the article? If you are working on an outline or numbered document, are the letters or numbers in consecutive order? Check the calendar to make sure days and dates given are correct.

13. It should not be necessary for anyone but the novice to proofread with someone unless the material is extremely technical. Even then, the expert proofreader can often do a more efficient job alone. The "buddy system" interrupts another person's work and should be avoided if possible.

Special Proofreading
and Editing Guides

439 | 8

Statistical and Technical Material

1. Proofreading numbers takes special care. Work back and forth with the original using a ruler as a guide if necessary. If the numbers are in a column with a total, the easiest method of proofreading is to add the numbers with a calculator and check the result against the given total.

2. When working from handwritten copy or dictated material, it is sometimes difficult to know whether to use upper or lower case letters in formulas and whether or not to space between units. Don't guess. Check with the author, if in doubt, and keep a technical reference guide handy if you do this type of work frequently. General guides:
   A. Do not space before subscripts or superscripts.
   B. Space once before and after addition ($+$), subtraction ($-$), multiplication ($\times$), division ($-$), and equals ($=$) signs.

3. When checking outlines, remember, there can be no "A" without a "B" or "1" without a "2." See OUTLINE FORMAT, p. 347.

Manuscripts and Bibliographies

1. The style of a manuscript must be uniform throughout. Style manuals are available that give detailed instructions on setup.

2. Make sure the format of a bibliography is consistent throughout. Two styles of bibliographies are shown in REPORT AND MANUSCRIPT FORMAT, p. 366. When bibliographies are run out from computer searches, there frequently is a variety of styles used. Sometimes all capitals are used in titles. Check for acceptability and uniformity.

Handwritten Copy

This is probably the most difficult material to proofread or edit. The letters "a" and "o" often look alike, as do "e" and "i."

Many authors do not dot "i's" or cross "t's." Look for "m's" that look like "w's." When typing from handwritten work, it is very easy to skip a line, so watch carefully for this error. You may find it helpful to use a straightedge to keep your eyes on the correct line.

To make the job easier, encourage authors to use ruled paper and to write on every other line. The originator should use a fine point pen. Avoid wide felt tip pens and magic markers.

Reading and editing the handwritten copy before you begin to type will familiarize you with the material and will make proofreading for meaning much easier to do.

Pretyped Copy

Pretyped copy is readily proofread by using a straightedge under the line of copy being read. Take special care to find rearranged words, sentences, and paragraphs. Also, renumbering should be checked for accuracy.

Transcription from Machine Dictation

In addition to following the general guides for proofreading and editing, the inexperienced machine transcriber may find it helpful to listen to the dictation while proofreading the transcription. While this is a very time-consuming procedure, it will help to insure correct transcription. After the operator is confident of transcription skills, this procedure should be discontinued. Double-check names, addresses, and numbers, and watch for minor articles, conjunctions, and prepositions that can easily be mistaken for similar sounding words.

Transcription from Shorthand Notes

Ordinarily, it should not be necessary to read shorthand notes before transcribing. In proofreading, check the notes only for dates, numbers, and technical terms. Because you are not checking against copy, it is especially important to read the transcription for meaning. Follow all other general proofreading and editing guides.

Proofreading and Editing in the Word Processing Setting

443 8

1. It is usually necessary to play out a copy to proof. On the draft, circle errors clearly and correct them before final playback. Often proofreading can be done while the machine is playing back other work.

2. If you are typing on rough draft paper, proofread and edit *after* removing the work from the typewriter when using display model word processors.

3. When proofreading revised copy, proofread only the new material that has been typed.

4. Be certain that all changes are clearly marked on the file copy each time revisions are made.

Some operators prefer to proof short documents on the screen. However, operators who find it difficult to proof on the screen should play out a draft copy. Lengthy documents should be proofed from a draft copy.

Words and Phrases to Avoid

445 8

There are a number of words and phrases that make business writing sound stilted or archaic. Avoid the use of unnecessary words and phrases and redundant expressions such as those listed below on the left. Suggestions for alternative choices are given in the column on the right.

thank you in advance	thank you
I remain	Do not use.
enclosed please find	enclosed is (are)
in regard(s)	concerning, regarding, about
I would like to say	Do not use.
per	a
hopefully	I hope, we hope
due to the fact that	since, because
at the present time	now, at present
on hand	Do not use.
our Mr. Bell	Mr. Bell, our buyer
communication	letter, memo
on the order of	like
and etc.	Omit *and*.
firstly, secondly	first, second
irregardless	regardless
off of	from
is because	is that
sort of, kind of	rather
cognizant	aware
for the reason that	because
for the purpose of	for
in order to, in order that	to, so that
make inquiry	ask
in a position to	can
meets with your (our, their) approval	you (we, they) approve
in the near future	soon
refer back to	refer to
restate again	restate, say again
free of charge	free, at no charge
utilize	use
tell Susan or myself	tell Susan or me

Revised Material
(Proofreader's Marks)

to cover completely	Transpose
of course	Insertion of word(s) as
We are interested	indicated
~~As you know~~	Delete as indicated
STET ~~As you know~~	Retain deleted material
¶	Make paragraph here
is fully illustrated. Most of the pictures	Run in—no paragraph
Market place	Close up—no space
Stock room	Leave space between words
←	Move to the left
→	Move to the right
The result however is	Insertion of punctuation indicated by circling
LC an Accounting Department	Small letters or lower case
federal or anniversary	Triple underlining of letter or word means all caps
sale	
ds	Double space
ss	Single space
Vt Sp.	Spell out in full—Vermont
extremely well made	Take out underscore
→ ←	Center on the page

Appendix

Standard American and Metric Weights and Measures Data

Standard American	Metric
Linear Measures of Length and Distance	**Linear Measures of Length and Distance**
Inch (in.) _____	1 millimeter (mm) = 0.001 meter
12 inches = 1 foot (ft.)	1 centimeter (cm) = 0.01 meter
3 feet = 1 yard (yd.)	1 decimeter (dm) = 0.1 meter
5½ yards = 1 rod (rd.)	1 meter (m) = 1 meter
40 rods = 1 furlong (fur.) = ⅛ mile (mi.)	1 dekameter (dkm) = 10 meters
320 rods = 1 mile	1 hectometer (hm) = 100 meters
3 miles = 1 league	1 kilometer (km) = 1000 meters
Fluid/Liquid Measures of Capacity	
1 minim or drop (min. or M)	1 milliliter (ml) = 0.001 liter
60 minim = 1 fluid dram (dr.)	1 centiliter (cl) = 0.01 liter
8 drams = 1 fluid ounce (oz.)	1 deciliter (dl) = 0.1 liter
16 fluid ounces = 1 pint (pt.)	1 liter (l) = 1 liter
2 pints = 1 quart (qt.)	1 dekaliter (dkl) = 10 liters
4 quarts = 1 gallon (gal.)	1 hectoliter (hl) = 100 liters
31.5 gallons = 1 barrel (bbl.)	1 kiloliter (kl) = 1000 liters
Dry Measures of Capacity	
1 teaspoon (t.)	
3 teaspoons = 1 tablespoon (T.)	
16 tablespoons = 1 cup (c.)	
2 cups = 1 pint (pt.)	(Metric measures are identical to liquid capacity measures)
2 pints = 1 quart (qt.)	
8 quarts = 1 peck (pk.)	
4 pecks = 1 bushel (bu.)	
Units of Measure for Counting	
1 dozen (doz.) = 12 units	
12 dozen = 1 gross (gr.)	
12 gross = 1 great gross	
25 sheets paper = 1 quire (qr.)	(No comparable metric units)
500 sheets paper = 1 ream (rm.)	
10 reams = 1 bale	

Standard American and Metric Weights and Measures Data *(continued)*

Standard American	Metric
Square Measures of Area	
1 square inch (sq. in.)	1 square millimeter (mm²) = 0.000001 square meter
144 square inches = 1 square foot (sq. ft.)	1 square centimeter (cm²) = 0.0001 square meter
9 square feet = 1 square yard (sq. yd.)	1 square decimeter (dm²) = 0.01 square meter
30¼ square yards = 1 square rod (sq. rd.)	1 square meter (m²) = 10 dekameters
160 square rods = 1 acre (A.)	1 square dekameter (dkm²) = 100 square meters
640 acres = 1 square mile (sq. mi.)	1 square hectometer (hm²) = 10,000 square meters
	1 square kilometer (km²) = 1,000,000 square meters
Cubic Measure of Volume	
1 cubic inch (cu. in.)	1 cubic meter (m³) = 1 cubic meter
1,728 cubic inches = 1 cubic foot (cu. ft.)	1 cubic centimeter (cm³) = 10^{-6} cubic meter
27 cubic feet = 1 cubic yard (cu. yd.)	1 cubic decimeter (dm³) = 10^{-3} cubic meter
	1 cubic dekameter (dkm³) = 10^3 cubic meters
	1 cubic hectometer (hm³) = 10^6 cubic meters
	1 cubic kilometer (km³) = 10^9 cubic meters
Circular Measure	
1 second (″)	
60 seconds (sec.) = 1 minute (′ or min.)	(No comparable metric measures)
60 minutes = 1 degree (° or deg.)	
90 degrees = 1 right angle	
360 degrees = circumference of a circle	

Standard American and Metric Weights and Measures Data *(continued)*

Standard American	Metric
Weights	
1 dram (dr.)	1 milligram (mg) = 0.001 gram
16 drams = 1 ounce (oz.)	1 centigram (cg) = 0.01 gram
16 ounces = 1 pound (lb. or #)	1 decigram (dg) = 0.1 gram
100 pounds = 1 hundredweight (cwt.)	1 gram = 1 gram
	1 dekagram (dkg) = 10 grams
2000 pounds = 1 short ton (s.t.)	1 hectogram (hg) = 100 grams
2240 pounds = 1 ton (t.)	1 kilogram (kg) = 1000 grams
Temperature	
32 degrees Fahrenheit (F.) = freezing point of water	0 degrees Celsius (C) = freezing point of water
212 degrees Fahrenheit = boiling point of water	100 degrees Celsius = boiling point of water
98.6 degrees Fahrenheit = normal body temperature	37 degrees Celsius = normal body temperature

METRIC PREFIXES	NUMERICAL VALUE
tera (10^{12}) = 1 trillion times	1,000,000,000,000
giga (10^9) = 1 billion times	1,000,000,000
mega (10^6) = 1 million times	1,000,000
kilo (10^3) = 1 thousand times	1,000
hecto (10^2) = 1 hundred times	100
deca (10) = 10 times	10
deci (10^{-1}) = One tenth of	.1
centi (10^{-2}) = One hundredth of	.01
milli (10^{-3}) = One thousandth of	.001
micro (10^{-6}) = One millionth of	.000001
nano (10^{-9}) = One billionth of	.000000001
pico (10^{-12}) = One trillionth of	.000000000001

Conversion Tables (Approximate)

American Standard Measures to Metric	Metric Measures to American Standard
1 inch = 25 millimeters	1 millimeter = 0.04 inch
1 inch = 2.5 centimeters	1 centimeter = 0.4 inch
1 foot = 0.3 meter	1 meter = 3.3 feet
1 yard = 0.9 meter	1 meter = 1.1 yards

Standard American and Metric Weights and Measures Data *(continued)*

Standard American	Metric
1 mile = 1.6 kilometers	1 kilometer = 0.6 mile
1 square inch = 6.5 square centimeters	1 square centimeter = 0.16 square inch
1 square foot = 0.09 square meter	1 square meter = 11 square feet
1 square yard = 0.8 square meter	1 square meter = 1.2 square yards
1 square mile = 2.6 square kilometers	1 square kilometer = 0.4 square mile
1 acre = 0.4 square hectometers (hectares)	1 square hectometer (hectare) = 2.5 acres
1 cubic inch = 16 cubic centimeters	1 cubic centimeter = 0.06 cubic yard
1 cubic foot = 0.03 cubic meter	1 cubic meter = 35 cubic feet
1 cubic yard = 0.8 cubic meter	1 cubic meter = 1.3 cubic yards
1 fluid ounce = 30 milliliters	1 milliliter = 0.034 ounce
1 pint = 0.47 liter	1 liter = 2.1 pints
1 quart = 0.95 liter	1 liter = 1.06 quarts
1 gallon = 3.8 liters	1 liter = 0.26 gallon
1 ounce = 28 grams	1 gram = 0.035 ounce
1 pound = 0.45 kilogram	1 kilogram = 2.2 pounds
1 short ton = 0.9 megagram (metric ton)	1 megagram (metric ton) = 1.1 short tons (2000 lbs.)
1 horsepower = 0.75 kilowatt	1 kilowatt = 1.3 horsepower
Degrees Fahrenheit to Degrees Celsius	*Degrees Celsius to Degrees Fahrenheit*
$(°F - 32) \times 5/9$	$(9/5 \times °C) + 32$

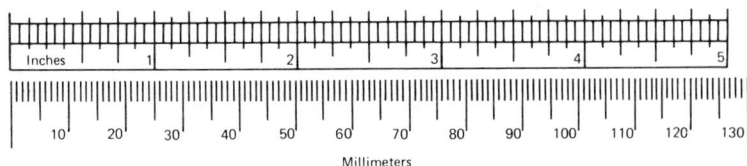

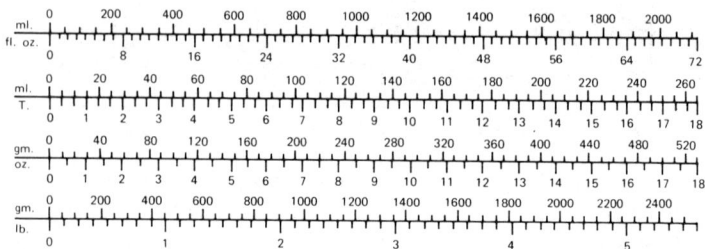

| ml. / fl. oz. | 0 | 200 | 400 | 600 | 800 | 1000 | 1200 | 1400 | 1600 | 1800 | 2000 |
| 0 | 8 | 16 | 24 | 32 | 40 | 48 | 56 | 64 | 72 |

(measurement conversion scales: ml./fl. oz., ml./T., gm./oz., gm./lb.)

Typewriting Style

American Standard Usage	Metric Standard Usage
In technical writing, units of weight and measure may be abbreviated without periods.	Metric units of weight and measure are always abbreviated without periods in technical writing.
In nontechnical writing, spell out units of measure.	In nontechnical writing, spell out units of measure—although there are some exceptions such as 35 mm film.
Plural abbreviations change form: for example, *1 in* but *3 ins*, *1 yd* but *3 yds*.	No distinction is made between singular and plural abbreviations: for example, *1 m* and *5 m, 1 km* and *5 km*.
Area and volume measures are expressed with the prefixes *square* and *cubic: square feet, cubic yard.*	Area and volume measures are expressed in exponential form: km^2 or m^3.
	If "l," the abbreviation for liter, will be confused with the number "1," spell out the word liter or use a capital letter (L).

Symbols Made at the Typewriter

Symbols that are not on the typewriter keyboard can frequently be made by using one or two keys as shown below.

ACCENT		
(apostrophe)		entrée
ASTERISK		
A + v		✿ Table II
BRACES		
( )		(Monday)
( )		(Tuesday)
( )	Days of the Week	(Wednesday)
( )		(Thursday)
( )		(Friday)
BRACKETS		
⎣		⎡ sic ⎤
CENTS		
c + 1		21¢
DEGREE		
o (lower case "o")		72°
DITTO		20 feet
" (quotation mark)		30 "
EXCLAMATION POINT		
' + .		The End!
FEET		
' (apostrophe)		27'
INCHES		
" (quotation mark)		36"
MINUTES		
' (apostrophe)		36'
SECONDS		
" (quotation mark)		60"

Mathematical and Engineering Symbols

DIVIDE
: + —   22 ÷ 2 = 11
DOES NOT EQUAL
= + /   22 ÷ 2 ≠ 10
EQUALS
-- (two hyphens)   =
FRACTIONS
/   3/4

> **NOTE:** Always be consistent within text. Do not combine typewriter fractions such as ½ or ¼ with made fractions.

> When typing mixed numbers with made fractions, space once between the whole number and the fraction (1 3/4).

PLUS
/ + —   3 ≠ = 6
PLUS OR MINUS
±   ± (Use variable line spacer)
SQUARE ROOT
v + / $\mathrm{v}^/$ (Use variable line spacer)
SUBSCRIPTS
  Place a half space below letter
  or number to which they refer $A + B_{10}$
  with no space preceding.
SUPERSCRIPTS
  Place a half space above letter
  or number to which they refer $A + B^{10}$
  with no space preceding.

INDEX